ALSO BY

GEOFFREY BIBBY

THE TESTIMONY OF THE SPADE

LIFE IN NORTHERN EUROPE FROM 15,000 B.C.
TO THE TIME OF THE VIKINGS

(1956)

A BORZOI BOOK
published by ALFRED A. KNOPF in New York

FOUR THOUSAND YEARS AGO

FOUR THOUSAND YEARS AGO

A World Panorama of
Life in the Second Millennium B.C.

by GEOFFREY BIBBY

1 9 62

NEW YORK : ALFRED · A · KNOPF

L. C. catalog card number: 61–14367

MHBC

PUBLISHED NOVEMBER 13, 1961
SECOND PRINTING, JANUARY 1962

TO MY MOTHER,

WHO SHOWS IN HER PERSON HOW SHORT A PERIOD

SEVENTY YEARS IN FACT IS

October 6, 1891 to 1961

INTRODUCTION

THERE HAS LONG BEEN a place vacant, on the history shelves of the world, for a volume covering the Second Millennium B.C. That millennium is the span of time in which some of the most well-known events in man's history occurred, in which some of the most renowned persons of antiquity lived. It is the period of Stonehenge and the Hyksos, of the Minoan and Indus valley civilizations, of the Hittites and the Argonauts and the Philistines, of the Trojan War and the Exodus, of Hammurabi and Abraham, Akhenaten and Tutankhamon and Rameses the Great, Moses and Saul and Samson and Agamemnon and Theseus and Tiglathpileser. Everyone has heard these names—and yet the history of the period remains vague, a jumble of disconnected stories.

This situation is out of date. For ten or twenty years we have had sufficient material at our disposal to write a connected history of this "lost" thousand years. All the same, this book is not the missing history volume. But it is an attempt to pull together into a connected whole all the well-known facts and figures of this thousand years, to place them at least into a chronological framework, to show who did what, and when, and where.

I have always found the time scale very difficult to grasp in conventional written history. In any history covering a thousand years or more there is a tendency for the author to jump easily over gaps of time in which nothing of significance happens. And this has worried me. When the historian casually writes "fifty years later," I have always had to stop and remind myself that if I had been twenty in the last paragraph I should now be seventy, and if I had been fifty I should now be dead. Similarly, that two events, unrelated, take place at the same time is not always brought out with sufficient clarity for my mind to grasp. It was long before I realized that the fall of Constantinople to the Turks (A.D. 1453) and the discovery of America (A.D. 1492) took place within a single lifetime. This is not perhaps important. But it was important to the people living that lifetime, and we cannot historically appreciate these people unless we adopt much the same measure of relative importance as they had.

It is to a large degree a question of scale. Archaeologists have been for some decades faced with the same sort of problem. In their drawings of plans and sections, in their photographs of minor objects and architectural features and town sites, they used to lay a graduated scale alongside the object or beside the building. They found that this not only did not help the viewer, but could even mislead; they recalled too well the shock of discovering that a photographed scale thought to be graduated in feet was actually in centimeters. Of late, archaeologists have been introducing something new into their pictorial records—the lay figure. On site photographs, a single workman will be standing stolidly, with pick poised, to give a human scale; small objects are photographed in the hand, or between finger and thumb; the "average man" is drawn into the sections and plans. A man is not as accurate a scale as a six-foot rule, but he is easier to assimilate. The scale of the structure is immediately related to things human and ordinary.

This book is an attempt to introduce a similar device into history, to give a human perspective to time scales. We are here dealing with a thousand years. And a thousand years is, after all, but fourteen lifetimes measured by the conventional scale of threescore years and ten. So alongside the tale of this thousand years are set fourteen "lifetimes"; fourteen lay figures will obtrude themselves in turn, chapter by chapter, to point the passage of time between the events recorded. This is, of course, the device of the historical novel; but here the human actors are for the most part anonymous spectators of and participators in history, purely —and it is hoped unobtrusively—present to give the scale of elapsed time in our journey from 2000 to 1000 B.C.

The year 2000 is a bad place to begin, and the year 1000 a

bad place to end. Three hundred years before 2000 B.C. the first of the great conquerors, Sargon of Akkad, had pushed to the Mediterranean from the land of the Two Rivers, showing the way for all future empires, while bronze was well on its way into Stone-Age Europe. And at the close of our story in 1000 B.C. the Assyrians were only beginning an expansion which was to end with the establishment of another empire in the Middle East, while the use of iron was beginning its spread from the east over Bronze-Age Europe. But anywhere at all is a bad place to start and a bad place to end. In this book we are not trying to follow a single thread or a single pattern in the embroidered damask of history; we are trying to view the whole cloth, the whole weft and woof, all the threads and patterns which go to form the long tapestry of mankind's story, and wherever we cut this cloth we cut across a multitude of patterns. Nor is there any special virtue in the years 2000 and 1000 B.C.—except that they are convenient dates for us to remember, and that a thousand years is a convenient length of cloth out of which to make a book.

This book is not meant for professional historians or professional archaeologists. But as some of these estimable people will be forced to read it for review purposes, it is seemly that I apologize in advance to them—to the historian because I tell him nothing new and because I take sides on questions where the responsible historian sits on the fence, with the perfect justification that the ground on either side of the fence is a morass with no certain footholds and that only from the fence can the footholds be reliably charted—to the archaeologist because I have frequently used the term "people" where he would use the term "culture." I am aware that he uses the word "culture" not as jargon or expertise, but precisely in order not to beg the question of whether a distinctive collection of artifacts, which is what he finds, presupposes a distinctive people. I have simply, and unscientifically, begged this question, as I have begged innumerable questions throughout.

My defense is that I have tried to give the situation as it probably appeared to the people *living at the time*. They *knew* whether what we now only know as a "culture" was a people or not; they *knew* which side of a now disputed historical question was the truth. And while I may be wrong in my choice of what appears most probably to have been the truth, I would certainly be wrong if I instead gave the impression that the people living at the time had the same doubts as we. I have tried as best I can, in italics at the end of each chapter, to confess to what degree I have misled my readers as to the reliability of my "facts."

G. B.

CONTENTS

BOOK I: BRONZE AND STONE

BOOK II: THE CHARIOTS

Contents

BOOK III: THE ARGOSIES

BOOK IV: BRONZE AND IRON

DRAWINGS

MAPS

DRAWN BY RALPH MARCANO

LIST OF PLATES

Book I

Bronze and Stone

ROCK CARVING FROM BOHUSLÄN, IN SOUTHWEST SWEDEN.

THE CITIES

THE FIRST RAYS of sunlight of the Second Millennium B.C. strike almost horizontally across the Arabian desert. They glow pearly white through the low mists that overhang the newly sown fields on either side of the Nile, which still runs strongly, though now back in its own bed after the autumn inundation. Above the mists the villages of square reed and adobe houses, each on the mound that raises it over the floods, are places of clear-cut light and shadow. Already they are stirring, thin pencils of smoke arising from the fenced yards, and the geese cackling against the muted sound of rubbing-stone on quern where women are grinding millet for the morning meal. Sleepily, and pulling his whitish linen loincloth around him, a man steps out of a doorway and looks towards the sun and the dissipating mists.

It is a morning like any other morning. For him it is not the beginning of a millennium; not even the beginning of a year. It is in fact almost exactly a month since he celebrated New Year's Day by his reckoning, and he is not to know that an era will begin precisely two thousand Gregorian years later. But the inundation is over; the fields have been plowed and sown with millet and barley and flax, as they have been sown after the inundation since the beginning of time; and now will follow the period of comparative leisure, with planting of vegetables and fishing and fowling, until the strengthening sun and the falling river make watering of the growing crops a long and wearying prelude to the harvest. So has it always been. So it will always be.

It has not always been so. The Egyptian farm laborer, standing in the morning sunshine on the outskirts of his village on the upper Nile, knows nothing of the time, probably even then five to six thousands years in the past, when the inhabitants of the Nile valley had lived altogether differently, ranging the edges of the forests that then stretched between the cliffs of the desert and the swamps of the river valley, living on the beasts and birds that they could bring down with their clubs and boomerangs and arrows, and dwelling in temporary villages of grass huts. To these hunting savages seed corn and sheep and goats and cattle had gradually penetrated from the delta to the north, together with the knowledge of sowing and harvesting, of milling and cheese and butter-making, of spinning and weaving. Centuries had gone to taming the river valley, to clearing the forest and draining the swamps, to laying out fields and dikes. Gradually irrigation systems had been developed to extend the belt of cultivable land up to and into the watching desert; the plow had been introduced from the delta, and the revolution of using oxen to draw it; corn had been improved, flax introduced. The papyrus reed had become a commercial crop, when papermaking followed the introduction from the east of the idea of writing and the development of the native Egyptian hieroglyphic script. Systems of government and land tenure had changed and changed again during the slow march of generation upon generation. Even gods had come and gone again, as the primitive animism of the hunting peoples was refined. The patron animals that formed the totem of each clan became the animal-headed gods which protected each shire, and then were amalgamated and related into a closeknit pantheon in which all the gods were common to all the land—though still particularly associated with their original shire—and each had its own attributes, its own sphere of the universal way of life to control and guard.

Of how all this had grown up the worker in the fields knows nothing. Though he has his legends and his myths.

The legends tell him that his earliest forefathers came from Punt, the Holy Land far to the southward along the coast of the Eastern Sea. He calls his country the Two Lands, and the greatest figure in his traditions is King Mena, who united the two lands, one the river valley and the other the delta, into one kingdom some fourteen hundred years ago. (It is as far in his past as King Arthur is in ours.) And he tells tales of the wars and kings that preceded the Union, of how the Falcon Kings of his own upper valley conquered the Reed Kings of the lower valley and united thereby the whole of upper Egypt into the White Kingdom under the white crown. Mena had worn the white crown before he had added the delta, the land of the Bee Kings, to his realm and assumed thereby in addition the red crown of lower Egypt. Since then for fourteen hundred years the wearers of the double crown had ruled the land, first from Memphis (near present-day Cairo), on the former frontier between the White Kingdom and the Red, and later from Thebes, three hundred fifty miles farther south along the valley and not far from the village where our farm laborer stands.

He knows but little of the history of the Memphis kings, and cares less—knows and cares at least as little as a man of our day knows and cares about the history of the corresponding length of our past, from the Anglo-Saxon invasions to the War of Independence. But just as he has listened all his life to legends of Mena, the great uniter of the lands, so he has heard tales of the mighty pharaohs of the Fourth Dynasty, who eight hundred years ago built the great pyramids near their capital. Pyramids, of course, he is accustomed to; every pharaoh builds one, starting to plan it as soon as he comes to the throne, or even before. The pyramid, the emblem of the sun-god Ra, is the recognized form for the burial monument of the king, who is son of Ra and Ra's earthly incarnation. But the great pyramids of the Fourth Dynasty, the pyramids of Khufu and Khefre and Menkure, were something different and worth traveling days to see. It is possible that our farmer has been to see them, as millions of tourists must already have done in the eight hundred years since they were built, and had stood awestruck before their colossal dimensions, ranging up to Khufu's four hundred eighty feet in height, and dazzled by their smooth white limestone facings. He would gaze on them from about the same distance in time as we look on Windsor Castle.

The people of the south, of the old White Kingdom in the main valley of the Nile, stand not a little in awe of Memphis as a whole. Though it ceased to be the capital of the country, even in name, over two hundred years ago, it is still a fabulous city, with its palaces and temples built by ten successive dynasties. Particularly famous was the He-Ku-Ptah, the "house of the spiritual materialization of Ptah," who was the god of learning and the regional deity of Memphis. It was so famous that it gave its name to the whole country, being written by the Greeks as Aigyptos and by us as Egypt. And Memphis was the door to the north for the valley dwellers, the gateway to the delta, to the old Red Kingdom.

The delta had always been more civilized than the valley to its south. It was in closer contact with the other old civilizations and with the growing Mediterranean trade; and it was more fertile and more populous. That agriculture itself, and with it many other revolutionary technical and economic innovations, had reached the southlands from the delta was forgotten long ago, but the feeling of belonging to a poorer, less urbane, yet more virile, culture (the same feeling as the Scotsman has towards the Englishman) persisted in the south. Yet Mena had come from the southlands, and now it was the southlands that once more ruled Egypt.

The history of the last three hundred years would be well known in general outline to even the least-educated laborer of the south. A combination of weak kings in Memphis and strong priesthoods in the delta had allowed the sheriffs of the shires to the south, who were originally officials appointed by the pharaoh, to obtain hereditary office and thereby set themselves up as barons in their own right, though nominally still subject to the king. For a long while they were held in check by internal rivalries. In particular the successive barons of Siut, loyal to the king, had time and again on his behalf put down incipient revolts of the more independent barons of Thebes. But about 2300 B.C. Intef of Thebes declares his independence and assumes the title of pharaoh. And apparently the kings in Memphis can no longer restrain him. His son, too, was called Intef and followed him on the throne of Thebes. After him came a succession of pharaohs called Mentuhotep, who appear to be another branch of the same family. For the line of Intefs continues, though they no longer rule. It is in the reign of the second Mentuhotep in the south that the old line of kings in Memphis ends, apparently

in a people's revolution and a sack of the palace by looters. Mentuhotep II seizes the opportunity and marches north, puts down
the revolution and takes over the government of the whole of
Egypt. He retains Thebes as his capital, and during his reign
and that of his three successors, all called Mentuhotep, an influx
of architects and sculptors from Memphis changes Thebes from a
provincial town to a worthy capital city with the palaces and
temples that befit the state. Mentuhotep III had a minister of
state called Amenemhet who traced his family to the line of
Intefs, and it may be his son, also called Amenemhet, who was
minister of state under Mentuhotep V.

We are now close to 2000 B.C., and it is only a year or two
ago that our laborer heard of the raids into the delta made by
desert tribes both from the east and the west. They coincided
with a popular rising probably, though we do not know, confined
to the delta. Both the invasions and the rising were firmly re-
pressed by the minister of state, Amenemhet. But Amenemhet is
ambitious, and perhaps believes that he belongs to the legitimate line of Intef. From the time when he suppressed the rising
he is the real power in the land and it can only be a question
of time before he deposes Mentuhotep V and declares himself
pharaoh. It is to rumors of dynastic change that the sunrise of
this morning ushers in the Second Millennium B.C.

The sun was already an hour up in the sky over Mesopotamia
when its first rays reached the valley of the Nile. Between the
valley of the Euphrates and the Tigris and that of the Nile lie
eight hundred miles of desert, and only rarely does news of what
is happening in one valley reach the other in less than four or
five months. The workers now going out to the fields of Mesopotamia know nothing of Amenemhet's rise to power, and
scarcely anything of life and customs and history in Egypt. They
have their own life and their own traditions.

They too, like the Egyptians, are descendants of the old
farmers. Over four millennia ago the hunters of the foothills to
the east of the valley began to burn off the grass and plant corn,
and build their small adobe villages in the north of the land.
They were not the first farmers in the world. That honor must

go, as far as present knowledge extends, to the people of Jericho in the Jordan valley north of the Dead Sea, who as early as 6800 B.C. already lived in a walled city and practiced agriculture. But it was not long before the science of sowing corn and taming cattle seems to have reached north Iraq. It was longer before the first settlers began to reclaim the swamps of the lower valley, where the Euphrates and the Tigris approach one another and form a single river system.

These days of early settlement are long ago forgotten, and we should perhaps refrain from complicating our narrative with the mention of forgotten things. Like the Egyptian, the Mesopotamian of 2000 B.C. knew that seedtime and harvest had existed from the beginning of things.

Yet farming was very different in Mesopotamia from what it was in Egypt—and very different in south and in north Mesopotamia. In the north, the area of Mosul and the Kirkuk oil fields, the first long-forgotten farmers had built their villages. This is a country of steep valleys and wide uplands, with cold winters and hot dry summers. And it is a region with winter rains. It is thus farmed more as we know farming, with extensive grazing, and with crops of barley and emmer, which can be sown with a reasonable expectation that they will get sufficient natural watering to grow and ripen. Provided that they are harvested before the parching heat of summer, they can be sowed at will, and it is fairly easy to get two crops a year.

In the south, from a little north of Baghdad down to the beginning of the swamps which, then as now, stretch down to the Persian Gulf, the situation superficially resembles that of Egypt. The water level in the Tigris and the Euphrates rises and falls with the melting of the snows in the Turkish and Persian mountains, and the Euphrates in particular carries much fertile silt when it is at its height. The rivers reach their highest level two months earlier than the Nile, in June and July, and will then, if unchecked, flood wide areas, just as the Nile does. But the Nile runs in a narrow valley, and the farmer of 2000 B.C. can watch the floods with satisfaction, knowing that within two months the river will return of itself to its old bed, and only such water will remain as he himself dams up for his own use.

The farmer of the immensely broad flat valley of the Euphrates and the Tigris sees the flood as a catastrophe. If uncontrolled, the waters will cover the land for months and never drain back to the river. For the Euphrates at least runs in a bed carved out of its own silt deposits, which often lies higher than the country around. Both rivers can very well decide to cut a completely new channel after the floods from the one they occupied before, and the change in channel can drown cultivation, or leave it high and dry, with its summer water supply miles away.

The problem for the first forgotten settlers of the south had been to tame the Twin Rivers, as the Nile had never needed to be tamed. And tamed they had been. Immense levees strengthen the banks of the great rivers, and huge canals lead off from them. The canals have a triple function. At the time of high water they give the rivers room for controlled expansion, leading off the dangerous waters. When the rivers begin to fall sluice gates are closed, and the water is retained for use in the dry period. And lastly the canals lead water to dry areas beyond the natural coverage of the inundations. Fear of uncontrolled water and a natural genius for harnessing it are as deeply ingrained into the southern Mesopotamians as they are into the Dutch today. A favorite theme of their storytellers is the mythical fight between the god Enlil and the water monster Tiamat, in which Enlil succeeds in subduing the monster to his will. And every child knows of the Deluge, the great flood which had drowned the world, all but Ziusudra, who had saved himself and his family and his livestock in the ark which the gods had bade him build. The Deluge is, in their minds, no mythical story, but a definite historical event of the remote past—and indeed archaeologists have found traces of catastrophic floods fifteen hundred to two thousand years earlier than the period we here describe.

The farmers who, this first morning of the Second Millennium B.C., are making their way out to their fields along the canal levees of south Mesopotamia do not consider themselves the inhabitants of a country. Egypt was the Two Lands, and, for all the internal rivalries between them, their inhabitants felt themselves as one nation. But the Mesopotamian was first and foremost a citizen of his city. It was natural enough. He farmed immensely fertile alluvial dirt, land which even according to his own tax returns (we have them) gave a yield of thirty-three times his outlay in seed corn. But to farm this safely and consistently he needed a complicated and expensive system of water control. And he needed tools. Elsewhere tools could be made on the spot, by the farmer, of timber and of stone. But the alluvial mud of lower Mesopotamia contains not a single stone, and could not support hardwoods. From the very beginning the settlers in this region had been faced with the urgent necessity of producing not merely enough to live on, but a surplus which could be traded for essential equipment, for hoes and sickle blades and spades and hammers. This involved at a very early stage the establishment of a central authority which could organize canal construction on an economically large enough scale, and which could arrange the marketing of the surplus agricultural produce in the regions outside the alluvial area, and the purchase there of the missing raw materials. The result was, again so long ago that its origins were lost in the mists of antiquity, the city-state, consisting of an urban center of trade, manufacture, and administration, supporting and supported by a surrounding area of farmland and farming villages. And the city-state is an independent, or semi-independent, political entity.

An incidental result, too, is that the farmer is not nearly so typical an inhabitant of Mesopotamia as he is of Egypt. The organized artisan and the organized businessman are very numerous—and very vocal—in the city-states. And just now they are becoming very much more vocal, for a most interesting reason.

The city-state has from the beginning been a closely knit administrative unity. And the form the administration has taken is one that undoubtedly by a present-day observer would be called communist. It is necessary to be very careful in applying modern terminology to earlier ways of life, and the parallel here is not of course point by point exact. But it is close enough to be very suggestive.

The means of production in the state are owned by the god of the state and administered by a governor who is also the chief priest of the god. The body of priests forms the administration acting on the authority of the governor. The inhabitants of the state may own nothing beyond their houses, their portable possessions, and the tools of their trade. The land is temple property, and the farmers either deliver a fixed proportion of their produce to the temple or else are direct temple employees. Crafts such as weaving and brewing and metalworking, carpentry and stonecutting and jewel setting, are carried on in temple workshops by temple employees for a fixed wage. The temple organizes trading caravans, and stores in granaries and warehouses the surplus wealth of the community, barley and wool and sesame oil and dates. It pays wages in barley to the many direct temple employees. The governor is directly responsible for the defense of the state, keeps a small standing army, and can call out the militia as required. The position of governor passes normally from father to son.

But just about 2000 B.C. all this is changing. What can only be described as a capitalist revolution is taking place. Probably not simultaneously, of course, in all the twenty or so city-states, but approximately at this time in them all. We suddenly find in the temple archives records of independent groups of merchants paying taxes on their imports and even financing private ventures by loans from the temple. And we find that large and small estates are being bought and sold in the open market. The temples continue, and their premises are enlarged; the revolution is apparently bloodless. Nevertheless, the whole economic structure is changing to one based on private initiative and ownership of property.

The people of lower Mesopotamia must have been conscious of this change—it was much too rapid to have been imperceptible. And they undoubtedly knew, more clearly than we do, the reasons behind the change. For the reasons lay in the course of fairly recent history, in events beginning, admittedly, all of three hundred years before, but culminating in the last two generations.

Throughout southern Mesopotamia there is at this time a mixture of two nationalities, Sumerians and Semites. They mix at all levels. If our farmers on the levee are clean-shaven, stocky, and talking among themselves in a rather staccato tongue, they are undoubtedly Sumerians. But they can equally well be taller,

leaner, with beards and long hair, and a speech which rolls out
fluid consonantal periods, by which we can recognize them as
Semites.

Just when the ancestors of each of the two races entered the
land they may themselves know. But we do not. We know that
more Semites have recently come in, Amorites from the deserts
to the west, but we know that there were already Semites in the
country more than five hundred years ago. There can be little
doubt that they, too, came from the west, from the great cradle
of the Semitic peoples in the Arabian peninsula. The Sumerians
may have been in the river country longer; at least the first written documents, of baked clay and already buried beneath the
debris of fifteen hundred years of settlement, are written in
Sumerian. Moreover, the script used was clearly designed to fit
Sumerian, and now that Semitic-speaking scribes are using it to
write their own tongue they are finding not a few difficulties.
It may well be that the Sumerians were the first to settle the
swamplands of the lower rivers, though they do not make that
claim themselves. Modern researchers tend to believe that they
originally came from the north, for in their language "country"
and "mountain" are the same word. And they call themselves
"the black-headed," presumably referring to their hair color,
which would suggest that they had at one time lived close to
fairer-haired peoples. All this would seem to indicate the Caucasus. And yet they themselves say that their ancestors came by
water up the Persian Gulf. . . .

However this may be, the Sumerians have a long tradition
of dominance in lower Mesopotamia. The Semites were less in
number and politically negligible. The communistic temple rule
was Sumerian in language and its power is exercised by people
with Sumerian names. But then about four hundred fifty years
earlier, as long ago as the Union of England and Scotland for
us, a number of city-states arose in the northern part of the
lower land, identical in pattern with the more southerly Sumerian
states, but Semitic in language. The next hundred fifty years
are troubled times, with almost continuous wars and intrigues
between the cities, both Semitic and Sumerian, one after another
claiming, and in some cases even enforcing, a temporary leader-

ship over the others. Some of the governors even begin to call themselves kings. Finally, three hundred years before the Second Millennium opens, the son of an official in Kish, the largest of the Semitic cities, usurps power in the north and rechristens himself the True King, Sargon. In 2289 he defeats the leader of the southern confederacy, and for the first time the whole of southern Mesopotamia is united under a single rule.

In the memory of the Mesopotamians of 2000 B.C. the reign of Sargon of Akkad three hundred years ago is their period of

SUMERIAN WAR CHARIOT DEPICTED ON THE SO-CALLED "STANDARD OF UR." IT WAS A SLOW AND CUMBERSOME VEHICLE, WITH FOUR SOLID WHEELS, AND WAS DRAWN BY ASSES. BUT IT WAS THE FIRST MECHANIZATION OF ANY ARMY, AND WAS THE BEGINNING OF FAR-REACHING CHANGES IN THE CONDUCT OF WARFARE.

glory. During his fifty-six-year reign he campaigned to the ends of the earth. He conquered northern Mesopotamia and followed the Euphrates westward and on over the mountains until his armies stood on the shores of the Mediterranean. To the south he claimed dominion over the gateway to the Persian Gulf. "From the lower sea to the upper sea," they boast, his dominions spread. It was an empire such as the world had never seen before, and it was to be a standing challenge to future conquerors.

Sargon, and his equally great grandson Naram-Sin, who after a period of revolts restored his grandfather's empire and held it for thirty years, are much clearer figures to the Mesopotamians of 2000 B.C. than the rulers that follow. Naram-Sin died less than two hundred years ago and his memory is still green. But his empire fell, attacked at its heart by tribes from the Persian highlands. They held Mesopotamia for a hundred years, though latterly the cities of the south for all practical purposes were independent. It was the ancient city of Ur which finally overthrew the alien rule and reunited south Mesopotamia. Though the Sumerians did not know it, it was the last time that they were to dominate the land. People alive in 2000 B.C. have seen the growing threat of Elamites to the east and Semitic Amorites to the west. And sixteen years ago a combined attack overthrew the Dynasty of Ur. Ibi-Sin, king of Ur, was carried off captive to Elam, and an Elamite puppet kingdom, with its capital centrally placed at Isin, now holds only a small area of the country. Kish is once more a center of a Semitic confederacy to the north, and the new Semitic Amorites have established a southern confederacy based on Larsa.

It is clearly this period of warfare, and the rising power of the Semites, that has unsettled the old-established temple communism. Sargon and his sons had rewarded their demobilized veterans with gifts of land, and the desert nomads, arriving with their flocks and herds, would feel no compulsion to hand these over to an omnipotent state. And once private ownership is even partially recognized, people are no longer content to be wage slaves of the state. When the priests lost their power to enforce temple ownership of the means of production, the capitalist revolution was carried forward by the momentum of a popular desire to own property.

The farmers whom we have seen this winter morning on their way to work, and who are now eating their barley cakes and dried fish in the lee of an embankment, with their woolen cloaks pulled over their heads, may thus well own their own land. But they are more probably tenant farmers, paying the owner a rental of one third of the net produce. It is the time of the barley sowing, and all the farmers are busy, too busy to hunt or fish, though they keep their bronze-tipped spears ready to hand. The times are unruly, and, besides, lions are not uncommon in the region of the Twin Rivers. Even wild elephants, though rare,

are not unknown. But the wild beasts rarely venture into the cultivated areas. The boundary between the desert and the sown, drawn before the dawn of history, is better respected by animals than by man.

The sun that rose over the Nile and the Twin Rivers is high in the sky over the valley of the Indus far to the east beyond the mountainous plateaus of Persia. The Indus valley contains the biggest river system of them all, broader than the Nile, longer than the Euphrates and the Tigris. A complex of parallel rivers and tributaries, the traditional Seven Rivers of the Punjab, many of which in our day have dried up, occupy the thousand miles of valley which drain the snows of Korakoram and the Hindu Kush into the Indian Ocean. It is a lush valley, a place of swamps and jungles, vastly different from the deserts through which the Indus flows today. Very likely the monsoon rains at this period extended farther north than in our day, and possibly there was more rain and snow in the mountains that feed the river. But the desert of today is largely man-made, the result of intemperate agricultural exploitation, followed by destruction and neglect. In 2000 B.C. the destruction had not yet taken place (we shall see it happen), but the agricultural exploitation was in full swing.

Like the valleys of the Nile and of Mesopotamia, the valley of the Nine Rivers is occupied by an old-established farming civilization. It covers a vastly greater area. Its small towns and fortified settlements lie along eight hundred fifty miles of coast, from the borders of Persia to the neighborhood of Bombay. And inland they stretch for over eight hundred miles, along the Indus river system and over the foothills that divide the head-waters of the Indus from those of the Ganges. Each town and village has its acreage of irrigated land, on which its livelihood is based; and these towns and villages are legion. Most of the inhabitants of the Indus valley live in these towns and in scattered dwellings amid the fields. The large, semi-independent cities of Mesopotamia have no parallel here. Instead, as in Egypt, the government of the whole area is centralized, though here, unlike Egypt, in two large cities. The lower Indus has its capital in Mohenjo-daro, on a great bend in the river two hundred miles from the sea. And the upper Indus is ruled from Harappa, almost five hundred miles farther to the northeast.

They are large cities by the standards of the time. It takes a full thirty minutes to walk from one end to the other, even along the broad thoroughfares which divide the cities into regular blocks. A visitor from Memphis or from Ur, used to the winding haphazard streets, broken by the colorful fronts of temples, of his native city, would find these wide straight dusty avenues, with their central drains and endless windowless façades of whitewashed brick houses, outlandish in the extreme, and highly monotonous. But the cosmopolitan crowd that throngs the streets knows no other type of city, and in any case the variegated costume of the inhabitants does much to relieve the austerity of the architecture. Many races are to be seen here: wool-clad Mongols from the northern hills; and dark, almost negroid, Dravidians in cotton robes from the south; beak-nosed Armenoids; and sallow dark-haired individuals who would not have excited remark on the shores of the Mediterranean.

The monotony of the buildings is broken by the massive walls of the citadel, rising, both at Harappa and at Mohenjo-daro, to the west of the town. The citadel is not merely the center of government. It is also the center of religion, and of trade and taxation. A countryman, entering Mohenjo-daro from the west, climbs up a steep staircase in the thickness of the citadel wall and, pausing for breath at the top, can see to his left the massive bulk of the municipal granary. There, on the ramp below, four-wheeled oxcarts are unloading sacks of wheat and barley, and perhaps bales of cotton, to be swung up on ropes to the granary floor above. He does not regard the grain merely as a food reserve. It is the universal medium of payment, and the granary is national bank and state revenue department in one, and therefore has its natural place in the citadel (or at Harappa close by). From where the visitor stands he cannot see the rows of brick grinding floors, where municipal workers pound the grain to the flour in which payment is generally made, but he knows that they must be hard by. He begins, on his way into the town beyond, to see the other state buildings of the citadel, the great bath lying between the granary and the temple, the bath in which the public cleansing ceremonies take place on the festival days prescribed by religion. And he makes a detour to the south to one of the seats of government, the immense pillared brick hall of assembly. And then he goes on, to buy the cotton cloth and oil for which he has come, in one of the large brick-floored shops of the merchants of the town, and to chaffer for the hire of a donkey to carry his wares back to the village.

We must admit that we know nothing of the form of government of the realms of the Indus, little of the religion, and almost nothing of the previous history of the region. This is largely because we cannot yet read the pictographic script which the men of the Indus valley used. It would be natural to imagine two realms, each governed from one of the two cities, like upper and lower Egypt before the union, or like Babylonia and Assyria in later times. The close association of the government buildings with the state granary and the public baths would suggest a priestly rule, or at least a state religion. Baths, both public and private, are such a prominent feature of the Indus cities that it is difficult to argue against the view that bathing had a religious significance, as it has in the Hindu religion of our day. The religion had many other facets. A large number of animals were considered sacred, chiefly perhaps the bull; and a god portrayed on several of the square stamp seals used by most of the merchants of the cities has many of the attributes now associated with the name of Shiva. In other words, many of the characteristic features of modern Hinduism seem already to be associated with the Second Millennium civilization of the Indus valley.

It seems likely that at least the southern realm of the Indus valley, with its capital at Mohenjo-daro, was known to its inhabitants as Meluhha. For the Mesopotamians knew of a land of that name, a land with many kings, out beyond the entrance of the Persian Gulf. And from Meluhha they imported gold and ivory and carnelian and lapis lazuli, products which can hardly have come from lands other than India. (That the later conquerors of the Indus valley civilization refer to its inhabitants as the *Mleccha* may possibly add confirmation.)

Just what background our countryman, standing at the top of the citadel steps at Mohenjo-daro, possessed we simply do not know. We can be sure that he possessed just as detailed, superficial, and romanticized a knowledge of the past of his own people as had the men of Mesopotamia and of Egypt. As he stood there, he was heir to at least five hundred years of city life and organized agriculture. So much we can prove; but it is extremely likely that the beginnings of civilization in the valley lands are many hundreds of years earlier still, that they lie so far back that they are beyond even the myths which begin the popular picture of his people's past. We can be sure that there are stories of kings and of wars, leading up by insensible degrees to the more immediate and detailed recollection of the previous genera- tion or so, and tying up with the present moment, the govern- mental structure, the decrees and opportunities and dissatisfac- tions of the first day of the Second Millennium B.C. in the valley of the Indus.

THE BRAHMIN BULL, HERE REPRODUCED FROM A HARAPPA SEAL, IS REPRESENTED ON MANY OF THE SEALS OF THE INDUS VALLEY CIVILI- ZATION, AND MAY WELL HAVE BEEN SACRED THEN AS NOW.

2

THE BACKWOODS

IN THE HUSH before the dawn the clearing lay silent. Against the paling sky to the east the pine trees at the forest edge stood black and sharply outlined. To the west, beyond the cleared fields and the marshes of the foreshore, the setting moon trailed a wake of silver across the waters of the fjord. In the clustered houses of wood and turf the settlers slept, rolled in their furs and homespun cloaks as near as possible to the banked central fire, the low doors shut tight against the midwinter cold. The new millennium came in unheeded across the forest settlements of northern Europe.

There was a watch, it is true, but he dozed over his fire in the lee of a store hut, conscientiously close to the corral in which the cattle and the sheep were penned. The natives were friendly hereabouts, had been friendly for generations. The watch was only a precaution against wolves or marauding bobcats, and the cattle could be relied on to give warning of their approach.

The settlement was typical of many along the deep fjords and scattered through the wooded lowlands of southern Scandinavia. It was new, its fields carved and burnt out of the forest less than three years ago. Yet it was not in virgin territory. When the last village had been abandoned, and the villagers had trecked the seven miles across the ridges to this new site that the gods had indicated, they had found massive old tree stumps among the lighter newer growth, which showed that, before the memory of man, other farmers had been there. There was even an ancient stone tomb where the hills gave way to the estuary flats, the immense capstone of the dolmen protruding above the low mound which covered its walls, its entrance choked with

brambles, and the wooden door rotted almost away. They had
cleared out the chamber beneath the capstone, and used it for
the first two burials within the community. But last year they had
completed a new burial place, an immense and lofty room with
walls of upright stones and a roof formed of no less than six
large slabs, approached by a stone passageway, and the whole
covered by a mound of turf. They were justly proud of the magnificent new tomb, with the green turf rising above the white
limestone ringstones—proud, and a little afraid; and never a
month passed without a procession to the passage-grave, and offerings and libations and jars of food and drink for the spirits of
the three dead ones who already lay within.

But though they venerated their fathers and grandfathers,
and punctiliously gave them their due of offerings, they gave little thought to the men of the olden days who had lived on the
site before. They had even unceremoniously cleared out the old
bones from where they lay thick on the floor of the dolmen
chamber, and dumped them outside to make room for their own
burials. For the signs of earlier villages were common along the
fjords and in the forests, half-overgrown clearings and collapsed
houses with moss-grown timbers. They well knew that a village
has no permanency; at longest every dozen years, when the
millet and barley began to fail, it was necessary to leave the
homestead and seek out a new site for cultivation. And as the
forest reclaimed the abandoned site, so the strength would return
to the exhausted soil, and it might even be possible, within the
lifetime of a man, to return to the overgrown fields and burn them
clear once more, and again raise crops there. For that was the
way one lived, here on the shores of the northern sea.

Though they had been long in the land, these builders of
passage-graves and sowers of the forest clearings, they knew from
the traditions of their people that their ancestors had originally
come from the south. They could tell the tale of the generations
back to the first settlers some five hundred years or so ago—
scarcely further back, after all, than the discovery of America is
behind us—and they maintained intricate family relationships
and family feuds with the people of the lands from which their
fathers had come even as far as the Hungarian plains. Adven-

turous youths would sometimes set out to retrace the old migration routes, spending years wandering from tribe to tribe among
their distant blood-brothers, and, if they returned, they would
bring back family news, and perhaps a wife, and perhaps an ax
or a spiral bracelet of copper as visible proof of the wealth and
sophistication of the fabulous southern lands. They were envied
and admired, these bearers of copper, for metal ornaments and
implements were hard to obtain. Some flat copper axes, it is
true, were brought in across the western sea by infrequent ships,
the ships which brought the architects of the passage-graves and
the expounders of the religion which demanded them. But only
the wealth of a lifetime could purchase such an ax, and if a young
man aspired to that symbol of wealth and culture he must go
out himself and earn it.

Others must make do with implements of flint. And the flintsmith had little to fear from the competition of metal. On the
contrary, he prided himself on producing, from the red-brown
native flint, axes and spears, and even halberds, which from a
distance of a few paces could hardly be distinguished from those
of copper.

In contrast to the rich and variegated urban life of the old
farming lands of the Middle East, with their specialized metalworkers and carpenters, jewelers and shopkeepers, scribes and
auditors and millers and weavers, these homesteaders of the
new lands had only one specialist, the flintsmith. Apart, of
course, from the half-alien priests. Beyond that, all the work of
the settlement was done in common, with only the century-old
division of labor between the sexes. The women undertook the
sickle harvesting and the grinding of the grain in the troughlike
stone querns, the baking and the weaving and the making of pots.
The men tended the cattle, and milked and hunted and car-
pentered, and perhaps sowed the grain. And it was they who
felled timber and chopped the underbrush, though in the actual
burning-off of the new sowing areas all the population took part,
except the youngest children, who were set to watching the pigs
rooting in the forest a safe distance from the fires.

This was the pattern of their lives, and they were not to
know that change was upon them. They had, it would seem,

a primitive vigorous democracy. There were elders, of course, and
a headman to each village, and village and village were united
in a loose confederacy of family relationships. But there were no
autocratic lords, and no palaces or manors. Slavery was accepted
as a natural institution, but slaves were few, because wars were
few. Whether the herds and the crops were held in common we
do not know, but it seems certain that they were tended in
common, and class distinctions are practically unknown. There
were, of course, the natives, the fishers of the foreshores and the
hunters of the less thickly wooded hinterland. But there the bar-
riers were down, had been down for generations. There had never
been any noticeable racial difference between the settlers and
the old hunters and fishers who had dwelt in the land before agriculture came. Now there was none, and few in the village
could not claim a portion of native blood. And while fishing and
hunting were still profitable occupations, the coastal villages on
their millennia-old shell heaps had adopted as much as they
wanted of agriculture and cattle herding, and were often practically indistinguishable from the colonist homesteads. Though,
as their fishing grounds held them to a fixed village site, their
agriculture gave poor returns and was never more than a subsidiary occupation.

The farmers had a knowledge of the outside world greater,
perhaps, than we reckon with. There were many travelers, and
they were not averse to earning the hospitality with which they
were met by giving the news of the places where they had been.
Seated under the great tree at the end of the wide village street
late into the white nights of midsummer, or grouped around
a hut fire in the autumn, the bearded villagers in their homespun cloaks would listen sagely to the latest traveler, and later
compare at length his news with those of other travelers or
with their own recollections of the journeys of their youth. And
the women would listen as they replenished the home-brew, or
prepared the evening meal, their heavy amber necklaces glinting
tawny in the firelight. They knew, vaguely, of the rich lands of
Egypt and Mesopotamia, as a Persian farmer of today knows of
New York, with little idea of direction but some idea of distance,
and they knew that it was too long a journey to be worth making.

What use was all the bronze of the east, if your children were grown men before you returned? But they knew central Europe well by repute as far as the Danube plain, for the people there were their kinsfolk from the dawn of time. And, as we shall see in a later chapter, ships came in every now and then across the North Sea, from Britain and beyond, bearing what trade there was and bringing the message of the passage-grave priests from the far Mediterranean.

By the same channels the farmers of England and Scotland and northern France and central Germany knew of the lands of south Scandinavia, though they may well have looked on them as backwoods areas, not far from the actual frontier regions where, in the valleys of south Norway and central Sweden, the impetus of colonization had died out, where the forests of oak and ash gave way to the serried ranks of the pines, and the short summers and severe winters made the life of the farmer hard and bitter.

In the milder lands of southern England life was good—though not radically different from that of the Danish home-steaders. On this night when the Second Millennium B.C. began, the earth ramparts of the corral on Windmill Hill lay deserted under a powdering of snow. Only twice a year, at the spring and autumn roundups, would the earthworks echo to the shouts and laughter of herdsmen and spectators. Now, in the sheltered wooded valleys below, the wattle villages lay snug and closely grouped. The cattle were out on the water meadows, with a mini-mum of herdsmen. For the weather was milder then than now, and there was no need, as in the more northern Denmark, to cor-ral them for the winter and harvest leaves for their feed. (And only with the worsening weather fifteen hundred years later would it be necessary to bring them into the houses for the win-ter.) The houses were lighter built, and less severely rectangular, than the solid timber structures of Scandinavia, but their furnish-ings were much the same. Bronze was, of course, more common, though still imported from outside and therefore employed mainly for ornament rather than wastefully for implements. Stone and wood and flint must still suffice for these, though in this lighter-timbered land the heavy flint felling axes of Scandinavia had no place. Nor was there any tie of kinship between these British farmers and those of Denmark. The farmers below the Downs claimed kinship rather with the peoples across the Channel to the south. From there, the folk tales of their people would relate, their forefathers had come about a thousand years ago. Over in the more thickly wooded Ardennes lived people with the same hilltop corrals, the same way of life, even an understandable language. In fact a tenuous relationship, a feeling of being of one blood, extended throughout the backwoodsmen of the whole of western Europe, to where the forests of France lapped the bastions of the Alps or petered out on the sun-baked hills facing the Mediterranean.

No one at this time could have explained that feeling of relationship, nor extracted from the legends and fairy tales into which it was woven the original folk tradition that over two thousand years ago the forebears of all the farmers of Europe west of the Rhine had crossed to a virgin continent from North Africa; whereas Europe east of the Rhine had been settled by colonists from Asia Minor who had occupied the Danube valley and from there spread out over the European plain. All that now survived was the feeling that the Western peoples belonged together and that the Danubians east of the Rhine were somehow different.

Still farther south and west, in the southernmost parts of Spain, the inhabitants of the hilltop towns would have protested with vigor at the appellation of "backwoodsmen." Though their sierras are sparsely pine-clad, they do not, like the barbarians of the rest of Europe, burn off their forests to clear new land for planting, nor move their villages from place to place every few years. Their stone-built towns are permanent, fortified with wall and ditch, and they cover several acres of ground. They are proud of being an ancient people, these dark slender Spaniards whose flocks of sheep roam the close-cropped hillsides, and whereas the British cattlemen look no farther for their origins than across the Channel, the Spanish shepherds have never lost the tradition that their forefathers came across the straits from Africa.

But they do not look to the past, but to the future. They do not consider themselves isolated communities on the edge of the uttermost ocean. They know that they are the shock troops of civilization. As we shall see, they are in touch with the civilized east, and in their own eyes they are well on the way to modernity. Within their towns—which are almost cities anyway—they have all the civilized paraphernalia of palaces and temples; they have a cemetery of collective tombs outside the walls quite as impressive as anything in Crete or Egypt. And, clearest of all signs of progress, they have home-produced bronze. It is only a few generations since the prospectors from the east discovered the lodes of copper and tin, but production is now in full swing, both for export and for the home market. It will not be long, they reckon, before they in their turn can begin to spread civilization to the benighted flint-using barbarians of the forests of the northwest.

SUGGESTED RECONSTRUCTION OF A VILLAGE IN SOUTHERN GERMANY AT THE BEGINNING OF THE SECOND MILLENNIUM, BASED ON AN EXCAVATED SITE AT AICHBÜHL.

They are not the only Europeans who consider themselves well on the way to civilization. In the Balkans and along the valley of the Danube there are also farming communities which have recently taken the (in their own opinion) most important step, the change-over from flint to bronze. Admittedly they are forest farmers, moving their villages to new clearings every few years in the way of the real backwoodsmen farther north. But their forests are the open woodlands of the great plains of glacier dust, where there is room for their massive ox wagons to maneuver between the trees. They move in style, with many possessions. And since the prospectors from Asia Minor discovered the copper lodes in their mountains, they have begun themselves to make axes and adzes of the metal. In their rectangular frame houses the housewives display proudly on wooden shelves pottery which is burnished and painted in spirals and meanders of white, yellow, and red, home-produced but quite as decorative as anything that can be imported from Asia Minor. And they talk with cultured sympathy of the primitive way of life farther north and west where pottery is undecorated, or at best decorated with chalk rubbed into grooved patterns to imitate their own sophisticated ware. And their menfolk wear signet stamps hanging from a cord around their necks. They understand the importance, now that communications with Asia Minor are becoming more regular, of being able to set their seal on their wares, and there has even been talk in the town council of sending young men south to learn to read and write.

Yes, things are stirring in Europe. The winds of change are blowing from the southeast, and the farmers of Europe are alive to the opportunities of the new age. The civilized lands have marvelous devices for sale, if only one had the wealth to buy them. And, who knows, if one could strike copper or tin on one's territories, or find some other marketable commodity, it might be possible at that. . . .

The farmers of Europe did not look beyond the civilized lands to the south and east. In that direction lay wealth and culture; in the other direction lay the cold benighted lands where, if one went far enough, even cultivation ceased. That there could be other lands, on the other side of the civilized world, never even occurred to them. (And we can hardly reproach them, for until very recently we too have paid little attention to the prehistory of regions other than those of the ancient civilizations and of Europe. Even now we know all too little of the state of the rest of the world at this arbitrarily chosen date of 2000 B.C.)

South of the Sahara there stretches, at this date, a broad belt of tropical grassland, from the fringes of the Guinea coast of Africa in the west, across the upper valley of the Niger to the Sudan, the upper Nile, and the mountains of Abyssinia in the east. To the north the grass fades out into the wastes of the Sahara, to the south it is swamped in the forests of the Gold Coast and the Congo. It is an area as large as Europe, and at the beginning of the Second Millennium B.C. it too is occupied—let us qualify that: there is evidence that it probably was occupied—by agricultural peoples.

They are dark of skin, these farmers of Africa (they are the ancestors of most of the Negroes of America), and they live in thatched huts in small communities, surrounded by their fields. They know no more of Europe than Europe knows of them, and their agriculture is very different from that practiced north of the Sahara and of the Mediterranean. They grow no wheat or barley, though the easternmost communities are in precarious, and often warlike, contact with Egypt, and are there learning of the existence of barley and millet. Their life is based on the cultivation of sorghum and ground nuts, gourds and watermelons, supplemented by hunting, for they have no domestic animals—though again in the east they have picked up from Egypt the idea of keeping sheep and even cattle.

In an area the size of Europe there is as much diversity as in Europe, and undoubtedly the Nubians in the Sudan regarded themselves as vastly more cultured than the semihunters, semigardeners of the far west. But over the whole range agriculture is so old that no tradition remains of its beginnings. We, too, know little of its origins. We are inclined to date the first beginnings to 4000 or even 5000 B.C., and we are allowed to speculate whether the idea of taming wild plants occurred independently to the inhabitants of this region, or whether the idea came—without the crops—from the old cultivators of the Nile valley and was merely translated in the Niger valley to the wild plants of that region. We shall meet the same problem elsewhere, and we need not take a stand with either the champions of diffusion or those of independent invention; whichever was the case, it happened everywhere long before our story opens. Again as in Europe, the African farmers use solely implements and weapons of stone and wood, with a little bronze (probably more than we guess) being traded for ivory into the Sudan from Egypt. The art of weaving, too, and potterymaking peter out as one travels from east to west, the westerners making do with gourds and baskets and fashioning such clothing as they need from bark. But even in the west they are no benighted savages. They have their village councils, their division of labor, their songs and legends and art forms; they have recited histories and genealogies going back hundreds of years into the past. We must not assume that they knew nothing of themselves merely because we know nothing of them.

In three other parts of the world, each of them an area comparable with Europe in size, there were at the beginning of the millennium groups of communities which farmed the earth for their livelihood. Each of them, too, must have had its histories and legends, its separate languages and nations, its wars and kings and dynastic struggles. And each was composed of individual men and women, working and playing, making war and making love, worrying about next year's harvest or the need to renew the house roof or to keep the gods benevolent. Each of them knew that his own community was the center of the universe, was actively conscious of the neighboring communities within a few days' journey, and was vaguely aware of the total extent of the farming area to which we, in our wisdom, ascribe him (though he himself would have protested that the distant peoples of "his" area were completely foreign, in customs and language and appearance—as different as a Labrador lumberman and a Mexican cattle rancher). And, with more or less interest, depending on how close he lived to the center of his area, he would know that there were other people outside the pale who had other ways of life, hunters or herdsmen, nomads or city dwellers.

In one of these areas, stretching from the headwaters of the Ganges across northeast India to Burma, Siam, and Indochina, the inhabitants were as actively aware as were the European backwoodsmen—and perhaps the African gardeners—of a literate "industrialized" civilization on their borders. The nearest towns of the organized kingdoms of the Indus valley lay in considerable numbers in the hill country between the Indus and the Ganges, and one or two new towns had recently been built close to the upper Ganges itself. Traders and prospectors must have followed the Ganges downstream, and goods from the city manufacturers must have been available, if only one could afford them. So bronze would be known to the farmers of farther India, as it was known to the farmers of farther Europe, but only as a fabulously expensive civilized luxury, to be aspired to as a native of Zanzibar or the Fiji Islands might today aspire to purchase a radio or an outboard motor.

Otherwise, the eastern Indians make do with the stone tools which their forefathers have used as far as legends go back, the polished axes and stone-weighted digging sticks and pierced stone clubs. The growing of corn is spreading eastward from the Indus valley, but by tradition these farmers are rice growers. When the first year of the Second Millennium B.C. begins, they are already preparing for the spring sowing. For the jungle must be burnt off during the first two months of the year. At the chosen areas on the hill slopes the larger trees were ringed the previous year, and they now stand dead and can be felled, or at least partly cut through, so that they will fall when the area is fired. The undergrowth and the smaller trees need not be felled, except in the fire breaks, which must now be cleared completely to prevent the flames from spreading to the whole jungle.

The days of the burning are busy ones for the whole population of the village. They move out in a body from their clay and bamboo houses and establish themselves in flimsy shelters near the chosen area. After sacrifice to the gods of fire and fertility, they set torches to the underbrush, working backwards into the wind so that the flames may not join force with the wind to jump the breaks. All the men and most of the women are out, naked to the waist, setting the fires, piling partly consumed branches and bushes together into individual bonfires, guiding the fall of the great trees. Afterwards, when the fires die down, the trees must be lopped and the branches burnt, while the trunks are rolled to the edges of the area to form the basis of the fence.

Throughout the work, which lasts out the two months, the children and the older folk are busy preparing meals, carrying water to the thirsty workers, and spreading and raking the ashes. Finally the area lies desolate, blackened and clear except for the charred stubs of trees. The men can return to their hunting, except for those who are to build the stout fence that will keep wild animals from the crops.

Now the area can be allowed to rest, the life-giving ashes to settle into the soil. When the rains begin in May, the sowing can start. Then it will be the women's turn. Beginning at the foot of the slope, they will work their way up, digging small holes six inches or so apart with their weighted sticks and dropping four or five grains of the mountain rice in each hole. Nothing more is needed. Except for weeding, the rice needs no more care until the harvest.

With the harvest there will again be a busy time for all the villagers. The rice will be cut with flint-edged clay sickles, parboiled in large earthenware pots and then mixed with sand, heated red hot in a beehive-shaped clay oven. When the mixture is dry, and the sand removed by sieving in wickerwork sieves, the rice will be pounded in deep wooden mortars to remove the hulls, and then winnowed by tossing in basketwork trays. Then the rice is ready for storage in the large pots sunk into the floors of the houses. Another year's harvest will be home.

Thus life goes on, with seedtime and harvest marked by the village feasts, with offerings of fruits and flowers and rice cakes to the gods who control the increase of the earth. It is a year like any other.

On the Yellow River, in northern China, life is more organized. It is the time which later generations will look back upon as the Hsia Dynasty, the first of the innumerable dynasties which followed the reigns of the three great emperors of the Golden Age, Yao, Shun, and Yü. But though there is an emperor, he is but the titulary head of a loose organization of farming villages confined to the wooded valley of the river. The villagers clear their planting areas from the forest with stone axes and with fire, for bronze, though known, is still rare. They plant millet and kaoliang and breed cattle, pigs, and dogs for the pot. Had they known it, it is a frontier agriculture similar in all respects to that of Europe. But they know nothing of Europe. They probably know whence came their agricultural way of life, for it cannot have been more than five or six hundred years since their hunting ancestors began to raise their own food. Unlike them, we can only guess. It seems unlikely that a way of life so like that of the other northern agricultural area was developed by independent invention. But it did not come from the south. For between north China and the southern agriculturalists of the Ganges valley lies all south China and Indochina, a land of mountain and jungle whose inhabitants know nothing of planting and harvesting. Only around the coasts are there scattered settlements of fishermen who have learned to plant taro and yams by the digging-stick methods of the rice growers—and they are more interested in expanding to the islands of the southeast than to the cold winters of the northern lands. We can guess that the idea of agriculture, and with it the millet seed and domestic animals, had moved slowly from oasis to oasis along the northern foothills of the Tibetan plateau, and across the half-desert grasslands which then covered the Taklamakan and the Koko Nor.

As on the coasts of south China, so on the coasts of Peru there are settled communities of gardener-fishermen. But it is hardly necessary to postulate a traffic across the Pacific bearing the idea of plant cultivation (though that would explain the presence of cotton on both sides of that ocean). These villagers live where their ancestors have lived for five centuries and more, upon the gradually mounting mounds of mussel shells and general refuse of their occupation, lying close to the sea at the mouths of the steep and arid valleys running down from the Andes. They live mainly on fish and shellfish, with an occasional sea lion or porpoise when luck is with their hunting. But in the low marshy meadows by the river they plant and harvest peppers and beans, squashes and gourds and cotton. Their shawls are colorful and attractively woven, and form their only item of clothing. They have no pottery and, of course, no consciousness that it is lacking from their inventory. What more, anyway, could they need than the gourds they grow and the baskets and nets they are so adept at constructing? After all, they are the most advanced people in the world as they know it, and they have reason to be proud of the fact.

3

THE OUTBACK

W E H A V E R A N G E D widely in the last chapter. Yet the greater part of the world remains untouched; many other men and women, of diverse physical types, saw the sun rise upon the Second Millennium B.C. In their diversity they have one thing in common: they accept the world as it is. They live on what the world, as it is, can provide, and do not, as the other peoples we have passed in review, seek to force nature into a more favorable pattern. Instead of planting the crops they wish to eat, they eat the crops which nature chooses to plant. Instead of herding and penning the animals whose meat and pelts they wish to use, they use the meat and pelts of the animals which happen to exist within their range. They are hunters and fishers, and collectors of the wild fruits of the earth.

Except for those who live close to the lands of cultivators and herdsmen, they are not aware of having any choice in the matter. No other way of living has ever existed; no other way of living is even remotely conceivable. Fish and game and edible plants are the only things that man can eat, and the only way to get them is—to get them.

The sun that aroused the cities and villages of the Nile to a new day, and was already brightening the sky above the melon fields and grass huts of the Nigerian cultivators, found hunting parties on the South African veldt already awake and preparing to take up the pursuit of their game at the point where the same sun, sinking on the Third Millennium, had interrupted them. A typical team, no more than four men strong, has been following a wounded giraffe for three days now. The tracks show clearly that the animal is weakening, as the poison from their fire-hardened arrows takes effect, and they are gradually regaining the distance they lost when the freshly wounded animal escaped their ring. With the first light of dawn they are on their way, following the faint spoor with scarcely a check, noting where the animal has stopped to rest with increasing frequency, and, as they go, scavenging almost automatically for anything edible, pouncing on lizards, flushing a lark from its fledglings, or pausing briefly to grub up a tuber.

They are small dark men, these bushmen of the veldt, almost pygmies in stature, thin but incredibly wiry, and they chatter among themselves as they lope along the trail. They are in high humor, for they know that this time their hunt will be successful. Before they started out five days ago the eldest of them had drawn a giraffe on the wall of the temple-cave. There is no doubt that it was that drawing which brought within range of their arrows the giraffe they now follow and that the drawing is still doing its work to bring the animal down.

Towards the afternoon they sight their quarry, standing with drooping neck and wide-straddled legs in the shade of a clump of trees. As they approach, it tries to run but stumbles and then wearily turns to face them. They stand at a distance, out of reach of the still dangerous hoofs, and aim their arrows carefully at the area of the heart. Even so, six arrows strike before one is successful, and the great animal quivers, runs two strides and falls, twitching, to the ground. The hunters close in, to deliver the *coup de grâce* with their stone knives. And while three remain to skin and partition the dead animal with the same knives, the fourth sets off on the long journey to bring the rest of the family group.

For such a quantity of meat cannot be transported to the family at its semipermanent home by the water hole below the outcrop ridge. The family must, as so often before, move to the meat. Some of it can be sun-dried for later use, but most must be eaten on the spot during the few days before it will become too "high" even for an experienced stomach. They will gorge while they can, and starve when they must. That is the way of the hunter.

So the family, the women and children and the old men, break camp when they hear the word. Their only possessions are a skin or two for the shelters, a bundle of arrows, and a basket or two containing spare stone knives and scrapers and a stock of roots for brewing arrow poison. These are carried by the women, while the oldest man bears the masks and monkeys' tails and paints which are rather more important than the weapons in ensuring hunting luck. And the whole party moves off, naked and in high humor, through the thorn scrub.

Throughout the warm lands the picture is much the same. In the rain forests of the Congo—and of the Amazon—different animals are hunted, different plants and tubers and small game collected. And the people have a different physiognomy and a different language. But the day-to-day problems and the day-to-day satisfactions are the same. In southern India and in Australia, and scattered throughout the chain of islands between them (but not in New Zealand or the Pacific islands, which are still unknown to man), recognizable cousins of the South African bushmen live a recognizably similar life. But the great migration that spread the Australoids across half the world is many many thousands of years in the past. It has dropped from the recollection of man millennia ago, and now the scattered communities know nothing of any land but their own. Their horizon is bounded by the extent—admittedly widespread—of their own hunting grounds, and each family group rarely meets even the next group—though it is the rule that men must seek their women outside the group.

We shall not meet these hunters of the tropics again in this book. For them the coming millennium brought no basic change in mode of life and except in rare cases no contact with the history we shall recount. But we should not forget that the hunters are there all the time; that they occupy much of the world's surface and comprise much of the world's population; and that while better-documented events are occurring in Europe and in Hither Asia, generation after generation of the hunters is being born, and living, and dying. They are as entitled to their place in the story of mankind as any literate citizen of Ur or of Thebes or of Harappa.

No sun rises over the Arctic regions this first day of January in the year 2000 B.C. But in the desolate lands looking out upon the polar seas people are living, huddled in half-underground sod and stone houses in the dim twilight of the arctic day, warm and cozy in the clear light and comforting heat of their blubber lamps. They sleep on while the dawn of the millennium sweeps round the world, for what is there to wake for? In the caches raised on poles out of reach of wolves and foxes there are provisions for weeks ahead, whole carcasses of reindeer and seal, and stocks of frozen fish. For the moment there is no need to hunt. It will be long, though, to the spring thaw, and it would be wise, if the wind drops, to go out to a breathing hole in the ice and, if the gods are kind, to harpoon a seal. One can, after all, never have too many seals, and the winter settlement is sited on the sea-shore with that very end in view.

In the meantime the womenfolk can prepare food over the lamps or at the hearth just within the doorway. And they can dress furs with their flint scrapers and sew them with bone awls and sinew threads into clothing which will withstand the bitter cold of the long wait by the breathing hole.

But when the gales rage, and the men are inside the rectangular houses, they sit around, desultorily repairing harpoon thongs or fashioning new points of bone and walrus ivory, or new knives or scrapers of flint or slate. There is time to spare in the winter, and they talk of the long days of summer, recollecting the year before and planning the year ahead.

When the ice goes out they will move, for then the seals can no longer be approached by stealth, and they must go abroad to find the reindeer. They will pull the roof from their house before they leave, to let the summer sun and rain sweeten the interior after a winter's habitation. And they will pack their skin tents and spears and harpoons in the big skin boats. It happens that they must travel far to find the reindeer. But it often happens that they travel farther yet just for the fun of traveling. For though they feel safer with a herd in the neighborhood, they can always get along on fish and hares and berries; or they may sight a walrus or a school of right whales and harpoon a feast for the whole boat family for several days. So they cover great distances in the summer along the arctic coasts, and think little of crossing from Siberia to Alaska, or from Baffin Land to Greenland, or from Nor-

way to Novaya Zemlya. It matters little if they do not return to
their winter settlement. They can build another, or repair an old
abandoned one somewhere else.

There are one or two appointments they must keep. There
is one with the reindeer at the autumn migration, where toll is
taken of the passing herds with harpoons and fall traps. There is
one with the salmon at the estuaries of the great rivers, where the
fish can be caught by hand and tossed ashore without need of
nets or lines. And there is one with the forest people at the great
autumn marts held by the estuaries after the salmon run.

They know the forest people well; the two peoples hold each
other in wary esteem. Throughout the year the arctic hunters
have been amassing a little store of trade goods, walrus and
narwhal ivory, pelts of polar bear and arctic fox, lamp blubber,
and carved knife handles of reindeer antler. And at the mart they
will exchange them for the goods of the forest people, the hollow-
ground stone adzes, the skins of otter and mink, and the birchbark boxes of molasses or honey.

The life of the arctic hunters has lasted unchanged for millennia and will last unchanged for millennia to come. Their ancestors had lived much the same life on the edge of an icecap
which, in an age now long forgotten, had stretched down to the
plains of Germany. And their descendants will live much the
same life when Alaska is incorporated as the forty-ninth state.

The forest folk, too, live a life based on thousands of years
of tradition. Through the great pine forest of North America, Russia, and Scandinavia they have moved along their game trails
during the long days of the previous summer. They have traditional camping places where they pitch their skin tents for weeks
at a time, fishing and hunting and gathering plants and berries
until the scarcity of game suggests a move. They live and move
in small groups of but a few families, except at the tribal meetings, where, on the banks of one of the rivers, hundreds of families, coming from all directions, pitch their tents and chaffer and
exchange news—and daughters—while the grown men gather
in council to discuss war and peace and tribal boundaries and
game movements and fishing rights and the succession of the

chiefs. There, too, the initiation ceremony takes place, when the young warriors who have endured the testing period without flinching are duly admitted to their place at the council. Then they disperse again, and the little groups of buckskin-clad, moccasined hunters make their way back through the endless forests to their own hunting grounds.

But now it is winter. The snow piles thick on the pines and spruces and lies heavily on the ground between. Only with snowshoes or skis is it possible to get around at all, and even so the hunters prefer to keep to their trodden trails, which make the round of their trap lines. It is the season for pelt hunting, to replace the fur garments worn out the winter before and to replenish the trade stocks depleted in the autumn marts. The people are now in their winter quarters, round tent-shaped huts of sod lined with birchbark, and they will not move until the spring. But here, where the sun sheds a little light and warmth in the middle of the day, there is more work going on than among the

THIS PICTURE OF A HUNTER PURSUING AN ELK IS CARVED ON THE ROCKS OF ZALAVROUGA IN NORTHWEST RUSSIA. ALTHOUGH OF UNCERTAIN DATE, IT IS OF IMPORTANCE AS SHOWING THE EARLY USE OF SKI (WHICH ARE ALSO ATTESTED FROM BOG FINDS IN FINLAND). THE HUNTER IS APPARENTLY ARMED WITH BOW AND ARROW.

arctic folk. It is the time for tree felling and carpentry. Dugout canoes are being fashioned, and the settlement echoes with the thud of the greenstone adzes with which the boats are being hollowed out. Sledges are being made or repaired, and the young men are exercising their dog teams in the difficult art of threading the tree stems at speed. Skins are pegged out and scraped; harpoons and chisels and axes are being fashioned from deer antler; knives, of slate or flint or wild-boar tusks, are being hafted. There is work, and to spare, to fill the short hours of daylight.

There is little hunting, for there are good stocks of dried fish and venison, supplemented by an occasional jack rabbit from the snares. The men have enough to do preparing their equipment for the following summer. Even so, they have time in the evenings around the central fire to add decoration to their tools and weapons, carving figures of animals on the bone or wooden hafts of their spears and axes, or finishing off their knife handles with the head of an elk or a reindeer, carved in the round. These carvings are eagerly sought after by the plainsmen farther south, and—who knows?—perhaps one of the elk-headed knife handles might end up adorning a blade of copper far away in the almost mythical regions south of the plains. The women are busy, too, looking after the children and cooking food, and curing and sewing furs. But now that the ground is frozen they are at least free of potterymaking, for the clay can no longer be dug or mixed. The pots they have now must last out the winter.

Actually, though, potterymaking is a favorite occupation. There is time for gossip while the clay is being fashioned, coil by coil, into round-bellied bowls and vases; and there is room for artistic expression in the decoration, for an elaborate composition of lines and pittings and commas, incised with whatever comes to hand, a pointed stick or a comb or a piece of whipcord or the cut end of a bone. And then the firing, in the constantly replenished clay oven, is always exciting, for many a masterpiece falls to bits in the kiln or comes out misshapen or discolored. Those that survive are eagerly compared and commented upon and shown around to the housewives of the other tents. Now, in the winter, the women must satisfy their artistic urges by sewing elaborate

Nubian mercenaries at all times formed an important part of the Egyptian army. About 2000 B.C. they were mainly employed as archers, auxiliary to the regular units of Egyptian infantry, who were armed with spear and shield. These foot-high wooden figures are from the grave of Mesehti, a baron of Assiut in upper Egypt, who lived about this date.

PLATE I

Many aspects of the life of the Egyptian baronial households about 2000 B.C. are illustrated by wooden models deposited in the graves of the nobles, to provide them with servants and retinue in the world to come. In this model grain store from upper Egypt the clerks in the anteroom keep tally of the sacks carried in.

PLATE II

This bronze head, discovered in a rubbish heap at Nineveh, is of the period of Sargon of Akkad. Although found five hundred miles north of Akkad itself, it is believed to be a portrait of that monarch who, three hundred years before the Second Millennium opened, established an empire stretching from the Mediterranean to the Persian Gulf.

One of the "Royal Graves" of Ur, of about 2400 B.C., contained, in addition to many human sacrifices, a "standard" of shell and lapis lazuli, bearing on its two sides pictures of Sumerian life in war and peace. This, the "peace" side, shows the king and his family feasting to music and song, while below them subjects bring tribute, bales of produce, sheep, oxen, and asses. The "war" side shows the infantry and ass-drawn chariots of the Sumerian army (see page 13).

PLATE III

The brick-built city of Mohenjo-daro, in the valley of the Indus, was divided into blocks by wide avenues with covered drains, one of which is seen on the left. The brick path to the right is modern, for the convenience of tourists, as are the steps in the distance, which lead up to two later street levels.

The great bath within the citadel at Mohenjo-daro is provided with an elaborate system of wells for filling and drains to remove the water. It is believed to have been built for religious purposes, and it may well be that the missing temple connected with it lies under a Buddhist *stupa,* two thousand years later in date, which is situated beside the bath.

PLATE IV

Raised stone slabs, with dry-walling between, ring the foot of the barrow of Grønhøj in Jutland, Denmark. The entrance, undoubtedly closed by a wooden door originally, leads to the passage-grave within, a large stone chamber which served as communal tomb for a nearby Stone Age village. This passage-grave was built about 2000 B.C. and was in use at the beginning of the Second Millennium.

PLATE V

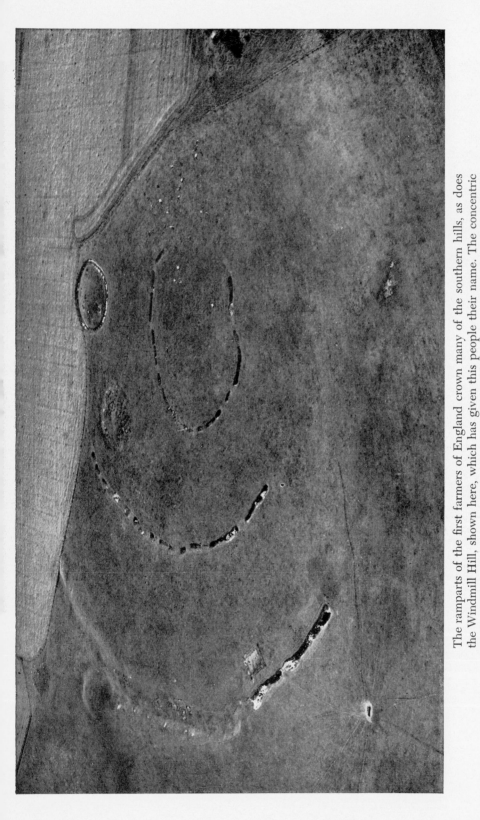

The ramparts of the first farmers of England crown many of the southern hills, as does the Windmill Hill, shown here, which has given this people their name. The concentric earthworks, with spaced openings, appear to have been used as corrals, probably at seasonal roundups.

PLATE VI

On the island of Bahrain in the Persian Gulf the merchant sailors of Dilmun raised a temple in the latter half of the Third Millennium B.C. It remained in use until well into the Second Millennium, and was twice pulled down and built on a larger scale. The temple stood upon an artificial platform held by high retaining walls. This photograph shows the wall of the terrace of the second temple and, in the foreground, the later terrace wall of the third temple.

PLATE VII

At Alaca Hüyük in northern Turkey relatives of the battle-ax peoples of the Russian steppes appear to have established a kingdom in the centuries prior to 2000 B.C. The rich graves of their princes contain a wealth of silver and gold bowls and vases, copper battle-axes, and solar symbols, and in addition a number of enigmatic foot-high figures of bulls and stags such as this, apparently intended as standards.

The barrows of the battle-ax peoples are found in thousands from central Europe to the Caucasus and beyond. In contrast to the rich graves of chieftains at Maikop and Alaca Hüyük with their gold and silver statuettes and copper standards, the simple graves of Denmark at the northwestern limit of their range contain little of wealth, perhaps only, as here, the amber buttons used to fasten cloaks and, of course, the battle-ax which gave the people their name.

PLATE VIII

fringes and thong embroidery upon the buckskin garments they are making. And here, too, there is much competition.

On the southern edges of the great forests the hunters make contact, at their fall marts, with the people of the plains. But though the hunters of the northern forests live much the same way of life all around the globe, the people with whom they meet are very different in America, Asia, and Europe.

In America they meet the buffalo hunters of the Great Plains. They are no mean hunters, these plainsmen. They take pride in choosing out and dispatching the largest of the bison, facing them on foot with their flint-tipped spears. And current still are folk tales from the time when their ancestors a thousand years ago trapped the great mastodons which then lived in the Mississippi valley.

In Asia the southern neighbors of the forest dwellers are the herdsmen of the steppes. We shall meet in a later chapter these shepherds and cattlemen who ranged over the wide plains from the Black Sea to Mongolia, driving their flocks of sheep and herds of cattle and horses from valley to river valley and from water hole to water hole.

In the south these herdsmen are in trading contact with the bronze-using cultivators of the Middle East, and from them they have heard of the ass-drawn carts used by the Sumerians in warfare. They are at this time experimenting with modifications of this radical invention, heavy four-wheeled wagons to be drawn by oxen, and light two-wheeled chariots which they are training their horses to draw. But only the vaguest reports of these technical wonders reach the southern fringes of the forest, just as the copper weapons known to be current among the rich herdsmen of the south rarely reach the north, though stone imitations of the copper battle-axes are not uncommon.

In Europe the pine woods end not in plains but in the oak and ash forests which cover the low-lying coastlands around the North Sea and stretch down over the flatlands of central Europe. Scattered through the forests are the clearings of the backwoods farmers, some abandoned and overgrown, others cleared and ready for the wheat and barley to be sown among the tree stumps. By the cleared fields stand square two-roomed houses of timber or of wattle and daub. But by fjords and seacoasts lie other settlements of a very different type.

Though the cultivators have been living in the forests for a thousand years and more, they know that their ancestors came from the south and occupied a land that was not their own. The people who dwell in the shell-heap villages, they know, are the real "natives," who were here when their forefathers came. These people are clearly different, fairer of hair and larger of bone, and they speak a different language.

Only a stone's throw from the beach stretches the long low mound on which the fishing village lies. It is grass-grown except around the circular wattle huts, where the scuffing of dogs and children has brought to light the grey-white oyster shells of which the whole mound is composed. This is the debris of thousands of years of occupation, the remains of the daily meals of a hundred and twenty generations. And to the lee of the huddle of huts the current rubbish heap, spilling down the side of the mound, is still mainly composed of oyster shells, with among them the bones, broken for the marrow and well-gnawed by the dogs, of many a red deer and aurochs. Pigs root along the edges of the mound, turning the drifts of dead leaves in the hope of finding a forgotten acorn, and the dogs lie out in the winter sunshine, curled up with their bushy tails over their noses.

The men are coming in from the marshes now. They saw in the millennium crouched in dugouts in the reeds, waiting to catch the wild fowl on the lake at dawn. And over their shoulders they bear a bundle of ducks and coots brought down by their flint-tipped arrows. They bring enough meat for the day, and the women reflect thankfully that today at least it will not be necessary for them to wade through the icy water out to the mussel banks. While they begin to pluck the birds, the men warm their frozen hands at the hearths and refresh themselves with beakers of beer from the barrel which, together with the beakers, they had bought the previous week from the farmers at the price of a fat roebuck.

Continually there is trade between the farmers and the shell-heap dwellers. Whenever more game or fish is taken than can be used for the pot, it is carried or paddled the six miles to the nearest farming village. The villagers are always glad for a change of diet, and a willing customer can always be found to trade for a length of homespun cloth, a polished flint ax, a pot or two, or a measure of corn or of beer.

Sometimes a young man from the shell heaps will take service for a season with the farmers, hunting for them and lending a hand with the harvest. For a summer's service he can earn a cow, and many of the young men have begun, desultorily, to keep cattle, and even to clear and sow a field. But the regular work entailed in farming is uncongenial to them. Whenever the weather is fine, they set out in their dugouts to the fishing banks; and at any time a school of right whales or porpoises, or a seal or two, may be sighted, and every man turns out to drive the beasts ashore. So agriculture hardly gets the attention it deserves, and most attempts to introduce it peter out.

They travel long distances in their dugouts, or in the larger boats covered with sewn skins. They even occasionally visit their cousins in the marshy lands of eastern England, sailing out on a northeast wind with the big square sail set. For in the fens of England there are also settlements of hunting, sealing, and fishing folk, and many of them have come, within living memory, from Denmark and Sweden. They are daring sailors, these fishers of the North Sea, and some are already talking of signing on in one of the big foreign ships that every now and then come into local waters. They have talked about it to the local priest of the passage-grave religion in his house in the nearby village of the farmers. . . .

4

THE SEA

AROUND THE SEABOARDS of the world more ships than one would guess saw the Second Millennium begin. They are galleys for the most part, broad in the beam and castle prowed and sterned. The majority are drawn up for the night on open beaches, perhaps beneath the tall walls of a seacoast city, perhaps on a naked foreshore to a naked hinterland. Their crews sleep soundly, wrapped in their sea cloaks, beside the oar benches or beneath the poop deck. Many ships, though, lie at anchor in sheltered coves, where the shores are too steep for the vessels to beach; and on these the watchmen blink at the lightening sky and yawn as they greet the new day. And some, caught out on a harborless stretch, or commanded by a devil-may-care captain, fight out the night at sea, with bows turned to meet the waves and with short-hauled oars just giving steerageway. There the dawn is doubly welcome for the view it gives of the coast, which has been muttering menacingly to leeward all night. With the coming of the sun the watch below is roused, and with fully manned oars, or with the approximately lateen sail shaken out to catch a favorable wind, the ships beat onward to their distant goals. By the beached ships the crews await the tide that will aid them afloat again, or load or unload bales and ingots, skins of water and sacks of barley under the direction of the sailing master, while the merchant officers are ashore in the city, completing the final documentation with their agents or negotiating exchanges with the local dealers.

It is predominantly mercantile, this shipping of the turn of the millennium, and we still know far too little about it. But every new discovery, whether of a coastal townsite or of a hoard of

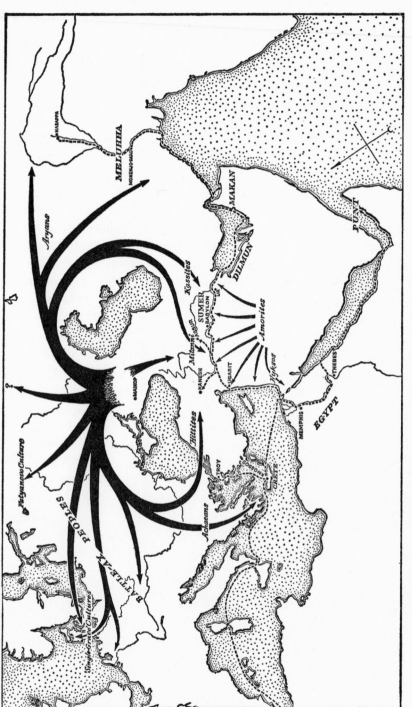

EUROPE AND THE MIDDLE EAST AT THE BEGINNING OF THE SECOND MILLENNIUM B.C. TRADE ROUTES ARE SHOWN BY DOTTED LINES. THE HISTORY OF THE NEXT FIVE HUNDRED YEARS IS TO BE DOMINATED BY THE EXPANSION OF THE INDO-EUROPEAN SPEAKERS FROM THE SOUTH RUSSIAN STEPPES, AND OF THE SEMITIC-SPEAKING AMORITES FROM THE NORTH ARABIAN DESERTS.

cuneiform tablets, seems to add weight to the argument that
sea trading at this time was large-scale, organized, and frequent,
with regular sea routes over distances which, even by our own
standards, are of impressive length.

As with the inland settlements, so, too, of the seaward trade
in the Far East, Africa, and America we know practically nothing. But we can no longer assume that lack of evidence means
that there was no sea trade along the coasts of India, Malaya,
and the Chinas, to Africa and even to America. Written evidence
supported by archaeology confirms such trade in the Red Sea,
the Persian Gulf, and the Indian Ocean, and archaeology alone
is sufficient to demonstrate it throughout the Mediterranean and
the northeast Atlantic. But these are the areas where archaeologists have had a hundred years and more to look for evidence. It
would be surprising if comparable data were not to be found in
regions where they have not yet looked. Be that as it may, we
must not anticipate the evidence—providing only that it be
clearly understood that the account which follows of the merchant adventurers of 2000 B.C. does not imply that none were to
be found outside the areas described.

With a following wind—and the wind blows almost always
from the north in the Persian Gulf—it was a three-day run from
Ur to Dilmun. Despite the dangers of the voyage (squalls are sudden and pirates not unknown), the merchant captains must
have heaved a sigh of relief when their vessels cast off and started
the long drift down the Euphrates. For the moment they could
forget the financial juggling needed to get the voyage started at
all with a full cargo. Deposited at the Ishtar temple ashore are
the documents recording the profit-sharing partnerships and the
direct loans against interest which alone made the voyages possible. At least the complication of money has not yet been invented, and the clay tablets are straightforward enough: "In exchange for thus-and-thus many bales of woolen piece goods the
partners undertake, on the return of their ship from Dilmun, to
pay such-and-such a weight of copper in ingots of good quality.
No responsibility is assumed for loss in transit." No responsibility,
indeed! The captains, who belong to the guild of Dilmun-farers

resident in Ur though many of them are natives of Dilmun or of the lands beyond, are full of scorn for the fat merchants ashore who rake in the profits and refuse to share the risks. But the sight of the sails straining to the fresh breeze, and the conscious-ness of a full cargo of woolens aboard, serve soon to banish the cares of shore life, while the bends of the river and the frequent sandbanks force them to keep their attention on the helmsmen at the large steering oars astern.

In the afternoon they cross the bar into the open waters of the Persian Gulf and as the sun goes down make landfall at the island of Failaka off the Gulf of Kuwait. There, on the sheltered southern shore, is a little town of colonists from Dilmun, and there the ships can be drawn ashore for the night, the captains gladly paying a toll on their cargo for the protection of the town-ship, rather than face the risk of a cutting-out expedition from the piracy-addicted mainland if they anchor farther down the coast.

There is no such security the next night. After a day of coast-ing along the ocher shores, they must anchor in the lee of one of the sandy headlands and hold nightlong watch against raiders from the Bedouin tribes ashore. It is with relief that they see the dawn break and start out to sea once more on the last day's voy-age to Dilmun.

Dilmun is the island now known as Bahrain, and on its north-ern coast the limestone defensive walls and temples of two large cities stand out clearly, from the sea, against the dusty green of the date palms. With its abundant springs of fresh water and luxuriant vegetation, Dilmun has been famed for a thousand years for its health and fertility. The seamen know and, as they walk the ship up the shelving beach, recite in monotonous sing-song the lays of Dilmun, the blessed land of the gods; how it be-came the home of Ziusudra, whom the gods saved from the Deluge, and how Gilgamesh found there, and lost again, the se-cret of immortality.

On the beach many ships are drawn up, most of them larger than the ships from Ur. These are the ocean-going ships, ships from the mountainous land of Makan, beyond the entrance to the Gulf, and ships from Meluhha, the Indus valley itself, a whole

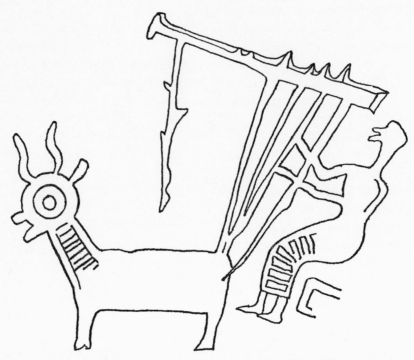

WITHIN THE CITIES OF DILMUN THE SAME CIVILIZED LIFE WENT ON
AS IN CONTEMPORARY SUMER. THIS SCENE FROM A SEAL FOUND AT
FAILAKA, KUWAIT, SHOWS A MUSICIAN PLAYING A HARP OF THE TYPE
FOUND IN THE ROYAL GRAVES AT UR, WITH A SOUND-BOX IN THE FORM
OF A BULL'S BODY AND ORNAMENTED WITH A BULL'S HEAD.

month's voyage away to the east. There is lively talk among the
crews in pidgin-Sumerian and scraps of half the languages of the
east, while the captain is away within the walls of the city con-
tacting his agent and arranging for the stowage of his cargo.
Many of the crews know each other well. Not only have they
met before in Dilmun; the ships from Ur have themselves sailed,
on occasion, to Makan, and both Makan and Meluhhan ships not
infrequently sail to Mesopotamian ports. And Dilmun-owned and
Dilmun-manned ships sail from here to all ports of the known
world.

For the fact of the matter is that the civilized peoples whom
we have already met, in Egypt and Mesopotamia and the Indus
valley, were essentially farming communities, in spite of their

large import and export trade. There were others, no less civilized, whose main means of livelihood was international trade, and whose prosperity, and even existence, depended on keeping open the seafaring routes that they had done so much to establish. The first among these sea-trading powers was Dilmun, the first to appear in history, and the first to fall. We shall later in this chapter meet the second, Crete. The third, Phoenicia, will not come seriously into the picture for several hundred years.

The men of Dilmun were first and foremost sailors. Though their island was well watered and fertile, and already famous for its dates, and though its seas furnished the pearls that were traded, under the name of "fishes' eyes," to the north, neither the harvests of the land nor those of the sea could support the large population that crowded its numerous towns and villages—the population whose burial mounds lie to this day in tens of thousands on Bahrain Island. Dilmun lived by trade. Lying astride the most important sea route of the age, it sent out ships to Mesopotamia and to the Indus cities, and welcomed to its open roadstead and shelving beaches ships of all the coastwise nations of the Indian Ocean. Within its walls was one of the greatest markets of the eastern world, and there were exchanged the staple commodities and the luxury goods demanded by the great civilizations to the north and east. The bulk trade was in textiles from Mesopotamia and copper from the mines of Makan—probably, though Makan has not yet been located, on the coast of Muscat. A very large proportion of the copper worked by the bronzesmiths of the Sumerian cities undoubtedly came from Makan by way of the Dilmun markets. But there was a luxury trade, too, in the products of the Indus valley. When the copper ingots were stored in the holds, the merchant captains would take on board a deck cargo of Indian timber, mangrove poles for building, or perhaps teak. And finally they would fill their chests with the small heavy ingots of gold, and with ivory combs, figurines and boxes of ivory, and soft leather bags of carnelian and lapis lazuli from far Afghanistan by the headwaters of the Indus. Even jade was occasionally offered, and no one knew where *that* came from. Often the chests in the cabin below the poop were worth more than all the rest of the cargo, and they would be sealed se-

curely with the round stamp seals of the Dilmun merchants and
guarded by two of the more trusted members of the crew while
the heavily laden vessel beat northward against the wind, back
to the security of Failaka and the waiting capitalists of Ur.

A thousand miles away to the west, across the breadth of
Arabia, other ships were sailing the Red Sea, on another of the
important trading routes of the world of 2000 B.C. We know little of this route, but that is more by the accident of circumstance
than because the route was unimportant. We know it only from
the records of the kings and of the upper civil servants of Egypt,
and it was only on occasion and as an exception that they were
interested in recording overseas commerce. The records of the
independent merchants, if such existed, would be written on papyrus and have perished, unlike the records of the Dilmun traffic, which are stamped on imperishable baked clay. And no serious archaeological investigations have yet been made along the
line of the route, or at its destination.

The destination of these ships was the land of Punt. And the
location of the land of Punt is anybody's guess. Yet Punt was
well known by hearsay to the Egyptian of 2000 B.C. He himself
had no doubt as to where it lay. Far longer than tradition could
record (*we* know that it was well over a thousand years) goods
from Punt had been reaching Egypt, and for at least as long as
three hundred years Egyptian ships had been sailing the route
thither.

They sailed from the point on the Red Sea coast closest to the
Egyptian capital, Thebes—and it can hardly be accidental that
Thebes lay on the great bend of the Nile, where the river approaches within a hundred miles of the Red Sea coast. From there
they sailed south, for an indefinite distance. The state records tell
us only of the state-sponsored expeditions to Punt, but surely
there were also private merchant adventurers, here as in the Persian Gulf, who would make the journey for the profit to be won
from the merchandise they could bring back. For the merchandise brought back by the royal convoys is rich enough in all conscience. Gold and ivory and ebony, frankincense and myrrh, apes
and leopards and slaves, particularly dwarfs, are listed; and

these goods all commanded a high price in the Egyptian markets. They give us, too, the only indication we have of the location of Punt. Frankincense must have come, as it comes to this day, from the Hadramaut on the south coast of Arabia. Gold and ivory and ebony must have come from central Africa. The dwarfs, too, to judge by the pictures preserved on tomb paintings in Egypt, are probably the pygmy bushmen of Africa. Yet the ordinary inhabitants of Punt, who are also illustrated (with their hands tied behind their backs) are not Negroes, but are painted in the red color which by Egyptian convention is reserved for the Hamitic races. It would seem that we are on the track of another sea-trading emporium like Dilmun, a mercantile empire which, centered somewhere near the outlet of the Red Sea on either the African or the Arabian coast, sent its own ships to gather trade goods from the coast of Arabia and far south into Africa. Its ships, at this dawn of the Second Millennium b.c., may well have been as numerous on the waters of the Red Sea and the Indian Ocean as those of Egypt, sailing the produce of the southlands to the markets of Egypt and returning with the linen and manufactured goods of the north.

Far to the north, across the isthmus of Suez and three days' sail from the mouths of the Nile, lay the greatest mercantile nation of them all, Crete. From its high limestone cliffs and headlands the inhabitants of the tiny villages could look out over the blue Mediterranean and see no land in any direction. But the white sails which dot the sea would tell of the lands below the horizon: to the south, Egypt; to the east, Asia Minor; to the north, Greece; and to the west, a whole world.

The men of Crete have been sailors as long as they have been farmers. And that, though they can scarcely be aware of it, is well over a thousand years. Their traditions do not tell them where their ancestors came from, and even today we cannot supply the answer. But the earliest traces of man on Crete are of stone-using farmers, farmers whose implements and pottery show a bewildering mixture of Near Eastern and Egyptian characteristics. These first farmers may therefore have come from two directions, but wherever they came from they must have come in ships.

Now they populate thickly the steep valleys and the terraced hillsides, in innumerable small villages and large isolated farms, growing their grain and olives, cultivating their orchards, and pasturing their cattle and pigs in the valleys and their goats on the hills.

On the seacoasts lie the larger villages and towns, with fishing boats pulled up on the narrow beaches, together with an occasional larger cargo vessel. The craftsmen in gold and copper and precious stones, sitting in their open-fronted shops of brick and timber, can look down the steep streets to the bustle on the beach and beyond to the blue sea curving up to the horizon. And they talk, as shopkeepers and craftsmen will, of the difficulties of trade, how raw materials cost more than they used to, and labor is hard to come by, and the margin of profit infinitesimal. They speculate on the destination of the ship now loading on the beach, and tell the latest news and rumors of their sons and brothers overseas. For there is scarcely a family among them which has not several members abroad. A coppersmith has a brother up north at Troy; he has been there five years now, living, as beseems an alien, outside the walls of the prosperous little stronghold at the entrance to the Dardanelles. He is buying up raw copper, and occasionally gold, from the hinterland of Asia Minor and from the merchant sailors who run the coastal trade of the Black Sea, and he sends it on, at a handsome profit, to his brother and the other members of his guild back home in Crete. It is always difficult to get raw materials at reasonable prices, they complain, and dream dreams of the profit that will accrue when the two ships which left a year and a half ago for the almost mythical lands of the west come sailing in, loaded with Spanish copper, and with tin traded in from somewhere beyond even Spain.

Travelers' tales of the whole Mediterranean, of the Black Sea and of the wastes of the Atlantic can be heard in this little Cretan coastal town. Many of the craftsmen and merchants sailed far in their youth, and never weary of saying so. Some spent years in the service of the kings and nobles of Egypt; others have traded their jewelry and bronze daggers and axes among the coastal villages of Greece, to the islands of the

Aegean, or to Cyprus and the Levant. It had been an adventurous life, but not without reward, both material and spiritual. By favor of the mother goddess—and they look toward the squat stone figurine in the niche in the wall—they have, until now, been regarded as citizens of some eminence, with their small but well-built houses and their family burial chambers outside the town.

Now things are changing, and they do not like the change. Farther up the hill behind the town a palace is rising, swarming over the slope in an ostentatious complex of roofs and colonnades and broad staircases. We do not know, at our distance of four thousand years, why, just at this period of Crete's history, the old, apparently egalitarian, pattern of small uniform houses gives place to towns dominated by these extravagant palaces. Simultaneously at three places they rise, at Knossos and at Phaistos and at Mallia, and they must betoken the rise to power of individual ruling princes. There is no break in the archaeological record that would suggest foreign domination. On the contrary, the continuity with what went before is obvious.

Not that the rise of princes need surprise us, though it probably surprised the members of the craftsmen's guilds. Any system of private trading bears within itself the seed of oligarchy. Under such a system only crushing taxation can prevent the rich from getting ever richer—and taxation on such a scale was then unknown. It is probable that it was the millionaires of Crete who now bought themselves into power and erected the palaces. Certainly the palaces appear in plan to be more factories than fortresses. They are centers of mass production of consumer goods, warehouses and counting houses, and at the same time luxurious dwelling places. No defenses were built, either to the palaces or to the cities they dominate, and in that we can see an indication both that the succession to power was peaceful and that the ships of the strongest maritime power in the world were defense enough for the land of Crete.

The ships of Crete that sailed out to the far western lands found there a world completely unlike the one they had left. They were part traders and part prospectors, these wide-ranging sea captains. But though they scarcely realized it, they were most to make their mark as missionaries. By their works we know them, and it is more than a little difficult to see behind the works to the people who were their cause.

The crews, we may imagine, were not entirely Cretan, but were drawn from all the islands of the Aegean and from the scattered cities which, like Troy, stood on the Aegean coast of Asia Minor and made their living by trade. The ships may not all have been Cretan-owned, and it is probable that the western trade was financed by merchants from the whole of the Aegean. The sailors must have been deeply religious, as events are to show. They carried images and amulets of the great mother goddess of their homelands, strange exaggerated violin-shaped female figurines, and they came from lands where the burial customs, undoubtedly of deep religious significance, involved the practice of collective burial in rock-cut tombs or in round vaulted chambers built above ground. They took these customs with them.

There were many routes which the captains could follow. Their first port of call could be in Malta, or in Sicily, or on the southeast coast of Italy. And there they would find small trading stations of their own people. There may not have been more than a Cretan factor, with two or three assistants, perhaps recruited from among the natives; or there might be two or three families of Aegeans, supplementing their trading by fishing and farming. The ships from home, calling in two or three times a year, would land supplies and trade goods, and take on board such local products as the factor had collected since the last visit. There would rarely be a full cargo, and the ships would sail on, bound for Sardinia or the south of France or southern Spain.

The Spanish trading posts were perhaps the most important on the whole route, for in Spain copper could be obtained, and even gold and tin. In most cases a bulk cargo could be obtained for the voyage home, and most ships would undoubtedly turn round here. After all, the voyage from Crete to Spain was long enough. A place now called Los Millares was at this time the greatest center of eastern Mediterranean culture in Spain, and from Los Millares to Knossos was almost exactly as far as from Ur to the mouth of the Indus river. But some ships, it would seem, went on, through the Straits of Gibraltar, beating up along the coast of Portugal against the Atlantic rollers, crossing the Bay of Biscay to Brittany, and sailing on to the north, to the sheltered waters of the Irish Sea, to make landfall on the Irish or the Welsh coasts. This voyage took them as far from Los Millares as Los Millares is from Crete, and only the lure of the red gold panned from the rivers of Ireland could have induced the more venturesome of the ships' captains to brave the perils of the Atlantic and the whole lee shore of Europe. Yet some, it would seem, went farther. Sailing through the Channel, or by way of Scapa Flow, some ships from the Aegean would appear to have reached Denmark across the North Sea, there ending a total voyage of over four thousand miles. And these voyages, it should be emphasized, were not isolated exploits of daredevil captains. All the evidence tends to show that, seen from the time which we now survey, ships from the Aegean had first begun to call at the coasts of northern Europe and the British Isles at least two hundred years ago, longer ago than, for us, the Boston Tea Party.

The evidence for these voyages is slender and lends itself to several explanations. Since it is important to the events of the following thousand years, it is only reasonable to review it here in some detail.

Along the whole course of the voyage here described, in Malta and in Sicily and in Sardinia, on the west coast of Italy and the south coast of France, along the south and west coasts of Spain and Portugal, in Brittany, Wales, Ireland, and Denmark, a remarkable type of burial monument is found, beginning at all these points in the century or two or three prior to 2000 B.C. This burial monument consists of large tomb chambers for communal burial, approached by a passage, sometimes cut in the living rock, sometimes built of dry stone walling with vaulted roofs, sometimes of upright slabs of stone roofed with similar stone slabs. Sometimes the monuments show combinations of all these factors. The resemblance to the communal graves of Crete and the Aegean is immediately obvious, and it is the greater the closer these sites lie to the eastern Mediterranean. Moreover, mother-goddess idols, and carved reliefs of the goddess, are found in many of these passage-graves, or in the settlements associated with them, and here again the incidences are more numerous the closer one comes to Crete. On the other hand, direct Cretan imports are rare in these areas in this period. They are in fact as yet only attested in Italy, Sicily, Malta, and Sardinia. In Spain and Portugal copper daggers are found which would appear to be local imitations of Cretan types. But north of Portugal no bronze or copper is found, although stone axes and daggers, clearly copies in stone of copper originals, appear in the graves.

This is the evidence to which it is necessary to fit an explanation. It appears clear that a burial practice native to Crete and the Aegean is introduced about 2200 B.C. into areas to which it is foreign, all the way around the coasts of Europe, but not inland, from Italy to Denmark. (It later extended, by cross-fertilization, to other areas, both coastal and inland.) The worship of a Cretan goddess accompanies the burial practice, but is not always, particularly not in the north, attested. And actual objects made in Crete do not penetrate (or at least do not penetrate in sufficient numbers to appear in the archaeological record) more than a quarter of the distance reached by the burial practice.

It has been suggested that this circumstance must mean that the voyagers who reached the north were not traders but missionaries. However, the difficulties involved in financing a voyage of such a length for purely missionary purposes would probably have been even greater then than now, and the ships must at least have paid their own running costs by trade. The most probable explanation of the lack of Aegean trade goods in northern Europe during the spread of the passage-grave religion is that, in coastal-trade voyages of that length, there would be several complete turnovers of cargo. Like the Arab coastal trader of Muscat and Dubai today, who sails yearly to Zanzibar and back, calling in at every port on the way, the Cretan traders of four thousand years ago probably exchanged their cargo at the first port of call, taking on local products, perhaps things so prosaic (and perishable) as wheat or hides or broadcloth, which would command a market at the next port of call. Thus the process would go on, and at each turnover the captain would bank a profit—converted to more easily transported valuables such as gold and tin and semiprecious stones. It is in fact only the possibility of making a profit several times over which could make a voyage of this length, to parts of the world still poor in this world's goods, commercially feasible at all. And thus we would expect to find, at the end of the voyage in Denmark, not copper daggers or silver chalices of Cretan origin, but the products of the last port of call, the flat-cast copper halberds and axes and the golden lunulae of Ireland. And this is in fact what we find.

But the ships and crews which beached at the coastal villages of Ireland and Wales and Denmark would be nonetheless Cretan. And it would be they who preached their religion of mother-goddess worship and of communal burial places—even though the gradually changing style of burial chamber, from vaulted dry-stone structure in the south to megalithic slab construction in the north, would suggest that the local representative of the Cretan traders, the factor left behind to collect produce for the next ship to call (and in his spare time to organize the new religion), was not himself a Cretan but rather an ex-apprentice, a native from one of the nearer countries.

The sea routes of the world, then, are well established at the opening of the Second Millennium before our era. They are perhaps not so old that their beginnings cannot be remembered (though every new discovery tends to make them older and wider). The Mesopotamian trade to the east and the Egyptian trade to the south would seem, by present showing, to be some five hundred years old at this time, about as far in the past as the discovery of America and the beginnings of trans-Atlantic trade for us. And the Cretan trade to the west and north is not more than two or three hundred years old, corresponding in our history to the discovery of Australia. Such old-established trade inevitably means a closely knit world. It would not be impossible for an Indian to reach Scandinavia and return within a space of two or three years. How far he could travel in the other direction only future research along the coasts of the Far East can tell us.

We have ended our survey of the world of 2000 B.C., a world as rich in contrasts as at any period in history. We have seen the settled civilizations of the great river valleys, the Nile, the Eu-

A ROUND STAMP SEAL FROM BAHRAIN, SHOWING TWO HUMAN FIG-
URES, A DATE PALM, AND A GAZELLE. THE GAZELLE, IN PARTICULAR,
IS VERY FREQUENTLY DEPICTED ON THE SEALS OF DILMUN.

phrates and the Tigris, and the Indus, with their millennia-old
irrigation agriculture and their sophisticated city life. Their political and social organization took for granted the use of bronze
and of writing, the production of an agricultural surplus sufficient to support priests and kings and soldiers and craftsmen,
and the augmentation of their own products by the import of
luxuries and necessities from abroad.

Extending outwards from this central civilized area we have
seen the belt of subsistence farmers, the users of stone tools, who
have gradually during the last three thousand years extended the

area of cultivation towards the west, and probably towards the east and south, until the pioneer frontier now stretches along the Atlantic seaboard of Europe and up to the edge of the pine forests of the north. We have guessed a little at the extension of the pioneer farmers into India and China and Africa, and looked at the puzzle of contemporary cultivators in Peru.

We have seen how the knowledge of husbandry also passed the Caucasus to the north, and there resulted in the conversion of the hunters of the Russian steppes into cattle herdsmen and horsemen. And we have looked at the hunters and fishers and gatherers of plants, the practicers of the immemorial policy of collecting what the earth produces, unasked, of food. These gatherers have not yet entirely perished from the earth, even in our day. Four thousand years ago they formed the majority of the earth's population, and covered the greater part of its surface. But they did not remain unaffected by the new agricultural way of life; we have seen how they came to terms with it on the peripheral area of the sown.

Finally we have looked at the sea lanes which bound together the civilized areas and which, extending out to the seaboard frontiers of colonization, kept the pioneers in touch with the centers of civilization. And we have seen how maritime trading cities and empires, as wealthy and cultured as the old-established civilizations, existed to carry on this trade, and spread their religions and cultures far across the world.

Much was to happen to all these peoples during the next thousand years.

Book II

The Chariots

A HORSE CHARIOT CARVED ON THE SLABS OF AN EARLY BRONZE AGE
TOMB AT KIVIK IN SOUTH SWEDEN.

5

THE HORSEMEN OF THE STEPPES

2000–1930 B.C.

T O   T H E   S O U T H   marched the mountains of the Caucasus. First the low green hills up which you could gallop and scarcely wind your horses; but then, if you pushed on, the forested slopes, the rock outcrops, the steep scree-swept valleys where fodder was scarce; and finally the precipices and pinnacles of grey stone, reaching up against the blue of the sky, streaked with snow and crowned with the hanging snouts of glaciers, where no man went. The mountains marched from sea to sea, all of a ten days' hard drive, and they were unbroken, save by a steep pass near the western end, which brought you in three days, leading your horses almost all the way, down to the blue haze of the western sea, and the little estuary where the bronze traders came.

The nomads (let us call them the battle-ax people; it is more than possible that that is what their neighbors called them) were uneasy—as yet—when too near the mountain barrier of the Caucasus, or the rocky shores of the Black Sea and the Caspian, which hemmed them in on the west and the east. But to the north it was different. There rolled the endless plains, the grasslands, parched brown in summer and white with snow in winter, but in spring green as far as the eye could see. To the north and northwest the grasslands stretched, only broken by the great sluggish rivers of the Volga, the Don, and the Dnieper. Even the swiftest messengers of the nomads, with unending relays of horses, would take a month or more to traverse them and to reach the pine forests beyond, which in their turn stretched unbroken, it was said, to the Ice Sea of the far north.

To the north, then, the battle-ax people were free, to roam at will with their herds of small dark cattle and with their thickset muscular horses. The horses were their pride, and were regarded with a worshipful awe, the reason for which was long forgotten. For it was already many generations since the notion of cattle-keeping had permeated by word of mouth through the mountains.

The ancestors of the nomads had lived by the chase, hunting on foot with their dogs the antelope and wild cattle and wild horses of the plains. It was in the deep south, in the fabulous valley of the Two Rivers far beyond the mountains, that the keeping of cattle and sheep in captivity had begun, long before the memory of man. When the idea was brought, not very many centuries ago, to the hunters of the grasslands, it was seized on avidly. Cattle were rounded up in large numbers, but not only cattle. The horse, too, a beast unknown in Mesopotamia, was domesticated, at first solely for the sake of its meat and milk.

But then wanderers from the south brought in a new notion. They told how, in the southern lands, domestic animals, oxen and asses, were used to draw wheeled carts and sledges. And the new herdsmen tried out the idea. Oxen proved tractable, and could pull fairly heavy wagons at a walking pace. But the horse was a different matter. It took time and complicated ritual to break in a horse, and even then it could only draw the lightest carts. But it could draw them fast. Two horses, harnessed to a chariot capable of bearing two men, could travel at speeds never before achieved in the history of man, far faster certainly than a man could run.

No wonder, then, that the horse is worshipped as the servant of the gods. Clearly, the sun-god himself, the chief of all the gods, who can traverse the heavens from horizon to horizon in a single day, must be drawn on his path by horses.

With the invention of the horse-drawn chariot the fetters of distance are loosened, and the herdsmen are given the freedom of the steppes. The result is an explosion. Cattle herding had already caused a phenomenal increase in the human population, an increase which strained the resources of the original home pastures. Some two hundred years before our story opens, even before the harnessing of the horse, the first emigrants had already left the steppes, and had gone south, attracted by the wealth of metal and the skill of the metalworkers in the lands south of the Caucasus. They had carved out for themselves a kingdom in northeast Asia Minor, and there, at Alaca Huyuk, the shaft graves of their kings have been found, wooden chambers below ground in which the princes lay, surrounded by a wealth of the metal they had come to seek.

Now with the advent of the oxcart and the horse-drawn chariot the battle-ax people begin to move north and to fan out east and west. The land into which they move is not empty. Outlying communities of herdsmen, and tribes still in the hunting stage, are overrun, learn the new art of chariotry, and join the advance.

By the year 2000 B.C. the outward expansion of the herdsmen of the south Russian steppes has been going on for some three or four generations. The advance guards of the movement are approaching the Rhine to the west, and washing against the Ural mountains to the east. Some semblance of coherence is, nevertheless, preserved, and the loose confederacy of tribe with tribe, which had existed in the homeland between the Black Sea and the Caspian, still survives. The advance, though swifter than any movement of peoples before, is still not so rapid as to disintegrate tribal union. With the horse chariot messengers can, and do, travel from end to end of the expanding territory in a matter of a few months.

A child born in 2000 B.C. among the nomads grows up aware of a loose kinship with herdsmen over the length and breadth of central and eastern Europe. He will himself be a wanderer, probably never in all his life sleeping under a more permanent roof than the hide or felt tents of his people. As far as he regards anywhere as his "home," other than the place where he encamped last night, he looks back to the land north of the Caucasus, probably to the area of present-day Maikop, where the rich graves of the ancient princes of his people—resembling closely the wooden grave chambers of Alaca Huyuk—lie beneath their green turf barrows.

He will grow up in recognizably the same milieu, wherever

the grazing range of his nation may lie. Although archaeologists have succeeded in dividing the material remains of the battle-ax peoples into some seven different "cultures," the overriding similarities are vastly greater than the small divergencies of pottery types or burial customs on which the division is based. In any case, the divergencies increase as time goes on and as the separate "hordes" of the battle-ax people become gradually isolated from the main stem and differently influenced by the different peoples whom they meet and with whom they mix during their migration. The year 2000 B.C. is early in the migratory period, and homogeneity has not yet been lost.

It is not without reason that the nomads are known today as the battle-ax people. The battle-ax is their characteristic weapon. Every male throughout their range possesses one. He receives it at puberty, after a ceremony of initiation into the ranks of the warriors, a ceremony probably quite as elaborate and barbaric as those we know of among the Plains Indians. This tomahawk is his personal property, clearly possessed of a symbolic, and perhaps religious, significance far outweighing its practical utility, and on his death it is buried with him, laid immediately before his eyes.

The battle-axes are themselves works of art. The closer their owners live to their original homeland north of the Caucasus, the more likely they are to be of metal, heavily cast in solid copper with a shaft hole and a narrow drooping blade. It would seem that they were made by the metalsmiths south of the mountains, modeled on the work axes and adzes of Mesopotamia to the south, and traded north to the nomads in exchange for cattle and hides, and perhaps for the first horses to cross the Caucasus. Farther north copper cannot be bought, and the axes are made of stone. They are of the same pattern, slim shaft-hole tomahawks with trim lines, and are clearly made not merely to resemble but to counterfeit the axes of metal. The casting seams of the metal ax, the ridges of metal left by an imperfect fit of the two halves of the mould, are often reproduced in the stone, while frequently the type of stone chosen, reddish or green in color, seems a deliberate attempt to produce a passable imitation of copper. In other cases ornamental stone such as porphyry is used, and the color and grain of the stone are brought out by careful grinding and polishing.

The place of honor of the tomahawk in the graves is only one of the features of an elaborate ritual of burial which tells us much about the life and beliefs of the battle-ax nomads. The ritual is in essentials the same, whether the burial is of one of the early kings around Maikop or of a simple herdsman on the north European plain. The bodies lie always on their sides, with bent legs and with faces turned to the south. There is a difference between the sexes: men lie on their right sides with their heads to the west, women on their left sides with their heads to the east. And

A SILVER VASE FROM ONE OF THE MAIKOP BARROWS BEARS THIS RE-MARKABLE INCISED LANDSCAPE. IN THE BACKGROUND RISE THE MOUNTAINS OF THE CAUCASUS, AND A BEAR BROWSES IN THE FORESTS OF THE FOOTHILLS. TWO RIVERS FLOW FROM THE MOUNTAINS ACROSS THE STEPPES, ON WHICH ROAM WILD HORSES, CATTLE, AND LIONS.

in even the simplest grave there is, in addition to the ax, at least one drinking bowl placed convenient to the hand. But the graves are by no means always simple. The Maikop graves in particular, probably a century or so earlier than 2000 B.C., show a wealth of furnishings which clearly reveal their royal character. The richest consists of three wooden chambers beneath the earth. In the main chamber a man is buried beneath a canopy adorned with lions and bulls of gold and silver, decked in necklaces of lapis lazuli and turquoise and surrounded by bowls and vases of gold, silver, and stone engraved with mountain scenes and processions of animals, including horses and oxen. He has three socketed axes of copper. In the subsidiary chambers lie the servants of the dead man, a man and a woman, accompanied by less rich accoutrements.

From the relics of the dead we can deduce something about the life of these nomads of the steppes. We know from the many flint arrowheads in the graves that they possessed the bow as well as the ax. In the graves, too, we find proof, in the form of a two-wheeled cart, that they had already learnt to make and use vehicles, and to break their animals to harness. The frequent discovery of two large amber buttons lying close to the throat of the men suggests that a prominent article of their clothing was a loose cloak secured at the neck. Other evidence of clothing we do not possess, but we can assume that they were acquainted with the art of weaving.

They worshipped, it would seem, gods of the sky and the horizon, as is natural for nomads and pastoralists—whereas dirt farmers tend to worship gods and goddesses conceived of as dwelling underground or in natural features of the landscape. That their dead lay with their faces to the south suggests that they were in particular sun-worshippers, a suggestion reinforced both by their later history, which we shall see in due course, and by the presence of golden discs, representing the sun, in the graves of their cousins in northern Asia Minor. We have reason to believe that the horse was venerated, and we have already seen that the ax was an object of ritual and symbolism.

Who are, then, these people who in 2000 B.C. occupy half of Europe with their chariotry, and are still expanding their domains? We know from innumerable skeletons that they are a long-headed race and that the racial type is homogeneous from one end of their range to the other. Appropriately enough in view of their place of origin, they are of the type now called Caucasian, one of the main components at this day of the European and Middle Eastern peoples. We have every reason to believe that the language they speak is Indo-European, that genus of language to which belong most of the languages of Europe, in addition to Persian and Hindustani. One must be careful to distinguish language and race. When peoples of two races and two languages meet and mix, both races, as well as all grades of admixture between them, will survive. But normally one language

completely drives out the other. Language is therefore no cri-
terion of race, and it would be incorrect to describe the
battle-ax people as Indo-Europeans. It will nevertheless be done
frequently in the following pages; what is meant in fact is a people speaking an Indo-European tongue and containing a significant admixture of the Caucasian stock to which the battle-ax
people belonged. They are to be, after all, one of the principal
actors on the stage of the Second Millennium B.C., and it is necessary for them to have a name. We do not know what they called
themselves. They had no writing, and they have no history, save
what the archaeologist can recover.

In the lifetime following 2000 B.C. the spread of the toma-
hawk-wielding "Indo-Europeans" is the most significant thing
that is occurring. It would not have appeared so to the inhabitants of the agricultural and trading civilizations to the south. To
them the movements of peoples beyond the innumerable mountain ranges of eastern Turkey and western Persia, with the great
bulwark of the Caucasus beyond, are of little interest, and their
own domestic quarrels assume an importance which domestic
quarrels always do to the people intimately concerned.

In southern Mesopotamia, where, sixteen years before the
millennium opens, the rule of Ur over the whole area had been
overthrown, the king of Isin, Ishbi-Irra, relying on his alliance
with the rulers of Elam to the east, faces uneasily the king of
Larsa, Naplanum, who is backed by his kinsfolk, the Amorites
of the Syrian desert. Before the children born in 2000 B.C. are
grown to manhood, Isin has lost its southernmost possessions, the
cities of Ur and Eridu, to Larsa. It is of little importance—except
to the inhabitants of those cities. They are to change hands many
times during this and the following lifetime.

In Egypt the strong minister of state, Amenemhet, who has
been the *de facto* ruler of the land since the beginning of the
millennium, finally ten years or so later deposes the last ruler of
the Eleventh Dynasty, Mentuhotep V, and assumes the crown of
upper and lower Egypt as the first pharaoh of the Twelfth
Dynasty. It is a bloodless revolution and brings little change to
the people of Egypt. It is more important to the people of Palestine and Syria, over whom in the following years Amenemhet

extends his dominion in a series of campaigns extending as far as
the rising city of Ugarit near the borders of present-day Turkey.

In Crete the merchant princes are still adding to their new
palaces in these early years of the new century, and no news
comes to them of the events far to the northeast on the Russian
steppes. Their news comes by the sea routes, and only from the
farthest end of those routes do they hear vague reports of a new
people appearing. For it is in far-away Scandinavia that the
battle-ax nomads from Russia come into contact with the missionary traders from the Aegean.

In their outward wandering the nomadic herdsmen had over
a generation before come into contact with the farthest-east
settlements of the Danubian farmers of central Europe. Over the
swampy plains of the western Ukraine and Poland the villages of
the Danubians lay scattered, carved out of the forest and surrounded by fields of millet and barley. Often the villages were
on the higher ground, on spurs rising above the damp plains
and affording protection on three sides. There the villagers lived
in wattle houses thickly plastered with clay, perhaps forty houses
grouped in a circle. The houses are divided into two or more
rooms, with raised clay floors and the clay beehive ovens in which
the women prepare the food. It is the women, too, who—as we
have seen—manufacture the surprisingly sophisticated pottery
with its painted fronds and spirals in red and white and black.
The men use tools and weapons of stone and flint, though near
the coasts of the Black Sea traders from Troy and the Aegean
have introduced copper axes and pins and jewelry, and even a
little gold.

Between the villages of the agriculturalists the cattle herders
appear to have passed without let or hindrance. In fact, it is a
noteworthy feature of the movement of the battle-ax people
that nowhere is it accompanied by evidence of battle, murder, or
sudden death. The explanation is probably to be found in the
intrinsically small numbers of the farmers, and in the fact that
the herdsmen found the best grazing for their cattle and horses
on the lighter-wooded grasslands, while the farmers preferred the
heavier enriched loam of the forests. The two peoples were not

in life-and-death competition with each other, and there was land enough for all.

We should not, of course, envisage the farmers as welcoming the cattlemen. Clashes there must have been, and very considerable suspicion of motives, and resentment, and downright fear. But there could have been serious warfare between the settled population and the incomers; had there been that, we should have found traces of it in burnt villages and split skulls. In any case, neither side was equipped for serious warfare. The villages of the Danubians lay on the high ground, on ridges and spurs, or on peninsulas running out into the lakes. They could be easily fortified with stockade and ditch, and many were already so fortified. Around such a stockade the chariot warriors with their bows and tomahawks would circle in vain, their mobility and light weapons even more useless than those of the Indians against the forts of the North American colonists in the far future. On the other hand, if the farmers left their palisades to take the offensive, they would be at the mercy of the swift chariotry of the herdsmen.

It was, nevertheless, with no great force of chariots that the nomads pressed westward. It has even been doubted whether the first groups to reach the west possessed horses at all. But it is difficult to argue from negative evidence. As is to be expected with nomads, remains of their sites of settlement are exceedingly rare, and it is there that one would expect to find evidence of the horse. The graves of the battle-ax people are legion, but horses were too valuable to be buried with their masters. We know that the domestic horse was unknown before the coming of this people and was well known some generations after their arrival. It seems necessary and reasonable to postulate the horse in order to account for the rapid spread of the herdsmen through the lands of the settled farmers.

But the herders did not pass in the night. Though their movement appears fast viewed from our pinnacle of four thousand years in the future, they were not driven on by any consciousness of historic destiny, or by a compulsive urge to reach the utmost west. Where they found grazing they stayed, perhaps for ten years or so, perhaps permanently, leaving it to other tribes to leapfrog them onwards, or extending their range solely by a natural increase in their population and in their herds.

In the lifetime that commences in 2000 B.C. some of them reached the Rhine, and others pushed into Denmark and Sweden.

It was in Denmark that they met the builders of the stone passage-graves, the megalith peoples, with their trade and cultural connections extending by way of the sea roads to Crete. At first they did not mix with the passage-grave people. For these settled farmers lived near the coast and on the islands, among the heavy woods of oak and ash and elm. The battle-ax immigrants confined themselves to the upland backbone of Jutland, where the grazing would suit their herds. It was not an empty land. From time immemorial small bodies of hunters had inhabited this upland area, living on the booty of their flint-tipped bows and spears. With the coming of the herdsmen these hunters disappear, more probably absorbed than exterminated. It would seem that the truce between the cultivators and the herdsmen was more uneasy in Jutland than elsewhere. The battle-ax folk had reached the sea, and they could no longer move on when they exhausted their pasture. There is still no evidence of strife. But the child born at the beginning of the millennium among the first Indo-European-speaking herdsmen in Jutland would, before he died, see the passage-grave farmers of the coast abandoning their villages and moving out to the Danish islands. He would already be thinking of following them, while his cousins in south Sweden would by then also be looking to the Danish islands—from the other side.

To the south, on the Rhine, this lifetime brought different events and problems. For some reason the nomads went no farther than the Rhine. Perhaps the forests were becoming too dense, now that they were leaving the wide plains of glacial dust, the loess area, which gave them the grazing and the mobility on which they depended. Perhaps the country was already too densely populated by settled communities. And perhaps the expansion was simply losing impetus. Enough land had been overrun, and it was time to settle down.

The men who were young in the first years of the Second Millennium began in their middle age to consolidate their gains. Their movements were now only seasonal, from grazing ground to grazing ground within a restricted range. They made their peace with the farmers, and in the fraternization the usual crop of romances developed between the two peoples. The next generation would be of mixed blood, and of mixed culture. Differentiation would begin, as contact among the far-flung tribes became less frequent, and as their arts and crafts and ways of life were affected by the different peoples among whom they had settled.

The Indo-European speakers now cover an immense area. They have not only overrun the farmlands of half Europe; to the north they have spread up to and into the pine forests of the subarctic, the lands of the age-old hunters. A hundred and fifty miles northeast of Moscow the herdsmen who settled in the Fatyanovo area learned much of the lore of the hunters, and trapped bear and wolf and reindeer. At the same time, they seem to have retained especially close links with their original homeland nearly a thousand miles to the south. Their chieftains wield battle-axes of copper, and bear copper and silver armlets, necklets, and earrings.

From Fatyanovo to the Rhine, the men who were born in and around 2000 B.C., and who in their youth had taken part in the great migrations, will still in their old age look back on the steppes of the Kuban, north of the Caucasus, as their ancestral homeland—however divided the loyalties of their grandchildren may be. Their cousins still live in the Kuban, and are now the elders of the tribes that remained. Their grandfathers have told them of the beginning of the migration, and they have themselves seen it in progress, perhaps taken part in it before retiring in their old age to the old pastures. Now they sit outside their tents and discuss the past—and the future.

More and more they find their eyes turning to the south. There lie the mountains of the Caucasus, and beyond the Caucasus other mountains, and there is no grazing for cattle. But beyond all the mountains lies the wealth of the world, copper and gold and precious stones, fair cities and lush fields. It is from there that the traders come, with their bronze axes to be exchanged—if possible, for horses. The elders think of their kins-folk who three hundred years and more before (the distance in time that separates the Pilgrim Fathers from ourselves) had mi-grated to the north of Asia Minor and there founded a kingdom of their own; and they dream of controlling the riches of the south. And they talk to the young men of the opportunities be-yond the mountains.

Opportunity there is indeed for charioteers in the settled areas dotted with towns on the fringes of the great civilizations. Oddly enough, the chariot is not an offensive weapon. Against the walls of a town it is useless. But as a defensive weapon it is revolutionary. A force of chariotry *within* a city wall can sally out against a besieging force and shatter it, undefended as it is by earthworks, to pieces. And from a city an organized chariotry can dominate and control a very much larger portion of the sur-rounding country than can be held by an infantry force.

So the princelings of the tribes and townships in the moun-tains south of the Caucasus are eager to obtain horses and chariots. But that is not enough. The training of horses and their breaking to harness is a new art, a craft requiring very great skill and experience, and the control of a horsed chariot in the heat of battle is not a thing easily to be learnt. So the young men of the Kuban, brought up with horses and chariots from their

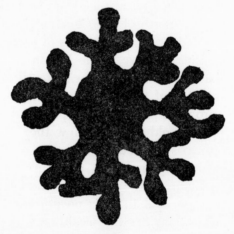

THE SUN DISC, THE MAIN OBJECT OF WORSHIP OF THE INDO-EUROPEAN SPEAKERS, FROM A SWEDISH ROCK CARVING.

earliest boyhood, have a career open to them in the southlands, if they desire it. And many of them do.

They are no ordinary hired warriors, these charioteers from the north, with their outlandish Indo-European language and their mumbo jumbo of horse lore and training. They are an elite, to be treated as nobles and ranked with the priests or the younger princes of the king's house.

Before the end of the lifetime that began in 2000 B.C. some of the young warriors have become more than a *corps d'élite* of a foreign king. By intrigue or by violence, by marriage or by treaty, not a few of them have become the actual rulers of the foreigners they had come to serve.

The Indo-Europeans are on their way south.

6

THE FRIEND OF GOD

1930–1860 B.C.

NOW THESE ARE *the generations of Terah. Terah begat Abram, Nahor, and Haran; and Haran begat Lot. And Haran died in the presence of his father Terah in the land of his nativity, in Ur of the Chaldees. . . .*

And Terah took Abram his son, and Lot the son of Haran, his son's son, and Sarai his daughter in law, his son Abram's wife; and they went forth with them from Ur of the Chaldees to go into the land of Canaan; and they came unto Haran and dwelt there. . . .

Now the Lord said unto Abram, Get thee out of thy country, and from thy kindred, and from thy father's house, unto the land that I will shew thee. . . .

And Abram took Sarai his wife, and Lot his brother's son, and all the substance that they had gathered, and the souls that they had gotten in Haran; and they went forth to go into the land of Canaan; and into the land of Canaan they came. . . .

The free city of Ur lay outstretched and prosperous on the banks of the broad Euphrates. The brown bare-legged children who scampered up and down the stairways and terraces of the ziggurat, the holy temple-mountain built of burnt and sun-dried brick by the great king Ur-Nammu nearly two hundred years before, could, when they threw themselves gasping on the flat summit beneath the walls of the tiled summit temple, look out over the flat sun-baked roofs to the new houses being erected on the level sand below the city mound, and could watch the wakes of the ships and boats approaching and leaving the river quays. Between the quays and the city proper they could trace the wall surrounding the merchants' enclave, the *karum* or free port area where the bigger businessmen had their offices and their bonded warehouses and their guildhalls.

The children were completely bilingual, chatting away quite impartially in Sumerian or in Semitic. Nor was it possible from their appearance, still less their practically nonexistent dress, to distinguish the two races which had lived together for centuries in the city and were now well intermarried. But there

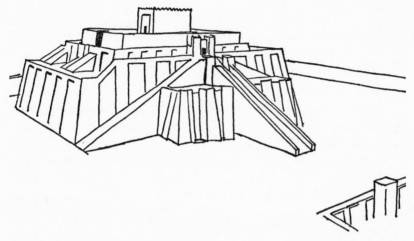

THE ZIGGURAT OF UR, AS IT APPEARED AT THE TIME OF ABRAHAM (AFTER WOOLLEY). IT IS ABOUT 70 FEET HIGH AND CAN BE CLIMBED BY THREE CONVERGING STAIRCASES.

were a few children among them, taller and leaner than the rest, who spoke Sumerian only haltingly and whose Semitic, even, was full of gutterals, which the other children joyously and ribaldly did their best to imitate. Though born in Ur, these children did not quite belong. They were second-generation immigrants, sons of the newcomers from the west, the Amorites.

It is not improbable that one of the boys playing on the ziggurat steps in the nineteen twenties B.C. was Abram, the son of Terah. And his play would not be disturbed by any consciousness of fate, any knowledge that he was to be regarded down the centuries as the patriarchal founder of two great races, that he was to be *khalilullah*, the Friend of God.

His father, Terah, would have a house down in the *karum*, as had most of the wealthier Amorites. But his spiritual home, and his actual home for much of the year, was in the tents of his tribe in the western desert. Abram, too, had spent almost every winter and spring of his short life in the tents, and following the

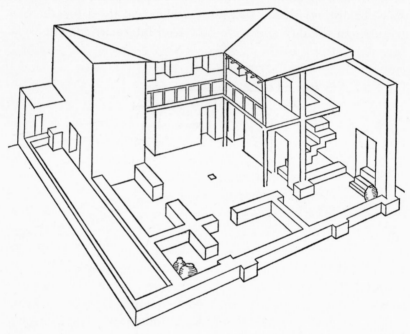

A MIDDLE-CLASS HOUSE OF UR AT THE TIME OF ABRAHAM (AFTER ROUX). THE ROOMS OPEN OUT FROM A CENTRAL COURTYARD OPEN TO THE SKY AND WITH A DRAIN IN THE CENTER.

sheep and goats, and the pack asses, on the long migrations up the Euphrates valley and across to the Mediterranean. For the Amorites were not only herdsmen but traders, and in their hands lay the overland trade from the Lower Sea to the Upper.

Their monopoly of the caravan routes was bringing them much wealth. Ur was the principal port of entry for all the wealth of the east. Down in the *karum*, not far from the caravanserai where the ass trains were gathered for the desert journeys, lay the

guildhall and offices of the *alik Dilmun,* the guild of merchant
adventurers who owned and captained the boats that sailed to
Dilmun down the Gulf. The sea trade with the east was still as
important as it had been seventy and more years ago, though
it had changed somewhat in character. For one thing, Dilmun
itself had captured a larger share of the trade. The ships from Ur
no longer sailed all the way to Makan at the mouth of the Gulf
to load copper, while only the older merchants could remember
seeing a ship of Makan ownership tied up at the quays. Now
the ships from Makan and the Indus sailed no farther than Dilmun, and there transshipped their copper and gold and ivory and
carnelian and lapis lazuli, exchanging it at the great market by
the beach for the silver and wool and piece goods brought from
Sumer by the *alik Dilmun.* Even Dilmun-owned ships were not
so common in the port of Ur as they once had been, and more
and more of the trade was carried in Ur bottoms, bringing double
profit to the merchant captains and the investors and share-
holders who financed the ventures.

It was an extravagant price the Amorite caravan masters had
to give for these luxury articles of the Indian trade, a price only
agreed to after a whole morning's haggling and negotiation, and
finally weighed out meticulously in silver against the standard
weights, weights shaped like ducks and often carved of semiprecious stone. But for all the high price of trade goods the
caravan business was profitable enough in all conscience. Even
copper fetched a good round price on the seaboard of the
Mediterranean, particularly when it was worked up into manufactured goods by the renowned coppersmiths of the Amorites.
And the precious stones and ivory of the East were beyond price.

We might well find Terah sitting in the shade of his warehouse, drinking beer with a fellow countryman from the north,
each using a long bamboo drinking tube from a common pot.
Their talk would range from trade to politics, always a matter
of speculation to the Amorites of Ur.

Most of them had not been many years in Ur. For Ur had until recently lain within the eastern sphere of influence, ruled by
the kings of Isin, who were the allies of the great kingdom of
Elam at the foot of the Persian mountains. Admittedly the

Amorites had been long in Mesopotamia, and they could recall tales of how their tribes, in the days of their great-grandfathers, had swept in from the Syrian desert, establishing their rule at Mari, on the great bend of the Euphrates, and then at Larsa. It was the Amorite king of Larsa, to the north, who had combined with the Elamites and their protégés in Isin to overthrow the rule of Ur over the whole of southern Mesopotamia. But that was long ago, a hundred and twenty years or so. Since then Ur had been the nominal vassal of Isin, ruled in the name of the Isin king by his nominee, the high priest of the Moon temple, the chief temple of Ur.

It had made little difference to the city. Whoever the overlord, trade still came to Ur and the city prospered. And the high priest was careful to avoid political entanglements. Just now, for example, Enannatum, the present high priest, though a younger son of the former king of Isin, nevertheless had sworn allegiance to King Gungunum of Larsa, who a few years back had overthrown the king of Isin, Enannatum's own brother, and now called himself king, not only of Larsa, but of Ur as well. Gungunum was an Amorite, and it was after his conquest of Ur that the number of Amorite merchants in Ur had increased so enormously.

But now there was a new and vigorous king in Isin, Ur-Ninurta, and it was questionable whether Larsa could continue to hold Ur.

In these surroundings the young Abram grew to manhood. He would attend the festivals in the temples, and even pay thank-offerings for successful trading ventures to the priests of Ishtar, though he would, of course, also have his own Amorite gods. Here he took Sarai to wife, and from here, at the beginning of most winters, he would set out with his family and retainers and his well-loaded pack donkeys (for the camel was not yet domesticated, and the horses of the Indo-Europeans had not penetrated farther south than the northwest mountains of Persia), to spend the winter grazing westward with the flocks of his tribe, aiming for one of the spring markets on the opposite fringe of the desert. By the end of spring he would be back at Ur, with a return load of silver and marble from the north, or linen from

Egypt or cedar wood from the Lebanon or frankincense from the deep south.

The return loads were not always the product of peaceful trading. Even the half-settled Amorites of Mesopotamia were only a few generations removed from the desert raiders who had pushed into the river valleys by force of arms, and once back in the desert they tended to revert to type. Between tribe and tribe, between family group and family group, there was a constantly shifting pattern of alliances and feuds, held in abeyance in the river valleys but kept alive by the unsettled nomads of the great desert. And on the winter journeys the young men of the cities plunged back joyfully into the old pattern, fiercely guarding their own flocks and baggage trains, raiding zestfully the possessions of their enemies of the moment, or banding together to attack an oasis or pillage a township on the fringe of the desert. They were raiders as well as traders, and only paid for their merchandise if it could not be got cheaper by other means.

If we are right in our guess that the life of Abraham can be approximately equated with this second lifetime of the Second Millennium B.C., then he was about twenty-four years old when trouble hit the Amorites of Ur. In 1906 B.C. King Gungunum of Larsa died, very likely killed in battle, and Ur-Ninurta, king of Isin, regained the overlordship of Ur. If not precisely this event, it was certainly some such political upheaval which brought the Amorites in Ur into disfavor, and decided Terah to take his possessions and leave the city.

This time it was not a trading caravan which left the gates of Ur and headed north along the banks of the Euphrates. Now it was a tribe on the move, perhaps three or four hundred strong, with the old men and women and the younger children traveling in four-wheeled bullock carts, with large flocks of sheep and goats grazing as they went, with several hundred pack asses, perhaps even with heavy goods carried by river boat parallel to the land movement. Tradition says that they traveled to Harran, and this can have been no chance destination.

The ancient town of Harran lay six hundred fifty miles away to the northwest, the whole length of the Euphrates away, in the foothills of the mountains of eastern Turkey. But for all its

length the route between Ur and Harran was well traveled and
well known. It was certainly not the first time that members of
Terah's family had traversed it. For there were long-standing
commercial connections between the two cities. Both Harran and
Ur were cities dedicated to the worship of the moon-god, Sin. For
centuries past (and for centuries to come) the moon temples
of Ur and Harran were famous throughout the Middle East, and
in the days of temple communism, still only a little over a
hundred years ago, when all commerce and industry was owned
and directed by the college of priests, the two temples of the
moon must have built up a close system of trade. For Harran
was the gathering point for the mineral wealth of the Turkish
mountains, just as Ur collected the wealth of the Indies.

It was principally the silver of the Taurus mountains which
passed through Harran on its way south; and we know that
silver was traded south from Ur in the ships of the *alik Dilmun*
to buy copper from Makan and gold from the Indus.

It is practically certain that the trade which linked the two
centers, carrying gold and copper north, and silver south, was at
the time of Abram in the hands of the Amorites. For the route
that trade must follow lay along the valley of the Euphrates, and
since the Amorites had pushed out from the Syrian desert in the
course of the last two lifetimes they had dominated the Euphrates valley all along its length.

The tribe of Terah, moving slowly on their two-month journey to join their cousins and business associates in the north,
would pass first through the territory of the small Amorite
city-states south of present-day Baghdad, probably camping a
night by one of them, a little village known as Babylon, and calling on its governor, Sumu-abum. And they would go on, entering
some fortnight later the territory of the important kingdom of
Mari, also Amorite and with ties of kinship and mutual interest
with the traders of the Great North Road. A fortnight beyond
Mari they would come to the confluence of the Euphrates and
the Balikh, and, turning north along the valley of the Balikh, they
would reach Harran in less than a week.

The tribe of Terah stayed in Harran, it would seem, for some
years. It is unlikely that the trading connections with Ur were

broken, though it may have been politic for a while to have non-
Amorite strawmen officially in charge of the southern end of the
business. And Abram probably learned to know the northern
trade routes, as he grew from youth to middle age, as well as he
had learnt the southern.

In Harran he would meet many traders, and among them not
a few from the Semitic, though not Amorite, kingdom of Assyria
to the east. Assyria lay in northern Mesopotamia, on both
banks of the upper Tigris. It was a small kingdom, at this time of
no great importance, and the language it spoke was akin to the
Semitic tongue of southern Mesopotamia and, like it, written in
cuneiform on clay tablets. Like all civilized countries at this time,
Assyria had extensive trade connections—along the Tigris to the
cities of the south, and westward along the foothills of Turkey
and over the Anti-Taurus range into central Asia Minor. This
latter route went by way of Harran and on, a farther two hundred miles or so, to Kanesh.

Kanesh lay in central Asia Minor, on the fringes of the
Taurus mountains. Its inhabitants we know little about, and
when the archaeologist calls them Cappadocians he is merely
giving them a geographical label for convenience of reference.
But Abram probably knew the inhabitants well, and very likely
visited the city. When he did so, however, he would not stay
in the city proper. For outside the city lay a *karum*, established
by Assyrian merchants perhaps a hundred years ago, a concession
area run by the Assyrian merchant guilds, with a large degree of
extraterritorial privileges.

We have met the *karum* already in Ur. And it was probably
a feature of most of the cities of the world at this time. But at Ur
the *karum* seems merely to have been an area set aside, for administrative convenience, as the office and warehouse area for
merchants who were largely citizens of Ur, subject to the laws
and the taxation of Ur, with no more special privileges than has,
for example, the City in London today. In more backward
regions, on the other hand, such as Kanesh, the *karum* corre-
sponded more closely to the "factories" of the early European
trade with the east, or the "foreign concession" in Chinese towns
until recently. They were self-governing colonies of foreign

traders, small walled suburbs with their own administration and probably their own defense forces.

As the trading caravans of the Amorites of Harran traveled from *karum* to *karum* in these years, they would follow closely the politics of the areas through which their trade passed. They would hear of the coalition formed in 1895 by a certain Sumu-abum, whom Abram might remember having met before, among the small city-states on the middle Euphrates, and they would wonder perhaps that he sited the capital of the coalition at his own little town of Babylon instead of at the historic city of Kish nearby. And they may perhaps have heard of a people towards the north of Turkey, a people who were not at that time called the Hittites though they were later to take that name. If the caravans heard of them at all, they undoubtedly attached no importance to the fact that these people's rulers spoke an unknown language and were said to have come from the north; or that they owned a small number of chariots drawn by horses.

We do not know when Abram's tribe decided to move south from Harran. Nor do we know why. There may have been commercial pressure from the Assyrians. There may even have been military pressure from the people who were to become the Hittites. For at a date which is thought by some to be 1872 B.C. the *karum* of Kanesh is destroyed by fire. And there is some slight evidence that its destroyers came from the north.

At that time a man born at the beginning of our second lifetime would be fifty-eight years old. We have assumed for the purpose of this chapter (most unscientifically, for we have no evidence) that Abram son of Terah was of this generation, and it would therefore seem that he was in late middle age when he led his tribe once more on migration, this time south and west, along the trade and grazing route leading through Canaan to Egypt.

It was again a not unnatural route to take. For Harran lay not far from the nearest point under the direct cultural influence of Egypt.

At this time Sesostris III was pharaoh of Egypt. Some hundred twenty years have passed since Amenemhet I had assumed the crown as the first pharaoh of the Twelfth Dynasty. It has been four generations of increasing prosperity and bureaucracy within Egypt, and extending influence abroad. In the time of the fathers of the present generation, Amenemhet I and his son Sesostris I had introduced a series of careful measures to reduce the independence of the hereditary barons of the nomes, the administrative districts, of the Nile valley. They established in each nome a taxation officer, responsible to the crown, to supervise the collection and transmission of taxes, although the actual collection was still in the hands of the barons. The introduction of a census at fifteen-year intervals reduced the possibilities of graft in the tax returns, while the appointment of a board of ten judges responsible to the head of the civil service, the vezir, also served to curb the power of the nobles.

The present lifetime had on the whole been a peaceful time for the people of Egypt. Sesostris I had died in 1927 b.c., when those born in 1930 were scarcely more than babes in arms, and they had grown to manhood during the thirty-two-year reign of his son Amenemhet II. While Abram in Ur and later in Harran had been organizing his caravans and raiding his neighbors' caravans along the trade routes of Mesopotamia and the Syrian desert, Amenemhet was developing the copper mines of the Sinai peninsula and the gold mines of the eastern Sudan, a region conquered by his grandfather fifty years before. He sent trading expeditions to Punt at the southern end of the Red Sea, and he had commercial attachés in the growing cities along the Lebanese coast.

Amenemhet II died in 1895 b.c., when Abram, in Harran, was thirty-five, and was succeeded by his son Sesostris II. Egypt is now strong and wealthy, with a centralized government which itself engaged in the production and exchange of raw materials and manufactured goods. The ships of Sesostris II sailed the length of the Red Sea and the Levant coast, as far north as Ugarit, a thriving coastal town well north of the Lebanon. Ugarit is less than two hundred miles from Harran, and Abram probably visited it frequently, along the trade route by way of Carchemish and Aleppo and Alalakh.

It is not impossible that Abram had himself visited Egypt in his youth. Certainly the Amorite tribes were spreading westward as well as eastward, and it is during Abram's lifetime that they

raid into Palestine, destroying the small walled towns of the
Canaanites, driving them to the shelter of the cities of the coast,
and themselves taking over the rich pastures of the inland hills.
The trading families of the Amorites being by no means averse
to a little brisk warfare, we may well believe that Abram, by now
a tribal chieftain with a very considerable following, brought his
tribe down from the north with the main object of sharing in
this campaign and in its plunder.

However that may be, Egypt was too strong to fear the raids
of desert tribes, and when Amorites came to Egypt it was in small
parties, for peaceful trade. In 1892 B.C., when Abram was (by our
fiction) thirty-eight, just such a party, visiting Egypt, was im-

PART OF THE FAMOUS TOMB PAINTING AT BENI HASAN, SHOWING A
PARTY OF AMORITE MERCHANTS IN EGYPT IN 1892 B.C. THAT ONE
OF THE MEN CARRIES A HARP AND ONE OF THE DONKEYS BEARS AN
ANVIL SHOWS THAT THE MERCHANTS WERE ALSO MINSTRELS AND
ITINERANT COPPERSMITHS.

mortalized in a painting on the wall of a tomb at Beni Hasan.
We can there see in very clear detail the appearance of the
smaller trading parties from Amorite tribes such as that of Abram.

Both men and women travel on foot, the men in sandals and
loincloths, or in knee-length woolen tunics patterned in stripes of
bright colors. The women are barefooted, with ankle rings and
rather longer tunics which leave the left shoulder bare. Their dark
hair falls over their shoulders and is held by a band across the
brow. The older children walk with them, while the youngsters
ride two by two in the saddlebags of the pack asses. The men
bear spears and bows and throwing-sticks, and one of them is a
weaponsmith, with his anvil borne by a donkey. And one man is
carrying a harp.

Thus they traveled through the lands of the Middle East, slowly, stopping for days at a time when grazing was good, dropping in at towns to transact business with their kinsfolk in the *karum*, banding together for a raid, or for a punitive expedition in reply to a raid, and then splitting up again into groups of fifty or a hundred to wander hundreds of miles along the trade routes which they monopolized. They must have been a quite incalculable factor to the settled peoples on the fringes of their immense range. While they played an essential role in the economy of the time, carrying as they did much of the luxury articles and staple consumer goods, they were a standing menace to that economy, liable to combine into raiding and plundering armies whenever the vigilance of the settled areas relaxed.

The story recounted in the fourteenth chapter of Genesis clearly belongs to the last phase of the period dealt with in this chapter, to the period when Abram is settled as the head of a tribal confederacy in the interior of Palestine (and now calls himself Abraham, readopting the fricative of West Semitic which the East Semitic of Mesopotamia had dropped). The story is clear enough, and shows us how Abraham, for all his wanderings in south Turkey and Palestine and Egypt, has not completely escaped out of the orbit of the troubled politics of south Mesopotamia, where he started. It is recounted how the king of Elam, and three kings confederated with him (including one who claims to be king of Sumer), had forced the "kings" of the Syrian desert and the Jordan valley to submit to them. After thirteen years they rebelled, and the following year the king of Elam sent a punitive expedition. This expedition defeated the rebel sheikhs, and carried off many prisoners and much booty. As this loot included the person, family, and possessions of Abraham's nephew Lot, Abraham gathered his tribesmen and, in a night attack, succeeded in freeing the prisoners and regaining the booty.

The whole course of events is typical of desert warfare and tribal skirmishing—were it not that it has troubled historians to find the kings of Sumer and, in particular, of Elam so far away from home. We can be fairly sure, however, that it did not surprise Abraham in the least. The jockeying of the Amorites and of Elam for the political dominance of southern Mesopotamia was something he had seen for himself in his boyhood. It is quite likely, as has been suggested, that the transfer of Ur from the Amorite sphere of influence under the king of Larsa to that of the Elamite protégé, the king of Isin, had determined Abraham's father to migrate north. But the struggles of Amorite and Elamite had continued.

The new confederacy of Babylon held the northern part of lower Mesopotamia under king Sumu-la-El, who had seized power after the death of Sumu-abum, and this confederacy was Amorite. But to the south Elamite influence was waxing. We do not know the precise details, though Abraham undoubtedly did. (But we do know, as Abraham did not, that thirty years from now the king of Elam will not only dominate Isin but will also establish his son as ruler of the former Amorite stronghold of Larsa.) It need not surprise us, then, if a king of Elam, dominant on the lower Euphrates, extends his conquests over the Amorite tribes of the desert as far as the Jordan valley. And the latest research into the complicated chronology of just this period even appears to show a gap of twenty years between the reigns of Sumu-abum and of his successor Sumu-la-El in Babylon, a gap which may well denote a period when Elam was dominant over the whole of Mesopotamia south of present-day Baghdad. There may well have been a brief Elamite empire stretching almost to the Mediterranean coast where the Egyptian-dominated cities lay. For Egypt at this time had no interest in the hinterland of Syria and Palestine. Even in the coastal towns Egypt's interest was purely commercial, but the towns there were undoubtedly strong enough to discourage attack from the Elamite confederacy, at the end of very long lines of communication, even without military aid from Egypt. Sesostris III of Egypt was anyway at this time engaged in the deep south, in protracted campaigns against the Negro tribes of the Sudan.

But after Abraham's success against the withdrawing army of Elam, we hear nothing further of Elamite adventures in Palestine. It is the end of the seventy years of this chapter. In the final years we may imagine Abraham firmly established with his growing tribe in the pasturelands of Palestine. His people still have close contacts with their kinsfolk over a wide area, and his two eldest sons, Ishmael and Isaac, take wives respectively from Egypt and Mesopotamia. But he was undoubtedly content, in his old age, to sit outside his tent beneath the evergreen oaks of Mamre and must have appeared to himself, as he has appeared to subsequent generations, as a patriarch and the father of his people.

As he looked back over the span of his life, there must have seemed to have been little change in the world as he knew it. Perhaps Elam had increased in power; perhaps Egypt, with its now well-established dynasty, could be regarded as dangerous under its new and warlike pharaoh. But Elam after all had for many generations been the great power of the east, and Egypt had never seriously ventured beyond her copper mines in the Sinai peninsula. Abraham could not have the prescience to know that the future lay neither with Elam nor, for many hundred years, with Egypt. He would have no reason to see that the significant events of his lifetime were the appearance of the charioteers of the north in the hinterland of Asia Minor, the establishment of the little Amorite confederacy around the new town of Babylon, and the movement, in which he had been one of the prime movers, of the Amorite tribes into Palestine.

And yet perhaps he did see, in fact, the possibilities inherent in that westward settlement of his own people. For had not his god promised him that his seed should be numberless as the stars and that he should be the father of a multitude of nations? There was, of course, nothing remarkable in such a promise; every tribal god proclaimed at every opportunity the glorious future in store for his worshippers. The only remarkable thing was that in this case the promise was to be fulfilled.

But, like most old men, Abraham probably thought less about the future than about the past. In his long lifetime he had traveled many hundreds of miles. Now, sitting beneath the oaks of Mamre and watching his flocks grazing on the home pastures, he must frequently have looked back upon his childhood,

at the long-legged boy who used to scramble up the ziggurat
steps of faraway Ur of the Chaldees.

*Abraham is—let us admit it—not a historical character at
all, insofar as he is not named in any contemporary document
and is first mentioned in a book admittedly written down many
hundreds of years after his time. Yet, knowing the careful way in
which genealogical and tribal-historical tradition is transmitted
by word of mouth among nonliterate peoples, we can assume
with considerable certainty that he did in fact exist and that the
main events of his life are as recorded. His date is a more difficult question. He is clearly an Amorite prince, and his life and
movements must be fitted into (or at least not be allowed to
clash with) the main stream of Amorite history. It has thus
seemed reasonable to make him a contemporary of the establishment of Amorite kingdoms along the Euphrates and of the
appearance of nomads in strength in Palestine, both of which can
be dated to the period of this chapter. (See W. F. Albright:*
The Archaeology of Palestine). *A later date has been suggested,
on an assumption of the complete historicity of his war with
Amraphael and an identification of Amraphael of Shinar
(Sumer) with Hammurabi of Babylon, 1792–50 B.C. (see Chapter 8). This does, however, run us into quite considerable difficulties of later chronology.*

7

THE SUN TEMPLE

1860–1790 B.C.

THE TOW-HEADED CHILDREN, born in the shadow of
the mountains of northwest England at the time when Abraham
was seventy years old, must have played with axes before they
could walk. On the long trek up the Langdale valley they had
been carried on their mothers' backs, or had ridden gleefully
on the sledges pulled by the menfolk or by oxen. They had
traveled up from the wattle village by the lakeside, following the
track through the woods beside the tarns of the lower valley;
and then they had left behind them the scattered oak trees, and
come out into the tussocky waste of heather and cotton grass
and sphagnum swamp, choosing the better path along the slopes
of sheep-cropped turf which steepened to the crags below Dun-
geon Ghyll and the Pikes.

Where the valley turned to the north they had sighted the
summer encampment, with the smoke from the fires rising from
among the skin tents towards the low grey clouds which almost touched the top of the Langdale Pikes and obscured the
summit of Bowfell across the dale. (Bowfell and Langdale and
the rest are, of course, modern names given by a later people no
more than a thousand years ago. But the axsmiths of 1860 B.C.
would have their names for the dales and the fells, and their
names went at least as far back in their traditions as the present
names in ours.)

And now, while their mothers grind the flour and prepare
the meat for the substantial evening meal, and their elder
brothers and sisters roam the steep scree slopes collecting rocks of

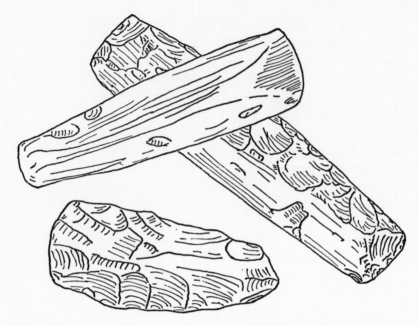

GREAT LANGDALE AXES. THE TWO UPPER SPECIMENS ARE THE FIN-
ISHED ARTICLES, FOUND AT A SETTLEMENT CLOSE BY; THE LOWER AX
WAS FOUND AT THE "FACTORY" SITE ITSELF. IT IS UNPOLISHED AND
IS PROBABLY A REJECT.

the right size and quality, the youngsters sit around the chipping-
floors, watching fascinated as their fathers turn the chosen rocks
against the anvil stones, shrewdly striking off flake after flake to
this side and to that. With wide eyes they see the axes take
shape, first as roughly rectangular blanks, and then fined down
at the edges and narrowed at the butt, until finally the cutting
edge is shaped with meticulous taps and much examination of
the natural grain of the rock. Then the finished ax, slim and a
foot or more in length, will be tested, a flake or two struck off
from the sides to improve the balance, and it will be laid with
the others in the growing pile, to be carried down in the evening to the tents in the valley. It is work which holds the youngsters absorbed, and the older ones will imitate the grownups,
striking a rejected core with a pebble until a misplaced blow
causes them to howl and suck their thumbs, while the men look
up and grin at their discomfiture.

And so the day wears on, while the sun bakes down on the chipping-floors, sited in sheltered gullies high up among the scree slopes, or while the low clouds scud overhead, spilling an occasional shower that brings the buckskin hoods over the heads of the men and sometimes, though rarely, drives the children to the shelter of the nearest rock face.

When the call comes for the evening meal, the men will pack their axes into leather bags and sling them on their backs, and, with the laughing children astride their shoulders, plod down the slope to the camp. There the results of the day's work will be spread out, for inspection by the master smith, and each man will have his tale of finished axes notched on his tally stick, before the axes are packed away, to be taken on the morrow to the polishing yard down the valley. There the final edge will be given to the stone axes, and they will be put aside against the arrival of the traders and the great fall market.

It is no trade for weaklings, that of axsmith. The rhyolite boulders of the scree slopes are a tough material to work, well able to raise blisters on the horniest hands, and they weigh heavier and heavier as the day wears on. The off-days are eagerly anticipated, when, for a change, the men will take their flint-tipped spears and arrows and go hunt the red deer over the moors of Watendleth and through the valleys running down to Borrowdale.

Hunting is more than a mere holiday. Although they live mainly on the produce of their sheep and cattle, and although their importance to the economy of this time (and to prehistorians of a later era) lies in their seasonal manufacture of stone axes, the people of the Langdale fells look upon themselves primarily as hunters, and know, without thinking much about it, that hunting has been their people's way of life from time immemorial.

The land of Britain belongs to this people, and to their cousins across the length and breadth of the country. That they are the original Ancient Britons they could, of course, hardly know, though they are in fact the linear descendants of the hunting and fishing tribes who had entered the country from the south and east thousands of years earlier, on the heels of the retreating

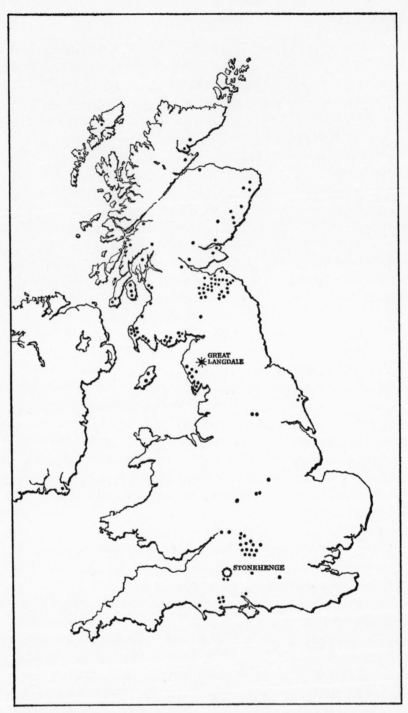

"SALES CHART" OF THE AX FACTORY OF **GREAT LANGDALE.** EACH DOT REPRESENTS THE PLACE OF DISCOVERY OF ONE OR MORE AXES SHOWN BY PETROLOGICAL ANALYSIS TO HAVE COME FROM GREAT LANGDALE.

icecap, at a time before the waters had broken through to form the English Channel and the North Sea. But in a dim unformulated way they look upon the farmers of the south and west as newcomers, even though these have been in Britain for a dozen centuries now.

They look upon the settled farmers with a mixture of envy and contempt. They well realize that these "foreigners," with their substantially built villages and embanked camps and corrals on the sand and chalk uplands of the soft south, enjoy a higher standard of comfort than they themselves do. But, while they will occasionally raise a crop, they feel no urge to tie themselves to the rhythm of seedtime and harvest, or to leave their fish-stocked rivers and coasts, and their game-stocked forests, for the bare Downs where alone cultivation is possible. The "foreigners"—and despite centuries of occupation they are still at least so foreign that they speak a different language—in truth only hold a very small part of Britain. On the Downs and the Cotswolds of the south their causewayed camps lie thick, and they have colonized, too, the northeastern chalklands of Yorkshire and Lincolnshire. And along the estuaries of the west coast, all the way to the north of Scotland, the seagoing settlers and traders from Ireland (who ultimately have come from the Mediterranean) are coming in increasing numbers, and are still building new passage-graves of immense stones alongside the old. But all these are fringe areas; the heart of the country, from the great valleys of the Thames and Severn in the south to the highlands and islands of Scotland to the north, is the domain of the "natives."

The youngsters whom we have seen around the Langdale chipping-floors will have traveled much of England before ever they reach manhood. They wander much with their tribe, which, as befits a race of hunters, ranges over a wide, though strictly defined, area of northern England. They rarely stay more than a couple of months at any one of the recognized camping sites, and often move every day or so, following their grazing sheep and cattle, or the slow seasonal movements of the deer and the wild cattle. They grow adept in breaking camp, packing the skins and poles of the tents on the ox sledges and solid-wheeled

carts, together with the boxes and baskets and coarse punch-
decorated pottery containing their gear and supplies. On the
march they drive the oxen, until they are old enough to accompany the men and dogs who shepherd the flocks over the rough
pasture of the Pennine moors or follow the spoor of a spear-
wounded stag. But every summer they return to the ax factory in
Langdale, to put in a month or so making the axes to buy them
the wheat and barley that will keep them in bread and beer the
winter through.

There are always some older boys who feel the urge to
travel farther. Many take service for a season or two with the
traders who come with the corn sacks to fetch the axes, and with
them they will take the month-long journey to the south and
east. Their destination is the earth-banked villages and stockades of the "foreign" agriculturalists on the south Downs, and by
these tiny timbered towns, often overlooking the waters of the
English Channel, they will pitch their tents, lay out their axes,
and spend their days in bargaining.

They will meet other traders of their own race, who speak
dialects akin to theirs. There will be other ax traders, with stocks
of granite axes from the factory in the mountains of north Wales,
and with them there will be interminable technical discussions
of the relative merits of the two stones. And there are traders in
flint, with stocks of knives and chisels and picks bought from
the miners who extract flint from shafts sunk thirty feet deep and
more in the chalk of Norfolk or the Channel coast.

It is overwhelmingly likely that other goods are displayed
for sale in the traders' camps outside the stockades, but what
these are we of a later age can only surmise. Ornaments of jet
from Yorkshire are attested, and we may guess that there were
furs and buckskin shirts and moccasins and mats and baskets.
That these goods are bartered for corn is similarly only a con-
jecture, but there appears to have been little else that the settlers
could offer. The woolen cloth and piece goods which are a
staple of contemporary trade in the Middle East do not figure
here, for the settlers do not, apparently, weave cloth. Very occasionally more exotic articles of foreign origin may have appeared at the marts, for bronze and gold, though scarce, can-

not have been entirely unknown to the villagers, while the itinerant traders occasionally had opportunity on their way south to
pick up a necklace or two of Scandinavian amber.

It is not unusual, in fact, for the traders to make a detour on
their way south, first visiting the agricultural settlements of Yorkshire, and then paralleling the east coast until they reached East
Anglia. For there, among tribes of their own people, they could
meet groups of newcomers from beyond the North Sea.

There has always been considerable traffic across the North
Sea between Scandinavia and England. Of course the great ships
of the passage-grave builders, coming from the Mediterranean,
had for many generations been making their voyages once or
twice a year, sailing around the north of Scotland to a landfall
on the Danish coast. But in addition the "native" fishers on
both sides of the water frequently cross over in their large and
seaworthy skin boats, rowing and sailing the distance in two
or three days, and keeping alive a contact which (though they
did not know it) was older than the North Sea itself.

But of late the traffic has been all one way. And the boats
which reach the English east coast from Denmark and Sweden
are deep laden with women and children and household goods.
The crews of these boats are refugees, settlers in search of a
new home. And where they arrive they tell, in their almost in-
comprehensible dialect, of the havoc spread through their homeland by new waves of battle-ax-wielding herdsmen.

The battle-ax people had first appeared in Jutland from the
southeast in the time of their great-grandfathers. But they had
come in small numbers, and had not interfered appreciably with
the life of the original inhabitants. Now they are flooding in,
invading Jutland from Germany and passing on to the Danish
islands, where they meet others of their own race coming by
way of Sweden. The newcomers to Britain tell graphically how
the settled farmers of Denmark and south Sweden, with their
acres cleared and burnt out of the forest, their timber villages
and stone passage-graves, are gradually being overwhelmed by
the incoming herdsmen, with no means of escape because they
have no boats. They tell how they themselves, seafarers from time
immemorial and accustomed to long voyages on sealing and

whaling expeditions, had decided to get out while the going was good and seek a new place to settle among their cousins across the North Sea. And the traders listen sympathetically to their hard-luck story, and unobtrusively raise their prices for the axes that the refugees will need to clear their new village site, taking in exchange whatever valuables—and it is often amber—the Scandinavians have managed to salvage.

There will be many tales to tell when the young north-country men return to their families in the Lake District after years on the trade routes. But they will probably attach little importance to one of their minor experiences, the occasion when they were present at the founding of Stonehenge.

It was on their way south to the Downland farmers that they had first stopped over with their kinsmen of the upper Thames valley. And there they had seen, and maybe taken part in, the religious ceremonies of that people. Like traders and young men of any age, they are not overly fanatical themselves in religious questions, though they are (far more than we) very conscious of the presence all about them of unseen forces and both benevolent and malevolent influences. These they are very careful to propitiate, by the ritual and offerings appropriate to those engaged in the hazardous occupation of commerce. But they tolerate the religions of others, and naturally feel that it is wise to conform to the customs of the people among whom they happen to be, and to follow the rituals which are known by experience to placate the local gods, who are, of course, no less real or powerful than their own.

In this point of view they are conscious of differing from the settlers of the west coast, who with missionary zeal have for generations been insisting on the universal validity of their Mediterranean religion, with its squat cubical statues of a goddess whose face is dominated by a pair of eyes which seem to follow you wherever you turn, and with a ritual centered on the courtyards outside the entrances to their immense stone communal tombs. The ax traders do not feel that their own god will turn his face from them if they occasionally, when in the neighborhood, lay a dish of porridge among the offerings in the forecourts.

They meet, after all, many different religions in their travels.

They are not disturbed by the ritual cannibalism of the farmers on the Downs, for it is confined for the most part to the eating of dead relatives. But they do, as far as possible, arrange to be elsewhere when the rumor reaches them that a new encampment or village or temple of this people is to be erected, or when they see the long mound going up above a place of burial and know that a new burial enclosure is soon to be consecrated. For on such occasions it is the custom of the farmer folk to erect a stout post, or an upright stone, on the sunrise side of the area to be consecrated, and this upright pillar—everyone knows that it is a symbol of man's fertility—will be immensely more potent if the body of a freshly slaughtered boy or youth is buried in the hole in which it is to be raised.

But to everyone his own beliefs. The religion of the people of the upper Thames is no less strange and complicated, and is but imperfectly understood by the visiting traders and their apprentices. (We, nearly four thousand years later, are quite unable to reconstruct the ritual or the thought behind the ritual from the archaeological evidence, and even the deliberately vague picture given here is wild guesswork, much more likely to be wrong than right.) They have frequently seen the holy places of this widespread people, and have noticed their resemblance to the burial places of the farmers of the Downs, a fact which is enough to make them chary about inquiring more closely into the details of ritual. They know that the hill farmers lay out their dead in small turf or wooden chambers set within an oblong or oval ring-mound, often with the grim stone or wooden pillars standing to the east and casting their sunrise shadows across the houses of the dead. And when the death chambers are full, a high barrow is cast up above the bodies and a new enclosure is laid out. Though the temples of the valley folk are not primarily places of burial, they, too, are ring-mounds, round or oval or even laid out as a ring within a square. And here, too, standing stones or posts can be seen on the eastern side of the enclosure, while within the enclosure can be seen rings of holes, dug down through the turf and filled in again with white stamped chalk. They are all too suggestive of graves, and there is talk of bodies being burnt on the nights when the holes are dug. That is all that strangers passing through care to know of the rites which take place within the ring-mounds; the cautious traders give them a wide berth, and even the boldest apprentices never step over the shadow of the sunrise pillar.

On this occasion a new temple enclosure has been consecrated, the biggest that has ever been made. The tribes of the valley folk have gathered in strength for the occasion, and the Downland farmers, too, attend in great numbers. Where many people gather there is always business for a smart trader, and they also have gathered in force as midsummer day approaches. A vast concourse of people is come together in the broad hollow below the high ground of Salisbury Plain, and their skin tents and wattle shelters stand in scattered groups over more than a square mile of heather. On the broad spur near the bottom of the valley the chosen workers have already completed the perfect circle of the ring-mound, over a hundred yards in diameter, with its surrounding ditch. It stands out with the white of virgin chalk against the green. Now they are engaged in erecting the Hele stone, the immense monolith sited just outside the only gap in the ring-mound, on the northeast side of the circle. The young men from the north have watched, from the slopes above, how the great stone is pushed up on rollers to the edge of the reinforced hole prepared for it, and levered upright by the united efforts of scores of men hauling on ropes and straining on poles. There is some very intricate final adjustment of the bedding of the stone, with much sighting by the architect in charge from the center of the circle. But this is only to be expected; everyone knows that it is necessary that the rays of the Great Sun, rising on midsummer day, shall cast the shadow of the stone exactly upon the center of the ring-mound. In the meantime the architect's assistants are measuring out the interior of the ring, with ropes stretched from the midpoint, and placing pegs at exact intervals in a circle within the mound. And workers are following them, digging circular holes half a man deep and over a yard across at each point marked by a peg. And the priests are everywhere, surveying the work done, blessing the tools and the workers at each day's beginning, pouring libations, and reading omens.

On midsummer's eve no one slept. Though the traders and other noninitiates are not allowed near the enclosure, they lie out on the hillsides in the moonlight and look down upon the ceremonies taking place below. They can see the dark mass of worshippers crowding the ring-mound, and the ritual fires and the dim shapes of the dancers within the circle. The chanting, and the drums, continue all night, and the watchers shiver as they imagine the unknown sacrifices taking place below them. As the short night draws to a close and the light grows stronger, the chanting increases. It rises to a mighty hymn of praise at the moment when the sun breaks clear of the horizon and casts the shadow of the Hele stone exactly to the feet of the chief priest standing in the center of the circle of pits. The Sun-God is risen again upon His land, and His worshippers within the henge bow down before His glory.

This is the story that the young men in the service of the ax traders bring back to their families in the north. They have grown tall, these youths, in the years they have trodden the earth roads of England (though, if we may venture to give to the radio-carbon date of 1848 B.C.—plus or minus 275 years!— for the first construction of Stonehenge a hypothetical accuracy which it almost certainly does not in fact possess, the boys who were born at the beginning of this chapter's lifetime would still only be in their teens on their return).

In the years that follow their return, most settle down to the hunting and herding and quarrying routine of their fathers, the marrying and begetting of children and the struggle for subsistence and position which is the common lot of man. Some become priests, and some become carpenters or fishermen, and many die, of sickness and of accident, for nowhere in the world is the average length of life even half of what it will be in future centuries.

Some go permanently into trade, and continue to follow the seasonal routes that they trod in their early years. Or they try other routes to gain fresh experience, trading their axes to the deer hunters of the Scottish hills as far as the underground villages of the Orkneys where wood is unknown and furniture made of stone, or sailing over to Ireland in the skin boats that put in on the Cumberland coast. In Ireland they find the third of the big ax factories, in the mountains of Antrim, and they meet as well, farther south, settlements of the passage-grave builders larger in size than any on the coasts of Great Britain. Some of the more adventurous spirits certainly come even farther afield, taking advantage of being among the passage-grave people to sign on in the coastwise ships that call there from Spain and the seas of the south. So that men of the northern lands could not impossibly be met on the quays of Crete, be cheated by Egyptian guides to the Pyramids, and even meet the younger grandsons of Abraham on the Canaan coast. For (though there is no proof of such contact at this period) travel is in the blood of these descendants of the nomad hunters. Home has always been where they are at the moment, and they feel no compulsion to return to their point of departure.

For those remaining in Britain time passes—not uneventfully, for no life is uneventful, but without cataclysmic change. The rhythm of the seasons and the rhythm of the years plays on. The generation of 1860 B.C. are grown men now, the fathers of families, settled in their ways. We may speculate—it is an instructive exercise—to what degree they are in touch with what is happening elsewhere in their world, while bearing in mind the danger of generalizing on the word "they." There would exist all degrees of intellectual—and commercial—curiosity, from the farmer who never raises his eyes from the furrows scratched by his straight wooden plowshare to his neighbor who will eagerly devour and embroider every rumor from distant lands.

They know more than we bargain with. Even the most sedentary peasant of the Downs or the remotest hunter of the Caledonian forest is in periodic touch with wanderers, not only traders but storytellers and mercenaries looking for a paymaster and men looking up second cousins and just plain tramps, who had covered the length of the country and the nearer parts of the continent—and who had there met other wanderers from at least as far afield in the other direction. Fishermen cross the North Sea regularly to and from the Low Countries and Scandinavia. The builders of the great stone graves along the west coast, who are in close touch with the people of the hinterland, have still their regular sea communications with the Irish and Spanish coasts and, somewhat less regularly, with the Mediterranean. And of the few adventurers who are bitten of wanderlust and really travel far, one or two in every generation will return.

So the men of England, such of them as are interested, will have some sort of picture of their world. They probably know Crete and Egypt by name, and have some idea of how far away they are. They will look on them as their superiors in material wealth and comfort, and will know that Cretans and Egyptians use bronze for their tools and ornaments and weapons. They know, of course, that metals exist, and will themselves have handled bronze—rather wistfully—more than once. They will not have heard of Babylon, even as a name, though they will be aware that there are other civilizations beyond Egypt and Crete. Closer home their picture of northern and western Europe will be much clearer. They will be vaguely troubled by stories of the ever-increasing numbers of battle-ax people pushing into the farmlands along the Rhine, the polders of the Netherlands, and the coastal regions of Scandinavia. And they will hear of the beaker traders of western Europe before ever the first of them sails across from Brittany and lands on the south coast of England.

It is the ax traders who actually meet the beaker people first, on an occasion when they have taken a consignment of Welsh axes, as they sometimes do, across the Channel to one of the markets in the north of France. It is the day after the British traders have settled in, and while they are making the rounds of their old friends and customers, that the caravan from the south arrives. First an advance guard, a middle-aged man to pick the campsite, and four young men as a bodyguard. They are foreigners, that anyone can see, slight and swarthy, with round heads and black hair and speaking an unknown language. But what impresses the crowds that flock around them is their assurance of bearing and their splendid clothing and equipment. They are dressed in woven cloth, which though not unknown is a rarity in these northern countries. Flowing cloaks, dyed in reds and blues, are clasped at the neck by real bronze buttons. The young men bear bows on their shoulders and quivers on their backs, and on their left wrists broad leather straps bearing a plate of bronze or stone to protect their hand against the snap of the bowstring. And on a belt at their waists they each wear a broad-bladed bronze dagger. Among the buckskin-clad and stone-armed crowd the newcomers in their woven finery and weapons of bronze stand out like beings from another world.

And then the main party arrives, a train of covered oxcarts and of pack asses. They are the first donkeys that many of the northerners have seen, and they arouse excited comment, until it is stilled by the sight of the goods being unloaded, with carefully casual ostentation—and under a strict guard of bowmen. As they see bolts of cloth and skins of wine, and finally bundles of bronze daggers disappearing into the newly pitched tents, the traders of stone axes at last realize the competition that they are faced with, and, as one man, they turn their backs and make for their tents to discuss their tactics in the face of this new threat to their livelihood.

The apprentices whom they leave to keep a watch on the newcomers are less troubled, though more excited, and they discuss among themselves whether the dark strangers can be real Egyptians. But the middle-aged traders—they are the same men who as apprentices had seen the consecration of Stonehenge—know better. They have heard of the activities of the new trading companies from Spain, and guess that the caravan has been sent from one of the newly established trade posts in central France.

It is a bad market for the ax traders. Though they have with one accord reduced their prices, and do a deal of trade among the poorer farmers, the bulk of the trade goes to the beaker people. (That is our name for the Spanish traders, for they used, and were buried with, richly ornamented bell-shaped drinking cups of pottery.) For the prices demanded by the new traders, though high, are not extravagant, and they know just what they want in exchange, furs and semiprecious stones such as jet and amber and the local callais. They have even set up a forge, and two bronzesmiths work there all day long, producing daggers or bracelets to order, or, for a consideration, resmelting and recasting such bronze as the community has got hold of in earlier years.

The upcoming trade in bronze appears likely to ruin completely the established trade in stone, and the ax merchants predict gloomily that it will not be long before bronze is there to stay. Indeed when they return—in reduced numbers—to France for the market the following year, they discover that the beaker folk have replaced their tents by a permanent timber trading post. The Spaniards' wives and families have come up to join them, and the post has a disquieting air of permanence. Thereafter the ax traders stop visiting France altogether.

But next year a party of beaker people arrives in a chartered boat on the south coast of England. And within a very few years a network of permanent trading posts covers the whole of southern England. There can be little doubt that the expansion is part of an organized trading campaign, with regular caravans running by stages all the way from central Spain, bringing the bronze and other wares to the outposts, and returning with the goods from the north. Indeed, the beaker people make no secret of their widespread organization. They boast of their connection with north Africa, from which many of them come, and of the trade routes all along the African coast from Egypt. And they tell how their people have spread their network far to the east, into Italy and the basin of the Danube and the Rhine valley.

But for all their wealth and organization they are not a standoffish people. They have clearly come to stay, and around their trading stations small farmsteads and neat fields begin to spread. They have many skills, and in particular the bronzesmiths among them can do more than cast the new metal. It is they who first recognize the presence of copper ores in England and identify, with great excitement, outcroppings of tin in Cornwall. And they encourage the local chieftains to mine these new riches. Clearly they are bringing wealth to the country, and their popularity increases accordingly. It is cemented by an increasing number of marriages between the dark handsome southerners and the tall Downland farmer families. And as the years pass, and the men who had seen the Stonehenge embankment raised grow old, a new generation begins to grow up around the beaker settlements. And dotted over the Downs small round barrows begin to appear, piled above the graves of men who had been born in Spain or Africa, but who had made their homes in England.

Through their merchandise convoys the south British settlements keep in close touch with events in Europe. While the old men in the Pennines deplore the recession in the ax trade, the new generation of their competitors is beyond the Rhine, demonstrating the superiority in close fighting of the bronze dagger over the stone battle-ax which is the traditional weapon of the cattle herders there. On the Rhine and in Holland, as in England, the beaker trading posts are by now a score of years established, and there too a new generation is growing up, taking its traditions, and often its blood, both from the Spanish merchants and from the horsemen who, generations ago, had wandered out from the Russian steppes. Many of the young men growing up here are looking to the untouched markets and reputed mineral wealth and fertile soil of the north of England and Scotland. And the younger generation of northern England is prepared to welcome them. For they see no future in the manufacture of stone axes or in subsistence hunting and herding. The future lies with the metal industry, and this only the beaker people are at this time able to develop. Unlike their metal-less neighbors in Scandinavia, who are now abandoning the battle-ax and imitating the new close-fighting weapon, the bronze dagger, in flint, the men of northern England are already looking forward to the day when they will be able to produce, and perhaps even export, genuine bronze daggers of their own.

The ax factory of the Langdale valley, like those of Graig Lwyd in Wales and Tievebulliagh in northern Ireland, are facts, and the ways of life of the manufacturers are well attested. The areas to which the axes from each factory were distributed have been identified with certainty by microscopic examination of museum specimens. The earliest form of Stonehenge has been determined by recent excavation. We know little, on the other hand, about the ritual associated with its first construction, the religion it was meant to serve, or indeed the purpose of the earliest monuments of the henge type. We are in fact on shaky ground in any discussion of the beliefs of the prehistoric Euro-

peans. The evidence for human sacrifice and, at least on occasions, cannibalism in England is, however, so strong as to be almost irrefutable. Stuart Piggott in The Neolithic Cultures of the British Isles *gives in great detail all that is known of Britain at the time of this chapter, while R. J. C. Atkinson's* Stonehenge *is a new and standard work on all aspects of that monument.*

8

THE LAWGIVER

1790–1720 B.C.

I T IS 1790 B.C. The Second Millennium B.C. has already lasted longer than the independent existence of the United States. Much has changed in these two centuries, and many changes are in progress now. We have seen the first appearance in Europe of the Indo-European-speaking charioteers from south Russia, and their gradual assimilation by the farmers already settled there—with some drift of refugee families, mainly of the "native" fishing and hunting stocks, towards the west. And we have seen the beaker people from Spain and Africa pushing deep, in small organized groups, into central and northern Europe, establishing as they go the beginnings of a regular trade in bronze among the Stone-Age peoples whom they meet.

Movements of peoples, conquests and assimilations, spreadings of ideas and state religions, trade and manufacture and war was the pattern of the background against which the European of 1800 B.C. lived out his intensely personal life. In the Middle East the same pattern regulated the run of men's lives (as indeed it regulates our own), and a warning is in place. In Europe we can only talk in general terms, of peoples with names we have ourselves given them (beaker folk and battle-ax people and the Windmill Hill culture and the users of Peterborough ware) and of events of a so indefinite date that it is only with reservations that we can even ascribe them definitely to one lifetime rather than another. In the east, on the other hand, we know what people called themselves, we have the names of individuals and nations and cities, accurate comparative and actual dates of events, and even to some degree the recorded thoughts and opinions of people then living. But the difference is unreal, it is in us and the state of our knowledge, not in the time of which we tell. We should never forget that the peoples of Europe had their own names for themselves and their lands, that their movements involved actual battles and treaties between actual people occurring on actual dates. No controversy raged at the time about the date of the building of Stonehenge, and the king who ordered its construction was as real and powerful a person as the king who, less than a hundred years later, wrote on a tablet that can be seen in the British Museum: "I am Hammurabi the mighty king, king of Babylon, king of the world. That which from days of old no king had built for his lord, I have accomplished gloriously for my lord the Sun-God."

A hundred years and more have gone by since the tribal family of Terah, migrating northward from Ur along the Euphrates to Harran, had encamped a night or so by the little walled village of Babylon. The grandsons of Abraham are now the chieftains of considerable nomad tribes in Syria and Palestine, the length of the desert away. And Babylon has become a considerable city, carrying weight in the affairs of the valley of the lower Euphrates and Tigris. There is a new king now sitting in the palace on the eastern bank of the Euphrates. He is a young man who succeeded his famous father only two years ago, and no one knows what he will make of his reign. His name is Hammurabi.

He comes of a long line of kings. For his great-great-grandfather was Sumu-la-El, who had usurped the throne of Babylon from Sumu-abum, in whose reign Abraham had passed by. It was Sumu-abum who had organized the little confederacy of Amorite-occupied villages, with Babylon as its capital, and had thereby first raised Babylon to something more than an obscure village. And the dynasty that followed him had been strong, and had needed to be, in order not only to preserve the independence of the Babylon confederacy but to extend it into a power of local, though not negligible, significance. It was Sumu-la-El himself who had defeated the ancient and neighboring

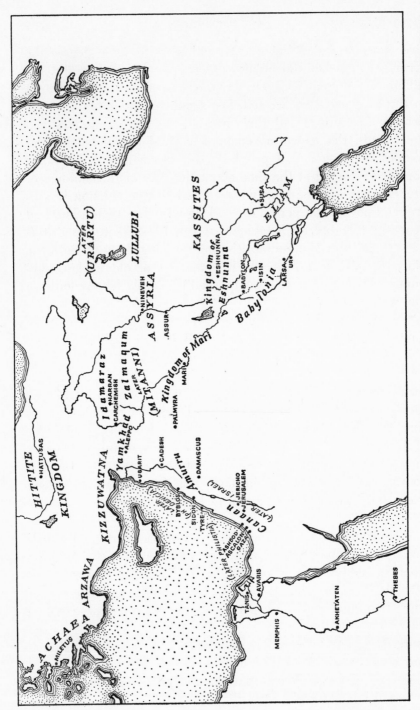

THE NEAR EAST IN THE TIME OF HAMMURABI. THE KINGDOMS IN UPPER AND LOWER CASE ARE UNDER AMORITE RULE.

city of Kish, the ruler of which had believed that the claims of history gave him paramount right to rule the Amorite confederacy. And in the reign of his son, Zabum, in the lifetime of old men still living, the threat of Elam, the great power to the east, had reached new proportions.

While the ax traders were wandering the green roads of England, and the beaker folk were pushing deeper and deeper into Europe along the river valleys, the kings of Elam had been watching the fluctuating struggle between the rulers of Isin and of Larsa for the control of Mesopotamia south of the Babylonian confederacy. They had continually interfered in the war, sometimes cold and sometimes hot, between the two tiny principalities, and finally, in 1836, within the recollection of most people now alive, the king of Elam, Kudur-Mabug, had captured the weakened Larsa, cynically assumed the title of Protector of the Amorites, and installed his son, Warad-Sin, as king there. Isin still existed, under a succession of weak usurper kings, but its power was drastically reduced. And even Babylon, farther north, had lost land to Elam, and had had to tread warily to retain its independence. Thirty-four years ago, after a reign of twelve years, Warad-Sin of Larsa had died, and had been succeeded by his brother Rim-Sin, an energetic monarch who still occupied the throne of Larsa and held firmly all Mesopotamia south of the confederacy. That had been the position when Hammurabi's father, Sin-muballit, had succeeded to the throne of Babylon twenty-two years ago.

The inhabitants of Babylon regarded Sin-muballit as one of their greatest kings. In defiance of the claims of Rim-Sin to the overlordship of all south Mesopotamia, he had held the confederacy intact, and even recovered the territory lost to Elam by his father. Eight years previously there had been an open clash with Rim-Sin, and many of the men of Babylon looked back with pride to their part in the victorious battle against the combined armies of Larsa and of Ur. Rim-Sin had retired, and had been forced to bolster his prestige by a move against a weaker foe. The following year he attacked Isin, still nominally independent, and brought to an end the two-hundred-year-old dynasty there.

But the garrison he left in Isin was weak, and two years later Sin-muballit was able to designate the year 1795 officially as "the year of the capture of Isin." Though Sin-muballit made no attempt to hold the town, there seemed little doubt that in the struggle for prestige Babylon had won two successive tricks. But now Sin-muballit was dead, and his son, an unknown quantity, sat on his throne.

Hammurabi, looking out from his yellow brick palace across the yellow waters of the Euphrates to the palm-fringed farther bank, was well aware that the Larsa-Elam alliance to the east and south was only one of the dangers facing his kingdom. To the north and west lay another great and aggressive power, Assyria, and only resolute and well-co-ordinated action could save Babylon from being ground to fragments between the upper and the nether millstones.

When a hundred years ago Abraham had traveled northwest from Ur to Harran, and southwest from Harran to Palestine, he had been moving all the way among his own people, the Amorites. In the generation before Abraham the Amorites had spread outwards from the deserts of north Arabia into the fertile lands to east, north, and west, and occupied a great half-circle of territory bounded by the Mediterranean coast, the mountains of south Turkey, and the mountains of west Persia. Only the might of Elam had held them on their eastern flank, and the power of Egypt on their western.

Since the time of Abraham this closely knit confederation of small nomad tribes had crystallized into a ring of Amorite kingdoms, centered around the capitals of ambitious and jealous monarchs. Since the Amorite kingdom of Larsa had fallen to Elam, Babylon had been for forty-five years the easternmost of these states. To its north lay Eshnunna, and north of that again lay Assyria, holding the headwaters of the Tigris. From there the kingdoms ran westward. The center of the line was occupied by Mari, on the upper Euphrates, and beyond it lay Idamaraz, with its capital at Carchemish, and Yamkhad, ruled from Aleppo. To the south of Yamkhad, along the Mediterranean coast, lay the kingdoms of Ugarit and Qatana, and finally the tribes of Canaan ruled by Abraham's sons and grandsons, facing Egypt across the Sinai desert.

Twenty-two years ago, when Hammurabi was a boy—the very year that his father had succeeded to the throne of Babylon—the northern frontier had gone up in flames. The king of Assyria, Ila-kabkabu, had died, and his second son, Samsi-Adad, had raised an army on the southern frontier, attacked Eshnunna and captured its northern provinces, and then with his victorious army marched upon Assur, the capital of Assyria, deposed his brother Aminu, and himself assumed the throne. In the following year he took Mari, and installed his younger son as regent there. And in the years that followed he had pressed farther and farther west, campaigning against Idamaraz and Yamkhad, until his armies stood on the shores of the Mediterranean.

After reducing the rulers of the northern string of kingdoms to vassalage, Samsi-Adad had of late been turning his attention to the south, and the only thing that had saved Babylon from sharing the fate of Aleppo was that the king of Eshnunna, Ibal-pi-El, had proved an unexpectedly hard nut to crack and, though he had lost all his northern territory to the Assyrian armies, had stubbornly resisted all attacks on his actual capital.

It was obvious to Hammurabi, a shrewd and realistic young man, that one or other of the veteran warriors to the north and south, Rim-Sin of Larsa or Samsi-Adad of Assyria, would attempt to take advantage of the death of his famous father to make an easy conquest of the important middle Euphrates area. He determined to give them other things to think about.

A diversionary move against Samsi-Adad was easily arranged. The king of Mari, deposed twenty years before, had a son, Zimri-lim, who had grown up in exile. Now he was encouraged by Yarim-lim of Yamkhad and Hammurabi of Babylon to return and claim his inheritance, and in 1790, two years after Hammurabi's accession, Zimri-lim expelled the Assyrian viceroy from Mari and re-established the kingdom of the upper Euphrates. To support him Hammurabi had conscripted his army and advanced north, establishing his frontier posts a full eighty miles up the Euphrates. They were not called on to fight. Without a

battle Hammurabi had completely stalemated the old king of
Assyria, re-established the balance of power in the north, and set
two buffer states between himself and any attack from that direction.

To the south was Rim-Sin of Larsa, and his strength lay in
his alliance with Elam. We do not know what envoys of Hammurabi climbed in secret the steep trails leading into the Persian
mountains, nor what messages they carried. But in 1785 Hammurabi's armies moved south against Rim-Sin and captured—and
this time held—the city of Isin. And Elam made no move, for
Elam had troubles of its own. A tribe known as the Kassites,
from the mountains of Luristan to the northwest, was suddenly
attacking with unusual vigor. At about this time the records of
Susa, the Elamite capital, break sharply off.

For the moment Babylon was safe, and already stronger than
it had ever been before, and for the first time in the seven years
since his accession Hammurabi could pause and take stock. For
the next twenty years there was peace in Mesopotamia.

In these twenty years the generation born at the accession
of Hammurabi grows to manhood. They do not remember the
tense days of their early childhood, when their fathers marched
with their young general to war, and the sack of cities. Now the
king, like their fathers, is middle-aged, and for a long while there
have been no battles. But the new generation of young men are
no strangers to marching and training with weapons. The price
of peace is eternal vigilance; every year when the harvest is in,
the muster roll is read out in the town squares and in the villages,
and men are called from pasture and from shop to serve their
king. No shirking is allowed, though exception may be made on
compassionate grounds or to persons in jobs of national importance. The remainder march out, with their spears and long narrow shields, some to relieve the units of the standing army manning the frontier forts, some to reinforce likely points of attack,
or to make carefully calculated demonstrations of strength along
the borders. For the months after the harvest are the traditional
campaigning season, and it does not do to forget it, or to let potential enemies forget it. It is a time of camaraderie and full
stomachs, of long hot marches and quiet warm nights under the

sheepskins around the bivouac fires, and military service is by
no means unpopular among the young men. To bear arms is
moreover a visible sign of rank, of belonging to the property-
owning class, which alone is officially entitled to call itself "men."
The menial work of the army, the carrying of supplies, the cooking, and the pitching of tents is done by the unarmed "poor,"
who do not own land, while the slaves, of course, are not allowed
to leave their work for any service at all.

The young men never knew why Hammurabi waited twenty
years before he launched his carefully trained infantry. And
they never realized the change which had taken place in Babylonia during these years. For they had grown up with the
changes. But their fathers, the men of Hammurabi's own generation, realized what had happened, and why Hammurabi had
bided his time. He had used the years to create a nation—and a
civil service.

They could remember, as their children born after Hammurabi's accession could not, that Babylon had been the head
of a confederacy. Each of the small towns owing allegiance to
Babylon had had its own king and its own particular god. The
"men" and the "poor" of each city worshipped that city's god
and served that city's king. And it was not yet quite forgotten that
generations ago the city and all within it and the land around
had been owned and administered by the city god and his
priesthood. Some of the cities, like Kish and Nippur and Sippar
and Isin, were of very much older standing than Babylon, and
Kish and Isin, in particular, had themselves been the rulers of
large confederacies before ever Babylon was thought of.

There had been a time when a subject could write to King
Zimri-lim of Mari (and the letter is extant to this day): "There
is no king who of himself is the strongest. Ten or fifteen kings
follow Hammurabi of Babylon, the same number follow Rim-
Sin of Larsa, the same number follow Ibal-pi-El of Eshnunna,
the same number follow Amut-pi-il of Qatana, twenty kings follow Yarim-lim of Yamkhad."

Hammurabi had changed all that. He had seen the danger
of vassal kings, who could change their allegiance, and he was
determined to be "of himself the strongest." The vassal kings were

removed and replaced by governors, ruling in the name of the Babylonian king, and themselves for the most part Babylonians. Hammurabi himself took over the administration and the judicial functions of the displaced kings, ordering personally the maintenance and repair of canals and the deciding of lawsuits. The governors collected the taxes, kept the muster rolls of the conscript army, and witnessed trade agreements. Gradually a staff of secretaries, messengers, and paymasters was recruited to manage the detailed work of administration, and a state police and a corps of excisemen kept watch on the roads.

The city gods had proved a more difficult problem than the city kings. For as long as they existed, the primary loyalty of the men of the minor cities was to their own temple and not to the capital. But Hammurabi had attacked the gods at their weakest point, by an order that the accounts of all the temples should be sent to Babylon for auditing. And he followed it by a planned aggrandizement of Marduk, the god of Babylon, up to now a god of little account. His temple was set up in every city, and great festivals in his honor were instituted. Clearly Marduk was now a great god, and it was wise for all men, and even for the local gods, to bow circumspectly before him.

In the course of these years, then, the confederacy of Babylon became the centralized country of Babylonia. The older men doubtless disapproved of the changes. But the young men had grown up with them.

Hammurabi, reading the tablets sent by his ambassadors and agents in the countries beyond his frontiers, knew that the time was ripe for the next step. It was perhaps even overdue. For beyond the Amorite fringe new things were happening.

The men of the mountains had never been negligible. The mountains, after all, overhung the whole civilized world. All the way north from the Persian Gulf through Elam and Eshnunna to Assyria, the mountains of Persia frowned down upon one's right hand. And as one turned west from Assyria by the great trade route that led through Harran and Carchemish and Aleppo to the Mediterranean and the ports where the ships from Crete came in, the mountains turned with one, and still rose on one's right, the mountains of Armenia and eastern Turkey. Even on the

sea journey to Crete—and not a few of Hammurabi's informants
made the journey regularly—the mountains could still be seen,
breaking in cliffs and headlands against the blue waters of the
Upper Sea. It was a fascinating and vaguely foreboding sight to
the Amorites, cultivators of the river plains and traditionally the
descendants of desert nomads.

The traders, though, put such thoughts from them. The
mountains and the people of the mountains were suppliers of primary products. All the silver and tin and lead, and much of the
copper and gold which was worked in the land of the Twin Rivers came from within the mountains. The villagers of the upper
valleys seasonally left their flocks of sheep and goats, and their
tiny terraced fields, and went to work the outcrops and galleries
and to operate the smelting ovens, amassing ingots—as a not dis-
similar people far away to the north amassed stone axes—against
the periodic coming of the traders. It was not difficult for Hammurabi to keep a sharp eye on what went on in the mountains.

The mountain people had lived there, they said, from time
immemorial, and they still worshipped their old gods, gods with
outlandish names like Teshup and Hepa among the Hurrians,
and Shipah and Harbe of the Kassites. But the chieftains and
their warrior-knights were of a different race, and though they
had ruled now for several generations, it was still well known
that they originally came from the north. They spoke a different
language, too, from their subjects (a language of the stock we
call Indo-European), and worshipped other gods, Mithra and
Indra and Veruna, Surya and Marut. They were a proud race,
these chieftains and their warriors, and their pride lay chiefly in
their horses and chariots. They practiced with their chariots all
day long, and at night, in their timber palaces or by the camp-
fires where they lay watching over their herds of mares, they sang
lays of the northern lands, of the endless plains beyond the mountains and of kings asleep in their barrows these three hundred
years and more.

With their light two-wheeled chariots they could, and did,
range widely even in the difficult terrain of the mountains, and
the younger princes often went on month-long journeys to the
chieftains of distant but related tribes. Thus they knew of their

kinsfolk who had wandered westward into Europe, and may even have heard of the expeditions now setting sail from the coasts of the Netherlands towards the eastern coasts of England. These, though, were a hybrid folk, intermarried with farmers and traders, and perhaps should hardly any longer be considered part of the family. They certainly knew of their cousins the Achaeans, who had made their way southwestward into the steep fjord-lands of Greece. And, closer home, other kinsfolk, who had crossed the Dardanelles, under the walls of the little fortress of Troy, and had established their kingdoms in the interior of Asia Minor, were close enough to be actually visited in their fortresses overlooking the river Halys.

But mostly the young warriors journeyed to the east. For there lay their closest kinsfolk, speakers of the same dialect, worshippers of the same gods. These were the tribes of the Aryans, who had pushed round the north of the Caspian Sea, across the plains of the Kara Kum, and up the broad valley of the Oxus into the mountains of the Hindu Kush. From there they looked down upon the headwaters of the Indus, and were already aware of the rich cities and cultivated lands of the civilization that held the valley farther south.

Hammurabi, too, knew, by other channels, of the network of relationships uniting the Indo-European warriors of the mountains. For the ships from Crete, which brought the eggshell pottery of that island to Ugarit on the Syrian coast and there met *his* merchants, had on other voyages met the Achaean settlers on the coast of Greece. And the merchants bringing copper from Ur and the other Persian Gulf ports had heard from the Dilmun ships' captains of the preparations for defense being made by the kings of the brick-built cities of the Indus.

That the Achaeans of the west and the Aryans of the east were related peoples, and the kin of the warrior leaders of the Hurrians to his north and the Kassites to his east, was strongly indicated by the fact that they all possessed the prized horse chariots.

Horses were no longer an unknown thing to the Amorites. It was a couple of generations or more since they had first appeared among the newer peoples of the mountains, and in Hammurabi's own lifetime they had been acquired by the Assyrians and by the kings of Mari. But horses were extremely expensive, particularly as it was necessary to import grooms and trainers with them from the mountain tribes. And the older generation looked with disfavor on the modern craze for speed at any price. Samsi-Adad, the old king of Assyria, now dead these ten years, had felt it necessary to remonstrate with his son for his extravagance in keeping horses, and the old state councilor of Zimri-lim, the king of Mari, had begged his master not to show himself behind horses on the roads of his kingdom.

That the horsemen of the north and east were a threat to Mesopotamia had long been obvious to Hammurabi. And now his agents told him of serious movements in the hills. The Kassites in the mountains of Luristan to the north of the great plain of Elam, who had once served his turn against Rim-Sin, were said to be too many for their pastures. And the Hurrians of Armenia were, he heard, wandering down from their hills into the northern marches of Assyria and Idamaraz and Yamkhad.

Hammurabi was an ambitious man, and he had long been working with the deliberate aim of uniting the whole of the Amorite fringe under one rule from the Persian Gulf to the Mediterranean. It now looked as though the incursions of the Hurrians into the northern kingdoms might well forestall his plans. It was high time to move.

In 1762 B.C. he ordered his armies to march against Eshnunna to the north. The young men born about 1790 B.C., now twenty-eight years old or so, must have formed at this time the backbone of his army. They had been trained for years with this day in view, and politically indoctrinated with a personal loyalty towards Babylonia and its king. For the first time in Mesopotamia a country, instead of a conglomeration of cities, was going to war.

Hammurabi led his troops in person, as was the duty and privilege of a king, and the soldiers would often catch a glimpse of his dyed sheepskin cloak and grizzled bearded face as he passed along the ranks in his litter, or driving, like a Sumerian king, in his four-wheeled ass chariot. From the frontier at Sippar they crossed the sandy grasslands between the Euphrates and the Tigris, a good day's march, were ferried across the broad Tigris (near present-day Baghdad), and headed northeast to meet the army of "the man of Eshnunna," as they contemptuously called him. When the battle joined, they were doubtless just as apprehensive as any raw soldiers before and since, and just as surprised to find that the tactics practiced on the exercise ground actually work when used against a real enemy. The army before them broke, Eshnunna opened its gates, and they encamped beside their first conquest, while their general imposed his terms on the city.

And then they were ordered east, much to their surprise. To the east lay the Persian mountains, the country of the Kassites. But as they marched along the foothills, trending southwards, it became obvious that their objective was not the Kassites, but Elam. This was not, however, a serious threat. By this route Susa, the capital of Elam, was too distant for attack. This was a demonstration in force, designed to overawe the Kassite hillmen and to divert the Elamite forces to the northwest, away from their southwestern allies in Larsa. When the army returned home to Babylon after successful skirmishes in Elamite territory, Hammurabi could claim the conquest both of Eshnunna and of Elam. But Eshnunna he held, with a governor and a garrison.

The next year, when the harvest was off the fields, the soldiers were again called to the colors, and this time they marched southeastward along the Euphrates. There could be no doubt about their destination. The question was to be settled once and for all, whether Babylon or Larsa should rule in Mesopotamia. Rim-Sin, king of Larsa, was a very old man. He had reigned for sixty-one years, since the time of Hammurabi's grandfather, and since he had overthrown Isin thirty-five years ago he had had no rival to the dominion of the old empire of Ur. But now his power over his confederate cities had waned, and one after another they submitted to the invaders. And from his allies in Elam, overawed by the show of force the previous year, came no assistance. After a last battle, Larsa capitulated and the old king was taken prisoner.

Hammurabi was now master of a rich and populous country, full of large and ancient cities accustomed to rule themselves with little or no interference from their nominal overlord. It took him three years to impose his new ideas upon them. The most noticeable sign of the new order, apart from the presence of the soldiers of the garrison, was the spate of new building, religious and secular, in the name of the new king. And the setting-up in the market places of the black obelisks, bearing in long rows of close-set wedge writing the clauses of the new law, the Code of Hammurabi.

The Code contained little that was new, and the inhabitants of the conquered cities would have no reason to guess that Hammurabi's claim to fame in a far-distant future would rest largely upon it. In its detail it bears witness to the competence of the king's civil servants and legal advisers, but its significance lay in the fact that from now on one law ran throughout Mesopotamia, that Hammurabi was, as he put it, "the king pre-eminent among kings; may my justice prevail in the land."

As on earth so in Heaven. Just as Hammurabi claimed in the introduction to his code that the old gods of Sumeria, Anu, Enlil, and Ea, had entrusted him with a kingdom "the foundations of which are as firm as heaven and earth," so the great creation epic, recited at the principal temple festivals and particularly at the *akîtu* festival of Marduk at Babylon, now the chief religious ceremony of the year, was at this time "edited" to show Marduk as the god who rightfully enforces the commands of Anu, Enlil, and Ea. The gods of Sumer had abdicated their powers to Marduk, god of Babylon, just as the kings of Sumer had abdicated in favor of the king of Babylon.

By 1757 B.C. Hammurabi felt secure enough to turn his back on Sumer, and he led his now veteran army to the conquest of his former ally, Mari. And two years later, after deposing King Isme-Dagan of Assyria, he records victories in the north of Assyria, on the borders of the Hurrian country.

For the first time since the legendary days of the great kings of Ur, four hundred years ago (as far back as the Conquistadores from us), the whole of Mesopotamia, from the mountains to the sea, was united under a single ruler. And yet it was too late. For the traditional next step, the campaign along the upper Euphrates and the southern edge of the Turkish mountains to the

Mediterranean, was barred. Across that route lay the horsemen of the Hurrians, now firmly settled in the lowland where their chariots had all the room they needed to maneuver; and their cousins, the rulers of the Kassites, lay waiting in the Persian mountains, to the rear of any westward movement from Mesopotamia.

And Hammurabi was an elderly man by now, and the weight of administration, to which he had always given an almost excessive personal attention, was heavy on his shoulders. We do not know exactly the date of his birth, but he must have been about sixty when he conquered Assyria, and about sixty-five when he died in 1750 B.C.

The men born in Babylon in the early years of his reign, in 1790 B.C., were forty years old when he died. For twelve years they had extended and held his empire, and now they were themselves middle-aged, and their children were growing up into a changed world. Samsu-iluna, Hammurabi's son, was himself of approximately this conquering generation, and had marched with the armies against Larsa and Assyria. The small standing army was loyal to him, and the people of Babylonia, who, when needed, formed the bulk of the army, accepted him without question as the inheritor of the empire. For four years seedtime and harvest, temple procession and canal maintenance, trading caravan and municipal brickyard carried on without interruption. And the frontier guards, who had learnt from history to expect invasion and revolt when a king died, leaned on their spears and looked out from the brick watchtowers upon empty plain or peacefully grazing flocks.

Then in 1746 the watchers beyond Eshnunna saw the smoke of fires in the hills. And next day the horse chariots fanned out from the valley mouth, and behind them came spearmen and bowmen and creaking ox wagons. Word went back to Babylon by relays of runners that the Kassites were raiding in force.

Gandash, the Indo-European chieftain of the Kassites, knew better. This was no raid in search of booty. His men had come to stay, and he knew that, a day's march behind them and with its own guard of charioteers, the main body of women and children and flocks and herds and tents and furniture and household gods was on its way down to the plains. For Hammurabi, the great king, was dead, and the lush land lay open to whoever could take it.

With all the speed that horses could give him (though hampered by the new obstacle of wide rivers and a network of irrigation canals) Gandash threw his forces at Babylon. And Samsu-iluna called his veterans to arms, this time to defend their homes. Gandash had underestimated the new king and his experienced troops. Between the waters of Euphrates and Tigris the seasoned footmen of Babylonia met and defeated the charioteers from the northwest. The first serious clash between Indo-European and Semite, between horse and foot, ended in favor of the latter.

But it was only a partial victory. Gandash retired behind the Tigris, but he stayed in the plains. Eshnunna and the Diyala valley became a Kassite kingdom. Samsu-iluna must almost have expected what happened next. Within weeks word came out of Assyria, to the north beyond the Kassite bridgehead, of revolting cities and slaughtered garrisons and of a new king proclaimed in the old capital of Assur. And then silence. Samsu-iluna prepared for revolt in the south.

Nevertheless, four years went by before it came, so well had Hammurabi done his work, four years of watchful garrisons and apprehensive governors in Sumer, and of border clashes between Kassite and Babylonian charioteers in the north. For Babylon was now beginning to develop for herself the new arm of chariotry.

In 1742, eight years after Hammurabi's death, a pretender to the throne of Larsa arose, calling himself Rim-Sin like the last king, and rallied Larsa, Uruk, and Isin to his side. Samsu-iluna was prepared, but he had to keep the bulk of his army facing the Kassites, and could spare little more than the local garrisons to cope with the revolt in Sumer. Even so, he succeeded, after two years of guerilla warfare in the swamps and reed jungles of the south, in capturing and executing the rebel leader. Once more there was an uneasy peace.

The position in the north stabilized as the years went by. By the time the Kassites had been ten years in the country, the permanence of their occupation of the eastern plains was accepted as a fact. With the horses acquired by the Babylonians had come renegade Kassite grooms, and now others of their people drifted over the frontier between the two powers, taking service as laborers in the towns and harvesters in the fields. Many of the soldiers who had served Hammurabi and who had taken part in the battle that saved Babylon from the first Kassite onslaught now found themselves, as elderly landowners, employing their former enemies on their estates.

Again the south revolted. In 1736 Iluma-ilu, a noble of the ancient royal family of Isin, which had lost its throne to the kings of Larsa over sixty years ago, claimed the kingship of the south and was accepted by the cities along the Persian Gulf. Samsu-iluna of Babylon raised another army and marched down the river to meet him. And this time the spirit of Sumerian independence defeated the Babylonian king. Although he could and did attack and capture the revolting cities, and even sacked the venerable city of Ur, the army of the rebels was a match for him. He was attacked in turn, and driven back, even beyond Hammurabi's frontier town of Nippur. And there he was forced to refortify a frontier line originally built by his great-great-great-grandfather over a hundred years before.

The Babylonians born in 1790 B.C., now sixty years old, looked back on an empire which had risen and fallen within their lifetime. They had, it seemed to them, fought in vain under their great general. The borders of Babylonia lay where they had lain before their first campaign. To the south the new dynasty of the sea-lands held the old realm of Larsa. To the north Assyria was risen again, and the kingdom of the "man of Eshnunna" was firmly in Kassite hands. Only Mari remained of their conquests, and beyond Mari the Hurrians held the upper Euphrates in ever-increasing strength.

The situation was obviously unstable, and sooner or later must break out into a decisive war. The sixty-year-old strategists argued fiercely that only a united Mesopotamia could hope to hold out against the chariot-led armies to the east and the west. Divided as they were, Assyria was bound to fall to the Hurrians, Babylonia to the Kassites, and Sumer to Elam. The position could not possibly remain static.

As the years slowly passed and Hammurabi's veterans grew older, they stated more and more positively that the cold war could not go on forever, that the status quo was untenable, that the uneasy balance was bound, sooner or later, to topple over into war. They were still protesting as their generation passed away. They were not to know that the uneasy peace in Mesopotamia was not to be broken for a hundred and twenty years.

The events of the reign of Hammurabi and his successors are exceptionally well documented by large numbers of contemporary tablets and inscriptions from Babylon, Ur, Mari, and Ugarit. There is little disagreement between them, and the events of this chapter can to that degree be regarded as history. (The suggested secret alliance between Hammurabi and the Kassites, designed to keep Elam engaged while he dealt with Larsa in 1785, is, however, only a suggestion.)

The big question, though, is—or has until recently been—the precise date of Hammurabi's reign. It is a question of very considerable importance to the historiography of the whole of the Near East, as Hammurabi is not only important in himself but is also the peg on which some three hundred years of earlier and later history can be hung. Until some ten years ago he was normally considered to have lived about 2000 b.c. (or even 2300 b.c.), but recent research and discoveries, particularly the Mari tablets, have made the date 1792–50 very probable—some would say certain. The main argument for this date is contained in Sidney Smith's Alalakh and Chronology, *while a full discussion of the various views is given in S. A. Pallis's* Antiquity of Iraq, *which also gives a very full account of life in Mesopotamia at the time of Hammurabi, and many details of his code of laws.*

9

THE PRINCES OF THE DESERT

1720–1650 B.C.

A FTER NIGHTFALL the inn became the center of village life. It lay on the edge of the village, immediately at the foot of the levee that held back the Nile waters from flooding the delta lands. The levee at the same time was the great trunk road, so the inn was well placed to receive both travelers from the boats which chose to tie up for the night on the other side of the embankment, and the wayfarers who journeyed on foot or on donkeyback along the road that led from the cities of the south to the coast ports or to the Syrian caravan routes.

It was a solid construction of yellow mud brick, with a high windowless wall surrounding both the buildings and the courtyard. In summer the business of the inn all went on in the courtyard, where the evening breeze stirred the awnings that had given shade during the day, and brought a welcome coolness to the air. As the darkness deepened, the fires would be lit here and there in the wide sandy enclosure, as much for light as for warmth or cooking; for most of the travelers bought their meals from the sweltering kitchens, spiced stews thick with barley, and lentil mashes, and broiled fish, and even—if you could pay for it— roast duck caught that very day in the marshes. The slaves ran hither and thither, dodging among the tethered groups of donkeys with the trays of food and the mugs of beer; and the scribe kept a watchful eye, noting down on his wax tablets the value— calculated, of course, in measures of barley—of everything consumed, so that he could make out the bills before the travelers departed on the morrow.

Soon the locals were beginning to arrive, as, returned from their fields or their fishing boats, they finished their suppers in their homes and made excuses to their wives to drop around to the inn to see if there was a bit of business to be picked up. They would saunter in casually, exchange a word with the innkeeper sitting on his string-bed by the gate, and go and squat on their haunches at one of the fires. The first pint of beer would be drunk in silence, for the most part, but then a casual inquiry about the state of the roads or of the harvest would start the talk rolling, and anecdotes and reminiscences and tall stories would be tossed back and forth across the fires until, around midnight, the locals would gradually drift back to their homes, walking rather steadily and deliberately. And the travelers would unstrap their blankets and roll up by the fires.

The children were always there. The innkeeper was careful not to see them as they sidled in, and once inside they stayed away from the circles of firelight, lying on their stomachs among the fodder bags and bales of flax or wool, listening to the stories told by the travelers or by their own fathers and grandfathers.

They were children of a new generation, born around 1720 B.C. And their grandfathers were contemporaries of the old soldiers who on the same evenings were sitting in Babylon recalling the great days when they had conquered Mesopotamia for Hammurabi. The children will, indeed, occasionally hear of Hammurabi and his empire, for in their time their grandfathers had followed his campaigns with some interest. But mostly the talk was of events closer to home and nearer in time. And there were tales enough of danger and sudden death to curdle the blood of the listening children.

It was all the fault of the secessionists in the South, the grandfathers were agreed. And for the benefit of foreign traders, who were new to the land and could scarcely speak Egyptian and knew nothing of Egypt's internal politics, they would tell the story—after their third beer—of the Civil War of nearly sixty years ago.

It had all started on the death of the last pharaoh of the great Twelfth Dynasty. They had been great and splendid kings in that dynasty, and the succession of Amenemhets and Sesostrises, for all that they had made their capital at Thebes in the deep and uncivilized south, had given Egypt two hundred years of peace and prosperity at home and expanding trade and political influence abroad. Up as far as Ugarit in the north of Syria their influence had extended, and the cedar of Lebanon and the gold of Nubia had adorned their palaces. But when Amenemhet IV had died, he had had no son to succeed him.

As was only right and proper, his wife-and-sister, Sebeknefrure, also of the blood royal, had continued to rule alone, until such time as she should select a consort to share her throne. And three years later she had done so. But the man she selected, Khutouire Ugafa, was a commoner, and what was worse he was from the delta. And the nobles of Thebes had refused to accept this perfectly legal succession, and they had set up a rival pharaoh, from a younger branch of the royal family, in Thebes, and the south had seceded.

The Civil War that had followed had been long and bitter, as the grandfathers could testify from their own experience. Several times they had been conscripted for campaigns against the south, or to withstand a threat from the southern armies. Twice the intermittent struggle had even invaded the delta, and the village had been burnt. And even when there had been no active warfare between the north and the south, there had been intrigues and plots, palace revolutions, and army mutinies fomented by the opposing sides. The old men could no longer count the number of princes and priests and generals who, after murdering their predecessor, had proclaimed themselves pharaoh, only to fall themselves to an assassin some months or years later. There must have been at least fourteen successive pharaohs, they reckoned, in the north, and ten or twelve in the renegade south. Both sides claimed, of course, to be the rightful rulers of the whole country, but once at least—it was the last time the village had been burnt—the southern usurpers had actually held control of the north for a space of years, under a king calling himself Sebekhotep III. That had been some fifteen—or was it twenty? —years ago, they explained. And the king of the north, the rightful pharaoh, had had to flee the country. But he had returned, with a force of Bedouin from the eastern deserts, and driven the usurper back up the Nile. It was, they reckoned, the first time the Bedouin had fought for the men of the north against the men of the south, and their long curved bronze swords had proved a new and irresistible weapon against the spears and daggers of the southern troops. —At this point in the story three black-bearded Ishmaelites from Arabia, in long woolen robes, grinned self-consciously as the men crouched round the fire turned and looked at the bronze scimitars hanging from their belts. And the eyes of the listening children widened as they realized that here in their midst was an actual party of the renowned desert warriors.

Yes, they were lawless times, agreed the old men. The war would not be over as long as there was one king in the north and another in the south. And it seemed as though the south, with its black mercenaries from the Sudan, was at least a match for the north.

The younger men of the district, the fathers of the children, disagreed. If the south used mercenaries, the north could do the same. The men of the desert had defeated the Sudanese once before, and could do so again. —The Ishmaelites glanced at each other, and said nothing. And next morning they went on, with their baggage asses, towards the northern capital at Itkt-toui.

There were frequently travelers from the Levant coast and its hinterland staying at the inn. For the village lay on the main road from Sinai and the bitter lakes of the Suez isthmus to the capital of northern Egypt. And for all the lawless state of Egypt there was still a good deal of trade between the two areas. And often, as the children listened, these travelers would interrupt the reminiscences of the locals to tell of their own country, and their own troubles.

Civil war was a bad thing, they agreed—though they had difficulty in understanding the compulsive urge of each of the rival pharaohs to defeat the other and unite the Nile valley under one ruler. They came themselves from a much smaller area, the Jordan valley and the hill country on either side, and they had existed happily for generations under any number of independent chieftains, and had felt no necessity to recognize the rule of a single man. Not until recently, anyway.

Yes, civil war was bad. But foreign invasion was worse. They were Amorites themselves, and proud of it, long settled in their grazing lands in the hills of Canaan, to which their forefathers had come from the north approximately two hundred years ago. They were not of the tribes of Abraham, they digressed to explain, though they were related, and had come to Canaan at about the same time. Their listeners knew a lot about the tribes of Abraham, for some twenty or thirty years earlier, following a drought in Canaan, they had crossed the Egyptian frontier and settled with their flocks not far away, on the grasslands between the delta and the eastern desert. One of their princes, a man called Yusuf (though he had now assumed an Egyptian name), had taken service with the pharaoh of the north and was now overseer of granaries in the delta.

For a while conversation turned to a discussion of whether it had been these "children of Abraham" that had supplied the mercenary swordsmen who had driven back the southern usurpers, or whether they had been recruited from farther east. But the Amorite travelers had talked of foreign invaders. It sounded interesting, and they were urged to explain.

Well, the Egyptians should understand that the Amorites of Canaan were no parochial villagers. Admittedly many of their number had now married into the families of the original inhabitants and settled down to farming, but the majority of the tribes still moved around, and had retained close contact with their landsmen up north, even as far as their old home of Harran, in the shadow of the Turkish mountains. And it was there, in the north, that the invaders had first appeared. They were tribes of mountaineers calling themselves Hurrians, and the spearhead of their attacks was a corps of elite warriors fighting from horse chariots. That they had to explain; for the Egyptian villagers had only a vague idea of what a cart looked like and had never heard of a horse before. In the thirty years or so since the Hurrian kings had come down out of their mountains, they had occupied a large area of northern Syria. Harran had fallen, and

they held now firmly the lands of the old Amorite kingdom along
the upper Euphrates, as far down the river as the marches of
the Babylonian king north of Mari. But of late they had begun to
push southwards again. Not in organized campaigns, but in daring long-distance raids, using to the full the mobility of the new
chariots. The Amorite nomads in the hills had been able to avoid
the raiders in the main, but the towns and villages of Palestine
had suffered severely before they had found the solution—building keeps and fortresses strong enough to defy the light-armed
horsemen and providing a refuge for the population when the
raiders were out. Now these adobe forts were springing up in
every village in Canaan and south Syria, and the raids were becoming less frequent. Moreover, under the threat from the north
both the townsfolk and the pastoral tribes were uniting, energetic
chieftains were being given the military command over large
areas, and there was even talk of a unified command in time of
danger. They had already captured both horses and drivers during the skirmishes, and were organizing their own squadrons of
chariots. The Amorites had always been warriors to reckon with,
they boasted, and in their new unity they would prove more than
a match for the Hurrian armies—or for anyone else who opposed
them.

The children of 1720 B.C. listened avidly, wriggling their
feet. And for months to come they played Amorites and Hurrians
up and down the embankments, charging and wheeling imaginary chariots drawn by fantastic fire-breathing monsters.

And life went on, with the yearly inundation followed by the
spring sowing and the harvest and the collection of taxes and the
next inundation. The children went out to help in the fields, to
scare birds with their throwing sticks and, as they grew taller,
to help to bear the barley home, to thresh and flair the ears, and
to winnow the grain from the chaff. And before they really knew
of it they were grown men, sitting themselves around the courtyard fires of the inn, drinking barley beer as they listened to new
tales from the travelers from the northeast.

There were more travelers these days. While merchants were
just as numerous as ever, there were now frequently bands of
mercenaries passing through, and occasionally whole army units

on their way from the powerful Canaan kingdom to the aid of
their Egyptian ally. For the war between south and north Egypt
had blazed up again, and the king of the south, Subkheferre Intef V, was campaigning well within the frontiers of the north.
The hard-pressed king of the north had made an alliance with
the new power of Canaan, and more and more troops from the
east were coming into the country. They were a mixed lot, Canaanites and Amorites and Arabians from the deserts, and they
were led by hawk-nosed arrogant princes who looked with
frankly covetous eyes on the agricultural wealth of the delta. The
Egyptians called them Hiku-khasut, the princes of the desert,
and they did not care much for them. (A later Greek historian
was to write the Egyptian word in Greek as "Hyksos," and mis-
translate it as "shepherd kings," a mistranslation which is still current today.) There were even Hurrians among them, though
quite how *they* found themselves subject to the rulers of Canaan
nobody could ever really make out. But when the Hurrian companies passed through, then there was excitement in the village.
For attached to their headquarters there was invariably a
squadron of chariots. And if the horses and chariots excited the
fanatical admiration of the impressionable young men, their
drivers and the spearmen who rode beside them aroused almost
equal admiration among the young ladies of the village. They
were clearly of a different people—and rumor said that they
spoke a different language—from the rest of the Hurrians, and
many of them had red or yellow hair and grey eyes. For months
after they had passed there was a vogue among the young men
of the village for close-trimmed beards and henna-dyed hair!

But already the same year, when the harvest was home, the
majority of the men of the village were summoned for service in
the army. In the cool of an autumn dawn they said good-by to
their wives and young children, assembled with their personal
weapons, bow, spear, and dagger, and marched off along the
levee.

In the barracks outside Memphis they were drilled in battle
tactics and in the use of heavier weapons, lances and maces and
the new cut-and-thrust swords of bronze. Not far away lay the
encampments of the Hyksos allies, and they met them frequently

during the long exercise marches, while Memphis seemed to be full of them when—infrequently—the Egyptian recruits were allowed leave to visit the city. Clearly a campaign was under preparation against the rebel south.

But something went wrong. Very wrong indeed. In the beginning of winter, according to plan, the Egyptian army moved out of barracks towards the south. And they had marched for three days when messengers overtook them from the rear. The next day they received no order to break camp and they spent the day around the tents, while wild rumors flew from man to man and the generals conferred with pharaoh all day long in the hunting lodge where he had taken up his quarters. And the next morning the troops were summoned to general assembly and told the news. It was serious enough, in all conscience. Two days after the army had marched, the Hyksos troops had broken camp and, instead of following them according to plan, had occupied Memphis and the other nearby cities and proclaimed the Canaanite king monarch of the whole of Egypt. The spokesman of pharaoh called on the troops to march north and expel the treacherous allies from the occupied towns—and added that envoys had been sent to the king of the south proposing an alliance of all Egypt against the common danger. With apprehension in their hearts for their families in the towns and villages now in the power of the new enemy, the troops set off back along the road they had come. They forced their pace, and on the afternoon of the next day they could already see the smoke of burning Memphis on the horizon. Between them and the city, drawn up with its right flank on the river, was the army of the Hyksos. For an apprehensive night they rested, with patrols in contact, and next morning they attacked and were defeated. It was an utter defeat. The recruits, whose first battle it was, were stationed in the second line, behind pharaoh's seasoned troops, and they never really got into the battle at all. For the Hurrian chariots on the enemy left enveloped their right wing, at the same time as the Amorite swordsmen broke their center. And the army of the Egyptians disintegrated.

For the next weeks the villages around were full of refugees from the battle, weaponless and often wounded, and hidden by the villagers whenever the patrols of the occupying power passed through. But gradually the district emptied, as the refugees drifted away towards their homes, moving by night and lying up by day.

The men who straggled back to the village by the levee were very different from the youths who had marched away in the autumn dawn. They were thinner, more mature—and very bitter. And the world to which they returned was very different too. There were no more convivial evenings at the inn. The troops from Canaan who passed through, in increasing numbers, were now quartered on the houses of the village, an imposition which the villagers, for the most part farm laborers and river fishermen living never very far from the level of bare subsistence, found very hard to bear. Particularly as the taxes on produce were increased the following year. The merchants still stayed at the inn, of course, and, after a "dead" period immediately following the conquest, trade had picked up again and was, if anything, greater than it had been before. But the men of the village no longer felt inclined to chat with casual strangers and they kept away from the inn. Besides, the merchants were now for the most part Canaanites, or Levantines from the trading cities along the Syrian coast, cities which had once been practically Egyptian. An increasing number of the traders, however, were of the tribes of Abraham, which now occupied a rather special position. For they were, of course, Amorites, and therefore reckoned officially as belonging to the conquering race. But they had lived in Egypt for a generation, spoke Egyptian as easily as their own Semitic tongue, and were to some degree accepted by the conquered Egyptians. They therefore drifted naturally into trade between north Egypt and the neighboring Asian lands. Many of them, too, were used as go-betweens by the conquerors, as interpreters and tax collectors and overseers of forced-labor gangs. They were not exactly popular.

But the conquerors themselves were hated with a bitter, impotent hatred (a hatred which was to reverberate down the centuries). They made no attempt to become Egyptian; on the contrary they clearly regarded northern Egypt as a subject province of their true homeland of Canaan. Some years after their conquest they moved their administrative capital from Memphis to the northeastern edge of the delta, to Avaris on the coast not far from the isthmus of Suez. There the king settled; from there he could rule the lands of both the Nile and the Jordan.

The building of Avaris brought a new and unexpected prosperity to the village, a prosperity which even the discriminatory taxation imposed by the occupation authorities could not entirely outweigh. For the village now lay on the main highway and waterway between the new capital and the told. A new inn was built at the other end of the village, and the old one put up a new wing and enlarged its courtyard. And the little shopkeepers along the single street, the baker and the charcoal seller and the bronzesmith and the potter and the carpenter, found that it paid them to stock the luxury items which travelers always seemed to be able to afford. There were even some shopkeepers who were heard to remark that the coming of the new rulers was not an entirely bad thing. And they learned to speak a sort of Semitic and were very obsequious to the Hyksos civil servants who stopped to patronize them. But these collaborators and fellow travelers were shunned by the majority of the villagers, and they formed a tight little clique of their own.

They were the only ones now who sat with the travelers at the inns of an evening, claiming that it was part of the duty of a man of the world to keep in touch with events beyond the village. And indeed quite a lot of news came in in those years, carried by the merchants and barge captains who transported inland the cargoes reaching Avaris by caravan from north Syria and by ship from Crete and Cyprus.

It was from these travelers that they first heard of the conquests of King Labarnas of Kussara, a small city-state in the center of Asia Minor south of the Halys. Labarnas and his people, it was said, were northerners of origin, of the same race and speaking much the same language as the rulers and charioteers of the Hurrians. It was only a few years since Labarnas had succeeded his father, Pu-Sarrumas, on the throne of Kussara, but he had already, in a series of lightning campaigns, conquered almost the whole of southern Asia Minor, and his many sons now ruled in his name over all the Mediterranean coast of Asia Minor from the borders of the Hurrian kingdom at Ugarit as far as the Cretan and Achaean settlements on the mainland opposite Rhodes. It was at the ports along this coast that the ships' captains in the coastal trade between Crete and Avaris had met the new governors and their garrison troops, and could confirm that a new great power had arisen in the north.

It was the same captains, too, who brought the news of the great earthquake in Crete, and of the revolution that had followed. But this time—it was a relief to hear—the events had had nothing to do with the aggressive peoples from the north. It was, they had explained, purely an internal readjustment, and had had no adverse repercussions on the export trade. The earthquake had, of course, disorganized things for a while. The great cities of Knossos and Phaistos and Mallia had been particularly hard hit, and in the confusion that followed, the prince of Knossos had established a united realm covering the whole island. The palaces of the former princes of Phaistos and Mallia were not rebuilt, but the palace now being built at Knossos for the new king of all Crete would, when it was completed, be of quite breathtaking magnificence. In many ways, they said, life in Crete was being rationalized under the new government. In particular a new script had been devised and was being introduced, clearer and easier for foreigners to write than the old hieroglyphs. This script could even be used to transcribe the cuneiform Semitic of Assyria, which was the language of commerce from Crete to the Persian Gulf.

The shopkeepers in the village by the Nile politely expressed their interest in the introduction of a new script in Crete, and turned the conversation to the possibilities of importing a better quality of olive oil from Cyprus or farther north. And the other villagers carried on with their work in the fields and the vegetable gardens and the fruit plantations, much too occupied with paying the tithes required at harvest time by their landlords to summon up any interest in the world beyond the horizon.

In truth, their life was not much different from what it had always been. Already the memory of the disastrous battle above Memphis and the long journey home was growing dim with the years. Their landlords now were Canaanites or Amorites, and the

This head, in black granite and ,
inches high, so closely resembles t
portrait of Hammurabi on the st
bearing his code of laws (below) th
there can be little doubt of its identi

Hammurabi's code, carved on a column seven feet tall and three feet
around at the base, stood for six centuries in Babylon and was carried off
to Susa in 1165 B.C. by the Elamite
conqueror Shutruk-Nahhunte. The
top of the column, illustrated here,
shows Hammurabi standing before
the enthroned sun-god, whose multi-
horned headdress resembles a turban.

PLATE IX

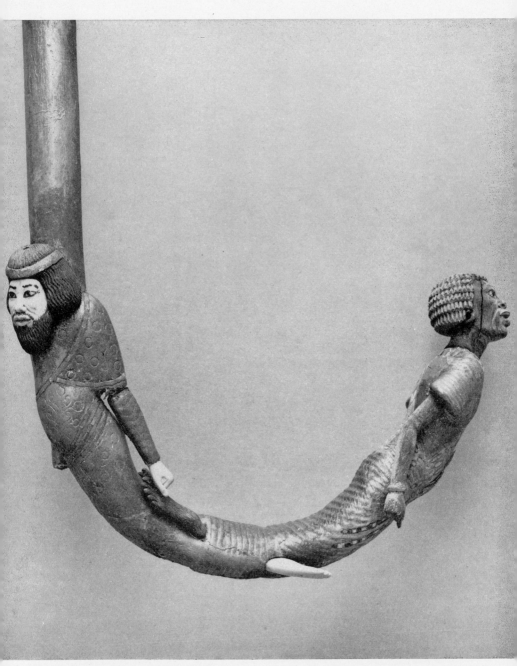

For centuries after the Hyksos invasion the peoples of Palestine and Syria were regarded as the natural enemies of the Egyptians, and monuments and accoutrements of the Egyptian pharaohs are frequently ornamented with figures of bound Asiatic prisoners. This walking stick, from the tomb of Tutankhamon, has a handle carved in the shape of both an Asiatic and a Sudanese prisoner.

PLATE X

The east gate of the citadel of Hattusas, the capital of the Hittite realm, is still guarded by this figure in high relief. In addition to the sword at his belt he bears a battle-ax, appropriate in view of the relationship of the Hittites to the battle-ax peoples of Europe.

PLATE XI

The "sun-wagon" from Trundholm in north Zealand, dating to a little after the middle of the Second Millennium, is one of the prized possessions of the Danish national museum. It represents the sun's disc drawn by a horse, both mounted on a six-wheeled cart, and is of bronze, though much of the sheet-gold covering of the solar disc is preserved. A little over two feet long, it is undoubtedly a model, constructed as an offering, of the image and wagon drawn in religious processions connected with the sun-worship of Bronze Age Europe.

PLATE XII

The ziggurat of Ur still stands, thirty years after Sir Leonard Woolley excavated it, as the most imposing of the monuments of that city. Built a hundred years before the Second Millennium B.C. began, it must have towered above Abraham's city, an artificial mountain with its temple on the summit, and its terraces, it is believed, clothed with bushes and trees.

PLATE XIII

Sun symbols, horses, ax-bearing men, and ships innumerable are carved on this slab of rock, with south exposure, at Vitlycke in Bohuslän, Sweden.

PLATE XIV

At Aspeberget in Bohuslän, Sweden, this carving of four men, armed with swords and holding battle-axes aloft, occurs among sun symbols and carvings of ships. It is probable that a ritual dance is here portrayed, especially as the four-spoked wheel, one of the symbols for the sun, is used for the bodies of the men.

PLATE XV

Queen Hatshepsut of Egypt (1502–1480 B.C.) built this mortuary temple beneath the frowning cliffs which border the Nile valley at Deir al-Bahri west of Thebes.

PLATE XVI

former Egyptian landlords had been killed or enslaved or had fled to the south. But they had rarely seen these landlords anyway—they had lived in their town houses just as the present landlords did, and the agents and overseers who managed the estates had not, in the majority of cases, been changed. They did not like their new rulers, but, as life went on and their children grew up in a world where the Hyksos had always ruled, the first burning resentment died, and was succeeded by apathy.

But not in every case. There were men in the villages, and even more in the towns, who consciously kept alive a spirit of resistance and who, meeting in secret, discussed ways and means of freeing Egypt from its foreign rulers. They saw their hope in the south.

The Hyksos had never succeeded in putting into effect their claim to be the rulers of all Egypt. South of Memphis and the Fayum, where the cliffs closed in on the valley of the Nile, the chariots which were by now the major arm of the Hyksos army could not effectively be deployed. And the rulers of Thebes had held their own in an almost yearly succession of campaigns. Fierce battles had taken place between the Semitic troops of the delta and the Negro companies of Thebes, the tall black spearmen and bowmen from the Sudan who formed the elite corps of the army of the south. Nor were the "princes of the desert" always defeated. Many times the southern armies were forced to retreat and retreat again, fighting at every ridge or major canal until the Hyksos, far from their bases and short of supplies, had to turn back from the unprofitable struggle. And more than once they captured Thebes itself; but Thebes was less than halfway to the southern frontier of upper Egypt, and sooner or later the northern troops gave up the chase, and the south rallied and expelled the garrison left in Thebes. And the Hyksos were back where they started.

So the men of the north looked forward to the day when the south would be strong enough to carry the war the other way. And not a few of the more resolute of the Egyptians of the delta packed up their possessions and, traveling by stealth, made their way south, to join the princes and nobles and landowners of the north who had fled to Thebes at the time of the conquest, and who now formed a sort of government in exile at the court of pharaoh at Thebes.

But time passed, and the counterstroke never came. The Hyksos king who had commanded the original conquering host had been dead these many years, and his successor, too. The new king—and *his* successor, too, for he reigned only a few years— began to make some attempt to bridge the gulf between the Egyptians and their conquerors, and to introduce a modicum of Egyptian culture into their courts. To their good Semitic names of Yakob-bael and Yakob-hat they added, in the manner of the pharaohs, an Egyptian throne-name. They and their nobles sealed their letters with scarab seals, just as though they were real Egyptians, and did not care that the "inscriptions" cut on the seals by their own jewelers were meaningless scrawls with only a superficial resemblance to the hieroglyphic script which they had never bothered to learn.

They were more successful with a piece of religious propaganda, when they officially identified their own chief god Sutek with the Egyptian god Set. Set had been worshipped in the delta, and particularly in the Avaris district, for as long as records went back. With the rise of the Theban kings in the south, however, the worship of Set had fallen into disrepute. For the Theban monarchs were worshippers and earthly incarnations of the hawk-god Horus, and Horus and Set were the two protagonists in a popular cycle of legends which were well known to refer to a struggle between upper and lower Egypt at the beginning of time, when the gods walked the earth in their true shape. And with the Horus kings on the throne of Thebes Set had been recast as the villain of the whole Osiris and Isis legend, an embodiment of all evil. But his worship had survived in the delta, and it was an astute move on the part of the Hyksos monarchs to pose as the champions of the age-old delta god against Horus and the Horus-kings of upper Egypt. And the propaganda did indeed succeed in persuading a number of the younger men of the conquered people to identify their loyalty with the alien government of the north and to regard the southerners as heretics attempting to impose a false theology upon the delta.

But the men who had lived through the conquest and fought

in the one lost battle against the Hyksos were not persuaded. They were old men now, too old to work the fields, content to sit in the sun outside their adobe huts and to remember the time when Egypt had been its own master. And often as they sat their gaze would turn towards the south, as though something might some day appear there.

This chapter is largely myth—but with a very solid basis of fact. It is acknowledged fact that the Egyptian Twelfth Dynasty ended with Sebeknefrure, wife of Amenemhet IV, in 1776 B.C. (the date is only disputed within very close limits), and that the succeeding Thirteenth and Fourteenth Dynasties reigned simultaneously in the south and north, from Thebes and Memphis respectively. Somewhat untrustworthy lists name a large number of kings in both dynasties; the names suggest that both claimed continuity with the foregoing Twelfth Dynasty.

The invasion of the Hyksos is a historical event, and later Egyptian writings make clear the bitterness with which it was recalled. Lists of kings, inscriptions, and later histories are agreed that the Hyksos came from the east, that some at least of the kings had Semitic names, and that, while there were Bedouin among them, there were also peoples of previously unknown race. That the Hyksos introduced the horse chariot into Egypt is a fact, though it is uncertain whether they possessed it at the actual time of invasion. The precise date of the Hyksos invasion is disputed, within the range of about 1730–1660 B.C. While I have tried not to be too precise, I have assumed the date most generally agreed on, about 1700–1690. I have assumed an Amorite–Canaanite–North-Arabian–Hurrian–Indo-European mixture for the Hyksos, the result of the formation of a strong Semitic power in the Palestine region under pressure from the Hurrians now established in northern Syria. It is not my own idea, and would be generally accepted by students of the period. It is confirmed by the strong castles that archaeology attests were being built at about that time in Palestine. The entry of the Hyksos as the allies of the north against the south, and their usurpation thereafter of power is unsupported by evidence, but is inherently not unlikely. Nor is it my own original idea. There is some discussion as to whether the Hyksos, in the period covered by this chapter, controlled southern Egypt. There is no evidence that they did, and some that they did not.

The role of the Biblical patriarchs in the events of the period is, in my version, hypothetical. The story of Joseph is generally accepted to have some relation to the Hyksos. Some authorities would date him somewhat later and assume that the pharaoh he served was a Hyksos king. Some would even equate the coming of Jacob and Joseph's brethren to Egypt with the Hyksos invasion, though the Bible account in no way suggests that this movement was other than peaceful. I have taken it rather as evidence of a peaceful penetration of lower Egypt by Semitic elements prior to the actual Hyksos conquest.

Contemporary events in Asia Minor are attested by documents of only slightly later date. The destruction of the Cretan palaces is known from excavation, and the concentration of power in Knossos is assumed from the fact that only that palace was rebuilt.

Suggested further reading: Albright's The Archaeology of Palestine; *Gardiner's* Egypt of the Pharaohs; *Aldred's* The Egyptians.

10

THE WIDE VIEW (I)

For FIVE CHAPTERS we, the writer and—I hope—the reader of this book, have been living among the people who inhabited the world between 2000 and 1650 B.C. The temptation is strong to write "living *down* among the people. . . ." The tendency to "rise above" the scene and events being described requires conscious resistance; it seems proper for us of a later day to see the events of the far past from a viewpoint which it feels natural to call "above," or at least "outside."

We are, of course, "outsiders." We were not there. Through the period with which we are dealing events were occurring in three dimensions of space and one dimension of time. The space dimensions were exactly as extensive, and movement along the time dimension was just as slow, as in our own space and time. Mesopotamia was as far away from Great Langdale then as it is now, and a century was a hundred years of 365 days of precisely the same length as one of our own days. But it does not feel like that. We sit outside the space-time continuum of the period, and see the nations of the world in a moment of time and the life of a man as a brief flicker of a candle.

This situation of godlike detachment is bad for the soul, and undoubtedly bad for the judgment. For one thing, it permits us to use our judgment—and we are not competent to judge. Unearthly wise after the event, we see "trends," and apparently irresistible marches of events, irresistible purely because they were not, in the event, resisted, or not adequately resisted, or perhaps not desired to be resisted. In any history covering a large extent of space and time such trends cannot entirely be disregarded; nor is it proper that they should be, for they are facts, they did happen. But they happened to, and by the agency of, people; and if, in studying the trends, we forget the people who imple-plemented and were influenced by them, we are not really study-ing history at all.

When Gandash made his decision to lead his Kassites down from the mountains of Luristan into the Mesopotamian valley and the kingdom of Hammurabi's son, he was, more than likely, influenced by "historical necessity." But it is doubtful to what de-gree he was aware of it or influenced by his awareness. Undoubt-edly one of the principal "trends" of the first third of the Second Millennium B.C. is the spread of the horse and of the Indo-European-speaking people who had tamed it. Within the first cen-tury of the millennium they had spread from their homes on the Pontic steppes over the whole of the great plains of central and eastern Europe and central Asia, and were bounded by a colos-sal ring of natural obstacles, the North Sea, the Rhine, and the continuous west-east sweep of mountains, the Alps, Carpathians, Balkans, the Turkish mountains and the Black Sea, the Caucasus and the Caspian Sea, the Elburz mountains and the Hindu Kush. The next century and a half saw the penetration of these obsta-cles, the occupation of England and Holland, the Balkans and Greece, Turkey, Persia and Afghanistan. And in the last hundred years we have seen the beginning of the "spill-over" into the low-lands beyond the mountains, into north Syria and Mesopotamia and the valley of the Indus.

Every move in this long succession of expansions must have involved decisions by chieftains like Gandash, decisions to move rather than sit still, and to move in one direction rather than in another. To what extent did each of these chieftains realize that he was part of a "trend"?

The importance of answering questions of this sort is the jus-tification for the division of this book into arbitrary chapters, each a lifetime long. This division, inconvenient in many ways, does indicate, within limits, what anyone at any one time might rea-sonably be expected to know. It has been stated before, and will be stated again, that people alive at the time covered by one chapter experienced the events of that chapter in their own per-sons and that they knew the events of the preceding chapter from immediate hearsay, from having talked to people who had lived through them. The events of perhaps the two preceding chapters were inaccurately known, idealized, transposed, and perverted; but they *were* history, in the sense that they were known to have occurred. Anything that happened more than three chapters ago is largely to be regarded as legend, of at least doubtful authenticity. And anything that appears in the next and following chapters *has not yet happened.*

Thus we have already, a third of our way through the Second Millennium B.C., reached the point where the events of the first lifetime of the millennium are legendary, their main features known but known as romantic stories rather than as real happened events.

At the time of Gandash, a hundred years ago now, they were closer and more real. He probably knew the history of his people, could trace his family tree and his tribal connections back to their original home in south Russia. He was almost certainly aware, not only that his own ancestors (from approximately his great-great-great-great-great-grandfather on) had gradually moved southwards, but also that related people—related in the sense of blood-brotherhood or descent from a mythical common ancestor—had moved in other directions. He would know the distance they had gone, and would in fact have a fair knowledge of the area held by these interrelated Indo-European speakers, the battle-ax peoples.

So the "trend" was to that degree a reality for him. Tribal and intertribal "history" would be full of the exploits of other chieftains moving ever farther from the original homeland; if he wished to emulate them there was only one thing he could do, only one direction he could go. What we see as a "trend" he would be more likely to see as a "fashion" or as a legitimate ambition or as the path of glory. A man of honor could do nothing else.

But what he could not, of course, know, is whether he would succeed. His was after all not the only "trend."

Samsu-iluna, Hammurabi's son and the ruler of Babylonia at the time when the Kassites came down, would hardly have as clear a picture as the Kassite chieftain of the scope and progress of the expansion of the Indo-European horsemen. Yet even he could see it as a "trend." The horse had first come to Mesopotamia in his father's time (it was as new as the automobile is to us), and the Kassites would still be regarded as newcomers to the Persian mountains, even though they may have been there for about a hundred years. And he would know that the Kassites were no isolated group of newcomers. He lived at the center of a network of trade routes extending from Crete to India; and all along that line he would hear of horse-driving newcomers in the mountains to the north.

But Samsu-iluna was himself part of a "trend." Just as the battle-ax horsemen had expanded eastward and westward and southward during this third of a millennium, so the Amorite shepherds, of whom he was conscious of being a descendant, had expanded eastward and westward and northward. From their origin in the sparse grasslands of the Syrian and Transjordanian plateau the Amorites had fanned out within the first century and a half of the millennium to occupy the Levant coast and the valley of the Euphrates and Tigris. Their kingdoms, still consciously related, occupied the whole crescent facing the mountains, from the Mediterranean to the Persian Gulf. And if Hammurabi's son believed in "historical necessity" and the irresistible march of events—as he may well have done—there was just as much reason for him to expect the Amorite advance to continue and occupy the mountains as to expect the battle-ax people's advance to continue and occupy the plains.

At the end of the first third of the millennium, in 1650 B.C., the issue had not been decided (in a way, it has not been decided to this day). The Kassites held their enclave in central Mesopotamia, and the Hurrians had advanced to occupy much of north Syria; but on the other hand the Semitic kings of Assyria held the northern valley of the Tigris between the two and had extended their rule well into the mountains of Kurdistan.

It was an uneasy stalemate. And it is at such times, when "trends" cancel each other out, that the deciding factor becomes the character and action of individual men. From our vantage point of four millennia, which we have chosen to occupy for one brief chapter before "descending" again to attempt to see history through the eyes of those that lived it, we can see that, if Hammurabi had moved faster to organize the Amorites into a single kingdom, the "irresistible march" of the Indo-European speakers might well have been halted and reversed in the mountains of Turkey and Persia.

In a way, the Hyksos invasion of Egypt is the latest example of Amorite expansion, and shows just how much life and strength and initiative is to be found among the Semitic-speaking peoples of this period. Had the Hurrians been weaker and Egypt stronger (which is much the same as saying, had Queen Sebeknefrure, a hundred years earlier, not married a commoner and plunged Egypt into fifty years of civil war), the strength of the Amorites might well have been turned north rather than south, and even then reversed the trend of Indo-European expansion.

But, we have represented the Hyksos as being themselves partly Indo-European. There is every reason to believe this to be the case, and the fact illustrates a trap that it is very necessary to avoid. Just as easy as it is to talk about trends and movements, so is it to talk about "races," as though they meant something. Let me make it clear that there is no question here of an "Indo-European race" spreading southward and clashing with a "Semitic race" in the Near East. "Semitic" and "Indo-European" are names of two groups of languages, the various languages within each group being so closely related as to suggest a common origin. The original Semitic language would appear to have developed in north Arabia, the place of origin of the Amorites, and it is therefore possible to stretch a point and to call the original Amorite invaders a Semitic people. Similarly the original Indo-European language appears to have been spoken by the horsemen of the Pontic steppes (it is one of those things which cannot be proven), and these horsemen might perhaps not too improperly be called an Indo-European people. Even at that, it would be most unwise to use the term "race," since even within their countries of origin the Amorites and the battle-ax horsemen were probably a mixture of many races.

In any case, both peoples left their homeland some three hundred fifty years ago. And much has happened to them since. The Hurrians and Kassites who came down from the mountains did not even speak an Indo-European language, and were in no way related to the battle-ax people; they had merely been picked up on the way.

They were probably related to each other, though this is not certain. The Hurrians spoke a language of which we possess a number of documents, clay tablets in cuneiform script, but it is only possible to say that they spoke neither Indo-European nor Semitic nor Sumerian, and that they belonged apparently to a group of peoples which had inhabited the mountains of eastern Turkey before the coming of Indo-European and Semitic speakers, a group which is normally termed "Asian" merely for convenience. The Kassites may have spoken a language akin to Elamite, but only a few words of it are known.

But in both cases they were led, at the time of their invasion of the Amorite area, by an aristocracy which spoke an Indo-European language. This aristocracy comprised the ruling princes and chieftains, and in addition a warrior elite with a name whose significance is still in dispute but which, it seems, can best be translated as "knights," with its connotation both of minor aristocracy and of horse users. This Indo-European-speaking aristocracy was undoubtedly descended from bodies of battle-ax people who with their horses and chariots had penetrated southward and fought their way to leadership of the "Asian" tribes of the hills. But purity of language cannot be taken as signifying purity of race. The small body of Norman soldiery which conquered England from the Saxons spoke Norman French, and for over a third of a millennium thereafter Norman French was, in England, the language of an aristocracy which regarded itself as the descendants of the knights who followed Duke William to England. And yet we know that within the first generation there were many Normans, even within the royal family, who contracted marriages with daughters of the dispossessed Saxons, and that before a hundred years had passed there was more Saxon than Norman blood in the "Norman" aristocracy. Similarly we can be sure that the "Indo-European" aristocracy of the Kassites and the Hurrians, for all that they retained their language, was by now more Kassite and Hurrian than "Indo-European."

The case was no different with the Amorites. In south Mesopotamia they settled among a population of mixed Semitic, Elamite, and Sumerian speakers; in north Mesopotamia and Syria, among a population of mixed Semitic-speaking and "Asian" origin. In the course of the twelve generations which is three hundred fifty years they must have completely lost whatever racial purity they may have started with. If it had been possible to disentangle the complicated racial origins of a typical Hurrian and a typical Amorite army such as must often have faced each other on the banks of the northern Euphrates during these years, both armies would probably have been proved to be predominantly "Asian" in origin—in race and in physical appearance indistinguishable from each other.

They would not fight each other any less fiercely for that. They would think of themselves as Amorites and Hurrians—and the charioteers of the north, for all their "Asian" mothers and grandmothers, would feel themselves a race apart from both and akin to the battle-ax peoples beyond the Rhine and the Aryans beyond the Indus.

The battle-ax people beyond the Rhine were by now no more pure-bred "Indo-Europeans" than were the rulers of the Hurrians. Over the length and breadth of Europe five major ways of life were in process of coming to terms with each other, and in the process integration and disintegration were the order of the day. Archaeologically the picture is fairly clear, but the absence of written documents induces a mental block, hindering the translation of the archaeological record into history. The people who crossed the Alps from central Germany into Switzerland were no less real than the people who crossed the Zagros from Luristan into Mesopotamia. But the latter we know called themselves Kassites, and they immediately become in our minds a people. The former we have to be content to call Saxo-Thuringians, and they obstinately remain a "culture" rather than a people and their leader refuses to come into focus at all. Of course, we know nothing about him at all—but we know nothing about Gandash either, except accidentally his name. And given a name we can imagine a personality.

Of the five ways of life that now were reacting upon each

other, three had already been doing so for centuries before our millennium opened.

The first was the ancient hunter strain, the original "natives" of the European continent, nomadic trappers following the seasonal movement of the game, or fishing communities settled along the salmon rivers or on the sheltered estuaries and fjords of the coast.

The second was what we have called the "backwoodsmen," homesteaders and colonists, long settled on the lighter-wooded plains and low hills, but still comparatively few in number (probably not very much more numerous than the "natives") and not yet firmly planted on their own soil. They were always moving on, clearing with stone ax and fire a new sowing area every generation or so, dependent largely on their millet and barley, to a lesser degree on their sheep and cattle, mixed farmers, marginal cultivators.

And the third way of life was that of the passage-grave settlements along the coast, folk with their spiritual home in the warmth and civilization of the eastern Mediterranean, but with only an occasional ship trading from point to point along the coast to keep the lifeline open. They were factors and farmers and missionaries, and possessed no higher standard of life than the people among whom they had established their stations.

These three ways of life had been acting upon each other for longer than memory went back, for periods which we can measure as, in some areas, five hundred or so, in others several thousand years. But during the first third of the Second Millennium B.C. their life had been further complicated by the intrusion of two new peoples. We have met them both; one was the battle-ax people from south Russia, cattle herdsmen, charioteers, apparently unacquainted with the growing of grain or with a settled life; the other was the beaker people, spreading east and north from Spain into all western and central Europe in small bands of bronze traders, shepherds, prospectors, and smiths.

By 1650 B.C. the two latest arrivals were no longer newcomers. Even at the extreme limits of their ranges they had been settled for two or three generations, and, willingly or not, the original inhabitants had come to terms with them. In eastern and central Europe the Indo-European-speaking battle-ax people seem to have rapidly achieved the same position as in the hill-lands of the Middle East. Over a dozen "nations" are distinguish-able in the area stretching from Greece through the Balkans and Germany to Scandinavia. (The archaeologist prefers, of course, to call them "cultures," but one assemblage of artifacts sufficiently different from another to merit the name of a separate culture must imply a different political entity.) And all of them—with at most one exception—reveal, mixed with the Danubian artifacts of the earlier inhabitants, the incursive artifacts of the battle-ax people; and in this mixture the battle-ax components are domi-nant. We need no written documents to see the Indo-European speakers established here, too, as a warrior aristocracy over the original inhabitants.

What we do not know is how it happened. In India, where at this time the Indo-European-speaking Aryans were planning their conquest of the city civilization of the Indus valley, there have survived, in the Vedic literature, what in effect are the vic-tory hymns of the conquerors. And they show that the Indo-Europeans had no scruples about conquest and enslavement of native populations. But in Europe there is no evidence—like the scattered skeletons in the streets of Mohenjo-daro—of battle and sudden death. Perhaps the sheer strength of the invaders made resistance impracticable, perhaps the warriors were wel-comed as allies and mercenaries, and peacefully usurped power. The fairy tale of the prince who, appearing from beyond the frontiers, performs great and beneficial exploits and wins as his reward the hand of the princess and half the kingdom is pecul-iarly widespread in southeast and central Europe. It may well date back to this period, and give us a hint as to the way things may have gone—particularly as there is evidence that the suc-cession to the throne among societies derived from the Mediter-ranean may well have been matrilineal, descending not from father to son but from father to daughter's husband. And this would be a very convenient custom for land-hungry (and pa-trilineal) warriors coming from abroad.

Whatever the process, the results were the same. All the peo-ple who inhabited the eastern half of Europe three hundred fifty years before were still there—the fisher-farmers of Greece, under direct Cretan influence; the farmer-prospectors of the Balkans, pushing into the mountains from their bases in Asia Minor, looking for and mining copper and tin; the widespread slash-and-burn cultivators of the Danube valley and the great European plain; the passage-grave builders of Denmark and south Sweden. But without exception they appear now in the archaeological record as relying more than before on cattle-herding and hunting, as being more warlike and less egalitarian, with a greater gulf between the aristocracy and the commonalty. And everywhere the aristocrats bear the now typical armament of the Indo-European speakers, long straight daggers (almost a stabbing sword in length), battle-axes, and spears. And everywhere the horse appears, though rarely as yet in the north. We may imagine Europe east of the Rhine as a large number of small princedoms, often at war with each other, occasionally united into a larger confederacy, their princes all speaking the same language, which is gradually permeating down to their subjects.

Life for these subjects had probably not changed for the better during these three hundred fifty years. They lived still in a Stone Age, reaping their millet and barley with flint sickles, felling their timber and building their houses with flint axes and spokeshaves, cutting their meat with flint knives. The knowledge of copper, and even bronze, had spread during these centuries; bronze was known in the Balkans, and copper as far as Austria and Hungary. But it was reserved for the aristocrats, fashioned into their daggers and spearheads and axes, their trinkets and necklets and the long pins with which they held their gowns. North of Austria it was only rarely that even the aristocracy saw copper, and at this time the superb flintsmiths of Denmark begin to copy the bronze daggers and spearheads of the south in copper-colored flint, flaking the stone to the thinness of the metal prototype, and even reproducing in flint the curved scimitars of the Hyksos.

Typically enough, the only community in central Europe which appears to have escaped the actual physical dominance of Indo-European speakers is a truly "native" people, probably, like the rest, of well-mixed origins, but mainly descended from the original forest hunters. They are known by the cumbersome name of the "globular amphorae culture," and in the same way as the descendants of the hunters in England they had adapted their way of life to trade. From their home in central Germany they spread out over much of Europe, trading in flint, in amber, and even occasionally in copper. They were also great pig-keepers.

It was on the Rhine and the upper Danube that the Indo-European speakers came into contact with the beaker folk, men of another language but equal determination. And there, where their cultures met and clashed, it was the beaker people who triumphed.

In the last two hundred years the beaker people had spread out from central Spain, reaching as far as north Italy, Poland, and Scandinavia. They were small, dark, and roundheaded, and they traveled apparently in incredibly small groups, of a dozen or so. The fact that their pottery, including the drinking cups after which they are called, shows no variation at all throughout their range suggests that they traveled fast, and that they kept up communication between the extremes of their outposts. They were in fact not settlers, interested in finding a home and staying there. Their way of life involved movement, for it seems clear that they were essentially traders. They were, undoubtedly quite consciously and deliberately, introducing the Bronze Age into central and northern Europe.

Spain had for centuries been in close contact with the bronze-using civilizations of the eastern Mediterranean. Ships from Troy and Cyprus, from Crete and probably from Egypt, traded regularly to the south coast of Spain, as well as to Sicily, south Italy, and Sardinia; and in all these lands the original farming communities had adopted a Bronze-Age economy, at first importing copper and later exploiting their own and neighboring countries' ores. They had also adopted the religion of the east, with its communal stone-built grave chambers. Spain, with its rich lodes of copper, lead, and silver, had been particularly well equipped to achieve self-sufficiency in metal production, and now this production demanded markets in its turn, and a secondary expansion from this center into the northern lands resulted.

But trade is a two-way exchange, and the beaker people were clearly interested not only in selling but also in buying. Their need for agricultural produce was small, and it was necessary for them to persuade their potential customers to produce other things for sale. So they were not merely traders and smiths; they were also prospectors and exploiters. They were constantly on the lookout for suitable trade goods. The metals which were rare in Spain, such as gold and tin, stood first on their list, but it was also they who first realized the potentiality of such semiprecious substances as jet, callais, and amber.

Throughout their range their activities produced revolutionary changes out of all proportion to their numbers. Though bronze was still too expensive, for tin was scarce, objects of copper were now within the economic reach of the wealthier members of the farming communities, and flat-cast axes and short daggers of copper were soon in general use, while copper jewelry was even more widespread. It is interesting to see, too, that with the spread of the beaker people there is a sharp upswing in the amount of barley grown. There is a strong possibility that the bell-shaped beakers which are the hallmark of the Spanish traders are the outward sign of the spread of beer into Europe. It had been known for thousands of years in Egypt and Mesopotamia, and undoubtedly reached Spain together with the ships from the east. Now the farmers of Europe began to devote a proportion of their land to growing the grain from which the new and potent liquor could be made.

It is not surprising that, after the beaker people first met the Indo-Europeans in the Rhineland, the mixed population which arose in the course of two or three generations (undoubtedly also with a large proportion of the original farmers and even of the aboriginal hunters) was culturally dominated by the beaker folk.

Nor is it surprising that the influence of the beaker people spread far beyond their actual physical range. Though only three actual bell beakers have been found in Denmark, the south Scandinavians at this time abandoned the practice of burying battle-axes with their dead, as their Indo-European-speaking ancestors had done on the Pontic steppe, and began to bury fine flint daggers with them instead.

The mixed people of battle-ax and beaker ancestry in the Rhineland and Holland must have had a double share of wander-lust in their blood and in their traditions, while from the original coastal fishermen of Holland they derived a knowledge of how to build ocean-going boats. It was from Holland and the northwest coast of Germany that this people, in successive waves over about three generations, crossed over to the south and east coasts of England, following the pure beaker people who had crossed from France not long after the first construction of Stonehenge. These later invaders were, in most aspects of their culture, also beaker people, but racially they must have been a mixture of all the strains that had met on the Rhine, the battle-ax strain being particularly prominent. By 1650 B.C. this hybrid culture domi-nated the whole of south and central England and east Scotland, and, in true battle-ax tradition, an aristocracy of the invaders

IN THE PASSAGE-GRAVES OF SPAIN AND WESTERN EUROPE THERE ARE MANY REPRESENTATIONS OF A RATHER OWL-FACED GOD, OFTEN THE EYES ALONE BEING DEPICTED. THIS DRUM-IDOL OF CHALK, FROM AN EARLY BRONZE-AGE BURIAL MOUND AT FOLKTON IN YORKSHIRE, ENG-LAND, IS OF IMPORTANCE BECAUSE IT IS OF A LATER PERIOD THAN THE PASSAGE-GRAVES, IN FACT OF ABOUT THE DATE WE HAVE NOW REACHED IN THE SECOND MILLENNIUM. CLEARLY THE RELIGION OF THE PASSAGE-GRAVE BUILDERS WAS STILL PRACTICED AT THIS DATE.

ruled over the original farming communities of the Downlands, and even over the "native" traders of the north and Midlands.

Under the double impact of beaker and battle-ax peoples even the communities of passage-grave builders along the coasts of Europe begin to lose their identity. It is over four hundred years since they were first established as trading posts along the shipping routes from the Mediterranean, and they are no longer consciously the foreign agents of a higher civilization. Though they still retain occasional contact by sea with their sister communities, they are now, in fact, groups of farmers, sailors, and fishermen assimilated to the peoples among whom they originally settled. Their religion is still very much alive, and new passage-graves are still being built. But on the coasts of northern Spain and northwest France the people buried in these communal graves are often beaker people, whereas in England, Scotland, and even occasionally in Ireland, they are of the hybrid beaker invaders. In Denmark and south Sweden the process of assimilation has gone further. Here the battle-ax people have been in the country for three centuries, and the two strains are no longer separate. Passage-graves have given way to stone cists, which in effect are the single graves of the battle-ax folk translated into the stone construction of the passage-grave people.

But if the builders of the stone graves have assimilated beaker and battle-ax customs and material culture, the invaders have equally assimilated the art of building in stone. It is at about this date that the beaker people of England take over the sanctuary of Stonehenge and build within the circular rampart and ditch of the original founders a temple of stone. Some two hundred monoliths, brought by boat from the mountains of south Wales, are now erected in a double circle in the center of the rampart. The sun had always played an important part in the ceremonies that took place in Stonehenge, as the placing of the Hele stone shows. But whether the sun was actually worshipped there, or whether it merely acted as clock and calendar for ceremonies in honor of other gods, we cannot say. The pits dug within the rampart and the burial in one of them of human remains would, in fact, suggest that it was rather a cult of the earth mother or the underworld that celebrated its rites there.

But now, with the advent of the mixed people of beaker and battle-ax origins and the building of the monolith circles, Stonehenge becomes beyond doubt a temple of the sun. For the battle-ax peoples were sun-worshippers. Wherever they spread in Europe and Asia, we find religious myths later current telling of the great sun-god who rides daily across the sky in his fiery chariot drawn by the horses of the sun. The association of the sun with the horse chariot points unmistakably to the battle-ax charioteers as the bearers of this religion, and, as we shall see, the evidence for sun-worship mounts steadily through the great period of the Bronze Age which is to come.

Thus, while in the Near East Semitic-speaking peoples hold

COMPARE WITH PAGE 151 THIS COMPOSITE JAR AND LID FROM THE SECOND CITY OF TROY, DATED TO ABOUT 2300 B.C. SEPARATED BY NEARLY SEVEN HUNDRED YEARS AND ALL THE LENGTH OF EUROPE, THESE TWO DEMONSTRATE THE WIDE-RANGING VITALITY OF THE PASSAGE-GRAVE BUILDERS' RELIGION.

the great centers of ancient civilization ringed around by new nations led by Indo-European speakers, throughout Europe the shape is appearing of things to come, with the use of copper and bronze penetrating north from the Mediterranean coast and being widely spread in the west and center by the traders from Spain, at the same time as the Indo-European speakers from the east are introducing the horse and chariot, the worship of the sun, and the languages which are going to be general over all Europe at the time when history opens, and which are still the languages of Europe today.

But we must not forget that Europe and the Near East were no larger a part of the whole world then than they are now. It is unfortunate—it is in fact disgraceful—that we know so little about what was going on thirty-six hundred years ago over the rest of the world, but our ignorance must not tempt us to believe that nothing at all was happening there. At this time there were people living in Africa, in China, and in Greenland, in Indonesia and in Australia and America, whose lives, did we but know the details of them, were just as important as the lives of Hurrian horse grazers in the Euphrates valley or beaker-using tradesmen on the upper Danube.

We catch a few scattered glimpses, and must guess the rest. In Egyptian tomb paintings we meet the tall black herdsmen of the Sudan, warrior tribes under kings of their own who raid the Egyptian frontier regions on average two or three times a generation. Much work needs to be done here, to determine how far south into Africa the practice of agriculture and the influence of Egyptian culture had spread at this date.

Into Farther Asia we know that agriculture had spread very far from its cradle in the Near Orient. Beyond the Indus valley, whose civilization at this time was preparing to meet the threat of the Indo-European-speaking Aryans, the settled agricultural communities of the valley of the Ganges could almost by now rank as a civilization in its own right, and must, could we but know it, have had a history no less detailed than that of Europe.

By now agriculture has also reached the steppes north of the Caucasus, the original home of the battle-ax herdsmen. The descendants of the herdsmen who remained in their homeland now begin to grow wheat and millet on the plains by the rivers, and bury their dead in chambers cut into the barrows of their ancestors of three hundred fifty years ago.

Not far to the north, where the great Siberian forests begin, agriculture and even stock raising cease. In the forest still live the trappers and the hunters of deer and wild forest oxen, wandering their range from the settled areas of the plains as far as the polar tundra facing the Arctic Ocean. And on the arctic coasts live the hunters of seals and walrus and reindeer, with their skin boats and bone harpoons. They are the descendants of the people we met in these regions three hundred fifty years ago, removed by just as many generations as have succeeded each other in the lands of the south. But their lives are the same as they have been for these many years, and they are to be the same for their descendants for millennia to come.

Beyond the mountains of the Tien Shan and the sparse grasslands of the Gobi and the Taklamakan, the agricultural communities along the Yellow River are becoming an organized civilization under a centralized rule. From the province of Shantung, the coastal region around the estuary of the Yellow River, a new people has in these centuries been spreading westward along the river valley. Like the people they conquer, they are village farmers, users of stone tools. In the archaeological record the change is shown merely by the appearance of fine black burnished pottery and by the introduction of sheep and the horse to the area formerly inhabited by keepers of pigs and cattle. It is possible that we should see in this change of "cultures" the rise of the first of the legendary dynasties of China, that of the Hsia emperors.

As in the Old World, so in the New these three hundred fifty years have been full of births and deaths, battles and movements of peoples. But we have no records to tell of them, nor has archaeology yet been able to provide a sharp enough chronology for wars and kingdoms and hunting ranges to be identified. On the surface, America was unchanged since 2000 B.C., with its arctic-coast fishers and its forest and plains hunters. And on the coast of Peru the enigmatic fishermen-gardeners still dwell upon their shell heaps, now a good twelve feet higher with the debris of three hundred fifty years.

We have paused at 1650 B.C., and for a chapter have borrowed the chariot of Apollo, surveying the whole world from the viewpoint of the gods. But to the people living, dying, and being born in 1650 B.C. there was no perceptible pause. Life went on, and with it history. It is time that we descend to earth again.

Book III

The Argosies

THE "LONG SHIPS" OF SCANDINAVIA, WITH ANIMAL HEADS AT THE
PROW, CARVED ON THE ROCKS OF SOUTHWEST SWEDEN.

11

THE GREAT KING

1650–1580 B.C.

THE FORTIFICATIONS were going up on the ridge between the deep gorges where the Halys and its tributary had cut down into the central Turkish plateau. The whole line of the wall was already marked out on the ground, enclosing an imposing area. It stretched three quarters of a mile from east to west, and ran from the junction of the rivers for over a mile up the ridge to the south. And it dwarfed into insignificance the original city of Hattusas, destroyed in the recent war, whose ruins stood desolate in the midst of the area marked out for the new city.

The citadel was already completed on a spur jutting out to the east, its walls of five-foot blocks of rough-hewn stone towering up against the deep blue of the Anatolian sky. And King Labarnas of Kussara had already taken up his residence there. It was to be his new capital, meant to mark symbolically his inheritance of the power and prestige of the ancient kingdom of the Hatti. And further to stress the point he had already begun to call himself Hattusilis, the builder of Hattusas, retaining his ancestral name of Labarnas merely as a title, and as a reminder of his great father. For the name Hattusilis harked back to something much more ancient and venerable.

The Hatti had been a people of proud traditions. These traditions, often recited—in the old Asianic tongue—told how, before the Amorite had pushed up from the south and the Indo-European penetrated from the north, the Hatti had been a power to be reckoned with not merely here in central Asia Minor,

but far to the south in the coastal lands. Some said that their people had stretched to the frontiers of Egypt (and certainly there
was a tradition current in far-off Canaan that Abraham himself,
the forefather of the sons of Israel and of Ishmael, had bought
land there from the men of the Hatti when he first came to
Canaan two hundred fifty years ago). Their legends told how
they had fought against Naram-Sin of Akkad during the days, six
hundred and more years ago, when the Mesopotamian empire of
Sargon had stretched to the Mediterranean.

But now the glory of the Hatti was departed, and another
king of another race had conquered their ancient capital.

The kings of Kussara, to the south of Hattusas beyond
the Halys, were of the new race, with the new language, which
had pushed into Asia Minor a century ago, more or less, from
the northwest. Tribal chieftains of the newcomers, each with his
small striking force of horse chariots and tomahawk-armed infantry, had captured many of the old Asianic cities and established themselves as rulers of the farming communities in the
valleys around the cities.

It was a rich territory they had conquered. For though the
upland plateau of Asia Minor was bleak and treeless, covered
deep in snow every winter and parched every rainless summer,
the valleys were deep and sheltered and fertile. Here grew millet
for bread, and barley for beer, and here grew the vines which
provided a different, and some thought a better, intoxicating
drink. Here was ample grazing for sheep and cattle, and for the
newcomers, the horses. And in the mountains there was an
abundance of metal, silver and lead, and a bare sufficiency of copper. Silver was so abundant that it was used as a means of payment even for small items that elsewhere in the world would
be paid for in barley. It was carried in rings and ingots and
weighed out to buy the necessities and luxuries of life. The people
of Anatolia were world-famous smiths, forging ornaments and
tools and weapons of the metals which their mines produced.
Their bronze was well wrought and hard (though they had to import the tin to alloy with the copper), and some among the
smiths even had the secret of smelting a grey-black metal out of
a red ore. But iron needed a very hot furnace, and the finished

product was brittle and could not be wrought. It was inferior to bronze in every way, only suitable for making occasional rings and ornaments as a curiosity.

It made little difference to the miners and the smiths, the farmers and the traders, the carpenters and the potters and the stonecutters that they now were the subjects of new and foreign kings. They were liable to periodic forced labor in state projects, and occasionally to military service, but that they had always been. They were still governed by their councils of elders; and life went on as before. There were perhaps more wars than there had been, for the new rulers of the cities were no lovers of peace and strove among themselves to extend their powers and their lands. The warrior aristocracy, who had come with the princes and who stood closest to them, had been given large estates and court titles, and it was they who did most of the fighting, being liable, in return for their estates, to render military service and to keep the assigned number of chariots prepared and manned.

But it was not always against rival cities that the fiercest battles were fought. The newcomers had, it seemed, no fixed order of succession to the city thrones, and on the death of a king it was the rule rather than the exception that there be strife between rival claimants, each supported by a clique of the feudal nobles.

The first Labarnas of Kussara, the father of Hattusilis, had himself only won the throne after a bitter struggle with his relative and rival, Papadilmah, but once he was firmly in the saddle he had succeeded in promoting a harmony among his large family of brothers, half-brothers, and brothers-in-law which was already well on the way to being legendary. And he had embarked on a career of conquest which had united the greater part of central Asia Minor for the first time, and had even extended his sway to the Mediterranean coast to the south. His relatives and his sons had been appointed viceroys over the conquered cities, and had held them—it was still remembered with amazement—without ever questioning his overlordship. And on his death, only a few years ago, his son, the second Labarnas, who now called himself Hattusilis, had succeeded to his throne without opposition. Now he, in turn, had extended his frontiers, and had captured finally the old royal city of the Hatti.

It was at this time, while the immensely strong fortifications of the new capital were being built up of mighty stone blocks, that a prince was born to the royal house. The birth of Mursilis occasioned no great rejoicings. He was not a son of the king, who had no children, but of one of his sisters, and in his early years he was of little account in the large royal household.

He grew up with the new city, watching the houses and streets being built, training in the use of spear and ax and short curved sword beneath the frowning walls of the citadel, learning to guide his chariot on the flats beside the river, and taking his turn as a cadet officer at manning the towers and massive gate-

ONE OF THE FORTIFIED GATEWAYS OF HATTUSAS, AS IT MUST HAVE APPEARED AT THE TIME OF MURSILIS.

ways of the city wall. Almost every year, with the coming of spring, he would see the muster of the regiments of infantry and squadrons of chariotry, and watch them march off for the summer campaign. Often this would only amount to a show of force along the frontiers, but sometimes there were more serious campaigns, against the kingdom of Arzawa to the southwest or against the unruly tribes of the Gasga lands beyond the northern mountains. And every winter, when the army returned, he would accompany the king on his round of temple ceremonies.

In the realm of the new Hatti (whom we call the Hittites) there were many gods. Every city within the kingdom had its temples and divinities, gods and goddesses of the old people from before the coming of the new ruling class. And of course these gods and goddesses were no less powerful now than when the former rulers lived—on the contrary, they required extra propitiation if they were to accept rulers of an alien language. And besides these old gods there were the gods who had entered the land with the conquerors, the mighty sun-god who was always the first to be invoked in any official pronouncement, and the weather-god with his bull chariot and his ax and his thunderbolt. There was no difficulty about uniting the worship of the native gods with that of the newcomers. Nature was full of gods; on the earth and under the earth and in the heavens there was room for an illimitable pantheon. Mursilis even found it in no way incongruous that the royal entourage could proceed from a ceremony in honor of the sun-god at Hattusas to a festival of the sun-goddess at Arinna less than a day's journey away. He was too young to speculate whether they were different aspects of the same divinity, or whether there was room in the sun for both a god and a goddess.

Standing in his yellow acolyte's robes behind the king and queen, as they ate their ceremonial meals before the cult statues of one after another of the gods of successive cities, he would more often find himself dreaming of the time when he would be old enough to lead his chariot squadron out on daring far-flung raids beyond the Hittite frontiers. And he looked enviously at Prince Labarnas standing in the forefront of the attendant court. For Labarnas, though only a nephew, like himself, of King Hattusilis, was the prince-elect, the officially appointed successor to the childless king, and already a grown man with several campaigns behind him.

Prince Mursilis knew that he was one of the aging king's favorite nephews. The king had often watched his weapon exercises, and had many times talked to the eager boy about the prospects of military glory and a viceroyalty in some frontier province. But he knew nothing of the intrigues going on among the adult members of the royal family, nor of the fate that the weather-god had in store for him.

Things came to a head when he was fifteen and had only three years to go before he would be allowed to take part in his first campaign. King Hattusilis fell ill that year, and lay long in his sickbed within the palace. Prince Labarnas automatically assumed the regency, but much too eagerly and thoroughly for the sick king's liking. He proceeded to reorganize the affairs of state according to his own ideas, dismissing the old king's officials and appointing his own, confining the king to the palace and neglecting to consult him, clearly waiting only for Hattusilis to die and for his own proclamation. He misjudged things badly, for Hattusilis recovered and with the support of his loyal palace guard arrested Labarnas and his supporters.

Summoning his warriors and court dignitaries to an official council of state within the palace, Hattusilis made an official proclamation (which he later caused to be recorded in cuneiform in the royal archives). "I had fallen sick," he said, "and the young Labarnas, whom I had proclaimed my successor and exalted and called my son, showed himself cold and heartless. He shed no tears and showed no pity. He did not listen to the words of his king, but only to the words of the serpent, his mother. Enough! He is my son no more! I have granted him a house and an estate and flocks, and there let him dwell. Only if he causes no trouble may he come to the city.

"Behold, Mursilis is now my son, and when a call to arms goes forth you, my servants and leading citizens, must give him aid. And you, Mursilis, must obey my word. Eat only bread and drink only water. So will Hattusas stand high and my land be at peace. And be on the watch for the intrigues which, since my grandfather's day, have beset our family. Neither delay nor relax. For if you delay the same old mischief will come upon you. Lay this up in your heart, my son, and act always upon it."

In the years that followed, as Mursilis grew to manhood, he took an ever greater part in the administration of the Hittite kingdom. Hattusilis recovered his health completely, and together the old king and his heir toured the country, exercising the army along the frontiers and in the disputed regions beyond during the long warm summers, and in the winters moving from city to city, taking advantage of the temple festivals to confer with the viceroys and councils of elders governing the cities and provinces, judging disputes and assessing taxes and awarding fiefs. Often the two would sit long into the night discussing the problems of empire and the international situation beyond their frontiers. For the kingdom of the Hittites, now in control of the great metal-mining districts of central Asia Minor and the Taurus mountains, kept in close touch through its merchants and caravan leaders with the situation outside its borders.

To the west and south the Hittite realm was secure. South lay the land of Kizzuwatna along the Mediterranean coast, a friendly dependency. The great kingdom of Arzawa in the southwest was within the Hittite sphere of influence, officially at least a vassal. In the northwest, on the Dardanelles, the rich city-state of Troy was primarily a maritime power, interested only in maintaining its monopoly of sea-borne trade between the Aegean and the Black Sea and in challenging the paramount position of Crete on the commerce lanes of the eastern Mediterranean. Troy had no ambitions in the interior of Asia Minor. In the lands to the north, along the Black Sea coasts, the Asianic tribes of the Gasga were always making trouble, and no punitive expeditions appeared to subdue them permanently. But they seemed incapable of organizing themselves into a unity, and unless they combined they were a menace which could be kept under control by vigilant frontier fortresses and an adequate mobile reserve.

But to the east and southeast the Hittite realm was open to attack, and here by forces mightier than hers.

Due east, in the mountains south of the Caucasus and around Lake Van, were the Hurrians. Their rulers and warriors were, Mursilis knew, of his own people, a related folk who, like his own ancestors, had migrated from the region north of the great Caucasus range over three hundred years ago. Their language could still, with difficulty, be understood by a Hittite, though they had for ordinary purposes adopted the completely foreign tongue of the people they ruled. That the rulers of the Hurrians (they called themselves the Mitanni) were distant cousins of the rulers of the Hittites disposed neither Hattusilis nor his crown prince to mistrust them the less; it was, anyway, almost an instinct in the Hittite royal family to distrust cousins. But there was peace between the two nations, peace and even a sort of unformulated alliance. . . . For the Hurrians had their interest directed towards the south, where they were moving in increasing numbers into the plains of the upper Euphrates, the lands which they had captured from the Amorites over a hundred years ago. The Mitanni kings of the Hurrians were probably not too pleased at the sudden rise of a great power among the former conglomeration of small tribes in Asia Minor, but their envoys to the court of Hattusilis protested friendship and pointed out the advantages of presenting a common front towards the Amorites to the south.

Hattusilis and his heir needed no exposition of the possibilities which lay open to them in the southeast. They knew very well the strength and weaknesses of the Semitic-speaking peoples who held the immensely fertile and attractive plains and coastlands to the south.

Far to the south lay the greatest Semitic power of all, the Hyksos kingdom of north Egypt and Palestine. But the Hyksos were tied up with a permanently rebellious population in Egypt and had at this time (it is about 1620 B.C.) committed their full strength to the task of finally conquering southern Egypt and putting an end to the rival government "of all Egypt" in Thebes. North and east of Palestine were the Amorite kingdoms, but strategically their position was very different from what it had been during the reign of Hammurabi a hundred years or so ago, when they had presented a united front from the Mediterranean to the Persian Gulf. Those that were left were, it is true, still in a sort of alliance, of which the leading member was, as always, Babylonia. In Babylon the great-great-great-grandson of Hammurabi, Samsi-ditana, had recently succeeded his father, but the land was still held in the hundred-year-old stalemate resulting from the presence of the Kassites in the territory of the former Amorite kingdom of Eshnunna to the north. And between Babylonia and the Amorite kingdoms of the Lebanon and Yamkhad the natural route along the Euphrates was barred by the Hurrians, and communication went only by Hurrian sufferance, or by the desert route through Palmyra to the south.

Hattusilis had his eye on Yamkhad in particular. It lay immediately to the south of his vassal state of Kizzuwatna and comprised the rich plain between the upper Euphrates and the

Mediterranean. In its capital, Aleppo, its kings had collected the wealth of a century of peaceful trading, for the city stood on the main road from the Euphrates and the east to the port of Ugarit, the Mediterranean, and the west. The country would be a rich prize, but no easy one. Its cities, and in particular Aleppo, were strongly defended with walls of immense height and thickness.

It took some years to plan the campaign and to devise and test the weapons, battering rams and mobile towers and protective screens, which could make an impression on the fortified cities. But finally Hattusilis set out, with squadron by squadron of chariots riding the rough mountain roads, descending into the coastal plain of Kizzuwatna, passing the frontier fortress by the Syrian Gates, and debouching into the plain of northern Syria. Mursilis, now a mature man and an experienced field commander, accompanied the expeditionary force.

The war went slowly. The men of Yamkhad refused all temptations to do battle in the open against the heavy chariots of the Hittites, and retreated to their walled cities. The attitude of the Hurrians was equivocal; they had mobilized an army on the frontier towards Yamkhad which could as easily be thrown in on the one side as on the other, and Mursilis detached the greater part of his chariotry to guard against Hurrian intervention while the Hittite infantry assaulted the Yamkhad cities. There was delay in bringing up the heavy equipment, the new siege engines, and they were not at first employed with full efficiency. But as the troops gained experience in the new techniques of siege warfare, one after another of the cities fell, and finally the Hittite army took by storm the capital city of Aleppo itself.

They failed to capture the king of Yamkhad. He escaped from the city and, given free passage, it was said, through Hurrian territory, appeared as a refugee at the court of Samsi-ditana in Babylon.

But Yamkhad was conquered, and Hattusilis and Mursilis were well aware that by that conquest the Hittite kingdom had for better or worse entered the play for power in the ancient civilized area that stretched from Mesopotamia to Egypt. So long as they held Yamkhad they would have new sources of revenue, and a whole new set of enemies. They must leave a very strong garrison behind with their viceroy in Aleppo.

The progress of the army north to Hattusas was not a little slower than its advance southward. The trains of slaves and the groaning bullock carts loaded with the wealth of Aleppo slowed the chariots to walking pace. But nobody minded that as they thought of the share they would receive of slaves and cattle, fine linen and pottery, gold and silver, furniture and ivory. The soldiers joked among themselves as they swung northward, and Mursilis had time to remember boyhood dreams of victory in the east.

That winter the ritual round of the temples became a progress of triumph and thanksgiving. The conquest of Yamkhad was the crown of Hattusilis's career, and in the few years that were left to the old king he was content to hand over more and more of the mechanics of government to his brilliant crown prince.

Even so, it came as a shock to the whole of Asia Minor when the heralds proclaimed six years later from the gates of the palace that Hattusilis was dead, and that Mursilis was the Great King, king of Hatti. For Hattusilis was the founder of the realm. He it was who had renewed the ancient glory of the Hatti, and the glory could not survive his death.

Mursilis summoned his squadrons, and in a brief but emphatic tour of his realm persuaded doubters that the glory of the Hatti was by no means a thing of the past. A punitive expedition against the Gasga of the north, always prepared to strike south at the first suspicion of weakness, re-established the inviolability of the frontiers in that direction—but cost a precious summer. And in the meantime trouble came to a head in the south.

The news of the death of Hattusilis reached Babylon with all the speed that relays of chariots permitted. The exiled king of Yamkhad had long prepared for this day, and within a week he was on his way up the Euphrates with an army of Babylonian "volunteers." Again the Hurrians gave him passage (and further "volunteers"), and his attack on Aleppo, coupled with a fifth-column rising within the walls, took the Hittite viceroy by surprise. Mursilis had scarcely secured his throne and his frontiers in Asia Minor before the messengers arrived to report that he had lost Yamkhad.

Mursilis knew that only prompt and spectacular action could prevent the loss of Yamkhad from sparking a series of revolts which could disintegrate the Hittite kingdom. He summoned his barons with the full muster of their feudal retainers, and with an army as great as that which had originally conquered Aleppo he started south.

This time there were chariot skirmishes over the north Syrian plain, and the first pitched battles between Hittite and Amorite. But the Hittites had slaughtered garrisons to avenge, and they carried all before them. Once again the walls of cities crumbled before the shock of battering rams wielded by sweating infantry bare to the waist, with only leather, copper-reinforced helmets to protect them against the arrows and spears rained down from the walls. This time the cities were sacked and their walls razed; they should not have the means to rebel ever again.

Once more, proud Aleppo fell to Mursilis—and once more the king of Yamkhad fled down river towards Babylon.

But this time Babylon was to be no refuge.

Since his youth Mursilis had dreamt of leading a swift mechanized attack across the plains to the east, and during the original campaign against Yamkhad he had repeatedly argued to Hattusilis that their conquest of north Syria would never be secure so long as Babylon remained an impregnable base for Amorite counterattack. Now he regrouped his forces and pressed on down the Euphrates to the east.

It was in many ways a rash venture. He must pass through the southern territory of the Hurrians, leaving his lines of communication dangerously vulnerable, should the Hurrians choose to attack. But it was a calculated risk, and it came off. As he had expected, the Hurrians had no desire to intervene to protect Babylon against attack. To the immediate east of the Hurrian lands along the Euphrates lay the Semitic kingdom of Assyria, athwart the upper Tigris. If Babylon were to be weakened, Assyria would be isolated and left vulnerable to Hurrian conquest.

The Hurrians therefore looked complacently on, and opened

a passage to the Hittite army, content that Mursilis should pluck their chestnuts out of the fire.

The war chariots of the Hittites swept down the Euphrates valley in controlled formation, with scouts ahead and to either side. It was a dash of five hundred miles from Aleppo to Babylon, almost twice the distance from Hattusas to Aleppo, and through hostile, or potentially hostile, country all the way. It could only succeed by virtue of surprise, and through the ability of the horsemen to live off the country. But along the Euphrates there was fodder and water enough and to spare, and the army took its supplies where it found them. In less than three weeks the Hittite striking force appeared completely unannounced at the gates of Babylon.

There was no time to prepare defenses. The walls of Babylon had, of course, been kept in repair, but King Samsi-ditana had no standing army of any size, and it was too late to mobilize his conscripts from the fields. The battle for the gates was sharp and fierce, and then the invaders were in the streets. Before evening fell, Babylon was ablaze and the Hittites in control of the city.

The year is 1595 B.C., and Mursilis (if we may assume for the purpose of this chapter that he was born in 1650—it cannot be very far out) is now fifty-five years old. Exactly three hundred years have passed since Sumu-abum founded the Amorite confederacy with Babylon as its center. (As long a period has elapsed since the Restoration of Charles II. The great days when Hammurabi had carried the arms of Babylonia to victory and ruled from the Turkish mountains to the Persian Gulf are as far in the past as the American War of Independence.) During all these three hundred years Babylon had never fallen to a foreign foe. Old men could remember their grandfathers telling them how, in their boyhood, the Kassites had swept down from the Persian mountains and threatened the city. But now the Kassites peacefully farmed their lands east of the Tigris; their nominal rulers, up in the mountains, showed no desire for further expansion, and in any case had enough to do manning their eastern frontier against the warlike tribes (warlike and Indo-European seemed synonyms these days) who had pushed in from the northeast. The frontier with the Kassites had been wide open as long as men could remember, and Kassites formed a considerable proportion of the working population of Babylonia. To the south lay the rebel states at the head of the Gulf, forming the kingdom of the sea-lands. But they had seceded soon after the death of Hammurabi, and no one really thought of them as rebels any longer. They were a separate state, as they had been for centuries before Hammurabi, and only hotheaded advocates of a Greater Babylonia still asserted the divine right of the Babylonian kings to rule old Sumer. Babylon had looked to the west, where their fellow Amorites ruled as far as the Upper Sea, with the realm of their relatives, the Hyksos kings of Palestine and Egypt, to the south.

But now out of the west the storm had come, and great Babylon was in flames, Samsi-ditana was slain, and a three-hundred-year-old dynasty was no more. The people of Babylon, herded into detention camps outside the walls, had nothing to look forward to but the slave markets in faraway Asia Minor.

Mursilis, as he watched the heaps of booty mounting and the cattle and prisoners being driven in, had other things to think about. He was a long way from home, at the end of impossibly attenuated lines of communication. He could not hold Babylon—nor had he ever intended to. His aim, to break the power that could support a resistance movement in Yamkhad, had been accomplished. The problem was now to extricate his forces.

To the south of his line of retirement lay the Syrian desert, the homeland of the Amorites. And if the kinsmen of the Babylonians, the Hyksos from Palestine or the dimly known tribes of Arabia, were to desire revenge they could attack from the southern desert at any point on the return march. To the north lay the Hurrians. He could expect no gratitude from them for the removal of their principal rival in the east. Now that Babylon was destroyed, they might well feel that the Hittites, too, would be safest out of the way.

Weighing the dangers, Mursilis gave orders that the strongest flank guard should be stationed on the north.

It was well that he did so. When the smoking ruins of

Babylon were a week's march behind them, the report came through to the heavily laden columns of trudging slaves, ass trains, and bullock carts that hostile contact had been made between the chariots of the Hittites and the Hurrians. From then on the retirement on Aleppo was a running fight, with the screen of heavy chariots put out by Mursilis repeatedly assailed by the more numerous, but lighter, chariots of the Mitanni kings. Losses were heavy in the skirmishing, but the Hurrians avoided a pitched battle against the heavy infantry that guarded the convoys of booty. And finally, after weeks of forced marching along the Euphrates banks, Mursilis won through to the cover of the army he had left to hold Yamkhad, and knew that the gamble had come off. With the greater part of the loot of Babylon still in his possession, he took the now-familiar road from Aleppo to his capital of Hattusas.

Behind him in Mesopotamia he left a vacuum where Babylon had been. The refugees who returned and began slowly to rebuild their shattered city were in no shape to hold the realm of which Babylon had been the center. The nearest power capable of rapid action was the king of the sea-lands to the south. And without opposition the rule over Babylon was assumed by the king of the south. Once again the whole of south Mesopotamia, from present-day Baghdad to the sea, was under a single rule.

Mursilis returned in triumph to his capital amid the acclaim of his people. And within a matter of weeks he was murdered.

Mursilis had forgotten the charge that his foster father Hattusilis had laid upon him—to be ever on the watch against intrigue within his own family. The assassin was his own sister's husband, Hantilis, who had taken advantage of the long absence of the king to gain the support of the great nobles to his own aspirations. Believing that the removal of Mursilis would put an end to the burdensome foreign wars which the conditions of their fief required them to take part in and largely to finance, the nobles proclaimed Hantilis Great King of Hatti.

But neither Hantilis nor his supporters realized that Mur-

silis had started something that his death could not stop. And
that only a strong army and a vigorous monarch could hold what
a strong army and a vigorous monarch had won.

The Hurrians had had the fact rammed down their throats
that the Hittites were their rivals for dominion of the fat valleys of the south. And their rulers, the king and the nobility of
Mitanni, sat in their new capital of Wassukkanna, where the
Khabur river debouches from the mountains into the Syrian
plain, and laid plans to strike at the heart of Hittite power.

It was not so easy to take Hattusas by surprise as it had
been to take Babylon. In the mountain country chariots were
ineffective, and the frontier garrisons of the Hatti were strong
and well positioned. Still, the Hurrian attack was powerful and
dangerous. Hantilis was forced to call out his nobles to take the
field once more, as reports came in by mounted messenger of
fortresses taken by storm. When two cities only a day's march
away to the north of the capital were besieged and captured, the
artisans of Hattusas, too, were conscripted to strengthen the
walls of the city.

It never came to actual siege of Hattusas. The campaign
season ended with the capture of Nerik and Tiliura, and with the
first snows of winter the Hurrians withdrew eastward to their own
country.

But the myth of Hittite invincibility was shattered. During
the remaining dozen years or so of this chapter there were re-
peated revolts among the subject provinces which Mursilis and
his two predecessors had added to the kingdom of the Hatti.
Many broke away completely, for Hantilis had no desire for pro-
longed campaigns at a distance from his capital. He had learnt
that assassination is a two-edged weapon, and he lived under
the constant (and, as it proved, justified) fear of palace revolution.

And the Hittite soldiery, who had marched and ridden with
Hattusilis and Mursilis on the long campaigns, looked in bitterness at the renewed independence of Yamkhad, and even of
Arzawa and Kizzuwatna closer home, and wearied their sons and
grandsons with the tale of how they and their commander rode

against Babylon, and what *they* would do if *they* were Great King.

There is more evidence for the events of this chapter than would at first appear. While the only confirmed date is that of the capture of Babylon by Mursilis in 1595 B.C., and it is therefore somewhat conjectural to equate the life of Mursilis with the duration of the chapter, the main sequence of events is well attested, much by the royal archives of Hattusas, now in Berlin. Hattusilis's speech at the adoption of Mursilis is extant, and reveals that he was earlier (and still officially) called Labarnas. The foundation of Hattusas, the campaign of Hattusilis against Aleppo and its subsequent revolt, its reconquest by Mursilis, and the Babylonian expedition are all known facts. Even such things as the covert support given by the Hurrians to Yamkhad, and the early inefficiency of the Hittites in using siege machinery, is suggested by a "war-correspondent" report. That the Babylonian expedition was occasioned by support given by Babylonia to Yamkhad is surmise, but surely not unwarrantable. That Mursilis and the Hurrians came into conflict is strongly suggested by a single defective tablet, and the subsequent Hurrian attack on the home territory of the Hittites is historical, as is the murder of Mursilis and the accession of Hantilis.

The best brief accounts of the Hittites are furnished by O. R. Gurney in The Hittites *and* Seton Lloyd in Early Anatolia. C. W. Ceram's The Secret of the Hittites *gives a very readable account of the discovery of the Hittite Empire.*

12

THE RESISTANCE MOVEMENT

1580–1510 B.C.

T HE SUMMER SUN burnt down on a river crowded with boats of every shape and size. For forty miles in both directions, along the broad thoroughfare of the Nile the people of the villages were converging on Thebes. Along the dusty banks trains of donkeys, palanquins, and thronging white-clad crowds pressed in the same direction. From the smaller roads which led from the villages up under the cliffs lining the valley of the upper Nile, groups of farmers and their families shouldered their way into the throng on the main road.

In Thebes the crowds choked the narrow streets. All the shops were shut, and the merchants and artisans, the slaves and

BOATS SUCH AS THIS, OF PAPYRUS REEDS BOUND TOGETHER, WERE (AND ARE TO THIS DAY) A COMMON MEANS OF TRANSPORT ALONG THE NILE. THE RELIEF FROM WHICH THIS DRAWING WAS MADE WAS FOUND IN A TOMB AT SAKKARA, AND DATES TO ABOUT 2250 B.C. (SOME SEVEN HUNDRED YEARS EARLIER THAN THIS CHAPTER).

porters, the fishermen and builders' laborers, together with their wives and children and sweethearts, were all out on the streets, converging on the great pillared temple of Amon. Today, for all the anxiety about the future, there was a feeling of celebration in the air. And of expectation—even a degree of optimism. For today great Amon was to acknowledge publicly Amose as his son and as the true shepherd and ruler of both upper and lower Egypt, the rightful wearer of the crowns, both white and red. And there were many who believed that Amose could make the claim good, expel the foreigners who so long had occupied the northern kingdom, and unite both Egypts at last beneath an Egyptian ruler.

The actual ceremony would take place, of course, within the temple, the offerings of fruit and flowers and barley cakes, the anointing, and the expounding of Amon's will by the high priest, the assumption of the double crown and the taking up of the crook and the flail. The crowds who slowly massed tighter outside the temple were waiting to see the sequel, the presentation of the new pharaoh to his subjects. No one who could walk would fail to be here today, and the first impression of many a baby in arms would be of the hot sunshine and the tight-pressed crowd waiting to greet the resistance leader fresh from his assumption of divinity.

The new king was already within the temple, had been there since early morning, and his chariot, with its two magnificently plumed horses, stood in the shade of the pylons, with the grooms at the horses' heads and a detachment of tall Sudanese auxiliaries standing guard around, men of the same regiment as, stationed at intervals of three paces, kept clear the platform before the temple upon which the king would appear. The pennons on their lances, and on the flagstaffs before the temple, drooped in the still air.

As they waited, many in the crowd discussed, unemotionally as befits experienced campaigners, the chances of the coming struggle and the events which had led up to today's ceremony.

The north had been long under foreign occupation, so long

that even the oldest men present could only tell that when their grandfathers were young the rule of the Hyksos, too, had been young.

There were men in the crowd who still counted themselves northerners, because their great-grandfathers had escaped to the free south during and after the occupation, and who still laid claim to lost estates in the deltalands, although their families had now lived for three generations in the narrow river valley of the south. There were other more recent arrivals too, families who had lived under the occupation in the north but who during the recent fighting had thrown in their lot with the liberation forces so openly that they had been forced to flee, aided by the underground movement, to the liberated lands of the south.

But the southerners were quick to remind these embittered refugees that upper Egypt, too, had had its time of oppression; that it had not lasted so long as the martyrdom of lower Egypt was solely due to the devoted resistance of the southern armies in the years following the fall of the north. For a hundred years southern Egypt had retained its independence, until, forty years or so ago, Klian, the powerful king of the north, had organized an immense army in his garrison city of Avaris and in one irresistible campaign had overcome the desperate resistance of the kings of Thebes.

All but the youngest of those who formed the crowd around the temple had grown up during the thirty years of oppression that had followed, when a black-bearded Canaanite governor had sat in the royal palace at Thebes, and regiments of foreign-tongued troops had garrisoned every town. The earls of all the nomes into which the land was divided had fled to the Sudan with the royal family, or had been executed, and their estates had been granted to northerners or Palestinians from the Hyksos nobility. Much of the temple lands of Amon had been confiscated and granted to the new temples of the Hyksos god Sutek, and many thought that the victory of the powers of darkness was thereby made absolute. For Sutek was said to be but another name for the old god Set, the archenemy of the hawk-god Horus who from ancient times had been the special protector of upper

Egypt and its kings. Taxes had been levied, even impiously upon the diminished estates of the southern temples, to pay for the occupation; the copper mines had been manned by forced labor and by political prisoners; and many had been enslaved without cause and been sold down the river, to disappear for ever.

But the government in exile beyond the cataracts had never given up the struggle. It had maintained itself precariously in existence, with the good will of the Sudanese kings of Nubia, and had kept up clandestine contact with such of the old nobility and priesthood as had escaped the Hyksos proscription. Gold had secretly been collected, and men had slipped away to join the growing army of liberation. And finally, ten years ago, Sekenenre, a scion of the royal house of Thebes, had raised an internal revolt, aided by the patriot forces abroad and by the famous mercenaries of the Sudan.

The many veterans of the revolt present in the crowd recalled how the first shock had thrown the Hyksos garrisons out of Thebes and all the principal cities, and how feverishly constructed defenses and hastily armed militia had held off the counterattack that followed. The god Amon, with his temple lands restored, had declared Sekenenre his royal son, and his wife Ahotep his royal daughter, and the new king and queen had for nearly ten years held Thebes and the lands to the south against yearly attacks by the Hyksos armies of the delta. But just over a year ago Sekenenre had fallen in battle, and his body, with the skull cloven by a northern battle-ax, had only been saved for the embalmers by the courage of his two stepsons, Kamose and Amose, experienced warriors who had led an immediate counterattack and saved the day for the southern forces.

Kamose and Amose were sons of Queen Ahotep by a previous marriage, and so, though Ahotep was the divine queen, not strictly in the line of succession (though on this day no one expressed *that* thought openly). But they were both renowned captains of armies, whereas Sekenenre's own sons by Ahotep were too young to take command in these desperate times. And Ahotep was herself a heroine of the liberation, in addition to being divine—and a determined woman. It was not unreasonable, therefore, that Amon, her father, had chosen Kamose, the elder brother, to succeed the fallen pharaoh.

All last winter Kamose and his brother had spent training the army with which they hoped to reconquer the occupied north. And in the spring they had marched north along the river valley, to carry the war for the first time into enemy territory. They had won a hard-fought victory against the southernmost vassal of the Hyksos, Teti, baron of Hermopolis. And they had captured Hermopolis, and Kamose had established his head-quarters in the palace of the conquered nobleman. But there he had suddenly died, poisoned, as many thought, by Teti's wife, whom he had made his slave.

The death of the newly crowned king had prevented the army of the south from following up its victory, but the bulk of the army still stood beyond the northern frontier, while Amose had returned with his Sudanese bodyguard, summoned by his divine mother and the god Amon to assume the crown of both Egypts. And everyone knew that as soon as today's ceremony was over he would return to lead his forces to the liberation of lower Egypt. And the prayers of the south would go with him.

The sun was already casting long shadows from the pylons across the temple platform when the trumpeters stationed at the temple gates sounded their fanfare, and the crowd grew still as a little group appeared from the darkness within. First came the high priest of Amon, and then behind him came Amose, wearing the double crown of upper and lower Egypt and bearing the crook and the flail crossed before him. Beside him walked his royal wife and sister Nefertari, also crowned with the double crown, and behind them the dowager queen, their mother. The shout that greeted the royal party rolled over the city and gave echo from the distant hills that lined the river valley.

And then the crowd fell silent again as the high priest stepped forward to speak. In the age-old formula he testified to the might of Amon, and to the god's recognition of his true son and daughter as the rightful rulers of his two realms of Egypt. Throughout the recitation of the formula Amose stood rigid, his eyes gazing far beyond the temple confines. There were many among the spectators who remarked afterwards that he appeared to have grown in stature (for he was not a large man), but that may well have been the effect of the tall crown upon his head.

When the priest was finished, the fanfare sounded again and Amose and his queen mounted the chariot and drove to the palace along the path cleared by the bodyguard, while the crowd cheered wildly and cast flowers and barley before the horses.

The celebration in the streets of Thebes went on far into the night. But at dawn the next morning the king left the palace, still wearing the double crown but otherwise in his service armor, and, accompanied by the half-dozen or so chariots which was all the south could muster, set off to join his army. The two queens, Ahotep and Nefertari, as was right and proper, took over the regency in his absence. The crowd dispersed to the fields and fishing craft, to the shops and workshops. And the women went back to grinding their millet on the heavy stone saddle-querns, to baking their pancake bread in the beehive-shaped clay ovens, to their spinning and weaving, and to the care of the children whose lifetime is the story of this chapter. And their thoughts were far away, with their husbands and brothers marching and fighting with the king in the occupied provinces down river.

As the weeks and then the months wore on, messengers came through ever more frequently by river boat, bringing dispatches from the front to the queens-regent, and when the boats with the royal insignia were seen to pass, their sails spread to catch the north wind, silent crowds would gather outside the palace to await the release of the bulletins. Each time they brought news of further advances, of provincial garrisons defeated and towns captured, of new provinces liberated. And in the waterfront inns of an evening the crews of the messenger boats added details to the story. They told of uprisings in the northern lands at the approach of the army of Thebes, of tumultuous welcomes and garlanded troops parading through the liberated cities. But they told, too, of bitter struggles, with garrisons holding out to the last man, of summary punishment meted out by the populace to collaborators and Hyksos landlords. And they brought rumors of the army that Apopi III, the Hyksos king, was assembling in far-off Avaris, the grand army with its thousand chariots that was to strike back at the invaders. And the women bit their knuckles, and went back in silence to their work.

That year the army did not return for the inundation, and while the Nile rose and ran high and brown no boats came up the river from the north.

The flood passed on, the sowing was carried out by the old men and the women and children. and the green shoots of millet and barley began to appear. And still no news came.

Until one evening in early summer a chariot rolled by along the embankment road, its plodding horses drooping their heads as wearily as the young man who stood beside the driver. The man was recognized by many as a nobleman of the earldom a day's journey south of Thebes, a member of Amose's personal staff. Like a thatch fire the news ran through the town, and almost before the chariot passed the gates of the palace a crowd had gathered. In less than half an hour a palace scribe and a herald appeared at the gates and proclaimed the news.

Eight days ago the army of pharaoh had confronted the main host of the Hyksos monarch not far from the holy city of Memphis. The battle had raged for two days, and on the evening of the second day the Hyksos chariots had wheeled and fled. The chosen of Amon was even now in hot pursuit of the fleeing enemy, and should by now be approaching the stronghold of Avaris.

No more work was done that evening or the following day, and Thebes rejoiced in the exuberance of its relief. Palace slaves, who had heard the full story from the driver, told in the town of the booty and prisoners, the stores of weapons and the chariots which had been taken. The messenger chariot itself was part of the spoils of victory.

Clearly, though, there had been other dispatches with the messenger. For orders went out from the palace calling up many of the older men, particularly the artisans, carpenters, and smiths. The garrisons left behind in upper Egypt were drastically reduced, new contingents of Sudanese mercenaries marched in, and even the criminals who worked in the mines were ordered north under guard. It became clear that the war was not over, and the men and stores being sent to the front were obviously destined for the siege of the fortress capital of the Hyksos.

That year the harvests, too, were gathered by the women and the old men. But now both river and roads were open, and the picture in the north became clear.

Amose, with the largest army Egypt ever had known, lay before Avaris. But his sappers and miners had been unable to make any impression on the moats and ramparts of the fortress city, and his fleet of river vessels could not maintain an effective blockade on the seaward side. The Hyksos were effectively contained, however, and the rest of Egypt had submitted with enthusiasm to a king of Egyptian race.

There were exceptions. In a number of the nomes, the earldoms into which Egypt had from ancient times been divided, the nobles appointed by the Hyksos still ruled. They were often collaborators, members of the hereditary nobility of the nome who had made their peace with the Hyksos and kept their lands, even in the south, but who, when Sekenenre's rising commenced, had changed sides sufficiently promptly to retain their position, at least until Amose had time to deal with them. One of these, Aata, from a province up-river from Thebes, showed his hand while Amose was tied down before Avaris and upper Egypt was denuded of troops. He raised his own army of retainers, manned a river fleet, and sailed north against Thebes.

He had reckoned without the queens. The dowager Ahotep and her daughter Nefertari gathered what troops they could and held off the rebel. And Amose, leaving the bulk of his army to continue the siege, hurried south by river with a picked force and, fighting from his ships, cut the fleet and army of Aata to pieces. Then he hurried back to the siege, with scarcely time to visit Thebes and confer with his mother and wife before he left.

The following year the Hyksos king capitulated—on terms. He would surrender Avaris, but he himself and his whole army were to be allowed to march out and to cross unmolested into their native realm of Palestine.

Amose accepted the terms, waited until the Hyksos troops had passed the frontier—and then followed. Both he and his army were well aware of the folly of allowing the Hyksos king to regroup and rearm his army on his own ground, and of giving him the opportunity to choose his own time and place for a bid to regain Egypt.

Across the isthmus of Suez and by the coastal road over the desert of Sinai the army of the pharaoh, still mainly of spear- and mace-armed infantry, though now equipped with captured chariots, pursued the enemy. But the Hyksos army gained in safety the gateway fortress of Palestine, the embattled city of Sharuhen (not far from modern Gaza).

Amose's by now siege-trained army settled down to beleaguer the city, while the pharaoh returned to Egypt.

Here there was much to do. A whole new machinery of government had to be constructed to take the place of the Hyksos organization; his army must be reorganized and re-equipped, and the southern frontier towards Nubia strengthened; there were comrades of the liberation to be rewarded, and traitors punished; there was even another abortive revolt in the south to put down; and there was a foreign policy to be devised and implemented, and diplomatic contacts with the outside world to re-establish. But first Amose must return to Thebes, officially and in triumph, to give thanks to his father Amon for his victories.

The ceremony surpassed by far in magnificence the coronation of three years before—though in afteryears the children who were taken to both could never really distinguish them in their recollections. And this time the jubilation of the assembled crowds was unrestrained by fears for the future.

But the wildest outburst of joy came three years later when, following the fall of Sharuhen and a demonstration campaign in Palestine, the army came home. By now the new model army was a reality, and the old comrades of the resistance could be brought back to Thebes and disbanded.

Many of the veterans settled down on their tenant farms again, or bought a small business or a workshop with their gratuity, and their children, now six years old and more, grew gradually to accept the strangers as their fathers. Others were restless after their years of campaigning. They could not settle

down at home, and many, after a few months or a year, returned
to the army or joined the merchant ships or the trading caravans.

It was an unsettled period, these years following the liberation. The farmers and artisans were little affected, personally,
by the comprehensive reforms of the administration instituted by
the pharaoh, but that did not in the least prevent them arguing
endlessly about them.

On the whole they were favorably received. Everyone knew
that civil war within Egypt had opened the gates to the Hyksos,
and all were agreed that that must never again happen. It had
been the hereditary nobility of the nomes who, by supporting
rival candidates to the throne from within the royal family, had
turned a family squabble into a civil war. Nor was it unknown,
within the long and chequered history of Egypt, for a strong earl
to overthrow a dynasty and set himself up as pharaoh. Now was
the time to make a clean sweep of the old system of almost
independent earldoms. Much of the old nobility had been wiped
out by the Hyksos, and others, having made a profitable peace
with the occupying power, had now fallen with the fall of that
power, and had been executed or banished. Only nobles of
proved loyalty remained. Amose abolished the hereditary earldoms, and decreed that in future the nomes would be governed
by sheriffs appointed by pharaoh and responsible to pharaoh.

The people, hoping for less corruption in the assessment of
tithes and taxes, applauded. But in fact it made less difference
than expected, for the loyal nobility tended to be confirmed as
sheriffs in their own former nomes.

The Hyksos danger was by no means over. Beyond the present frontier, well up in Palestine, the new king of the Canaanite
confederacy, Maaibre, still called himself pharaoh of Egypt,
adopted pseudo-Egyptian manners, and inscribed his name on
scarabs with the royal "cartouche." And there was still a large
minority of Asiatics in the delta, who had immigrated during—
and even before—the Hyksos occupation, but who had been
peaceably settled so long that there was no real pretext for
expelling them. The most numerous of these were the "children
of Israel," as they called themselves, the descendants of some

Amorite chieftain of that name, whose original family home had alternated between north and south Mesopotamia, but who had migrated into Egypt about three hundred years ago. They were peaceable enough folk, but no one could say which way they would jump if the Hyksos king attempted to regain his lost empire.

In general Amose was not happy, it seemed, about his northeast frontier. As the young sons of his resistance veterans began to reach military age and to be taken for army service, the majority of them found themselves doing their tour of duty in the dusty plains of the Negeb or the coastal towns of the Gaza strip. And when they returned home they had a fair idea, picked up from the crews of coastal craft or the drivers of the donkey caravans, of the position deep beyond the frontier there.

The Hyksos of Canaan, they said, had strong allies in their rear. To their north lay the Amorites of the Lebanon, and north of them again the Amorites of Yamkhad. Some forty years ago Yamkhad had been conquered by a powerful king who had appeared out of the mountain country to the northwest, but his chariots had retired northward again and had not reappeared, and Yamkhad had recovered. The same mountain king had also raided and destroyed the greatest of the Amorite nations, Babylonia, on the Euphrates to the eastward. Babylonia had not recovered, but was still under the rule of a moderately peaceful mercantile kingdom around the head of the Persian Gulf. The most powerful of all the nations to the north was beyond doubt the Mitanni kingdom of the Hurrians, who occupied with their chariots the wide plains of the upper Euphrates. But these were of a different race and language from the Semitic speakers farther south, and were no danger to Egypt as long as the Semites lay between.

The older men in the towns and villages along the upper Nile listened with amused respect to the account given by the returned soldiers of these nations beyond nations of which they, in their time, had scarcely heard. They had, after all, had other things to think about. But now there was peace in Egypt, and such dangers as there were these days lay beyond the frontier.

Twenty-two years after the coronation of Amose news came

to the resistance veterans in the villages along the Nile that their great commander was dead. And the heralds who brought the news announced at the same time the accession of his son Amenhotep. The news was not unexpected, for Amose was in his sixties, and had been ailing for some time. Yet it seemed to the older generation that with his passing Egypt was once more left defenseless, and they looked anxiously again to the north. Admittedly Amenhotep's mother, the divine wife and sister of Amose, Nefertari, was still alive, and the old queen Ahotep, the heroine of the liberation, was as active as ever within the palace, though she was now over eighty. Both the dowager queens were legendary figures who had ruled the land with firmness and courage while Amose had been away at the front, and surely they could advise the young Amenhotep, if troubles should come again.

Whether Amenhotep needed, or heeded, the advice of his mother and grandmother was never known outside the palace. But the number of "royal and divine" ladies within it was the subject of comment, and of daring jokes, along the river. It was of course right and proper, and enjoined by law and custom, that Amenhotep should marry his full sister, for it was after all the daughter even more than the son of the divine rulers who contained within herself the spark of divinity. But Amenhotep carried it rather to extremes. Amose and Nefertari had three daughters, Ahotep—called after her grandmother—Merit-Amon, and Sat-Kamose, all full sisters of Amenhotep, and it was undoubtedly because he knew that anyone whom one of his sisters married would thereby become a not impossible rival to the throne that he proceeded to marry all three of them himself. As royal princesses they all three, of course, counted as divine wives and reigning queens, and the problem of precedence among the five queens in the palace must, it was agreed, give periodic headaches to the master of the household.

Amenhotep reigned for twenty years, and, historically speaking, his reign was uneventful and prosperous. The new system of delegation of authority instituted by Amose worked well, taxes came in regularly, and there was little discontent and no civil disturbance. On and beyond the frontiers there was peace,

though not always a completely easy peace. The Hyksos pretender to the northeast held his hand and before the end of
Amenhotep's reign had even officially given up any claim to
Egypt. The pharaoh showed himself regularly, as was fitting, at
the head of his army, and twice even crossed his frontiers. For it
is the duty of a divine pharaoh to spread the fear of Amon to the
unenlightened. One of the campaigns was against the Sudan,
where the tribes had been restive and had raided Egyptian territory; Amenhotep defeated a Nubian army there and captured its
chief. Some years later he campaigned in the western desert,
deep into Libya, and met no organized resistance from the
small principalities along the coast or the grazing tribes of the
interior. Otherwise he kept the peace, with a well-equipped
army and a watchful eye in the direction of Syria.

It was an uneventful twenty years. But of course for the men
and women who had been born in 1580 B.C. it was the most important twenty years of their lives, the period when they grew
from being young men and women of twenty-two to being middle-aged men and women of forty-two. It was the time when
their families were growing up, and when they themselves made
either a success or a failure of their lives.

For most of them success or failure was measured in unambi-
tious terms. To be a success in Egypt involved no more than living
no worse than your parents had lived before you, tilling your
landlord's fields or keeping your family shop, bringing up your
children to reverence and to be favored by the gods, and burying your parents, when their time came, in a decent grave in the
cemetery, with all the ordained ceremonial which would ensure
that they safely reached the hereafter to which you yourself
would in your turn come.

But there were some of this generation who, after their
turbulent youth, had greater ambitions and a more restless seeking after this world's goods. Now that the Egyptians were again
masters in their own house and peace reigned along the frontiers,
there was a considerable increase in the volume of overseas
trade. There was much rebuilding after the wars, and a ready
market for imported luxuries sprang up among the new nobility and the prosperous middle classes. The merchants, them-

selves a considerable proportion of this middle class, organized
their shipping lines and trading caravans to meet the demand,
while the manufacturers concentrated more and more on articles
for export to pay for the imported luxuries.

Great barges plied the length of the Egyptian Nile, working
their way down river with sweeps aiding the current, and coast-
ing up river with the north wind filling their sails. At Avaris and
the other estuary ports where the wind brought the tang of salt
to the nostrils of the fresh-water sailors, they exchanged their
cargoes, while scribes checked bales and crates against their
shipping lists and bills of lading, all written on papyrus sheets in
the swift hieratic script that had already lost most of its resemblance to the neatly drawn picture writing of the hieroglyphs.

The estuary ports were the clearinghouses for the growing
volume of overseas trade. They had a mercantile tradition running back for centuries, as their merchant-guild conventions were
fond of reminding themselves. Some of the earliest ships to sail
westward into the barbarian world of the western Mediterranean, and even beyond the Straits, had come from these ports,
and that was now nearly seven hundred years ago (as long ago
as the Crusades are removed from us). It was said that ships
from Crete still trafficked in that direction, and the Egyptian
merchants discussed half-seriously reopening their old western
trade. There was a good market in Egypt just now for anything
exotic, and native handicrafts from the primitive European tribes
would command a good price and could probably be bought
for a handful of beads.

A certain amount of European stuff did come in, probably
at vastly inflated prices, with the cargoes from Crete, and gave
them some idea of the products available in the north and west.
The native goldwork was quite good, when it did not try to
imitate Egyptian models, and there were even quite nice things
in bronze and wood. And there was jewelry, splendidly primitive and barbaric, made of new semiprecious stones which appeared likely to become fashionable—jet, which was shiny
black, and amber, which was like solid honey.

But the native handicrafts were for the specialist importer.
The bulk of the traffic was from nearer home. Just as in Hyksos

times, the coasters were now coming in again from Byblos and the other Lebanese ports, carrying mainly cedarwood, but with occasional cargoes of silver or copper or wines from Asia Minor.

The copper ships came in from Cyprus, too, or direct from ports along the south coast of Asia Minor, in Kizzuwatna and Arzawa. These countries had, in the boyhood of the older merchants, been subject to a power in the interior, the Hatti, the same power that had lashed out fifty-five years earlier and destroyed Babylon; but they had rewon their independence a few years before the Egyptians had expelled the Hyksos.

Perhaps the main trade, though, was with Crete. For Crete was the great emporium that dealt not only in its own products, oil and fish and fine pottery, but in all the staple products of the northern shores of the Mediterranean and even farther afield. The great broad-beamed merchant ships of Crete docked in northern Egypt deeply laden with timber and marble and wool, with tin and copper and dyestuffs, and sailed again with manufactured bronzes and linen, and bulk cargoes of barley and wheat.

And to the coastal cities of Egypt, too, led the overland caravan routes from the east. There lay the large caravanserais where the long trains of pack asses ended their journeys down the coast route through Canaan and across the Sinai peninsula. They brought bales of goods which had come all the way from the head of the Persian Gulf by the long route along the Euphrates. Some of the goods had even come from a distance down the Persian Gulf by sea to the ports of the Sea-land kingdom which now ruled in Babylon. These were dates for the most part, and occasionally pearls and carnelian beads.

But the price of carnelian has gone up to unprecedented heights, and the black-bearded merchants from the Gulf ports make no secret of the reason. These small consignments of the translucent red stones are likely to be the last to come through from India for a very long time to come. As the merchants toss the small leather bags of stones from one hand to the other, they tell of the disruption of the eastern trade.

Three weeks' sail down the Persian Gulf, they say, and across the sea beyond lies the land of Meluhha, where the Indus river, a river the size of the Nile, pours its waters into the Indian Ocean. The Egyptian merchants nod; they have heard of Meluhha.

From this rich land, went on the Mesopotamians, cargoes of precious goods had long been brought by the merchant adventurers of Ur and Dilmun, cargoes of gold and ivory, of teak and cotton and lapis lazuli. And of carnelian. Within the memory of man it had been a peaceful land, ruled by its great kings from the mighty capitals of Mohenjo-daro and Harappa. Far to the southeast its colonies spread, five hundred miles along the coast as far as the hills and jungles of the Kathiawar peninsula, and in the northeast new towns had been built by the upper waters of another river which was said to flow eastward for hundreds of miles to another sea. It had looked as though Meluhha could expand indefinitely, in size and wealth and power.

But in the time of their grandfathers an enemy had come over the northern mountains, mountains so high that they were thought to be the roof of the world. Like the Hurrians and the Kassites of north Mesopotamia, these newcomers—they called themselves Aryans—were nomads, with herds of cattle and of horses, and with squadrons of swift horse chariots. They were fierce warriors, great eaters of beef, and singers of songs. And since they appeared they had been pressing south.

Over a generation ago great Harappa had fallen, far to the north along the Indus, and since that time no lapis lazuli had come out of the mountains of Afghanistan. But Harappa was five hundred miles from Mohenjo-daro, and the length of Egypt away from the coast. The king in Mohenjo-daro had not been unduly troubled, perhaps not as troubled as he should have been, for he did not appreciate, as the Mesopotamians from long experience tried to warn him, the swiftness with which charioteers could move. Anyway, year by year the Aryans had moved southward, sacking and burning the townships of the Punjab, and recently they had been joined by kinsfolk coming from Persia into the hill country of Baluchistan. The ruler of Mohenjo-daro had realized his danger too late, when a coalition of Aryans and Asuras had swept in from west and north. The army of Meluhha had been shattered; the hastily improvised defenses of Mohenjo-daro, for centuries an open city, had been overrun; and the city had been stormed and sacked.

One of the merchants took up the tale. He had been in Mohenjo-daro, he said, with a party of Dilmun traders at the time of the sack, and he had barely escaped with his life—and two bags of carnelians. From the citadel he had seen the tall blond warriors storm along the wide avenues, which might have been built for chariots, spearing the panic-stricken civilians as they scattered. The wise ones of the population had taken to the fields at the onset, abandoning homes and possessions to the invaders. Those who stayed to salvage something of their wealth were struck down in the streets and left lying, still clutching their tusks of ivory or boxes of jewelry. And those who sought refuge in the underground chambers of the public wells survived only until the invaders dismounted and, intoxicated with slaughter, charged down the steps to complete the massacre. The eyewitness had seen the smoke from the looted and burning city staining the sky behind him for three whole days, as he paddled down river in the boat in which he made his escape.

Now no more ships sailed to India from the Persian Gulf, he said, and no more Indian goods would reach the markets of the west. For the invaders were no lovers of cities. Unlike the other Indo-European tribes, the Kassites and Hittites and Hurrians who were now accepted powers in the world, these Aryans left a wilderness where they passed, destroying rather than conquering. The Indian market was definitely closed to trade.

The merchants of Avaris listened respectfully, but cared little for tales of recession in Ur and Dilmun. In Egypt trade was booming as never before, in these twenty years of peace under Amenhotep.

As Amenhotep grew older, there had been much speculation about the succession. For all his three royal wives, pharaoh had no official son. But his daughter by Ahotep, called Amose after her grandfather, was now grown up, and the man she married would be, through her, the natural candidate for the throne. It had occasioned general satisfaction, therefore, when the princess Amose had some years ago been married to prince

Thothmes, who, though her half-brother, was only the son of Amenhotep by a slave girl. The divine blood of the royal house would be only a little diluted, and Thothmes was known to be an energetic young man with the expansion of the power of Egypt at heart. It was generally believed that the powerful clique of queens in the palace at Thebes was equally pleased. Amenhotep's mother, the famous beauty Nefertari, was now dead, but his grandmother Ahotep was still very much alive, vigorous despite her ninety-five years. And she and the three reigning queens saw with satisfaction that the feminine influence which had bulked so large in the present and previous reigns was likely to continue in the next, with the coming queen in fact more legitimate than her consort. It seemed even that Amon himself favored their sex, for the first child of the young couple was a daughter, the charming and vivacious princess Hatshepsut.

Amenhotep died in 1538 B.C., and those who, as month-old babies, had been carried to see the coronation of the liberator Amose, now as men and women aged forty-two attended the proclamation, from the same temple platform, of the succession of his grandchildren, his namesake Queen Amose and her consort Thothmes.

Thothmes was at this time a young man in his twenties, untried in war, and the Sudanese kingdom to the south, which had a defeat at the hands of Amenhotep to avenge, promptly invaded Egyptian territory. But the young pharaoh was not caught napping. He had inherited an efficient and well-equipped army from his father, and he struck back at once. Marching south from Thebes, he crossed the frontier, penetrated deep into the Sudan, and captured and sacked Kerma, the capital of Kush, the Nubian kingdom. From Thebes to Kerma is five hundred miles, but not content with this, Thothmes pressed on two hundred miles more, past the point where the Nile bends back upon itself to the north. He set the boundary stones of his empire there, by the fourth cataract of the Nile, proud of having, as his scribes undoubtedly told him, accomplished a march in hostile territory no shorter than that by which Mursilis of the Hatti had surprised and captured Babylon sixty years before. Leaving a garrison at

Napata by the cataract, he marched back to the third cataract, near Kerma, and halted there for some time while his troops raised a fortress for the garrison and governor who were to hold the newly conquered province for him. At the same time he ordered five reliefs commemorating his campaign to be carved on the cliff wall nearby.

When he returned to Thebes before the inundation, Thothmes had tasted victory and found it sweet. The young men of the army, and even the older veterans, men and officers of the 1580 class, had gained confidence in their leader. They responded eagerly when, a few years later, he led them in the other direction, towards Canaan.

Palestine was, in theory at least, subject to Egypt. Since the sack of the great Hyksos fortress in south Palestine forty years ago, the land had been broken up into a large number of small principalities, each prince building himself a mighty stone castle and intriguing for Egyptian support against the other princes, warring against them (or against Egypt) whenever he thought he could get away with it. True to Hyksos tradition, the princes were strong in chariotry, but they had devised new techniques of fortification to counteract the new weapon of attack. Their fortresses were built with a gateway that would only allow one chariot at a time to pass, and with a sloping glacis at the base of the wall which prevented the chariots from driving close in under the wall to discharge their spears.

The pharaohs had imposed tribute on these vassal princes, but payment of the tribute had been highly sporadic and the princes so unruly that there was ample excuse for Thothmes to interfere. He, however, saw farther than Palestine. Originally the principalities there had been thought of by his grandfather as buffer states against the Amorites of the north, but of late the Hurrians on the upper Euphrates, and their Mitanni princes and charioteers, had been making their presence felt farther south in Syria and had raided the territory of the northernmost of Egypt's Canaanite vassals.

Thothmes embarked on a second long-range campaign, and marched straight through the Canaanite principalities into Syria. He met no opposition, the princes retreating to their fortresses and hastily sending arrears of tribute, and the Hurrians retiring before him. Finally he halted on the banks of the Euphrates itself, conscious of the fact that he had led an Egyptian army farther into the eastern lands than any pharaoh before him. And on the Euphrates he set up his boundary stones, a full fifteen hundred miles from those he had planted by the fourth cataract of the Nile (the distance from San Francisco to Kansas City, or from London to Istanbul). This time he left no garrison, but accepted the submission of the local princes and confirmed them in their territory as the vassals of Egypt.

He returned to Thebes in triumph, lord—without a single battle—of more territory than any king of Egypt before him (and indeed, though he did not know it, lord of the greatest empire that the world had up to that time seen).

In the following years a landmark disappeared and a new landmark took its place at Thebes. Thothmes decided that the temple of Amon to the north of the city, at which he and his father and his grandfather had been crowned, was too small to house the majesty of the divine father of the ruler of so large an empire. He gave orders for it to be pulled down, and for a new temple of a more fitting size to be erected on its site. Over the next ten years the temple of Karnak grew in all its magnificence, to the wonder and admiration of the elderly men and women who could dimly remember Amose's coronation at the former shrine.

Thothmes made no more wars. He was rumored to be ill, though he still carried out all his official duties. But as the years went by, and Egypt's prosperity grew with the tribute now coming in regularly from its dependencies to the north and the south, and from the trade that followed the flag, Thothmes left Thebes ever less often.

Much had changed within the palace. The old heroine of the revolution, the great-grandmother of the pharaoh, Ahotep, had at last died, over a hundred years old, and of Thothmes's four children by Amose three had died, including both the young princes on whom he had relied for the succession. Only princess Hatshepsut remained in the line of succession, though there was a boy by a secondary wife, called Thothmes after his father. The pharaoh was clearly relying more and more on the quick judgment and acumen of Hatshepsut, whom, after the death of his sons, he had brought up almost as a boy. She was self-willed and temperamental, and had inherited the beauty of her mother and of her great-grandmother Nefertari. In 1518 B.C. Thothmes appointed her officially as his co-regent, and at the same time married her to her half-brother Thothmes. She was at the time twenty-four years old, and her husband was seven years her junior.

From that date Thothmes effectively retired from the throne, and Hatshepsut took over all the official duties of the pharaoh. The proprieties were still, of course, observed, for no woman could rule Egypt in her own name, and the name of Thothmes appeared together with that of his daughter on all decrees. But the invalid king never left his palace. The young Thothmes, too, was of weak health and seldom accompanied his self-willed wife when she drove out in her chariot on inspection tours of her realm.

Three years passed, and in 1515 B.C. Thothmes I died, and was succeeded by Thothmes II. But everyone knew that in effect the succession had devolved upon Hatshepsut.

On hearing that the pharaoh who had conquered them had died, the natives of the province of Kush made a bid for independence, and revolted.

The people of Egypt shared the outraged indignation of the new pharaoh and his consort at the ingratitude and temerity of the Sudanese. And most vociferous were the old people of the towns and villages of upper Egypt. They remembered—interminably—the victory parades when King Amose's troops returned from the war which had liberated Egypt from the foreign yoke, and the proud bearing of the Sudanese troops who then had fought side by side with the Egyptians for freedom. That, less than a lifetime later, the grandsons of these faithful allies should rise in rebellion against the Egyptian authorities showed the disruptive effect of modern education and contact with a higher civilization on the simple morals of a primitive people. Such a revolt would never have happened in their day, they said.

With the good wishes of the entire Egyptian people, the expeditionary force set out to relieve the besieged garrisons. With satisfaction the good people at home received dispatches telling of the defeat of Sudanese resistance armies, and of the summary execution of the male population of the revolted cities. Old and young lined the banks of the Nile to cheer as the returning fleet sailed by, with the captured chieftains of the rebels hanging head downward from the rigging, on their way to their well-merited execution before pharaoh.

The oldest men said that they could not recall having seen such popular enthusiasm since the day seventy years before when the army of Amose had marched north in revolt against the foreign oppressors of Egypt.

What the population of Kush thought is not recorded.

There is not general agreement on the precise dates of the events of this chapter. The dates given here are those accepted by C. F. A. Schaeffer in his Stratigraphie Comparée, *but some authorities (notably J. A. Wilson in* The Burden of Egypt) *would place the events twelve years later. There are in addition a number of minor points of uncertainty; the names of the Hyksos pharaohs at the time of the liberation and during the subsequent Palestine campaign of Amose are not with certainty those given here, though these names are recorded for Hyksos leaders living at approximately this time. It is not absolutely certain that Thothmes I was a son of Amenhotep I; he may have been a nephew or other close relative. The decisive battle near Memphis between Amose and the Hyksos is not historical. But there must have been a decisive battle, and it is unlikely that it took place farther into the delta than the old capital.*

Particular uncertainty attends the dating of the fall of the civilization of the Indus valley. Its fall is an undoubted fact, and the unburied skeletons found lying in the streets and the well chambers of Mohenjo-daro bear mute witness to its violence and to the fact that the city was not later reoccupied. It is now generally believed that the destroyers of the civilization were the Aryans, and that it is that destruction which is recounted in the poems of the Rigveda. *And these events can hardly have occurred earlier than 1800 or later than 1500 B.C. A date round about*

1550 B.C. is perhaps—on present, very slight evidence—to be preferred. The civilization is well described by Sir Mortimer Wheeler in The Indus Civilization. *The evidence for its date, and for the date of its fall, is—such as it is—admirably set out in D. H. G. Gordon's* The Prehistoric Background of Indian Culture.

13

THE AMBER ROUTE

1510–1440 B.C.

IN THE SUMMER the sun set almost due north, behind the headland. And the flaming gold and pearl pink of its setting moved slowly along the northern sky, with the pine forests on the hill crests sharp and black against the glow, until after at most three hours the light strengthened again and the sun rose again, a little east of north. It was never night, and the sun shone sixteen hours a day, and the grass and corn sprouted thick and green, and you could almost see the beanstalks growing. All living things reveled in the light and warmth after the snowbound winter and the cold wet spring.

The lads of the village spent most of their time in or around the water. They climbed over the rocks, dived into the pools, prospected high-level routes along the cliff faces, and paddled out on all manner of floats and logs and lashed-up contraptions of timber into the open waters of the Skagerak.

They said that they were working, and indeed they brought in a variegated and not unwelcome harvest from their expeditions. Gulls' eggs from the skerries and guillemot eggs from the cliffs alternated with crabs and mussels from the rocks and mullet and groupers from their fishing trips into the deep waters. Their parents looked indulgently on these jaunts and, remembering their own childhood, only when very hard pressed insisted on an occasional day's work in the fields.

The village lay in a fold of the grey granite hills, beside a broad inlet of the sea, on the coast near where now the border between Norway and Sweden runs down to the waters of the

Skagerak. The houses were low, of earth and stone, and the turf of their roofs caused them to blend with the grass of the meadows around. Only the manor farm, a collection of buildings in stone and timber a little way apart, stood out in the landscape at any distance.

Around the village and up the valley stretched the cleared pastures and the tiny cornfields, fenced in to keep the sheep and cattle from the young shoots. And beyond the fence lay the forest, broken by the crags and scree slopes which patterned the green of the trees with the grey of stone.

The fields, too, were far from level, running up the hillsides on either side of every stream, with everywhere outcrops of granite breaking the turf, huge boulders or steep slabs of living rock.

Along the shoreline lay the long low stone shelters, sometimes roofed with turf, into which the boats were drawn in the winter. But now the boats lay along the shore, except on the days when the wind and sea were right for fishing. Then the men would leave their fields to look after themselves, and take their boxes of mussel bait and their sinew lines and bronze fishhooks, and row out to the fishing grounds. For the village lived more from the sea than from the land, as the strings of fish hanging to dry in the wind and sun along every house gable gave evidence, both to the eye and to the nose.

The boats were seaworthy craft, clinker-built with overlapping planks sewn together with tight-twisted withes and caulked with cow hair and oakum. They were pointed, stem and stern, the bow and stern posts rising to a man's height and not infrequently elaborately carved. And it was a fine sight when they set out on a calm morning, with up to ten men at the oars and the steersman standing by the starboard steering oar, gazing at the lord of life, the sun, as he scattered the ritual grain upon the waters. And the morning chant would still reach the ears of the children along the shore, even when the boats were hull down to westward.

The children imitated the ritual faithfully whenever they launched their rafts and driftwood vessels, sacrificing a little of the barley bread that they had begged from the womenfolk

and casting it upon the waters with hand upraised to the sun-
god. And a favorite game was to act out the actual daily
journey of the god, galloping with the imaginary horses and
chariot of the day along the northern shore of the inlet as far as
the spit of sand, where they would be met by a raft representing
the boat of the night and paddled back to their starting point,
where the whole journey could begin again.

Their lives were governed by the weather-gods, as were
those of their elders. Even in summer the rain could sheet in
across the open sea and the mists scud low over the hills. The
god of the sea could wield his trident and send the waves thun-
dering against the cliffs, or the lord of the lightning hammer with
his double ax against the towering anvil-shaped thunderheads.
But in summer the mighty lord of the sun always won in the end,
riding his flaming chariot in triumph round the sky.

It was the four yearly festivals of the sun that were the high-
lights of the children's year, and on any day the height of the sun
at noon could provoke endless arguments and reckonings of just
how long it was to the next. Every festival was so different, and
yet each in its way was a message of hope and a time of good
cheer.

The most solemn was the seedtime ceremony, when the day
and the night were equal. Then the wooden image of the sun
chariot drawn by the horses of the dawn was taken out of the
temple and, mounted upon the creaking ox wagon, was drawn
from field to field, with the priest and his acolytes, wreathed with
new-sprung birch leaves, chanting the litanies, and the garlanded men and women following behind. And after the sacrifices came the ritual plowing. There the earl of the manor stood
for the king, and he harnessed one of his horses, the only horses
in the valley, to the wooden plow that otherwise only was
drawn by oxen, and, naked as the day he was born, plowed
the ritual three furrows in the temple field. He used a branch
in new-sprung leaf to urge the horse in its unaccustomed task,
and turned the furrows, of course, in the direction of the sun. And
in the furrows, along with the seed, were sown the crumbs of a
piece of yule cake, made from last year's harvest and kept all
winter in the corn bin.

The midsummer festival was more fun, though, when the bonfires were lit on every headland and along the shores, and the dancing went on all night long around the garlanded pole, and even the youngest boys regaled themselves on the cakes and ale until they could hardly stand. The night was scarcely long enough for the merrymaking (and love-making), and all too soon the sun-god arose in glory to give the signal for the sacrifice of the chosen beasts.

SOME OF THE ROCK CARVINGS OF SOUTH NORWAY AND SWEDEN ARE NOT EASY TO INTERPRET. IT IS POSSIBLE THAT THIS ONE REPRESENTS A MAYPOLE, WHICH TO THIS DAY IS A CENTRAL FEATURE OF SWEDISH MIDSUMMER-DAY FESTIVITIES.

The sacrifices were greatest, of course, at the harvest festival, held when the day and the night once more were equal and winter stood at the doors. For that was the time of the slaughtering of cattle and sheep and pigs for the winter larder. At that time the offering tables outside the temple grove were laden with acknowledgments to the sun-god who had given the harvest. There would be fish and meat and sausages and piles of grain and apples, dishes of nuts and berries, cheeses and bowls of milk. And after the god and his priests had taken their share, there would be the communal feast, a feast to be remembered long into the lean days of winter.

But best of all, the children loved yuletide, the midwinter day when the chariot of the sun once more began its climb up the sky and the night-time voyage of the sun beneath the earth from west to east began once more to shorten. Then the snow lay thick over the valley, and the cold bit harsh in the lungs, and the festival was celebrated inside the snug-built houses. But the tallow lamps and the central hearth burnt brightly on that day, and the cattle in the byre beyond the thin partition smelt warm and comfortable. Everyone, including the gods and the cattle, fed well on that day, with thick rich-smelling stews of dried meat and barley, with wheaten cakes, and with apples bobbing in the mulled ale. And the muffled priests drew the sun chariot on a sledge through the village, stopping at each house to chant their age-old songs of hope renewed, and to receive the gifts to the god in thanksgiving for the token that even the longest winter would have an end.

Punctuated by the festivals, the years took their course, and the boys grew older and began to talk about what they would do when they were grown men. Their talk was always of adventure far afield, and the timid ones who proposed staying to till their fathers' lands and to fish were laughed to scorn. Among the more daring, two ambitions were alternately in favor, to sign on in the ships for foreign parts, or to take service with the king and win renown on the field of battle. The popularity of either course depended much on recent events.

Most years the king visited the valley in his summer progress from his hall in the north. The first intimation would be the mounted messenger, always a young man in resplendent scarlet homespun cloak. The boys would feast their eyes on his rich bronze ornaments, the double spiral of his cloak clasp and the massive rings around his throat and wrists, and above all the sword at his side, while the older men would admire his sure horsemanship and recall the time when horses were regarded as too mettlesome to ride and suited only for the drawing of char-

iots. The earl would drive out to meet his lord at the head of the
valley, at the border of his demesne, and shortly afterward the
cortege would be seen winding down the rough road. It was a
magnificent spectacle, with the chariots, and the horse palanquins of the queen and her ladies, and the outriders, and the
spearmen and swordsmen on foot. Pennons flew, and everywhere
was the flash of bronze and of gold. Every year there seemed
to be more bronze accoutrements among the followers of the
king, bronze swords and even bronze helmets and bucklers. The
men of the village, while not aspiring to the splendors of the

THE PROBLEM OF REPRESENTING TEAMS OF ANIMALS DRAWING VE-
HICLES WAS TACKLED DIFFERENTLY BY THE SWEDISH ROCK CARVERS
AND BY THE ARTISTS OF THE NEAR EAST (SEE PAGE 13). AND THE
LIGHT TWO-HORSE CHARIOT WITH SPOKED WHEELS IS A VERY DIF-
FERENT THING FROM THE HEAVY SUMERIAN ASS CHARIOT OF SEVEN
HUNDRED YEARS BEFORE.

court, began to feel a little ashamed of the slim flint daggers of
which they had once been proud. Their wives, who without exception had succeeded in attending the banquet at the manor,
either as guests at the lower tables or as serving-women in the
kitchen, returned with tales of the bronze beltplates worn by the
queen and her retinue of ladies, and spoke pointedly of the arrival of the next ship and of the good prices paid—in bronze—
for amber jewelry.

When the king departed it was not unusual for one or two
of the older youths to leave with him, recruited into the service

of one of the nobles or chosen to wait upon the king himself. But it was when the ships came in that the largest numbers of youths left the village.

Ships were not infrequent. Perhaps three or four times a year a galley would enter the fjord and beach below the boathouses. Most often they were local ships, belonging to masters up and down the coast and sailing on the shorter routes, up the Baltic or down to Denmark or north along the Norwegian shores. But occasionally they were foreign craft, captained by dark-haired thickset masters of outlandish speech, from England or Spain or even farther afield. Their crews were a mixed bunch, speaking half the languages of Europe and even the Berber tongue of north Africa. But always there would be many of their own people, and more often than not there would be joyful reunions, when men who had left the village several years before reappeared, to unpack their sea chests and display the wealth they had gathered by astute bargaining in foreign marts.

While the ship lay on the beach, all work by sea and land stopped, and the whole population of the valley crowded to the market on the open land between the village and the shore. There were wonderful things to be seen there, rolls of cloth in colors which the local dyes could never produce, trinkets of jet and mother-of-pearl, blocks of flint of just the right size for axes or daggers, and, over and above all else, ingots and finished objects of bronze, or even of gold or tin. And the merchant captains knew what they wanted for their wares. Provisions for the ship, corn and dried meat and beer, they had to have, but that they paid little for. Furs paid better, and for a good foxskin you could even get a bronze pin. But for bronze in quantity you had to pay amber in quantity, and that everyone knew. Shrewd bargaining went on in the market and behind closed doors in the manor house for the lumps of raw amber which had been gleaned from the beaches after every winter storm, or for the ropes of amber beads which were the family heirlooms of the women, but which now were to be sold for the modern jewelry of the new metal.

When the ship put out again, there was little amber left in the village, but much display of new bronze weapons and tools

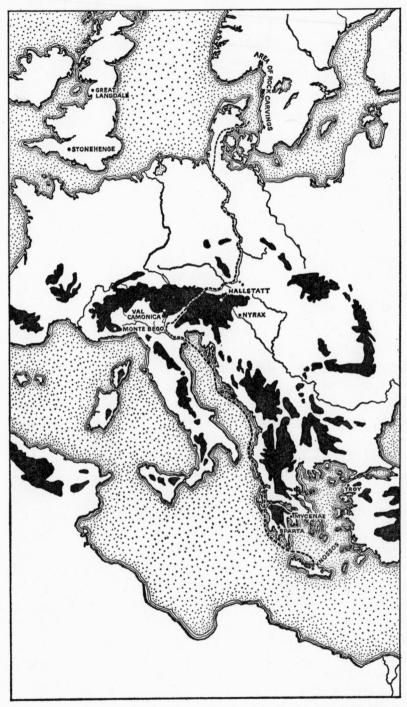

THE AMBER ROUTE ACROSS EUROPE (DOTTED LINE), AND A
NUMBER OF IMPORTANT CENTRAL EUROPEAN ARCHAEOLOGICAL
SITES.

and ornaments. The bronzesmith from the royal palace, the only smith within a week's journey—and a foreigner to boot—found it worth his while to come and stay a week or so in the valley, casting and hammering all day long, fashioning ornaments and swords which he swore were identical with those now being worn at the court.

And as usual four or five of the younger fishermen had signed on for a voyage with the departed merchantman. For such ships were always eager to engage the experienced seafolk of the northern coasts.

It was some years later, when the young men of the 1510 B.C. generation were in their late teens, that a new thing occurred in the valley. It was after a royal progress, when the king had talked long with his earl, that the lord of the valley called the experienced boatbuilders of his people together and gave his orders. The valley was to build and equip its own ship.

For a whole year the project dominated the valley. Fishing and farming were neglected, which mattered less than might have been expected, since the king—who had an interest in the venture—sent corn and meat for the workers by boat from the north. An overseer and two shipwrights also came from the court, though the boatbuilders of the village protested immediately that they could build a ship without the help of these foreigners. And certainly the ship was only a larger version of the boats that they had built for generations, with the same clinker construction and the same high bow and stern. But it was built for thirty oarsmen, instead of six or eight or ten, and it was broader in the beam, to give living space aboard and to accommodate the cargo. Much timber went into the vessel, pine and oak and ash, and willow withes to stitch the planks together. By the beginning of winter the hull was finished, and the following spring it was launched with all the appropriate sacrifices to the sea-god, and its thwarts and poop deck and oars added. There was even some talk of stepping a mast; the shipwrights claimed to know the art of setting sails to a ship, but it was felt that such an innovation would be beyond the powers of an inexperienced crew to control.

During all this time no visiting ship had been able to recruit a single sailor from the village. For all the young men, and many of the older ones, had determined to sail with their own vessel. Nor had trade been good for the visitors; the greater part of two years' gleanings of amber would sail aboard the new vessel, entrusted to members of the crew for private trade, or to the captain. He was already selected, a middle-aged houseowner who had sailed for nearly twenty years with foreign vessels and who claimed to know the sea lanes as far as Gibraltar and all the northern European rivers.

MOST OF THE SWEDISH SHIP CARVINGS ARE TOO CONVENTIONALIZED FOR US TO BE ABLE TO OBTAIN MUCH IDEA OF THEIR STRUCTURE. THIS IS ONE OF THE FEW THAT GIVES GREATER DETAIL. THE CLEARLY HUMAN FIGURES WIELDING PADDLES (OR BRANDISHING SWORDS AND AXES?) SUGGEST THAT THE ROWS OF UPRIGHT "POSTS" NORMALLY SHOWN ON THE DECKS OF ROCK-CARVED SHIPS (SEE PAGE 157) MAY BE CONVENTIONALIZED ROWERS OR OARS. THERE APPEARS HERE TO BE A DECKHOUSE TOWARDS THE STERN; THE "TREE" ABOVE THE CENTER OF THE VESSEL IS ONE OF THE VERY FEW HINTS THAT THE SWEDES MAY HAVE UNDERSTOOD THE USE OF MAST AND SAIL.

In the days before the ship sailed, the final preparations were duly interspersed with religious ceremonies, both private and public. The sacrifices to the sea-god rivaled in quantity those normally offered to the sun, while the other gods of wind and weather were not forgotten. And on the rock outcrops in the fields a wealth of new carvings appeared, hammered out by the men who were to form the crew, as a reminder to gods and men of the venture on which they were to engage.

It had long been the custom for the pious to carve pictures on the rocks. Often at the sun festivals a propitious rock surface, one which faced southward and was close to running water, would be adorned with a carving of some phase of the ceremony, the ritual plowing or the chariot of the sun or the night boat of the sleeping sun-god. Or the ax of the thunder-god would be portrayed, or more mundane subjects, horsemen or warriors or oxen or the beasts of the chase. It was known that these pictures called down the favor of the gods, bringing fortune to the portrayer or the person portrayed, bringing increase to the herds or luck in the hunt. But now everywhere appeared carvings of the ship, some but roughly chiseled, others detailed and accurate representations, all according to the skill of the artist and the time at his disposal. Surely with so many carvings the gods could not be unmindful of the vessel and the necessity of working actively for the success of its voyage.

With the sailing of the ship more than a score of the young men from this obscure little village on the Swedish coast—men who had been born around the time when Thothmes II of Egypt was, unknown to them and their people, waging victorious war in the Sudan—joined the growing company of the deep-sea sailors of the world. It was a cosmopolitan company, as it had always been, and its range was the whole known world and a good distance into the unknown. Ships sailed wherever there was trade to be done and cargoes to be acquired, and the sailors were not particular about where they hired, preferring a well-found ship and a "lucky" captain of whatever nationality. They changed ship at any convenient port, lugging their sea chest and their bedding roll with them and making themselves understood to their new shipmates in the bastard Cretan which was the lingua franca of the sea.

Scandinavians had been sailors for generations. They had fished from the coasts since before sun-worship, and the horsemen from the east who had brought it had come to their country hundreds of years ago. The young men had heard their grandfathers tell that in their day skin boats were still to be seen on the coast and men who were old then had recalled how they had crossed and recrossed the North Sea in them, to the coast of England and back. But the skin boats had gone out of use when the adzes of imported flint had made it possible to fashion planks and massive keelsons for wooden fishing boats. And now with the modern bronze tools a new era of shipbuilding had opened for Scandinavia, and the sailors need no longer take service in foreign vessels as they had done for so long as memory went back.

Where there are sailors and cargoes, said the old hands sagely, there will be ships. And sure enough from all the fjords of Scandinavia vessels were now taking to water, and already more than half the trade goods of the northern waters were carried in Scandinavian bottoms. And trade was clearly booming, and the shippers from the Swedish and Danish and Norwegian coasts were looking beyond the North Sea and the Baltic and the northern rivers.

For the first few seasons the ship kept to known waters and to short hauls. Its first voyage, admittedly, went to south England, where there was a good market for the collected store of amber. There the Wessex Downlands were ruled by proudly independent chieftains, rich in flocks and herds, magnificently armed and accoutred in their abundant native bronze, and adorned with massive throatbands of Irish gold. They were not too proud to trade, though, for trading was in their blood from distant southern ancestors, and here, where amber was scarce and bronze abundant, the Swedes were delighted to find that prices were much more favorable than on the beaches of their native land. The ship returned with a cargo of bronze and wool which almost paid, in one voyage, the cost of building the ship. But several of the crew did not return with the ship, lured instead by a short-handed Breton skipper bound for Spain.

For two or three years thereafter the ship stuck to the coastal trade, carrying flint from Denmark to Norway, and corn and hides and woolen goods and furs from port to port along the Scandinavian coast. They made one voyage up the Elbe to the limit of navigation in central Germany. Their object again was bronze, for in Germany there were now plentiful supplies, produced from the mines in Austria and the Carpathians. There they found a people who, though they worshipped recognizably the same gods and spoke a language that could with difficulty be understood, had a very different and luxurious way of life. Large timber-built towns surrounded by wide acres of grazing ground boasted booths and workshops where professional craftsmen produced intricate metalwork such as brooches and flanged axes and slim rapiers. And luxury articles brought over the mountains from the south could be bought in the permanent market places. For sale was burnished and even painted pottery, containing fabulous things like olive oil and wine, as well as jewelry of mother-of-pearl and of faïence and of gold.

It was here that the crew first heard precise details of the rich cargoes to be obtained in the Mediterranean coastlands, and while some adventurous spirits took the direct route thither, joining the portage gangs carrying goods by land to the Danube and the Adriatic, the rest returned home with the idea of sailing to the Mediterranean firmly planted in their minds.

They set off the following year, with a full cargo of furs and amber, on the long route round the western coasts, and it was many years before the ship was to be seen again in its home waters. The voyage was made with all speed, to save useless expenditure on provisioning, and only brief halts were made to engage pilots with a sailing knowledge of the next stretch of coast. Across the Bay of Biscay and along the Portuguese coast they had to strain to their oars against the awe-inspiring rollers of the Atlantic, but these they left behind on the great day when they passed the headland of Gibraltar and knew that they had entered the inland sea. They began to trade in a small way with the coastal towns of south Spain, where the inhabitants still built the stone graves which had gone out of fashion generations ago in the north. But the main cargo remained untouched, only a few bales of furs being exchanged for ingots of silver. (And two of the young men missed ship through drinking excessively of the Spanish wine in a dockside tavern.)

The voyage went on, past the Balearics, through the straits of Messina and round the headlands of Greece. And before winter came, the ship ran its prow ashore on the beach of Knossos in Crete.

Crete had been their destination from the start. For even

in the north it was well known that Knossos was the market place of the world, the home of the greatest merchant fleet on earth, the city where fortunes could be made and lost—and a holy city to boot. The Swedish sailors looked with awe at the white stone-built city rising tier on tier between the blue of the sea and the blue of the sky, and at the multitude of lateen-rigged ships crowding the fairway and beached along the shore.

But they caused some sensation themselves, for Swedish ships were not common at that time in the eastern Mediterranean. Swedish sailors were much more common, though, and there was a tavern near the shore kept by a retired Swedish bosun whose fame had reached the north. He was their first calling place on arrival, and he gave them much useful information about the land to which they had come.

There would be customs dues to pay on their cargo, he said. For the king in the palace three miles up country (he called him Minos) kept a sharp watch on the arrival of foreign ships, and his officers were probably already picketing the beached vessel. But once the tithes were paid, marketing was free, and the merchants would give good prices for luxury items from the north. Though if they would take his advice, he said, they would go easy on their sales, and reserve a good portion of their cargo for Egypt. For Egypt had grown wealthy under its present dynasty, and now under its female pharaoh was importing luxuries as never before.

Yes, it was true, he said, Egypt had a female pharaoh now, believe it or not. Of course, women had always had a lot to say in Egypt, and particularly the queens of the present dynasty had been a fine bunch of administrators (and good-lookers as well). But Hatshepsut was the most determined of them all. Ever since she was made joint ruler with her father thirty years ago (that was in 1518 B.C.) she had been the real ruler of the country. When the first Thothmes died, Hatshepsut's husband, also called Thothmes, had been the official successor, but he had been a weakling, plagued by ill health, and had not even been able to lead his troops in person when they conquered Nubia. He had died in his early thirties, some fourteen years ago, and had left no royal son to succeed him. He had a daughter, though, by Hatshepsut, and he had married her to his son by a slave-girl, still another Thothmes. So Thothmes III should have succeeded his father by reason of his wife's title. But Hatshepsut wasn't the woman to retire in favor of her stepson, who was only seventeen at that time anyway. She imprisoned the youngster in the palace, where he presumably still was, and, as cool as you please, proclaimed herself, not as queen, but as king! Why, she even wore a false beard when she appeared officially, and used all the masculine titles. And now she had reigned for fourteen years, and her renowned beauty was fading; but Egypt had prospered as never before, and that was the place to take a cargo if you had a cargo to sell.

The advice was taken. After three weeks in Knossos the ship sailed, with nearly half its original cargo and with a Cretan pilot, towards the southeast.

But these three weeks were a period of wonder for the crew. The stone buildings were no less amazing on closer inspection, with their frescoes of garden scenes and of fishing and dancing scenes, of acrobats and the sacred bull-baiting. Donkeys they had already seen in the Spanish ports, but here they were more numerous and did most of the portering within the city. But particularly the degree of nakedness practiced by the natives shocked—and delighted—the crew. That the men only wore a breechclout was reasonable enough in the warm sunshine that they scarcely recognized as winter. But the bared breasts of the women contrasted oddly and excitingly with their long flounced skirts—a direct reversal of the fashions among their own sisters back home, who wore decent high-necked blouses, but whose corded skirts scarcely went halfway to the knee.

They made good trade at Avaris, on the delta of the Nile, and were almost too sated with new impressions to do more than note idly the flat-topped houses of mud brick, the palm trees and papyrus rushes and the endless miles of cultivation. But the sight of Negroes in the streets aroused their comment. They had only heard of black people before, and never seen them. They were for the most part slaves, from the Nubian campaigns, and rarely had the chance to sign onto the crews of the Mediterranean ships.

By the beginning of summer—after a charter trip to Byblos
on the Lebanese coast to fetch cedar for Hatshepsut's new palace—the ship was ready to start the long voyage home with a
full cargo of manufactured goods, mainly of bronze, and with a
mast and sail new-fitted in the Lebanese shipyards. Less than
half of the original crew set off on the return voyage with her.
The young men in particular had been infected with the delights
of city life and the chances of making a quick fortune by sailing
between the centers of the civilized world. In Knossos and in
Egypt and in Byblos they had drifted off in twos and threes to
other ships, with vague promises that they would sail north again
on the next voyage. And the ship signed on in their place a few
Scandinavian sailors who felt homesickness after years in the
Mediterranean, and a number of young Cretans and Egyptians
and mainland Greeks anxious to explore the possibilities of direct sea trade with northern Europe.

In the years that followed it became impossible to keep track
of the men from the Swedish coast as they scattered over the sea
routes of the world. Occasionally two of them would meet at an
obscure port and exchange reminiscences over their wine. Some
of them were sailing the route between Crete and Sicily, and occasionally on to Spain. Others were on the cargo haul up and
down the Adriatic, carrying to Crete and Egypt the goods coming down to the neighborhood of Trieste by the river routes
across Europe; and among the cargoes they carried was a great
deal of amber which may well have been originally collected on
their own native beaches back in Sweden. Others sailed up to
Troy and beyond into the Black Sea. Perhaps the greatest number were in the coastal trade between Egypt and the Levant,
or the short route between Egypt and Crete. But a few could
tell of longer voyages, up the Danube into central Europe, or up
the other Black Sea rivers farther east; or down the Red Sea to
Punt, on the incense route to the Hadramaut and the ivory route
to the bushmen of east Africa. They told of trips to England to
fetch tin, and other voyages even farther out into the Atlantic.
One had sailed southwest from the Straits of Gibraltar, on one of
the infrequent trips to the Canaries, and he had strange stories
to tell. There were rumors in that part of the world, he said, that

farther westward there were other islands and even a great land
mass. Not long ago three ships had set out to find those lands,
on a prospecting trip financed in the hope of finding a new market for bronze across the Atlantic. But the ships had never returned, and no one knew whether they had reached their destination (it would be a rash man who, today, would claim to
know).

In 1480 B.C. there was a sort of reunion to celebrate the tenth
anniversary of the sailing from Sweden, though only six of the
original crew, who happened to be in Knossos at the time, managed to get together. They were now in their late twenties and
early thirties, broad-shouldered blond-bearded men, experienced
seamen—except for the odd man who had married a Cretan wife
up country and was contentedly growing olives and vines on the
terraced farm he had inherited with the girl. They all talked Cretan now by preference, and their own language sounded foreign
in their ears.

They were in the main prosperous men, with money invested
ashore or with part interests in the boats they sailed and the cargoes they carried. But that was not unusual. There was money
in sailing and in trade these days, they all agreed. For the past
twenty years and more there had been no major wars, and trade
had flourished as never before by land and sea. As the seamen
sat at their table under the vines in the warm summer evening,
looking out over the busy harbor and the blue sail-dotted waters, they felt the subconscious satisfaction of being at the hub
of the universe, at the center of an expanding economy, where
from year to year more primary products and more manufactured goods were being produced, and more of both were being
carried by an ever-increasing tonnage of trading vessels. Over
the whole world standards of living were rising, and no recession
was in sight.

To the north and west there was no frontier any more, and
those of the sailors who plied the Adriatic route, up to Trieste and
the mouth of the Po (where later Venice was to stand) could relate news of their distant Scandinavian homeland which was
scarcely more than a year out of date. Europe was no longer a

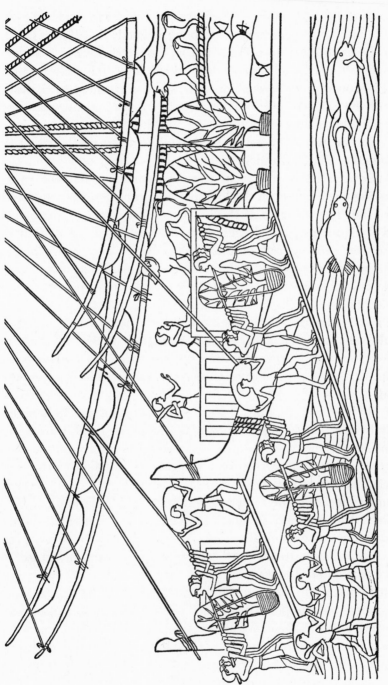

IN QUEEN HATSHEPSUT'S GREAT TEMPLE AT DEIR AL-BAHRI IS A RE-LIEF, A PORTION OF WHICH IS COPIED HERE, SHOWING EGYPTIAN SHIPS LYING OFF THE COAST OF PUNT AND LOADING MERCHANDISE, INCLUDING TREES FOR THE QUEEN'S GARDENS. THE BABOONS ARE PROBABLY NOT CARGO, BUT MERELY AN OCCUPATIONAL HAZARD OF THE PUNT TRADE.

land of stone-using cultivators scratching the soil for a bare livelihood, with no surplus to spare to buy the goods that the civilized
world was so eager to sell. Now it was an intricate jigsaw of independent and semi-independent kingdoms, with rich princes
and a growing middle class of traders and craftsmen. In the valley of the Salzach and in Transylvania copper and tin were being mined and alloyed into bronze; and the bronze crafts of central Europe were competing successfully in the north with the
products of England and Spain.

Down all the valleys of the Alps came regular caravans,
bringing trade goods on the long portage from the headwaters of
the Elbe. The villagers of the independent cantons of the Swiss
and Italian Alps, though they had little natural wealth of their
own, were growing rich on this carrying trade, even as the Scandinavians were growing rich on the sea hauls. There was not a
little resemblance in custom between the Alpine peoples with
their pile-built villages beside their lakes, and the Swedes in
their sod villages beside the fjords. And the Swedish captains
could tell of high valleys in the Alps, such as Val Camonica,
where the laden caravans passed rocks covered with carvings in
quite as rich a profusion as those of their Scandinavian homeland.

By land and sea Europe was being bound into a single economy by the merchantmen putting out from the coastal towns of
Scandinavia and England and Ireland and Brittany and Spain,
by the deeply laden river boats moving slowly along the great
navigable inland waterways, and by the slowly plodding ox
teams connecting the water routes. In the Mediterranean there
were Cretan emporia on most of the islands and along the coasts
from Spain to the Black Sea.

Immediately to the north of Crete, in the islands and inlets
of Greece and of the west coast of Asia Minor, many Cretan merchant houses had branches and representatives at the courts of
the numerous independent princes. The Swedish seamen had often sailed in the Aegean waters, which reminded them in many
ways of their own native fjords. They felt a kinship, too, with the
Achaean princes of Greece and Asia Minor, whose way of life
and traditions and religion and even language still bore out the

legends of a common origin hundreds of years ago with the sun-worshipping settlers of Scandinavia. And for all that the Achaeans had adopted much of the Cretan civilization, they had still not forgotten their warlike traditions. The massive citadels of the princes frowned down upon the Cretan merchant ships in the harbors, and their privateers were a constant menace to honest traders. Minos of Knossos was forced to keep a task force of warships almost constantly in Greek waters, and punitive expeditions were frequently necessary to keep the Achaean princes properly subservient.

To the northeast, beyond the coastal settlements of the Achaeans in Asia Minor, relations were friendly with the great kingdom of Arzawa and the small but rich land of Troy at the entrance to the Dardanelles.

In the interior of Asia Minor lay the kingdom of the Hittites. By their neighbors they were regarded as potentially dangerous, though more because of the tradition of their explosive conquests of over a century ago than by reason of any present activity. After a period of anarchy they had again been united into a strong kingdom some thirty years before, by king Telepinus. The Cretan merchants had little to do with the landlocked Hittites directly. Their contacts were closer with their southern neighbors and allies, the kingdom of Kizzuwatna, which held the coast north of Cyprus as far as the frontier with Yamkhad.

In the capital of Yamkhad, Aleppo, and its main port of Ugarit the sailors from Crete met the caravans from the east, as they had done for hundreds of years. The great Euphrates trade route was at peace. Beyond Yamkhad lay the strong kingdom of Mitanni, the southernmost of a confederacy of Hurrian states which stretched north almost to the Black Sea and the Caucasus. And beyond Mitanni, on the headwaters of the Tigris, was the Semitic kingdom of Assyria, sandwiched between the Indo-Europeans of Mitanni and the Indo-European chieftains of the Kassites in the Persian mountains and on the middle waters of the Euphrates and Tigris. And beyond the Kassites, from Babylon to the Persian Gulf, lay the Semitic-ruled country of Babylonia. For a hundred years, since the Hittite raid under Mursilis had sacked Babylon and put an end to the dynasty of Hammurabi, there had been peace between the Upper and the Lower Sea. It was a peace of convenience rather than of friendship, for more would be lost by an interruption of the trade routes than would be gained in booty by a costly war between closely matched powers. And lately, too, it had been clear that any strife between the four powers who shared Mesopotamia would only open the way for the greatest power of all, Egypt.

To the merchant sailors sitting over their wine in Crete—as to the soldiers of Babylon and Mitanni—Egypt was the arbiter of destinies. It was at once the greatest market, the greatest manufacturing country, and the greatest military power in the world. Only at sea was it inferior to Crete. In the hundred years since Amose had led the revolt against the Hyksos overlords, Egypt had steadily extended its wealth and influence under his brilliant descendants. Amose's grandson had set up his boundary stones at the fourth cataract of the Nile and on the Euphrates, and now his great-granddaughter had ruled for twenty-two years, alone— and many thought illegally and impiously. Amon and his priests had originally proclaimed her stepson and son-in-law Thothmes III as pharaoh, but the god had apparently changed his mind, for the high priest of Amon sat as vizier in upper Egypt, and Thothmes sat captive in the palace, as he had done for half his life. While Hatshepsut reigned, there was peace. The people of Egypt might very well be fooled by a false beard, it was commonly said, but the army of Egypt would not allow itself to be led to battle by a woman; and the army could not, by custom, move without a prince of the blood royal at its head.

Now the bluff of the "pharaohess" had been called. The main topic of discussion in the Knossos tavern this evening in 1480 B.C. was the recent declaration of independence by some of the cities of Palestine and Syria, cities which since the time of the first Thothmes, Hatshepsut's father, had been vassals of Egypt. If Egypt let this defiance pass, then the passive presence of the powerful Egyptian army, whose mere existence had kept the peace for so long, would be known for a hollow sham, and half the world might be at the throats of the other half tomorrow.

It was said that Hatshepsut had ordered her army out, and that the prisoner of the palace, her weakling stepson, had been

sent to lead it. There was much speculation as what would be
the outcome and how it would affect the Levant trade.

Before the year was out, they knew the outcome. Hatshepsut
was dead, and the prisoner of the palace sat upon her throne.
Thothmes had merely been biding his time, and with an army at
his back had proved a very different opponent from the weakling
who for twenty-two years had never left the palace grounds. He
had given orders that all mention of his stepmother was to be
erased from the records, and that his reign was to be reckoned
from his first proclamation twenty-two years before. Hatshepsut
was to be expunged from history.

During the next twenty years the Swedish sailors working
out of Knossos, and many another Cretan crew as well, saw much
of Thothmes III and his army. During these years the Egyptian
king made sixteen campaigns in Palestine and Syria. After the
first, in which he defeated a confederate Syrian army at Megiddo in Palestine and reconquered the coastal cities, he used
these cities as supply bases for his later campaigns farther to the
north and east. It was a profitable charter service for the Cretan
and Levantine coastal vessels, building up the stores at Gaza
and Jaffa and Byblos, transporting grain and hides and bulk supplies of arrowheads and spearheads and shields, sandals and
tents and harness, all the items required by the quartermaster
general, who, as much as anyone, was responsible for the success
of the pharaoh's campaigns. Chariots and horses they did not
need to carry north, although these by now formed an important
arm of the Egyptian forces; for two thousand horses and nearly
a thousand chariots had been captured at the fall of Megiddo
during the first campaign.

Each summer the pharaoh drove northward with his army,
confirming the loyal princes in their cities, appointing new vassals in the place of rebel princes who had fled north, ravaging
the market gardens and cornlands of such cities as held out
against him, and, where practicable, besieging and storming the
cities themselves. He rarely met an army in the open field during
these years, but each year he advanced a little farther, and people were already likening him to his grandfather, the first
Thothmes.

On his eighth campaign, in 1472 B.C., he captured Cadesh, the important city (a little north of a little village called Damascus) of the rebel ringleader. But though there were no further rebels to subdue, his realm still fell short of that of his grandfather. For since Thothmes I sixty years before had penetrated to the Euphrates the Mitanni kings had crossed the river, and their frontier now marched with that of Cadesh well south of the Euphrates. They had given open support to the Syrian revolt and now gave refuge to the king of Cadesh.

But for twelve years Mitanni made no move, while Thothmes reorganized Syria, taking the sons of the princes as hostages for education in Egypt and appointing political observers to report to him any breach of the terms of vassalage. Then, in 1460 B.C., with Mitanni support, the king of Cadesh came south, regained his city, feverishly rebuilt the walls, and again called on Syria to revolt.

It was a forlorn hope. Thothmes, now an experienced general in his early sixties, swept north unresisted, and took and razed the city. In the following two summers he led his army into Mitanni territory.

The rumors that reached the sailors at the Syrian ports suggested that he met no large Mitanni army, and in truth Mitanni was not yet strong enough to challenge Egypt in open battle. But an order came through to the quartermaster general for small boats to be collected and transported over the mountains and the plains beyond, to carry the pharaoh and his chariots across the Euphrates. It caused some excitement on the coast, for it must mean that Thothmes had achieved his ambition, and had reached and surpassed the northern limits of his grandfather's campaign. But more excitement was caused by a circumstantial story of a hairbreadth escape of the pharaoh from a charging elephant during a hunt of these rare beasts in the Euphrates valley. But that was the only moment of danger. The Mitanni armies still failed to appear, and Thothmes contented himself with punitive destruction of crops, and with the erection of his own boundary stone beside that of his grandfather.

His reign had now lasted as long as that of his stepmother,

and he had completely lived down the tale of his years of captive idleness in Hatshepsut's palace.

These years had seen no diminution in the prosperity of the Mediterranean peoples, and even the Egyptian campaigns in Syria had rarely interfered with the free passage of trade. Rather the reverse, for the capture of the revolted cities brought much stored-up wealth into circulation, and gave at the same time a great impetus to the slave trade.

Ships plied the Mediterranean and the northern European waters in undiminished numbers, and the river routes across Europe carried ever larger quantities of bronze to the developing metal industries of the north. Enterprising traders even pushed deep into Russia and into central Africa, exchanging the Egyptian glass beads for ivory and furs.

The sailors who had spent their boyhood around 1500 B.C. in the village on the coast of Sweden were—such of them as still lived—scattered over the world. They belonged now to the older generation. They were over fifty, and most of them had made their fortunes. They were tiring of the sea, and those who had not found abiding homes and raised families elsewhere now began to think longingly of their homeland in the north. More and more of them began to make their way northward across and around Europe, with their caravans or ships loaded with the proceeds of a lifetime at sea converted to the ready currency of manufactured goods of bronze or gold.

One at least of them chanced to be present at the rebuilding of Stonehenge. Coasting along the Britanny coast, he heard rumors of a stone-freighting job farther north and, always on the lookout for a short haul to cover sailing costs, he followed the rumor, taking a number of Breton stonemasons, too, as passengers. The report proved ill-founded. When the first stone temple had been built on the holy site, two hundred years and more ago, the stones had indeed been brought by sea, across the Bristol Channel from south Wales. And it was this tradition which had inspired the rumors. But the new and enlarged temple now going up, while incorporating the Welsh stones, was otherwise to be built of the local sandstone blocks which lay scattered over the plain, only a few at such distance that a river haul was of any advantage in transport. Still, the sea captain, talking familiarly of the transport and raising of the obelisks of Hatshepsut and Thothmes III along the Nile, got himself and his polyglot crew engaged by the Breton engineers who had been commissioned to raise the new monument. For weeks they sweated on the long land haul of the stones, and used their familiarity with block and tackle to assist in the raising of mighty uprights and capstones. The actual shaping of the stones was done by Breton and local masons, who scientifically battered irregularities away with stone mauls and finished the surface with bronze chisels. Even here some of the crew could give a hand, for it was after all the same technique as was used in the Egyptian quarries, where several of the sailors had served not entirely voluntary terms. And a couple of the Greek seamen with stonemason experience were even allowed, on their own suggestion, to increase the religious potency of the monument by carving their own holy symbols, reliefs of their native daggers and axes, upon several of the stones.

The priestly colleges of half the principalities of the British Isles had combined to raise the new monument, with funds and workmen contributed by all the rich princes of the south. For Stonehenge was the most venerable of all the sites of solar worship, a place of pilgrimage for all England and much of northern Europe. The embankment and the rough monolith beyond its entrance, in line with the midsummer sunrise, had been raised over four hundred years before (they were as old as Hampton Court Palace is now), and the concentric stone circles within had stood for two hundred years or so, built by the beaker chieftains of the downland. The wealthy priests and princes of south England had now been talking for some years of building a more imposing temple, and many schemes had been put forward. There had even been a tentative reconstruction, and the original stones had been taken down and partly re-erected in a new pattern. Finally it had been agreed, on the advice of travelers who had seen the mighty pylons of the Egyptian monarchs, that new and larger stones should be used, and the old stones piously incorporated merely as an inner circle between a great outer ring

of continuously linteled uprights and an inner horseshoe of immense capped pylons. This monument was to stand for all time,
to the glory of the lord, the sun, and as witness to the might of
the British princes.

And indeed, when, on midsummer day in this year of the
middle of the fifteenth century B.C., the monument stood complete and consecrated, it was an imposing sight even to those
who had seen the great temple of Queen Hatshepsut at Deir
al-Bahri. Five times the height of a man rose the central trili-
thon, and on either side two further trilithons graded downward.

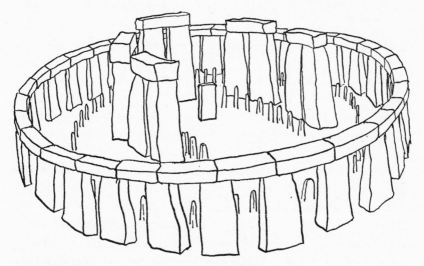

STONEHENGE, AS IT MUST HAVE APPEARED WHEN RECONSTRUCTED
AND ENLARGED BY THE WEALTHY BRONZE-AGE KINGS OF SOUTHERN
BRITAIN IN THE FIFTEENTH CENTURY B.C.

Around them ran the colonnade of the outer circle, framing with
its pillars the downs that rose on every side, downs dotted with
the burial mounds, new and old, of those who had desired—
and been able to afford—to be buried within sight of the great
sun temple.

It was no little thing to have assisted at the building of Stonehenge, as the old sea captain would tell his grandnephews in the
years to come. In the village on the Swedish fjord the retired
captains formed, in fact, an exclusive club (as they do in the
villages of Norway at this day). The village boys, who still

dreamt of their first voyage, and the young men resting between voyages would gather round at a respectful distance as the old men sat out by the boathouses on the long summer evenings, and listen to the wide-ranging reminiscences—of the mighty queen of Egypt, and of the chariots of Thothmes striking out into the Syrian desert, of the great pillars of Britanny and the dolmen tombs of Spain, of the white palaces of Knossos rising above the blue Mediterranean, and of the embattled stronghold of Troy, of the pirate nests of the Greek mainland and the fabulous amber route along the rivers and through the forests and mountains of central Europe. They had lived a rich life, these travelers of the middle of the millennium, and many were the pictures they carved on the rocks above the valley, as thank-offerings to the gods who had guided and protected them. And as the sun sloped slowly down for its brief rest behind the northern hills, the old men would wander up the valley to gaze once more on the picture book of the rocks, where forever the great fleets they had carved in their youth sailed onward over a calm sea of memory.

This chapter is fiction—as any account which attempts to show the cutters of the Scandinavian rock carvings as personalized individuals must be. But the background is authentic enough. Not merely were Europe and the Middle East as here portrayed in the middle years of the millennium, but they had in truth the trade connections here described—and we have the trade goods to prove it. Admittedly trade goods can pass through many hands, and the presence of Baltic amber in Crete or Egyptian faïence beads in England does not necessitate the presence of Scandinavians in Knossos or Egyptians in Wiltshire. But the tendency must always be towards a progressive elimination of middlemen; and in fact the archaeological evidence shows continuous contact between northern and western Europe and the Mediterranean since before 2000 B.C., the authenticated occurrences of trade goods rising to a statistical climax in the period 1500–1475 B.C. It is therefore no revolutionary hypothesis, but rather in agreement with the view of many distinguished archaeologists, to suggest that Swedish ships and sailors were not unknown in the Mediterranean at the period of this chapter.

The events of the reign of Hatshepsut and Thothmes III are authenticated, while the extent of Egyptian trade is evidenced by faïence beads found in England, Ireland, and Denmark, at Nakuru in Kenya, and on the upper Tobol river east of the Urals. (For more on this interesting trade see the article by J. F. S. Stone and L. C. Thomas in the Proceedings of the Prehistoric Society, 1956.) The rock carvings of the Italian Alpine region of Val Camonica are most recently described in Emmanuel Anati's Camonica Valley. The precise date of the building of the present Stonehenge is not known, but it must have been during or around this lifetime.

Let it be stated catagorically that there is no evidence whatever that ships from Europe or the Mediterranean ever reached America at this period. All that can be said is that Bronze-Age carvings on the Canaries show that they reached that far; that a thousand years later Carthaginian ships no larger than those of this period reached the Azores; that the set of wind and current, in the words of Professor Brøgger of Oslo (Opdagelsenes nye århundre, Oslo, 1936), "practically compels the discovery of Central America from Spanish and Portuguese harbors when once deep-sea sailing begins"; and that it would appear that the use of copper and gold commenced at or shortly after this period among the natives of central America and Peru. The discussion between those who favor theories of diffusion of culture and those who favor independent invention will doubtless continue, and no standpoint is here taken. It is reasonable to assume that there was no contact between Europe and America in the Bronze Age so long as there is no evidence that there was. But when the basic conditions for contact were present, it would be unscientific to reject the possibility completely.

14

THE FALL OF THE SEA KINGS

1440–1370 B.C.

W HILE OLD MEN in Sweden looked out over the waters of the Skagerak and remembered the Mediterranean, their sons and grandsons sailed and rowed galleys over the north Atlantic routes and frequently themselves ventured within the Straits of Gibraltar. They would often have messages, and cargo, for the families of former shipmates of their parents, now settled in the islands of the Aegean, the inlets of Greece, the crowded harbor cities of the Lebanese coast, and even at the port of Knossos itself.

The harbor town of Knossos, lying three miles north of the actual capital clustered around the palace, was full of all the races of the known world, and blond Northerners—or half-Northerners—excited no remark among the Egyptians and Amorites, Greeks and Hittites, Spaniards, Sicilians and Libyans, and the dark-skinned people who came from an unknown distance farther to the east or south. They were in fact normally taken for Greeks, for among the mainland Greeks blue eyes and blond or auburn hair were by no means uncommon. The rulers of Greece, after all, were a northern people, and even distantly related to the Scandinavians—or so they said.

There were always many Greeks in the harbor town, sailors and merchants and peddlers, porters and mercenaries and semi-official consular agents. The "real" Cretans of the inland city used to say that the harbor town was more Greek than Cretan, and complained that the Greek language, with its simple new script, was ousting Old Cretan entirely as a written medium among the businessmen, storekeepers, and tally clerks even in the capital itself.

Knossos proper was still predominantly Cretan in population. It lay an hour's walk up the valley from the coast, sited there, it was said, out of sight of the sea as a protection against pirates in the far-off days when Knossos had had no fleet to speak of, and was but a tiny principality among the many principalities of Crete. Now for almost three centuries the kings of Knossos had ruled all Crete, and received tribute—somewhat irregularly, it was true—from nominal vassals ruling most of the coastal towns from Sicily to Asia Minor. Knossos need no longer fear pirate attack.

It was predominantly the wealthier folk who lived in the city below the colonnaded palace. They were the shipowners, and the owners of vineyards and olive groves, the better-class craftsmen and the richer tradesmen. Fashionably dressed men and women moved leisurely through the paved streets, their dark hair and vivacious countenances set off by the brilliant colors of their costumes.

The men wore little more than a loincloth, belted at the waist and reaching halfway to the knee. It was a dress which went well with the long black hair and muscular bronzed bodies —though perhaps was scarcely so kind to the elderly and more prosperous of build. The women's costume, just as traditional as the men's, gave richer scope for variation of cut and color. From an impossibly narrow waist fell an ankle-length skirt, frilled or flounced or pleated to the heart's desire or the dictates of the latest leader of fashion. Above the waist the ladies went naked, save for a short-sleeved jacket fastened at the waist but opening above to reveal—or rather to display—the breasts. Hair styles were elaborate, and more subject to the whims of fashion than the clothes. And jewelry was worn in profusion by men and women. For here, at the center of the world's trade, the luxuries of three continents vied to demonstrate the wealth of their owners. Baltic amber and Yorkshire jet, set in Irish gold, gleamed against Nubian ivory and Dilmun pearls, carnelian from India and lapis lazuli from Afghanistan, and jade from the fabulous lands still farther east.

The children, even of the wealthy families, ran naked, except for an amulet, to give them the protection of the snake-goddess, the guardian of the caves.

It is the life story of these children, born in 1440 B.C., that we here shall follow.

It was a carefree childhood, in this sunny land among the

A RECONSTRUCTION (AFTER SIR ARTHUR EVANS, THE EXCAVATOR OF KNOSSOS) OF THE MARBLE-WALLED BATHROOM OF THE QUEEN IN THE PALACE AT KNOSSOS.

wealthy of the gods' own country. Many of the children admittedly went to school, particularly those destined for trade or the civil service. But there they learned nothing except to write the Old Cretan script (and, in the dangerously modern schools, the new script of the Greeks) and to recite interminable legends of the gods and heroes, tales of the birth of Zeus in the caves of Mount Ida, of the bull that had carried their forefathers to the island, of Daedalus who had built the rambling palace of Knossos for the first Minos. They were taught a little trade arithmetic, too; and those whose fathers were architects or surveyors were faced, in the upper grades, with problems of geometry and volumetry. But by then, of course, they were apprenticed, and were learning their trade, just like their contemporaries who were learning to distinguish and price precious stones, to calculate freights, or to make the simpler divinations from the livers of sacrificial animals.

There was nothing called history or geography in their school curriculum—there never had been in the age of the world, and it had never occurred to anyone that a knowledge of the present and past of the world should be taught in the schools.

But from listening to their parents, and to the many visitors from foreign parts who passed through Knossos, the children learned much of what was happening in the world outside.

Two countries in addition to their own were particularly vivid in their minds, Achaea to the north and Egypt to the south.

Achaea was not really a single country, but rather a conglomeration. It comprised the mainland of Greece, a collection of small states, where every city owned its fjord and its hinterland, and owed a sort of allegiance to the king in Mycenae and an even more nebulous allegiance to the Great King in Knossos. And it included the Aegean islands, and the settlements on the coast of Asia Minor, subject by racial ties to Mycenae but by proximity subject to the neighboring kingdom of Arzawa and in practice retaining complete independence of action by playing off the one against the other and the Hittites, the greatest power of Asia Minor, against both.

Egypt, on the other hand, was the power above powers, the greatest empire of all. The children learned at an early age the roll of the kings of Egypt, Amose the liberator, Amenhotep, Thothmes the conqueror of Syria, Thothmes the conqueror of Nubia, Hatshepsut the queen-pharaoh, Thothmes the Great, and now another Amenhotep. Feelings were mixed about Amenhotep II, the present king. In the first years of his reign, six or seven years before they were born, he had put down a rebellion in Syria with great severity, showing personal prowess and re-establishing in a single campaign the boundaries of his great father Thothmes. His expedition had swelled the slave market at Knossos, as it had swelled the slave markets throughout the Middle East, but not a few of the Cretan mercantile agents in the Levant had been swept into his all-too-widespread net and it had taken a while to re-establish trading connections. And then nine years later, in 1439 B.C., when the children were only a year old, Amenhotep had done the same again. Again he had had a rebellion in north Syria, up towards the Mitannian frontier, as an excuse, and again he had stripped the whole of Syria and Lebanon of everything of value, including manpower. The Cretan traders began to think it too much of a good thing, as they saw the market flooded with slaves and booty.

Since then Syria had not dared to lift a finger against Egypt, for all the diplomatic blandishments of the kings of Mitanni. Amenhotep's boundary stone stood undisturbed on the banks of the Euphrates beside those of his father and his great-grand-father, Thothmes III and Thothmes I. The three stones were a landmark to the caravans bearing the products of Mesopotamia and the east along the Euphrates route towards Aleppo, Ugarit —and Crete. But in recent years the merchants traveling along this route had had other worries besides that of making diplomatic gifts to sheikhs claiming to represent both Egypt and Mitanni. At either end of the route there was trouble. The Hurrians of Mitanni were pushing a pretender to the throne of Aleppo, which a score of years earlier had been conquered by the Hittites, as it had been once before in the reign of Mursilis the Great. And Babylon, great Babylon itself, which had also in its day fallen to Mursilis, had fallen again.

It was but rarely that Cretans traveled as far inland as Mesopotamia, and in their ears Babylon held all the mystery and glamor of the Orient. It was the queen of the east as Knossos was the queen of the west. It was the city of the almost legendary Hammurabi, and the capital of the oldest civilization on earth. Even Egypt, it was popularly believed, was not as old as the land of the Twin Rivers, and Crete was an upstart by comparison, for all its thousand years of history. For a hundred and fifty years, since Mursilis had brought to an end the dynasty of Hammurabi, Babylonia had comprised only the southern part of

Stonehenge, in south England, as it appears today. After a varied history lasting from the beginning of the millennium, with several building phases, this is what is left of the final reconstruction carried out in the fifteenth century B.C. By comparing this view with the temple of Queen Hatshepsut shown in plate XVI, it is possible to see a similarity of style which may not be entirely fortuitous.

PLATE XVII

In the western wing of the great palace of Knossos lie eighteen long narrow rooms, each over fifty feet in length, which served as the storerooms of the palace, and still contain many of the tall jars in which the products of Cretan industry and trade were stored.

PLATE XVIII

Very few, and none too trustworthy, representations exist of the merchant ships which plied the Mediterranean at the height of Cretan sea power in the fifteenth century B.C. This model, from the tomb of Tutankhamon, represents rather a river pleasure-craft than an ocean-going ship, but it gives some idea, with its lateen rig and double steering oars, of the probable appearance of the ships of the time.

PLATE XIX

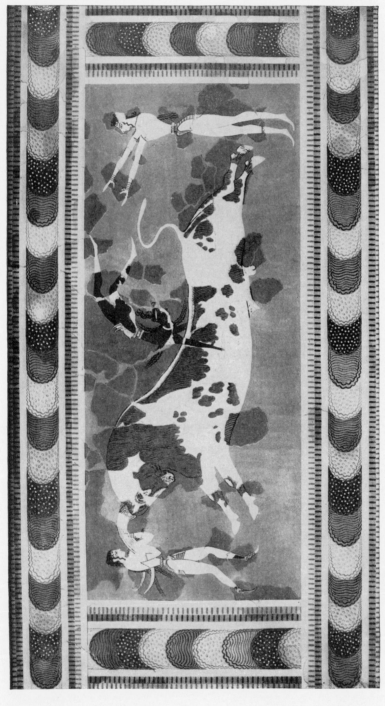

In a room to the east of the great central court of the palace at Knossos this spirited fresco was found. It shows three acrobats, the center one a girl, somersaulting over the back of a charging bull. Experienced Spanish bullfighters claim that the feat is impossible. Certainly the legends of the Minotaur (the Bull of Minos) suggest that the sport may have been engaged in from religious motives.

PLATE XX

Nefertiti, wife of the heretic pharaoh Akhenaten, and mother of Ank-hesanamon, is the best known of all the queens of Egypt, solely on account of this portrait bust, from the studios of Akhenaten's new capital at Tell al-Amarna. If, as is likely, Nefertiti was also Akhenaten's sister, she came of a long line of queens, and had clearly inherited the beauty and intelligence for which they were famous.

PLATE XXI

This panel, in beaten gold, forms the back of Tutankhamon's throne and was found among the other treasures in his tomb. Ankhesenamon, the queen, here anoints her husband with perfume. The whole scene is in vivid colors, as the gold is inlaid with silver, faïence, carnelian, and colored glass.

PLATE XXII

Tutankhamon and his queen appear to have been great flower lovers, and this charming and informal picture of the child rulers in their garden contrasts sharply with the official portraits of other pharaohs. It is from an ivory chest found in the tomb of Tutankhamon.

PLATE XXIII

This scene from the side of a wooden chest from Tutankhamon's tomb has all the crowded clarity of a Persian miniature. It shows the pharaoh, at the head of the disciplined ranks of the Egyptian army, attacking and routing a disorderly rabble of Egypt's traditional Asiatic enemies. On the opposite side a similar panel shows him defeating Sudanese enemies. It is almost certain that Tutankhamon took the field against neither.

PLATE XXIV

Mesopotamia, from the city of Babylon itself as far as the head of the Persian Gulf. To the north and east the land at the foot of the Persian mountains was held by the people of the mountains, the Kassites. And now news came along the trade route that the Kassites had emerged in strength from their mountains and had taken Babylon and the whole Babylonian kingdom. And now a Kassite king sat upon the throne of Hammurabi. The queen of the east had fallen to the mountaineers of the north.

To the Cretans the fall of a distant city to a distant conqueror was of little practical significance—and the ten-year-old children scarcely grasped what had happened at all. The Achaeans of the harbor town, though, made much of it. They resurrected the old legend that their ancestors five or six hundred years ago had inhabited the same land, north of the Caucasus, as the ancestors of the Kassite kings, and from there had spread out as conquerors over the whole of Europe and the Middle East. For a while they acted as though it was they who—by proxy—had conquered Babylon, and carried themselves with an arrogance that rather amused the less farsighted of the Cretans. But as the caravans continued to come through without interruption along the Euphrates route, it became clear that the change of rulers in Mesopotamia in fact changed nothing except the rulers. And Greeks and Cretans alike turned again to the serious business of making money and enjoying life.

The following years brought matters of more immediate concern to the children. As they reached the age of puberty they became eligible for initiation into the mysteries of Cretan religion. They paid their first visits to the caves in the hills, where the gods and goddesses of the underworld ruled. And there they made their first offerings and assumed the costume, and responsibilities and privileges, of manhood and womanhood.

The most eagerly anticipated privilege was that of being allowed to attend the annual festival of the bulls. It was the most colorful spectacle of the whole year, attended by everyone, Cretan and foreign, with Minos himself in the royal enclosure with the ladies and gentlemen of the court and the ambassadors and visiting princes. There was an air of thrilled expectation around the arena as the preliminary rites of propitiation were performed by the priests and priestesses, and then cheering and applause as the toreadors, picked teams of athletes, paraded round the ring. Finally came the roar of anticipation as the bulls were let in, great piebald beasts with wide-sweeping horns. Thereafter team by team the athletes entered the arena, youths and girls alike stripped to a minimal loincloth. To the gasps and applause of the crowd team vied with team in the brilliance and daring of its acrobatics, baiting the bulls to thunderous charges and then at the last moment grasping the horns and somersaulting to safety clean over the back of the charging animal. It was dangerous sport, and in the course of the day more than one acrobat, misjudging his—or her—timing, would be tossed, ripped and bleeding, high against the barrier of the arena.

There were famous names among the professional toreadors, for the greatest of the artists were popular heroes whose polished performances were anticipated long before the festival and discussed in detail for months afterwards. But there were also amateur performers, and many of the young nobles sprang into the ring in the pauses between the teams, to make a pass or two at one of the bulls and to retire to polite applause after a single somersault. And both among the amateurs and the professionals there were many foreigners. In particular the Achaeans from the Greek mainland, where the sport had been introduced a couple of generations ago, had shown themselves adept at the art, and of recent years picked teams from the mainland had competed with honor at Knossos against the best of the native acrobats.

But if the crowd gave acclaim to the best of the teams, they did not at the same time forget to give due honor to the bulls. Their points were eagerly discussed and their spirit and agility cheered equally with the spirit and agility of the toreadors. After all, the bulls were the chief performers, and the main point of the day's sport was the selection of the premier bull, the Bull of Minos, the Minotaur, which would prove its worthiness to be sacrificed on the morrow. And even the youngsters at their first bull festival knew why the finest bull in all Crete must be sacrificed yearly to Poseidon, god of the sea. One of the earliest stories they had heard—in all its scandalous detail—was how

Poseidon had sent up a bull from the sea for a sacrifice, and how the first Minos had impiously kept the bull for stud, with unfortunate results to his own marital relationships. But anyway, the blood of the sea bull ran in the bulls of Crete, and if the wrath of the storm maker, the earth shaker, was not to follow them by land and sea the best of his breed must yearly be sacrificed.

So it was with the double satisfaction of having placated the most influential of all the gods (for a maritime nation, at least)

BULLS AND ACROBATS ARE FAVORITE THEMES OF CRETAN ARTISTS. THIS SCENE IS TAKEN FROM A MINOAN SEAL, THE ORIGINAL OF WHICH IS ONLY 1¼ INCHES ACROSS.

and of having thoroughly enjoyed themselves in the process that the crowds streamed home from the arena, and the teen-agers went back to their apprenticeships, daydreaming of the thunder of hooves and practicing in their free minutes, with one of their number as bull, the last-minute sideslip or the split-second roll actually underneath the lowered horns.

The years passed more quickly for the youngsters now. By their late teens marriage was in the air, with much clandestine meeting of the young men and the girls, and conferences between heads of families and reckoning up of dowries and bride prices. And as often as not youth had its way in the end, for the Cretans were a lighthearted extrovert people, and the parents spoiled their children shamelessly.

But even so it was found prudent in quite a number of families to send the young men abroad for a while. They should gain a little more experience of the world, explained their parents, before they settled down for good to married life and the family business. And they arrived, with letters of introduction to agents and branch managers and business associates, in Egypt and Byblos and Ugarit, in Troy and Mycenae and Miletus. And the agents and associates welcomed them with many expressions of good will, and sent them off as soon as feasible, with their own younger sons as guides—and with letters of introduction to sub-agents—on a nice long sightseeing tour "to get the feel of the markets."

More than one of the young merchant princes of Crete, just out of their teens, was thus in Egypt in 1420 B.C. when Amenhotep II died. They understood nothing of Egyptian politics or royal protocol, and perhaps never really grasped why there was so much discussion around the succession of Amenhotep's eldest son as Thothmes IV. Their Egyptian hosts explained carefully that the young prince was of course son of the previous pharaoh, but not by his divine wife and sister Merit-Amon, but by a merely human wife, princess Tiaa. So much the Cretans, with their own matriarchal traditions, could to some degree understand. But when it came to the point that Thothmes's succession was supported by the priests of the sun-god Ra at his city near Memphis but opposed by the priests of the sun-god Amon in Thebes, they gave up. A multiplicity of sun-gods sounded very like blasphemy, and rival priesthoods contending for influence over the king was something outside their experience. They had simply not the background, said their hosts, to appreciate that the opposition between the priestly colleges was in fact a reawakening of the age-old rivalry between north and south Egypt, between the two capitals of Memphis and Thebes. And they sent their guests out to see the pyramids. . . .

There they were indeed impressed, overawed by the colossal monuments of an almost mythical age. For the pyramids were older than the beginnings of Cretan history (as old for them as King Alfred is for us). Twelve centuries looked down on them, said their guide, twelve centuries of continuous civilization, for over half of which Memphis on the other side of the Nile had been the capital of Egypt. And he took them to see the latest excavations, where gangs of workmen were digging the Sphinx free of its silted sand. The excavation was by order of the new pharaoh, for it was here, in the shadow of the half-buried colossus, that Ra had revealed himself to the young prince Thothmes and promised him the throne of Egypt if he in return would free the Sphinx of its covering of sand. Now the sun-god had fulfilled his promise, and Thothmes was fulfilling his. Most interesting, said the Cretan tourists, but somehow they felt that bull sacrifices were a better way of showing one's appreciation of divine favors than was archaeology.

Even so, when they returned to Knossos they retained an admiration for Egypt. And they found the contacts they had made there of great use to them in a business way, just as did the other travelers who had guested the rather barbaric princelets of the Aegean, or done the grand tour of the Syrian coast—and had had to return in a hurry, because a rebellion broke out once more in Syria against the union with Egypt. Thothmes, like his father and grandfather, led his army in person in a campaign of retribution against the rebels, and for a while Syria was an unhealthy place for foreign visitors—and for the natives.

The young men of Knossos, returned from their travels, contracted, most of them, sensible marriages, devoted themselves seriously to their family businesses, and began to acquire a family and a sense of responsibility.

And more years passed, prosperous peaceful years marked by the yearly returning festivals. Only from the Greek mainland was there news of trouble, and even this was only of family quarrels among and within the royal houses of the tiny principalities, each proudly independent though tending now to unite into leagues of equals under the leadership of one of their number, one year perhaps Attica, another Mycenae. It was just as well, thought the wiser Cretans, that they found it so difficult to stay united. For the Achaeans had a fighting tradition, and a fondness for booty, and by now a not inconsiderable fleet.

News came regularly from contacts in Egypt. They told that Thothmes had finally settled the disputed frontier along the Euphrates, taking the rather revolutionary step of accepting a prin-

IN THE HEYDAY OF CRETAN PROSPERITY THE ARTISTS OF THE ISLAND CITIES ACHIEVED A FREEDOM OF EXPRESSION NEVER PARALLELED IN THIS MILLENNIUM. THIS VIVID SCENE IS REPRODUCED FROM A CRETAN SEAL.

cess from the kingdom of Mitanni beyond the river as his bride to seal the bargain. This mixture of divine and mortal blood—foreign blood at that—was not entirely approved in Egypt, but of course the foreign princess was not accorded divine status or a regency. Anyway, in 1412 B.C., before the Cretans whose life we are following were thirty, the letters told of the death of Thothmes, after only eight years' reign, and of the unopposed succession of his son by his official divine wife and sister Muten-wiya. The son was another Amenhotep and for once fully legitimate on both sides. His accession was therefore peaceful, necessitating little more than a show of force in the Sudan and a state visit—with troops—to Syria. And another Mitanni princess disappeared into the harem of the new pharaoh.

Amenhotep III, and his energetic queen Teie, began a whole series of magnificent buildings at Thebes, the most imposing of them being a new temple to Amon. The correspondents, from lower Egypt, added to the news the rather disgruntled comment that it looked as though the rivalry between Amon and Ra had been settled in favor of the god of upper Egypt, though pharaoh appeared to be catholic in his worship and his wife had built a subsidiary chapel to a rather obscure aspect of the sun's divinity, Aten, the god of the sun's disc. But then Teie was rather a scandal in many ways. She had been proclaimed divine consort although she was not Amenhotep's sister, or even related to him at all. Some even said that she was of Syrian origin. The old order was indeed changing.

But it was all good for trade, and the Cretan merchantmen were profitably busy sailing Lebanese cedar south for the building program. The coastal towns of Syria, Lebanon, and Palestine were rapidly regaining their prosperity in these years. For the thaw in the relations between the two great powers of Egypt and Mitanni had given peace to the small principalities between Sinai and the Euphrates. No longer forced by geography to ally themselves to one sphere of influence, and to suffer retaliatory campaigns from the other, they could now devote themselves to their natural pursuit of trade. The following years of peace, with an artistic and luxury-loving pharaoh setting the fashion for his country, were compared favorably even with the prosperous days of Queen Hatshepsut eighty years before.

In this prosperity the Cretans had their share, as always. In Cyprus, along the Levant coast, and in Egypt itself they opened new branches of their trading houses or expanded those already in existence. And from them wealth flowed back to the metropolis of Knossos. Never had the palace and the city contained so much wealth. Never had the festivals been more magnificent. And foreigners flocked to Crete to share the prosperity. Among them were many Achaeans from the Greek mainland.

When the Cretans of this chapter's lifetime were about forty years old, the blow fell, completely without warning.

The festival of the bulls that year was of unparalleled splen-

CRETAN PREOCCUPATION WITH THE SEA SHOWED ITSELF, NOT IN REP-RESENTATIONS OF SHIPS, WHICH ARE DISAPPOINTINGLY FEW AND POOR, BUT IN MAGNIFICENT VASES PAINTED WITH ALL MANNER OF FISH, SEA PLANTS, AND CORALS. THIS VASE IS FROM GOURNIA, IN EASTERN CRETE.

dor. Many teams of toreadors had come from Greece to take part, and many Achaean princes, with their retinues, were there to watch their champions. Among them Prince Theseus of Attica was the most magnificent, and he distinguished himself by a polished amateur display in the arena against the chosen of the bulls, the Minotaur itself. And the burghers of Knossos retired to their

beds that night tired and excited, looking forward to the great
sacrifice on the morrow.

In the middle of the night they were awakened by shout-
ing in the streets, the clash of arms, and the roar of flames. As
men and women rushed out half dressed and only half awake
into the streets, they saw the great palace of Minos on the slope
above the town in flames. Around them flames were springing up
at half a dozen points within the town itself, and armed men,
in small groups with determined officers at their head, were moving purposefully through the streets, towards the houses of the
richest citizens, the barracks of the police troops, and the exits
from the city.

In that night of the long knives many of the citizens of Knossos lost their lives, struck down in halfhearted resistance to the
occupation and looting of their homes, or trapped in the flames
that spread rapidly through the tight-packed houses. Many more
were rounded up as they fled through the streets, and herded
into isolated houses under guard. Those who could escaped into
the hills around the city. And a surprising number, particularly
among the merchants with interests in the northern trade, were
left undisturbed, except for a guard of the attackers set to save
their homes from the looters.

It was only with the coming of dawn next day that it became
clear what had happened. Only then could the survivors, prisoners or in hiding, see that the armed men in control of the streets
were Achaeans, and were able to recognize among them many
from the Greek colony in the harbor town. And among the officers could be seen many of the Achaean toreadors and others
from the retinues of the visiting Greek princes.

With the light the occupation of the town became more methodical, and at noon the prisoners were herded out to the arena
where the bullfights had taken place the day before. There, with
armed guards patrolling the gangways and archers stationed on
the balconies, Achaean heralds proclaimed the incorporation of
Crete within the Achaean confederation. And to underline the
proclamation Prince Theseus himself carried out, there and then,
the sacrifice of the Bull of Minos to the god of the sea.

In the following days the occupation took on more and more

of a military and organized character. The city of Knossos, which had never known a foreign foe and had not for three hundred years experienced even domestic strife, suffered the same methodical looting and enslavement as had so often been the lot of the cities of the mainland. By oxcart and by pack ass the treasures of half a millennium of trade went down the sea road to the port. With them went the long trains of captives, white-faced and silent, facing the life of slavery which was one of the accepted risks of life elsewhere, but which no one who lived in Knossos had ever thought to experience.

Not all the inhabitants were enslaved. Even among those who had not fled there were many who came to an arrangement with the occupiers, ransoming themselves and their families with hidden wealth or by notes of hand for large sums invested abroad. And there were butchers and bakers and wagoners and gardeners who were needed to serve the occupying forces. And many who were too old or infirm to be worth enslavement. Others were favored for no obvious reason at all—except that it became clear after a while that the sudden conquest had not been entirely unexpected in certain quarters, that there had been a fifth column even among the wealthy native Cretans which had actively assisted Prince Theseus and his men. It was even said that there had been traitors within the palace, too, and certainly, when Theseus sailed for home a week or so later, with his captured fleet of heavy-laden ships, the state in which Princess Ariadne, daughter of the fallen king, traveled suggested to many that she was by no means an unwilling captive.

With the departure of Theseus something of the numbing shock that the blow at Knossos had dealt to Crete began to pass off, and feeling and the power of movement returned. A strong Achaean garrison remained, under a Cretan-born Achaean of princely blood, appointed by Theseus as confederate king, and to him the other towns and villages of Crete made hasty protestations of submission—lest worse befall. The Achaean prince, desiring to have a city to rule, ignored those of the citizens of Knossos who now began to creep down from the hills or to return from the nearer villages, and slowly to salvage and to rebuild.

But Knossos as a merchant power was broken. The great warehouses were empty, the war fleet was gone, and with it such merchantmen as had been in harbor. The capital to rebuild a trading empire had disappeared, but, more important, the confidence on which alone trade could be carried on had been destroyed in the flames. During the next month or so many a small boat slipped away from the obscurer beaches of Crete, loaded with the surviving representatives and the surviving assets of the great merchant houses of Knossos.

They went where they had assets abroad. Many went to Cyprus, or the southern coastal towns of Asia Minor. Many more made for the delta towns of Egypt. But by far the greatest number set course for the coast of Lebanon and Palestine. There they had branches and partners, there they had ships that it was vital to intercept before they sailed, with full cargoes, straight into the hands of the new masters at Knossos.

And in the following years the refugees built a new life at the foot of the Lebanese mountains, sending out their ships from Byblos and Tyre and Sidon as they formerly had sent them out from Knossos, rebuilding their shattered fortunes, and at the same time laying the foundations of a new period of mercantile prosperity for the Levant.

They met with competition. Even before the destruction of Knossos, the merchantmen of the Aegean ports had begun to be serious rivals to the ships of Crete. And there had never been any doubt in the minds of the refugee traders that the treacherous attack on Knossos had been as much motivated by a desire to remove a trade rival as by a hunger for plunder or a feeling of resistance to political dominance. Now everywhere in the Mediterranean from Spain to Cyprus ships from Mycenae and other Achaean ports, and among them ships from the new, Achaean-dominated Knossos, were trading the olive oil and wine and manufactured goods of mainland Greece to the markets which formerly had been the monopoly of the Cretans. And already they were looking beyond the Mediterranean, to the trade of the Black Sea and the Atlantic and northern Europe.

Between these usurpers of the trade routes and the refugee Cretans scattered over the eastern Mediterranean seaboard the

passage of years brought no reconciliation. Many of the refugees
had lost their families in Crete, and still had no means of knowing whether their wives and sons and daughters had died in
the night of terror, or whether they were even now, years after,
eating out their hearts as slaves in the households and workshops
of Greece. There could be no peace between Achaean and Cretan so long as such memories lay between.

But as the years passed, the exiles built up a new existence
for themselves. On the Lebanese coast they learned the Semitic
language of the Amorite inhabitants, and almost forgot their
own, though they met from time to time to recall in impassioned
or sentimental vein their lost motherland. They were beginning
to grow old now, these Cretans born in 1440 B.C., and their children, now themselves grown men, could only dimly remember
the night flight from the burning city. Many of the younger generation of refugees no longer felt themselves Cretans, finding
more satisfaction in merging their identity with that of their new
country than in vain regrets for a land they had scarcely known
and to which they could not hope to return.

There was, in any case, enough to worry about in Syria, without troubling with a lost cause in the Aegean. Amenhotep of
Egypt had just celebrated, with pomp, his thirty-fourth year as
pharaoh. But he was an old man, and clearly failing. To the north
a new king, called Suppiluliumas, had succeeded to the throne
of the Hittites. He had strengthened the fortifications of Hattusas, his capital, and his army had already had clashes with the
Hurrians of Mitanni. But it was more serious nearer home. Encouraged by the apparent weakness of the Egyptian overlord,
one of the princes in the interior of Syria, Aziru by name, had
risen in rebellion and was plundering the neighboring vassal
states. Although the mountains of the Lebanon lay between him
and the coast, there was always the danger that the revolt would
involve the coastal cities. The elderly merchants, who could remember the rupture of their trading connections forty and more
years ago when the old pharaoh's father and grandfather had
taken ruthless revenge on the revolting cities of the Levant, and
who now saw the possibility of being personally involved in a
repetition, did all in their power to persuade their rulers to avoid

a break with Egypt. Their rulers indeed had no desire, after forty years of profitable vassalage, to mix in political adventures, and they sent urgent letters to Amenhotep protesting their loyalty and requesting protection.

Amenhotep, despite his failing strength, answered their prayer. Though too ill to lead his troops in person, as was a pharaoh's duty and privilege, he sent an army which, without a battle, drove Aziru into the desert. The elderly exiles of Byblos and the other coastal cities breathed easily again.

But two years later came news that Amenhotep III was dead, and that his son had been proclaimed pharaoh as Amenhotep IV. And the new pharaoh was only eleven years old.

It is 1377 B.C. Those of the older generation of Cretan exiles who still lived were well into their sixties. They looked into the past rather than into the future, back to the golden age of their youth when the world was at peace and Knossos the center of the world. The future, indeed, looked black. The peace of the seas had fallen with Knossos, and it began to look increasingly doubtful whether Egypt could, or would, keep the peace on land. As the years went by, the more conservative of the citizens of the Levant coast had had high hopes that the young pharaoh, their overlord, would reveal with growth to manhood the old spirit of his dynasty and, by a show of force in Syria, confirm the dominion of Egypt there against the enemies threatening the country from within and without. But it became clear that the young Amenhotep was completely under the influence of his mother, Queen Teie, and it was even rumored that he had involved himself in strife with the priesthood at home.

As the Cretan refugees reached their seventieth year, there were already reports that Aziru had resumed his plundering, while the army of Suppiluliumas, the Great King of Hatti, was in Yamkhad, at the gates of Syria. In their lifetime they had seen the queen of the east and the queen of the west, Babylon and Knossos, fall to a northern foe, and now a third foe from the north overshadowed them. Surely great Egypt, though, could stem the tide that seemed everywhere to be sweeping southward.

.   .   .

It is generally agreed that some historic truth lies behind the story of Theseus, son of the king of Athens, who volunteered to join the tribute of youths and maidens sent yearly to be sacrificed to the Minotaur, half-man and half-bull, in the Labyrinth at Knossos, and who was aided by Ariadne, daughter of the king of Knossos, to slay the Minotaur and to escape, with Ariadne, from Crete. It seems probable that the story mirrors in some way the conquest, archaeologically attested, of Crete by the Achae-

REPRESENTATION OF A FLYING FISH FROM A MINOAN FRESCO AT PHYLAKOPI ON THE AEGEAN ISLAND OF MELOS.

ans of Greece around the year 1400 B.C. There have been many attempts to combine the archaeological evidence and the legend into a plausible story, and this chapter cannot claim to be more than another such attempt. The description of the course of events in Greece and Crete must therefore be regarded as archaeologically-based myth. For the course of events in Egypt, Syria, and Mesopotamia, on the other hand, there is a great deal of unimpeachable historical material, much of it contemporary.

The script used by the Greeks who conquered Knossos (referred to early in the chapter) was not the Greek script we know *today, but that normally called Minoan B, recently deciphered by the late Michael Ventris. It was not an alphabetic but a syllabic script, but the language it was used to write is recognizably Greek. It has long been believed that Greek tablets written in Minoan B script antedated, in Knossos, the Greek conquest of the city. The archaeological evidence for this has recently been challenged (see L. R. Palmer's forthcoming* Myceneans and Minoans), *but in any case there has never been any suggestion that the rulers of Knossos before the Greek conquest spoke Greek.*

Minoan B, as a script, developed as a simplified form of the so-called Minoan A script. The exciting work of deciphering Minoan A (on a foundation of our gradually increasing knowledge of Minoan B) is going on at the moment. All that can be safely said at this stage is that the language written in Minoan A was not Greek. The assumption must be that it was the language spoken in Crete before the Greek conquest, and it is in this chapter called Old Cretan.

15

THE PHILOSOPHER KING

1370–1300 B.C.

IN HER EARLIEST childhood years the princess Ankh-esenpa-Aten believed that the city stretched to the ends of the earth. It was but rarely that she went outside the palace grounds, which themselves seemed limitless, but when she occasionally drove out with her father and mother in the chariot, the wide streets seemed to go on for ever. And even when the houses and temples ended and the desert sand began, there was always the bustle of new buildings going up, and streets marked out into the distance, with architects busy with their red-painted cords marking out the plans of additional houses, and gangs of slaves pulling the sledges with piles of stones and bricks.

When Ankh-esenpa-Aten was born in 1370 B.C., the third daughter of the pharaoh Akhenaten and his divine wife Nefertiti, the capital of the two realms of Egypt was a new city, and growing fast. Akhetaten it was called, the city of the rising of the sun-god, and where it lay there had been, until but a few years before, only open desert between the Nile and the mountains. The court had moved in even before the palace was completed, living in the luxurious tents which still, in the heat of summer, were often pitched in the palace gardens, and her father had himself supervised the building of the palace and of the temple of the sun-god, the first buildings to be erected.

They were a happy family in these first years. Her father, tall, slim, and willowy, was most often gay, though he could be moody and preoccupied, and occasionally inexplicably ill. Her mother was the most beautiful woman Ankh-esenpa-Aten had ever seen. And the princesses tumbled all over the palace. There were six of them by now, and they were all, of course, gods, and treated as such by the servants and majordomos and ministers, which all helped to make life pleasant in the extreme.

THE "NEW ART" AT AKHETATEN. IN REACTION AGAINST THE CONVENTION OF PORTRAYING THE PHARAOH LARGER AND MORE HANDSOME THAN LIFE, AKHENATEN APPEARS TO HAVE ENCOURAGED HIS COURT ARTISTS TO PRACTICE A REALISM THAT BORDERS ON CARICATURE. THIS PORTRAIT OF AKHENATEN WITH ONE OF HIS DAUGHTERS WAS FOUND IN THE RUINS OF HIS NEW CAPITAL OF AKHETATEN (TELL AL-AMARNA).

She took her divinity for granted, for she came, she knew, of a long line of divine kings, stretching all the way back to Amose, the liberator of Egypt, over two hundred years ago. And she and her sisters were fully divine, for Nefertiti, their mother, was also of the race of the gods, full sister to their father

Akhenaten. They felt rather sorry for their half-brother, Tutankhaten, who was only a half-god, his mother being merely human. But they knew that that was only temporary. Some day, when their father took the long journey to his tomb in the eastern mountains which were the gateway to the abode of the god, Tutankhaten would certainly become pharaoh and be promoted to full godhood. By then he would, of course, be married to the eldest of the sisters, Merit-Aten.

Everything seemed bright and clear-cut in those days, preordained by the great god of whom they heard so much. Everyone talked all the time, it seemed, of the lord of life, the god Aten, who showed himself to mankind in the disc of the sun. Their father would take them on his knee and with shining eyes talk lyrically of the one god who ruled all the world, even outside the frontiers of Egypt, the loving father not merely of the divine family but of all humankind as well. Their grandmother, Queen Teie, was more matter-of-fact, and she it was who first told them of the struggle with the priests of the old religion and of the opposition that was still going on to the rule of the new god. Although she tried to explain in simple terms, they really understood little of the background which she sketched for them. She told them that the priests of Amon in the old capital, Thebes, had always had the privilege of proclaiming the new pharaoh, who was then believed to be the son of Amon, and not of Aten. It was now known that Amon, like Ra of northern Egypt, was only an aspect of the godhead which appeared in its fullest splendor as Aten, but at that time both were believed to be sun-gods in their own right, and Aten was even considered merely a minor aspect of Amon. Anyway, at the various times when the succeeding pharaoh had only been a half-god, the son of a human mother, it had been necessary for him to make great gifts and greater promises to the priests of Amon before they would agree to proclaim him. And in that way the priests in Thebes had become very rich and powerful, almost as powerful as the pharaoh himself. The priests of Ra in lower Egypt had been troubled by the growth of this ecclesiastical power in upper Egypt and, being themselves powerful and rich, had made great efforts to win influence over the pharaoh. Seventy years ago,

when Akhenaten's grandfather, the fourth Thothmes, had come
to the throne, they appeared to have succeeded, for he openly
acknowledged that Ra had promised him the throne on an occasion when he fell asleep at the foot of the sphinx of Memphis.

That had forced the Amon priests in Thebes to open action.
They had made it clear to Teie's husband, Amenhotep III, when
he in turn ascended the throne, that they would only recognize
his wife as royal and divine if he openly showed his preference
for Amon by rebuilding the great temple at Thebes. The eyes of
the princesses' grandmother grew hard as they recalled the
deadly insult which she had been forced to swallow, for the
temple had, in fact, been rebuilt. But in the replanning of the temple they had come across the little shrine to Aten, the god of
the solar disc.

Now, both Amon and Ra were believed to be gods of the
sun, explained their grandmother, with varying attributes, and
at first she and Amenhotep had believed that Aten was merely
another name for Ra. They had seen their chance for a subtle
revenge on the priests of Amon, and had enlarged the shrine of
Aten to the status of a temple. For if Ra obtained a foothold in
Thebes, they would be able to play off one college of priests
against the other. But with the guidance of the young priest Ai,
whom the Amon priesthood had appointed to the new Aten
temple, they soon saw that Aten was the only true sun-god,
though they had felt it politic not to recognize the god too
openly. They had even called their son Amenhotep like his
father, with a name incorporating the name of the old god.
And it was as Amenhotep IV that he had come to the throne in
1377 B.C., when the children's grandfather died.

Teie would pause in her story there and tell of the childhood
of her son, their father—how he had been a dreamy boy who,
tutored by Ai, had soon recognized the living presence of Aten.
He had only been eleven years old when Amenhotep III had
died, and for some years he had remained at Thebes, with the
government carried on in his name—not without conflict—by
Teie and the chief priest of Amon. But their father had never
been able to dissemble, said his mother, and he could not bear
to reign under a name which by implication recognized a false

god. As soon as he was officially adult he had, with the support
of Ai, proclaimed Aten as the only true god within his kingdom,
and changed his name to Akhenaten.

He had been surprised, and somewhat disappointed, when
the priests of Amon, instead of accepting the new revelation with
joy, had carried on as though the proclamation had never been
made. The idea of using force was abhorrent to him, for Aten
was a god of love, with no liking for war and blood offerings.
And so, again with the encouragement of Ai, Akhenaten had
retaliated by withdrawing his divine presence from Thebes, and
ordered the construction of a new capital in the desert halfway
between Thebes and Memphis, between Amon and Ra. There
he would wait, he said, until the manifest truth of Aten's godhead became clear to all Egypt.

All that the young princesses really gathered from their
grandmother's story was that the priests in Thebes were incredibly wicked and their father incredibly brave. It did not
make them like Ai, who, as high priest of Aten in the great
temple of the new city, was impatient of children and always
appeared to them much too full of his own importance. But
Thebes seemed far away, and life at Akhetaten was very pleasant.

The first shadow came with the death, shortly afterward, of
Makt-Aten, the second princess, Ankh-esenpa-Aten's nearest
sister. Akhenaten took it very hard, for he loved his children,
and even though he believed firmly that the little princess was
safe in the arms of the almighty father he was depressed for
several months. And the death of his mother, Teie, some years
later caused him to withdraw into himself.

He was worried, too, by the state of his kingdom. He had
confiscated the estates of Amon and his priests, and closed their
temples, but in retaliation the priests of Amon were preaching
that pharaoh had abandoned his people and been abandoned
by his father, the true god Amon. This was obviously a preliminary to an announcement, unprecedented in Egyptian history,
that Akhenaten was no longer pharaoh. But this they did not
feel strong enough yet to make, for the army and the civil service
were loyal to Akhenaten, and the machinery of government
worked undisturbed by religious doubts. The vizier of lower

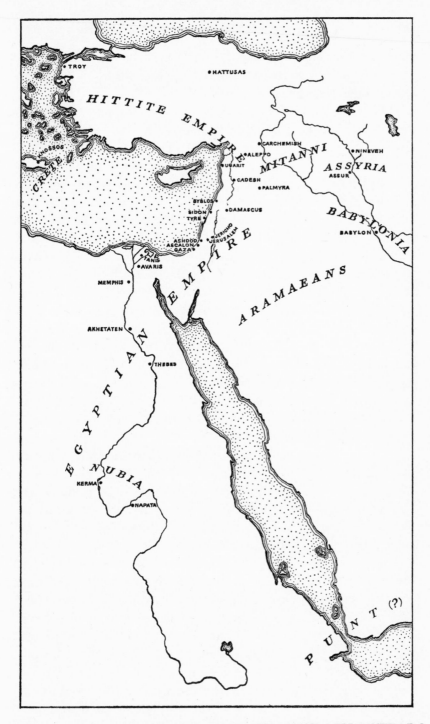

THE NEAR EAST IN THE MIDDLE YEARS OF THE SECOND MILLENNIUM B.C.

Egypt, Horemheb, frequently visited Akhetaten, and Princess
Ankh-esenpa-Aten met him often at court as she grew older and
began, as the custom was, to attend her parents' council meetings.
He was not worried about the state of Egypt, he said, but he had
much to say about the state of the northeast frontier. And the
emissaries who came with him, from the vassal princes of Palestine and Syria, reinforced his tale of troubles.

There was civil war in Syria. Aziru, the Amorite prince who
had been driven into the desert by Amenhotep III, had returned to his kingdom some years back and had gradually extended his rule over the nearer cities, in open defiance of the
power of Egypt. The loyal kingdoms were too weak to hold him
in check, and their envoys and letters begged repeatedly for a
punitive expedition from Egypt. But this Akhenaten refused to
send. He had also received envoys from Aziru, and Aziru had
protested his devotion to the great god Aten and his intention
of introducing the worship of the new sun-god throughout his
realm. Even the young princess, not yet ten years old, could see
the incompatibility between the envoys' tales of Aziru's treat-
ment of captured cities, and the universal love and brotherhood
which should reign wherever Aten was worshipped. But her
father, she was beginning to realize, had a stubborn streak, and
he refused to make war on his first avowed convert abroad.

The court at Akhetaten was full of envoys in these years
from the lands beyond Syria. Because there, it seemed—or at
least Horemheb explained—beyond the border of the Egyptian
empire a struggle for power was going on.

Until less than ten years ago, he said, there had only been
one power of importance north of the vassal states of Syria, the
Hurrian kingdom of Mitanni beyond the Euphrates. And the
Mitanni kings had long ago made their peace with Egypt and
sent their daughters to Egypt as pharaoh's wives. The children
nodded, for Princess Tatukhipa, who had joined their grandfather's harem as a young girl some twenty years ago and who
still spoke Egyptian with a strong accent, was in fact a great
friend of theirs.

Apart from Mitanni, went on the vizier, there was of course
Babylon, but Babylon, once the mightiest power in the east, had

been conquered by Persian mountaineers called Kassites nearly seventy years ago, and its Kassite kings now wielded little power, at least in the direction of Mitanni.

But just about ten years ago two other powerful kings had appeared in the north. Suppiluliumas of the Hittites, a people of Asia Minor who two hundred fifty years ago had taken Babylon by storm, had led his forces out of the mountains once more. He had captured the capital of Yamkhad, Aleppo, and then gone on to capture the capital of the Mitanni, Wassukkanna. The army of the Mitanni, however, had avoided battle, and their king Tushratta—Tatukhipa's father—had returned to his throne when the Hittite king retired. But Suppiluliumas had left his son Telepinus to govern Aleppo and the whole coastline north of the Egyptian vassals in Lebanon.

The other new monarch in the north was Assur-uballit of Assyria. Assyria, the Semitic kingdom on the upper Tigris, was an ancient land, though it was all of four hundred fifty years since Samsi-Adad, its king, had campaigned to the Mediterranean in the old days when Amorites reigned supreme and Indo-Europeans were still no more than a shadow on the northern horizon. For many generations now Assyria had been in the pincer grip of the new peoples, with Hurrians to the west and Kassites to the east. Since Hammurabi long ago had conquered Assyria, the kings of Babylon had claimed sovereignty over the country, but in fact it had until recently been a vassal of the Mitanni kings. Why, during their grandfather's last illness, said Horemheb, the king of Mitanni had sent him the statue of an Assyrian goddess, a certain Ishtar from a town called Nineveh, who was supposed to be able to cure illness but had not been as effective in Egypt as she undoubtedly was in her own country.

But now Assur-uballit, the present king of Assyria, was showing himself more than a match for his overlords. The latest news was that he had encouraged a younger branch of the Mitanni royal family to make a successful bid for the throne. Tatukhipa's father, the old king Tushratta, had been assassinated, and the Assyrian nominee, Artatemu, had proclaimed himself king. And that could be serious, said the vizier. For Tushratta had been a friend of Egypt, whereas Assur-uballit would be likely to use his influence with Artatemu on behalf of his fellow Semite, the rebel Aziru in Syria. It was high time that Egypt sent an army to the Euphrates frontier, to put an end to Aziru and to re-establish a friendly monarch in Mitanni. Otherwise they ran the risk that Mitanni would disappear completely between the Hittites and the Assyrians, and that those two powers would go on to divide Syria between them.

Though the princesses were impressed, Akhenaten refused to move. Aziru was his friend, and he had just received an envoy from the Assyrian king. Assur-uballit's ambassador brought a present of a silver chariot and two white horses, and the magnificence of the gift quite obscured the fact that the envoy entitled his master king both of Assyria and of Mitanni. The claim was not allowed to pass entirely unchallenged, though. Not many months passed before a deputation arrived from Babylon, bearing letters from King Burnaburias II. The Kassite king of Babylon protested that the king of Egypt had accepted gifts from "my subjects, the Assyrians," and had negotiated with them as though they were an independent country.

During these years, while the older princesses, and young Tutankhaten, took their first lessons in court procedure, many envoys came to the court at Akhetaten. Egypt, even under a pharaoh who seemed physically incapable of making up his mind to decisive action, was still the greatest power in the world. The pleas of the Syrian envoys grew more and more desperate, and in the end became ultimatums that if no help came they had no alternative but to make the best peace in their power with Aziru. And the embassies from the independent countries to the north, from the Hittites and from Arzawa and from the Achaeans who now ruled in Crete, became more and more aloof as, in their long journey up the Nile, they realized more and more clearly the growing gulf between Akhenaten and the people he claimed to rule.

It was in these years that the horizon began to contract around princess Ankh-esenpa-Aten. The city of Akhetaten, which had once seemed endless, began to appear to her as a little beleaguered enclave. The mountains that ringed the town to the east crept nearer until they seemed to overshadow the town, and behind them she could feel the world pressing in upon them, eager to overwhelm and wipe them out. And even inside their little community, dedicated to peace and harmony, there was no peace and no harmony any more.

The immediate cause of disharmony was Senkh-kara, a young architect who suddenly rose to be a favorite of Akhenaten. The scandal could not be hushed up. Akhenaten began to associate the name of Senkh-kara with his own as previously Nefertiti's name had figured. And to add legality to the association, he announced the marriage of Senkh-kara to his eldest daughter Merit-Aten, and proclaimed Senkh-kara his heir and co-ruler.

At the same time he disposed of Tutankhaten by decreeing his marriage to Ankh-esenpa-Aten.

Within his family, as within his kingdom, pharaoh was all-powerful. But Nefertiti was herself of the blood of divine pharaohs, and this humiliation she could not take. From this point events moved rapidly, and Ankh-esenpa-Aten, bewildered and not yet in her teens, found herself the sport of destinies which she was quite unable to control or even understand. Nefertiti left the palace, taking her daughter and Tutankhaten with her, and set up her own palace, which she called "the House of Aten." With her went the high priest of Aten, Ai, who for so long had had such influence over Akhenaten, but whose advice was now completely disregarded by the infatuated pharaoh. Ai was now a middle-aged man, stout and scheming, and he held long conferences with Nefertiti before disappearing suddenly one day in the direction of Thebes.

In the following months messengers were continually appearing at "the House of Aten" and leaving again as mysteriously as they came. Horemheb came once to Akhetaten and had a long conference with the pharaoh and another with Nefertiti.

Then, one day in the early months of 1358 B.C., word was brought to "the House of Aten" that Akhenaten and Senkh-kara had been found dead in their palace. Before the day was out, a boat arrived from Ai to take Tutankhaten and his young wife to Thebes.

Ankh-esenpa-Aten never did find out how her father died.

And she never saw the city of Akhetaten again. In Thebes she and her husband were met by Ai, who now in some remarkable way was a priest of the forbidden god Amon, and the same day her husband was declared pharaoh of both Egypts and she his divine wife. But in the declaration her husband was called Tutankhamon and she Ankhesenamon.

On the day of their proclamation the king and queen of Egypt, aged eleven and twelve, wandered hand in hand through the immense ancient palace of their ancestors, which they had never seen before, among the gangs of slaves busy sweeping and shoveling out the accumulated sand of fifteen years, and the masons and painters and carpenters repairing the damage which had been allowed to accumulate after the royal household had moved forever to their desert utopia. In the bewildering change in their circumstances only two things remained the same; they were together, as they had been all their childhood, and they were still, it seemed, divine, whatever name men used for the god who lent them divinity.

Nefertiti did not come to Thebes. Ankhesenamon never learned what part, if any, her mother had had in her father's death (it was not a matter into which she wished to inquire too deeply), but in the revolution that followed his death Nefertiti held fast to the worship of Aten and insured that Akhenaten received the burial which he had desired, in the rock-cut tomb in the hills towards the sunrise. And in the years that followed, as the royal household and the craftsmen and artisans and butchers and bakers moved away from the dying and accursed city of Akhetaten, Nefertiti remained with her priests and retainers in the House of Aten.

In Thebes no one was in any doubt that the real ruler was the priest Ai. He it was who held the seal and who instructed Tutankhamon in the responses he was to make. It was he who ordered the completion of the great temple of Amon which Amenhotep III had commenced, and he who formulated the decree that was to wipe out the name of Akhenaten from the pages of history. Everywhere his name was to be erased and his deeds ignored—with the result that Tutankhamon was officially

referred to as the son of Amenhotep III, although his grandfather had died eight years before he was born.

When the first shock of transition was over, it was pleasant
enough to play king and queen in the palace at Thebes. Tutankhamon and his wife were surrounded by every luxury, and crafts-

IN THE TOMB OF TUTANKHAMON WAS A WOODEN SHRINE COVERED
WITH SHEET GOLD EMBOSSED WITH SCENES FROM THE EVERYDAY LIFE
OF THE PHARAOH AND HIS QUEEN. AMONG THEM IS THIS CHARMING
SCENE, IN WHICH TUTANKHAMON POURS ROSE WATER OVER THE
HAND OF ANKHESENAMON.

men were always busy in the palace fashioning new "personalized" furniture and ornaments from costly materials. Model
ships and chariots in ivory or alabaster were made to amuse
them, and they posed in their garden for artists sketching the
design for the new golden throne, a touching scene of childhood
affection.

The embossed relief of the royal children drinking wine beneath the spreading rays of the sun-god was undoubtedly meant to be symbolic of the state of Egypt, carefree plenty under the guidance of the all-wise priests of Amon. But even the child-rulers, as they grew through their teen-age years, could see that this picture was false. The land was rich enough, but the priests of Amon exploited it with ruthless hand. The heresy which had reigned for fifteen years had extinguished all the human kindness that had once been a feature of the worship of Amon. The priests had been badly frightened, and for that the people should pay. In the name of the pharaoh and of Amon the priests conducted an inquisition over the whole land. And if in many cases the inquisitors proved less than incorruptible, and charges of heresy were levied or laid aside as it paid best, it should not be forgotten that Amon and his priests had also suffered material losses under the reformation, and it was only reasonable that the counter-reformation should make these good.

The inquisition tended, as inquisitions do, to vent itself most strongly on racial minorities. One of these in particular had been especially strongly infected by the heresy. The children of Israel, a Semitic-speaking Amorite and Canaanite minority living mainly in the eastern delta, claimed descent from a certain Abraham, whose grandson, they said, had entered Egypt with his people even before the Hyksos conquest, some four hundred years ago. And over the centuries this odd people had retained its individuality, as a caste of shepherds and traders, with its own language and its own religion. That religion had been the oddest thing about them, for they had only a single tribal god instead of the multitude of gods which every other people had. And during the Aten reformation they had been receptive of the new heresy, with its blasphemous talk of a single god ruling all mankind. Some of the children of Israel claimed that their own god Yahwa was identical with Aten; others that Yahwa, and not Aten, was the only true god of all mankind. In either case it was rampant heresy, and a fine of cattle and goods was imposed on the children of Israel, of sufficient size to ensure their insolvency and indebtedness for many generations.

Queen Ankhesenamon was not greatly interested in the

woes of the children of Israel. She was fascinated, however, by the colorful foreign embassies which now began to wait upon the pharaoh. News had reached the northern lands that the vizier Horemheb was training an army on the Palestine border with the intention of campaigning against Aziru and recovering the lost provinces of Syria and Lebanon. And the favor of Egypt was once more worth working for.

Seated on her throne beside Tutankhamon, the queen, now seventeen years old in this year 1353 B.C., gazed frankly and curiously at the black-bearded envoys from Assyria, the hook-nosed Hurrians from Mitanni, and the tall fair-haired Hittite ambassadors. The Hittites in particular attracted her. She questioned them, through the interpreters, about their country, and was interested to learn that, among them as among the Egyptians, the queen ruled in her own right beside the king. It was even said that originally, before the northerners had come among the Hatti, succession to the throne had been through the daughters of the king rather than the sons. She learned much of the Great King of Hatti, Suppiluliumas, and of his many sons, all of whom had been given kingdoms of their own, carved out of the border countries in the course of many campaigns. And now rumor said —and the envoys did not bother to deny it—that Suppiluliumas was preparing for a new campaign which would finally dispose of the kingdom of Mitanni.

The nobles of the Egyptian court were little interested in the tales of Hatti-land. But they examined with interest the swords which the Hittite envoys wore. For they were of iron, an exceedingly rare metal long considered too brittle to stand up against weapons of bronze. It appeared that the Hittites had mastered a new process of forging iron which produced a metal that need not be cast to shape but could be wrought, hammered, and tempered to a toughness and sharpness which made it superior even to the best bronze. It was a new and highly secret process, said the envoys, but before long even the ordinary soldiers of the Hittite army would be equipped with this ir-resistible weapon.

In the meantime they were pleased to present to Tutankh-amon, with the compliments of the Great King Suppiluliumas, a dagger of iron with gold and crystal hilt and golden sheath, and a set of iron awls and chisels, which would introduce his majesty's craftsmen to the advantages of this new metal.

Tutankhamon and his queen were by now completely habituated to the state ritual. They had grown up in it, through six years of audiences and parades, of religious ceremony and state processions. And outside the duty of the court, life was still very pleasant. Their childhood comradeship had grown into a very real affection for each other. Tutankhamon was a clean-limbed youth, fond of sport and hunting, and Ankhesenamon had inherited the beauty of her mother Nefertiti. Together they rode out in their chariots into the desert to hunt gazelle and antelope, or went duck shooting, with bow and arrow or with boomerang, in the papyrus swamps along the Nile. And afterwards in the evenings they would sit in the palace gardens, drinking the wine from the royal vineyards and listening to the flutes and harps of the palace musicians. In these halcyon years something of the warm feeling of peace and security that had permeated the palace at Akhetaten in the early days, before the dream of utopia faded, was re-created in the royal palace of Thebes.

Only one sorrow cast a cloud over their lives. Two stillborn babies lay in their tiny mummy cases in the palace chapel, waiting to be buried in their parents' grave. That grave was, of course, already prepared. Every pharaoh planned his grave chamber as soon as he ascended the throne. It was many centuries now since the pharaohs had built themselves pyramids, and in the Valley of the Kings, where all the pharaohs of his dynasty lay buried (except only Akhenaten, who lay in his lonely mountain tomb far to the eastward), the simple four-chamber tomb lay waiting, cut deep into the living rock. They did not know, then, how soon it was to be needed.

In 1350 B.C., at the age of nineteen, Tutankhamon died.

It happened suddenly, with no previous illness other than a couple of days' fever. And to Ankhesenamon it was the end of everything. The death of her father, even the death of her mother not so long ago, had not affected her so deeply. Now her bulwark against the world was gone. She stood alone, exposed to the cold winds that blow about a throne.

There was no successor. After eleven generations in which the kingship had descended from father to son, there was no son to carry on the line. Over and above her personal sorrow, Ankhesenamon knew that *she* was the successor, that through her alone the divine blood of Amose could be perpetuated, and that whoever married her would be the only rightful lord of the Two Lands. Even so, at least a fortnight passed, with the embalmers and funerary furnishers and goldsmiths and stonecutters busy on their preparations, before she fully realized that it was intended that her new husband should be Ai.

She had known, and disliked, Ai all her life. He had been priest to her father and her grandfather, and had practically run the court and the government, at least of upper Egypt, during the eight years of her reign. He was old enough to be her father— in fact his present wife was Tutankhamon's former nurse. But what chiefly shocked her was that he was a mortal, a commoner, without a drop of the blood of the royal house. It was at first unbelievable that a mere human could aspire to marry the daughter of Amon, the descendant of half a score of kings.

Ankhesenamon was in despair. A man of the people was to obtain the divine throne of Egypt as a dowry, just as in the old days the throne of the Hittites had gone with the hand of the king's daughter.

The memory of the tales of the Hittite ambassadors stirred the young queen—she was only twenty years old—to a desperate strategem to forestall Ai. She sent a trusted envoy with instructions to bear a letter with all speed to Suppiluliumas, Great King of Hatti. The messenger passed through Horemheb's army on the Palestine frontier, and made north as fast as relays of chariots could bear him. But it was not necessary to go all the way to Hattusas. He found Suppiluliumas encamped around Carchemish on the upper Euphrates. For the Great King had at last moved out with his armies. From his son's dependency of Yamkhad he had overrun northern Syria and was now at the gates of the Mitanni kingdom. He was preoccupied with his siege of the mighty fortress lying where the Euphrates leaves the mountains for the plains, and undoubtedly expected that any message from Egypt would be a protest against his occupation of territory which had been theirs until the revolt of Aziru thirty years before.

With surprise he read a personal message from the queen of Egypt: "My husband has died, and I have no sons, but of you it is said that you have many sons. Send me one of your sons and he will become my husband. I will on no account take one of my subjects; to make such a man my husband would be abhorrent to me."

Suppiluliumas, the shrewd master of strategems and diplomacy, scented treachery. Clearly Egypt wanted one of his sons as a hostage to deter him from venturing farther south into former Egyptian territory. He sent a trusted, but expendable, envoy to investigate the true state of affairs, and returned to his siege. He captured Carchemish after eight days—but those eight days lost him Egypt.

When his envoy reached Thebes, preparations for the funeral of the pharaoh were in full swing. All the personal possessions of Tutankhamon were being transported to his grave, and the widowed queen stood sadly by as the beds and the great golden throne, the bows and arrows and writing cases, the golden scimitars and the chests of clothing, the chariots and the inlaid gaming boards, all the relics of their life together, were carried out of the palace. The embalming was almost completed and the gold death mask was prepared, and every day courtiers and civil servants were delivering to the palace the wooden figures, covered with gold leaf, that symbolized their pledge to serve their master in the next world as they had in this.

To the Hittite envoy Ankhesenamon gave a second, hurried letter: "Why do you say I wish to deceive you? If I had a son, would I write to a foreigner and publish my shame? You insult me by speaking thus. He who was my husband is dead, and I have no son. Must I then take one of my subjects and marry him? I have written to no one but you. Everyone says you have many sons; give me one of them that he may become my husband."

And the messenger, realizing the urgency of the situation, left at once for Syria.

But before he reached the camp of the Great King, the funeral of Tutankhamon took place with all the pomp that traditionally attends the last journey of a pharaoh. The body of the king, dressed in all the finery that he wore in life, with rings and bracelets on his arms and his gold and iron dagger at his belt, was wrapped in linen and placed in the great gold coffin shaped to his living likeness. And in the alabaster sarcophagus he was taken across the river in the royal barge, borne down the sixteen steps to his tomb, and reverently placed within the gilded shrine in the inner chamber. With him went the golden statues of the gods and goddesses who would protect his passage to the world beyond.

The door to the inner chamber was sealed, and before it were placed two lifesize statues of the king to guard the portals. And all his possessions were piled up in the two antechambers, to await his pleasure in the world to come. With them went jars of wine and baskets of corn and dates and meats. And with them, too, went two great bunches of flowering oleander, which Ankhesenamon had cut herself that morning in the garden of the palace. And in the presence of the queen and the assembled priests, and to the mournful music of the horns, the passage to the grave was walled up and sealed, the last time that the seal of Tutankhamon would be used. Ankhesenamon felt that behind the sealed doors she had left her youth, and she wondered how many thousands of years would pass before any mortal eye would again see the treasures among which the happiest years of her life had been spent.

Not many days later she heard the announcement of her betrothal to the high priest Ai. It was announced by the priests of Amon as the expressed will of the god. And she could not reject the command of the god whose daughter she was. She could, of course, persuade the priests to persuade Amon to reconsider his decision, but that she could only do with an army at her back. And the army in the south was under Ai's command.

She looked often to the north in the days that followed. For she knew that no love was lost between Ai and Horemheb, who commanded the northern army. If a Hittite prince came at her summons, it seemed likely that he would come with the backing of the troops of the delta. Horemheb cared nothing for Amon, or for any god except his own hawk-god Horus, but he had always been faithful to the ruling dynasty, whether that dynasty worshipped Amon or Aten.

When the news came, it took her last hope. Suppiluliumas, who had made Hatti a power in the north and who now ruled from the Black Sea to the Lebanon, and from the Aegean to the Euphrates, had left until too late the greatest coup of his career. Ai had discovered what was afoot and had taken countermeasures. The Great King had indeed sent one of his sons (she never learned which), but before the prince reached the frontier of Egypt and the delta army he was assassinated.

Some weeks later, with appropriate pomp, Ankhesenamon was wedded to Ai, and Ai was proclaimed pharaoh.

It was never a marriage in anything other than name. Ankhesenamon was determined that there should be no children to perpetuate Ai's line. She set up her own establishment within the palace and was rarely seen. At the age of twenty-one, the young and beautiful queen in fact retired from the world.

She heard of her husband's official acts of government. Now that the priests of Amon were the open rulers of Egypt, much of the revenues of the country were directed officially to the building of temples and to increasing the estates of the existing temples. Of the corruption which accompanied this priestly rule she heard little. Now that the tax collectors and the royal inspectors were priestly nominees, there was no check on the rapacity of local officials. Fortunes were made through fraudulent returns and through bribes. And the middle class, the traders and small landowners, suffered the most. Even within the palace it was not entirely unknown that conspiracies were afoot, often associated with the names of prominent army officers, to overthrow the rule of the priests. More and more often the name of Horemheb was mentioned by the discontented.

For Horemheb held the north in a firm grip. At the accession of Ai he had neglected to send the customary congratulations to the new pharaoh and his consort, and Ai had not felt himself strong enough to insist upon them. In the north no corruption was tolerated, and the priests of Ra in Memphis held their temples and estates unsequestered.

For four years Horemheb made no move. But the army he had gathered and trained for the campaign to regain Palestine and Syria remained encamped on Egyptian territory. And around Horemheb a clique of high-ranking officers, prominent among them his chief of staff General Rameses, were in constant communication with the officers of the southern garrisons. Ai had shown them the way by which a commoner could reach the throne of Egypt, and what the priests had done the army, too, could do.

Finally in 1345 the army decided that corruption in the state had gone far enough. Horemheb declared himself governor of all Egypt and marched south from Memphis. The country was ripe for revolution, and the army was welcomed in every town along the Nile.

To Ankhesenamon in the palace at Thebes the news of the advancing army came almost as a relief. And yet—she had been queen of Egypt for thirteen years, and now her time as first lady of the land was clearly at an end. For Horemheb had married Princess Mutnesmet, sister to Nefertiti, and herself daughter of Amenhotep III. Through Mutnesmet Horemheb could make the same claim to the throne as Ai had made through her.

And so indeed it happened. The army of Horemheb was welcomed in Thebes without a blow, the palace was occupied, and Horemheb's officers took pains to ensure that Ai was accidentally killed. Thereupon the way was cleared for Horemheb to ascend the throne, and the priests of Amon made all haste to proclaim him pharaoh at the great Opet festival which was due in those days.

Ankhesenamon was treated with respect by the conqueror and by her aunt, the new Queen Mutnesmet. But her position was anomalous. To legitimize the right of the daughter of Amenhotep III to confer the crown upon her husband, it was necessary officially to ignore the previous descendants of that monarch who had ruled. As Tutankhamon had been proclaimed the direct successor of Amenhotep III and the reign of his father had been wiped off the slate of history, now Horemheb was similarly proclaimed the direct successor of Amenhotep III and the reigns of Tukankhamon and of Ai, as well as that of Akhenaten, officially ceased to have occurred. Ankhesenamon found herself relegated to the rank of princess in the royal household, and her thirteen years as queen were regarded as though they had never been. Horemheb's reign was reckoned from the death of Amenhotep thirty-two years before, and all the royal acts and buildings of those years were assumed to have been his. Even so, as a concession to the young ex-queen, Horemheb contented himself with ascribing his own name above the cartouche of Tutankhamon on the inscriptions, whereas the name of Ai was cut out as ruthlessly as that of Akhenaten had been thirteen years before.

The rest of her life Ankhesenamon lived in retirement. Indeed, she had packed sufficiently of joy and sorrow, excitement and disappointment into her first twenty-five years to fill more than a lifetime.

From her palace in the grounds of the royal residence at Thebes she followed the radical measures introduced by the new dictator of Egypt to restore order and prosperity to the country. Corruption was ruthlessly punished. Any attempt by the army officers to profit personally from their new position of power received short shrift. And the priests of Amon were curtly informed that there were other gods in Egypt.

Horemheb was a northerner. And the gods of the north, Ra and Ptah and even Set, were given places in the pantheon equal to those of the southern gods. Rameses was appointed vizier of the north, and Horemheb led his army south in a lightning campaign against the Sudanese, who had taken advantage of the troubles in Egypt to revolt, and even to invade Egypt itself.

But Horemheb did not consider the time ripe for further adventures abroad. It was necessary first to rebuild the shattered economy of the land. In the troubled times just past, Egypt's foreign trade, always dependent to a dangerous extent on goods of the luxury category, had slumped alarmingly, and a stable regime at home and peace abroad were absolutely necessary. A start was made by reopening the state-controlled trade with Punt to the south, and once more, convoys sailed the coasts of Africa, down the Red Sea and into the Indian Ocean. The northern trade could recover of itself, once relations with the new northern powers were stabilized. And Horemheb sent his plenipotentiaries to negotiate with Suppiluliumas.

The envoys left the delta behind them and crossed the desert of Sinai, with its nomad shepherds grazing the hills south of the great coast road. They passed the great frontier fortresses at Sharuhen and Gaza, and continued through the fiercely independent kingdoms of the Canaanites, lands which less than thirty-five years ago had been part of the Egyptian empire, and which still remembered that their forefathers had once conquered Egypt. Farther north they went by the rich coastal cities, Tyre and Sidon, Beirut and Byblos, cities still nominally subject to the old king Aziru in the interior but much more interested in the flourishing trade with the Achaeans of Greece, Crete, and Asia Minor. (The older-established trading houses had conveniently forgotten that the fathers of these same Achaeans had once plundered and conquered Crete, whence their own fathers had come.) And a little farther north, still well within former Egyptian territory, they reached the outposts of the Hittite empire in the former realm of Yamkhad, ruled from Aleppo by the son of the Great King. There they were given an escort, and passed on into the mountains of Asia Minor, up the Great North Road to Hattusas. At Aleppo they had heard of the war going on farther east, where the forces of another of the sons of Suppiluliumas, Piyassilis of Carchemish, were supporting a son of the murdered king Tushratta of Mitanni in a bid to oust his rival, Shutarna, from the throne of that land.

They found the Great King within his mighty fortified capital of Hattusas. Suppiluliumas was by now an elderly man and quite prepared to make a treaty of friendship with Egypt, particularly as this would recognize his rule over north Syria and leave him free to settle the affairs of Mitanni as he chose, and to deploy his main forces in the southeast against Assur-uballit of

Assyria. Both parties were, after all, equally interested in the revival of trade along the coasts of the Levant and in the eastern Mediterranean in general.

The envoys could return with the desired treaty of friendship—and the latest news, picked up in Aleppo, that a vassal king had been established by Hittite arms in Mitanni. But within the year other news came along the Great North Road. A pestilence had broken out in the Hittite capital, and Suppiluliumas, the Great King, had died, and his son and successor Arnuwandas had not long survived him. Another of the innumerable sons of Suppiluliumas had ascended the throne as Mursilis II, but he was young and faced with an insurrection in western Asia Minor, where the princes of Arzawa remembered their former independence and revolted. It was believed that the powerful kings of the Achaean confederacy were behind the revolt.

It looked for a while as though the north Syrian empire built up by Suppiluliumas would disintegrate with his passing. And indeed the old king of Assyria, Assur-uballit, struck at once into Mitanni, advancing with his troops clean to the banks of the Euphrates and the borders of the Hittite dependencies of Aleppo and Carchemish. But the brothers of the new king, who ruled these lands, stood firm while Mursilis campaigned in Arzawa. And before the storm could break, Assur-uballit, too, died. By 1340, when Horemheb had been ruling in Egypt for five years (and Ankhesenamon, now thirty, had been the same period in retirement), there was at last peace in Syria, with none of the great powers strong enough or united enough to venture on a career of conquest. The merchants of the coastal towns breathed easily, and began, hesitantly, to reopen the trade routes to the interior. In increasing numbers ships from the Levant docked at Avaris and the other delta ports, and trade and manufacture flourished again in Egypt.

In the years that followed, the ex-queen in the palace, now middle-aged, led a quiet existence, welcome after her stormy childhood and brief years as reigning queen. And in the towns and villages of Egypt a similar time of peace was no less welcome. Family festivals celebrated marriages and the births of children; and the yearly festivals of the gods followed one upon the other.

Inundation, seedtime, and harvest marked the passage of the seasons—and the years.

As the years went by, Ankhesenamon realized that the Eighteenth Dynasty was drawing quietly to a close. Both Horemheb and his queen were of the generation of her father. The queen could expect no children, and only through her royal and divine blood could the dynasty have continued. To the line which Amose had founded a quarter of a millennium ago, to the family which had liberated Egypt from the Hyksos, to the proud succession of Thothmeses and Amenhoteps—there was no generation to follow. In momentary periods of melancholy the princess remembered her two dead babies.

Horemheb, too, looked to the succession. But he was not of the divine blood. For him there was no mystique, but merely policy, in the blood of the gods. He had himself proved that the throne of the pharaohs belonged to him who was strong enough to take and hold it. And he was an ex-general, used to a chain of command which required no accident of birth to justify it. Horemheb had come to power with the support of the officers of the general staff, and it was the corps of officers which kept law and order throughout the land and held the frontiers secure. It was natural for him to choose as his successor his chief of staff, Rameses. As he grew older, he associated Rameses officially with his rule. For though Rameses was no younger than Horemheb, he had a son, Seti, who was of a caliber to bear the opening generation of a Nineteenth Dynasty.

Twenty-seven peaceful years went by before Horemheb, in his seventies, died. And Rameses, by now an old and feeble man, survived his old commander barely long enough to take up the crook and flail and assume the double crown. After a single year, in 1317 B.C., Seti succeeded his father. Princess Ankhesenamon, now fifty-three, felt herself the forgotten relic of an age that was past, and could herself scarcely credit that she was the same person who as a young girl had ruled with Tutankhamon thirty years before.

As the years went on, she lived more and more in the past. To her dowager palace in Thebes came little news. Though Thebes was still officially the capital, Seti came of a northern family and spent much of his time in the deltalands. He was ambitious, too, to use the efficient army which his father and Horemheb had built up, and to confirm in the eyes of his people his divine right to the throne by regaining the empire to the northeast which had been lost under Akhenaten fifty years before. After a punitive campaign against marauding raiders from Libya in the west, he crossed the frontier into Palestine.

It was a young men's expedition. The Egyptians of the ex-queen's generation, who had seen revolution and civil war and religious persecution in their youth, had no enthusiasm for a venture which at best must temporarily disrupt business and at worst could lead to an exhausting war with the powers in the north. But the young men and the professional soldiers were eager to try out in action the new system of independent brigades, each bearing the name of one of the gods and each equipped and supplied to operate alone. And the mechanized divisions with their squadrons of heavy chariots were believed to be a match for anything the northerners could produce, even for the iron-armed regiments of the Hittites.

In the end, though, no pitched battle was fought. The independent tribes of Palestine offered no resistance and the army marched along the coastal plain of Canaan into southern Lebanon. There, at the end of long and as yet unestablished lines of communication, they met the outpost troops of the Hittite provinces of north Syria, and indecisive skirmishes convinced Seti that further advance would be expensive and inconclusive. It would take time to reorganize the reconquered province of Palestine. He concluded a peace with the emissaries from Aleppo, acting for King Mursilis II of the Hittites, and established the frontier between the two powers just north of Beirut.

The young soldiers grew to middle age in the following ten years of peace and minor skirmishes along and behind the new frontier. But it was no longer a peace of exhaustion with war; it was rather a period of avowed preparation. From the Hittite country came reports of the successful campaigns of Mursilis against his insurgent frontier provinces to the west, north, and

east, and later of the succession of his son Muwatallis to a united
empire and a loyal army.

A new king, too, was on the throne of Assyria, Adad-nirari.
And he had secured his southern frontier by a campaign against
the Kassite king of Babylon and was marching through Mitanni
country to Assur-uballit's old frontier, the upper Euphrates.

Seti was not unconscious of the danger of these three powers
facing each other in north Syria, but Assyria and the Hittites
were hereditary enemies, and Egypt, with treaties of friendship
with both, could afford to wait. Seti devoted these years to public
works. By raising monuments on a scale which outshone the works
of the previous pharaohs, he would give an air of permanence
to the new dynasty and divert attention from the glories of the
former line, now represented only by the aged princess in the
palace at Thebes. The great pillared hall of the new temple at
Thebes, three hundred feet long with its rows of eighty-foot pillars, was to be one of the wonders of the world, and on its walls
Seti ordered a pictorial record of his Syrian campaign to be
carved. And to provide material and finance for these projects he
reopened the imperial gold mines four days' journey south of
Thebes and the stone quarries along the Nile.

For many years, in her old age, Ankhesenamon could sit and
watch the stone barges pass along the river. As she saw the
colossal temple buildings rising on the farther bank, she recalled
her earliest childhood, and the building of the graceful temples
of Akhetaten. Akhetaten, the accursed city, was no more, swal-
lowed up long ago by the desert sand. And with it had disappeared the stillborn idea of a peaceful and gracious world, united
under one all-loving and all-merciful god.

The old ex-queen, who in her lifetime had seen six pharaohs,
and herself been married to two of them, saw a seventh before
her seventieth year. In 1301 B.C. Seti died, and, in a swift palace
revolution, his eldest son, who had been nominated as his successor, was deposed. A younger son, a clever and ambitious man,
was proclaimed as Rameses II. And in the splendor of his coronation few noted the passing of the last of the royal line of Amose.

·   ·   ·

A considerable liberty has here been taken with history, in representing Queen Ankhesenamon as living out the seventy years of this chapter's lifetime. She may have done so, but in fact she disappears from the pages of history after the death of Ai, and we do not know what became of her. Up to that point, however, her life and the lives of her family are well authenticated, though some details are unclear. The cause of the death of Akhenaten is, for example, as unknown in fact as it is here represented as being unknown to his daughter. Nor is the date of Nefertiti's death known. And the mummies of two stillborn babies in Tutankhamon's tomb are not necessarily those of children of his with Ankhesenamon, though that is exceedingly likely.

There is some doubt as to whether Queen Nefertiti was a daughter of Amenhotep III and a sister to Akhenaten; but it was the practice for Egyptian kings, particularly of this dynasty, to marry their sisters, and the fact that Nefertiti was accorded all the honors of co-ruler makes this relationship overwhelmingly likely. Similarly the precise relationship of Tutankhamon to Akhenaten is rather uncertain. He may conceivably have been a nephew, but he is much more likely to have been a son by a nonroyal marriage, succeeding by reason of his marriage to a daughter of the royal wife as had occurred twice before in the history of the dynasty.

Finally, the reference to the children of Israel is completely unhistorical. The Bible is disappointingly silent about the events of the sojourn in Egypt. One would have liked to know what a monotheistic minority in Egypt made of an attempted reformation at court in the direction of a monotheistic religion. But no Egyptian document or inscription mentions the children of Israel. Yet it is generally believed that they were in Egypt during these years, and if so they should hardly be passed over in silence.

16

THE WIDE VIEW (II)

I N T H E L A S T five chapters the story of the central third of the Second Millennium B.C. has tended to be lopsided. During this period the main center of progress, and the best-documented chains of events, lie in the eastern Mediterranean, in Greece, Crete, Asia Minor, and in Egypt. And there is a tendency to look at the world from that center. It is time to redress the balance, and to re-emphasize that the people living in other parts of the world during these three hundred fifty years were no less real to themselves, no less alive and human, than those whose life stories we have recounted. All parts of the world which are inhabited now were inhabited then (with the exception—probably—of New Zealand, Iceland, and some of the Pacific islands). There were fewer people then than now, much fewer, but every one of them was an individual, with parents and families, worries and ambitions and bad habits, and as individuals they are worthy of respect—and study.

Outside of a very limited area of the world, we know practically nothing about them. It is unfortunate, and it is a situation which can and will be remedied. Let me be explicit. The purpose of this chapter is to summarize what happened *in the world* in the three hundred fifty years from 1650 to 1300 B.C. And this cannot be done. Within the area of the civilizations of the Near East very much is, as we have seen, known. Because contemporary written records exist. Over most of Europe the general outlines of change within this period are known. They are known, despite the absence of contemporary written records, because more than a hundred years of intensive archaeological research have brought them to light. Elsewhere—and elsewhere includes nine tenths of the inhabited world of the time—comparable research has not been done and comparable knowledge is not available. Over much of the world no research at all has been done into the history of this particular period, or even into any period at all. In other areas, specifically India, Asiatic Russia, and Central America, work has commenced. And therefore we have, as of now, knowledge of approximately what life was like in these areas at approximately the middle of the Second Millennium B.C. But the results are not extensive enough, or refined enough, for the period to be more closely focused, for us to perceive *changes occurring* within this third of a millennium. And so long as changes cannot be detected within a period as long as that intervening between the Pilgrim Fathers and our own day, then we are not writing history but only anthropology—and poor anthropology at that. (This is not a criticism of the researchers who are doing the essential preliminary work, but of myself. For where the material is not yet available to write history, it is unscientific to try.)

But let us do the best we can with what we have.

In the very widest terms the racial types of the world occupy at this period the same areas they occupied before the great reshuffling that accompanied and followed the European expansion of the last five hundred years. And over the greater part of this range men still hunted or fished for their food, or collected it from the wild-growing trees, bushes, and plants. In Australia the blackfellows were in 1300 B.C. hunting kangaroos, catching lizards, digging roots and chipping flint as they had done in 2000 B.C., as they had done for uncounted millennia, and as they do in the Northern Territories today. In Greenland and along the Arctic coasts of Canada, Alaska, and Siberia, Eskimolike peoples were still living an Eskimolike life, hunting seals from skin kayaks on a driftwood framework, fashioning carefully specialized weapons of bone and leather thongs, and carving walrus and narwhal ivory into exquisite, and often highly humorous, figurines. At the summer markets, at the points where the great rivers entered the Arctic Ocean, they still met yearly the deer hunters and fur trappers of the northern forests, exchanging their tools and onaments of bone and ivory for tools

and ornaments of wood and flint, and exchanging their seal-
skins for furs. And they exchanged news for news. For just as the
hunters of the arctic seas roamed hundreds of miles east and
west along the coasts, the hunters of the forest roamed hundreds
of miles north and south with the seasons.

At the winter end of this range the men of the forests met
the men of the Great Plains. In North America the plains people
were still hunters, small scattered groups following the great
game of the prairies on foot. But in Asia the men of the plains
herded—and now rode—horses, and possessed cattle in great
numbers. And they in their turn ranged widely with their herds,
as far as the mountains of the Chinese border and the plains of
Turkmenistan. And some distance into Europe. It was on these
borders of their range that they came into contact with farming
communities and there heard the news and met the commercial
travelers of the great cited nations farther still to the south.

It is these great concourses of peoples, plainsmen and
foresters and men of the coast and tundra, whose existence and
contact with each other we know of, but whose history we do not
know. While the way of life of each group of peoples may not
have been appreciably different in 1300 B.C. from what it was in
2000 B.C. or 1650 B.C., the individual men and women who made
up the groups undoubtedly experienced lifetimes full of the stuff
of history. Like the pre-Columbian Americans of A.D. 1300
(and for that matter the pre-Columbian Americans of 1300 B.C.)
the men of the plains and forests of Asia would be assembled in
nations, each with its own name and tribal entity, with its own
language and oral traditions. Nation would war with nation over
stolen hunting and grazing grounds, stolen cattle, and stolen
women. And nations would band together into confederacies,
under famous chiefs whose names and exploits would be sung
for centuries, but whose memory is now lost. The forest natives
would raid the cattle of the plainsmen, and the plains nations
would burn off the hunting grounds of the forest people. The
settled farmers of the south would build stockades and forts
against the grazing nations, and anxiously seek news of whether
the wandering herdsmen were disposed to peace or war.

But no nation was exclusive, and along the borders the peoples would mix. Undoubtedly there were complicated rules for marriage, such as we find among nomad and hunting peoples today. There would be patterns of marriage; wives should be sought within the nation, or outside the strict kinship group, or between cross-cousins and the like. But always there would be individuals who flouted the laws of their people for the sight of a pretty face. And along the borders there would be children with a foot in either camp.

Across and through the lines, in greater numbers as the centuries passed, moved the traders.

There has been some emphasis on traders in this book. And appropriately so, for these middle centuries of the Second Millennium B.C. saw such a volume of international and intercontinental trade as was not to be found again for fifteen hundred years. But it is time to define our terms, for trade is many things. Even in the most self-sufficient primitive communities there is a certain amount of specialization, and the hunter or herdsman or farmer will try to produce a surplus of produce which he can exchange within his community, for a smithy-made ax, a wife, a slave, or the blessing of the tribal medicine man. This is trade. When these communities tend to meet other communities with a different way of life, when herdsmen in their wanderings pass by the settlements of farmers, or hunters meet herdsmen, then the possibilities of exchange are much greater. Each community will have surpluses of its own produce, grain or hides or dried meat or fish or furs, which the other cannot produce. There will be seasonal markets for large-scale exchange, and for these markets each community will deliberately store up a surplus of goods for exchange. This, too, is trade. Moreover, specialist communities will attend these marts, communities which live by making stone axes or mining flint or copper or salt.

A third stage is reached when the nomad people attending a mart buy goods, not for their own consumption but to carry to another mart to sell again, at a profit, to another people. Now arises the professional middleman, the man or family or tribe who live exclusively on the surplus to be gained from buying in one mart and selling in another.

Now goods really begin to move. For an object's value is

largely a factor of its rarity, and its rarity is often proportionate to its distance from its place of origin. Goods begin to move from mart to mart, and on to more distant mart, first by a chain of middlemen and later by organized long-distance caravans (or caravels, for the movement at this organized stage may as well be by sea as by land).

This organized long-distance trade was clearly well established by the beginning of the Second Millennium between the centers of civilized city-based life in the Near and Middle East, between Crete, Egypt, Mesopotamia, and the Indus valley. And already it had been stretching out, through the medium of the megalithic missionaries, to the coasts of Europe.

We have seen how, in the first third of the millennium, the beaker people spread the use of and trade in bronze over Europe from their bases in Spain.

And in the last five chapters, through the web of wars and intrigues and conquests and changes of dynasty, we have been able to glimpse the spread of the activities of organized trading houses and shipping firms, reaching out farther and farther and dealing with ever larger and more varied consignments of goods.

This is the period of the ultimate spread of bronze, and there can be no doubt that bronze was the bait which induced many of the remoter peoples of the world to devote an increasing amount of their time to producing and collecting commodities that could be traded to the bronze-producing lands.

Bronze may well have spread far south into Africa during these centuries. The recurrent border wars between Egypt and the Sudan should not obscure from us the fact that between the wars there was active trade, gold and ostrich feathers and ivory and slaves being traded north against the metals and manufactured goods of Egypt. And often during this period state-sponsored trading expeditions sailed down the Red Sea to the unknown land of Punt. But in "black" Africa no independent bronzeworking center seems to have developed. The bronze that undoubtedly came south would be treasured, reused, and eventually worn out. It has not, at least, yet been found in archaeologically investigated sites south of the Sudan. But that trade stretched south of the Sudan is attested by the single bead of the fused quartz glass known as faïence found at Nakuru in Kenya, sixteen hundred miles south of the southern border of Egypt. Faïence is a durable and easily recognizable substance which had been known in the Middle East for about two thousand years. But in the middle centuries of the Second Millennium two very distinctive shapes of faïence beads, a star form and a segmented cylinder, are suddenly found in very large numbers, not merely in their homelands of Egypt and the Levant, but over a very large part of the Old World. The bead from Kenya is the southernmost yet reported, and in the other direction they have been found twenty-five hundred miles from Egypt, on the Tobol river in Siberia, which flows northward to the Arctic Ocean. The beads are found in large numbers in Europe, particularly on the upper Danube and in England. In themselves they were of little value, but they show that trade goods from Egypt, perhaps at second or third hand, did in fact reach into the heart of the Asian steppes and into darkest Africa.

But, as has been suggested in a previous chapter, it is by no means certain that Africa was uniformly "dark" at this time. If further investigation confirms the deductions made by botanists from later plant distribution, that at this period the peoples of west Africa were in fact cultivating gardens of gourds and sorghum and ground nuts, it would be reasonable to assume that they had received the idea of cultivation by word of mouth from the Nile valley.

The contemporary history of the Americas is a much more delicate question. Outside the tropics roamed to the north the hunters of the plains and the mesas, to the south the hunters of the jungles and the pampas. In between, not only now in Peru but also in Central America and Mexico, there were settled agricultural communities. They seem to have been at this period isolated from each other. In Mexico agriculture was some two or three centuries old; the staple crop was maize, and good pottery was manufactured. In Peru both maize and pottery were unknown, but cotton, gourds, beans, and peppers were cultivated. How is one to explain this? If garden cultivation of locally found plants in west Africa is to be regarded as a sign of the spread of the *idea* of cultivation, without the plants, from the Mediterranean, are we to regard garden cultivation of local plants in Mexico as the spread of the idea, without the plants, from Peru—or the reverse? For Peru is as far away from Mexico as the Niger coast is from Egypt.

And what are we to make of the Mexican pottery? Are we entitled to assume that the Mexicans invented both farming and potterymaking, not knowing that the same two inventions had been made (with an interval of two thousand years between them) millennia before in another part of the world which they did not know existed? Or are we entitled to assume that—somehow—the news of how one farmed and how one made pottery reached the Mexicans around this period from some other part of the world where both arts were practiced (and the nearest part was the coast of Portugal some five thousand miles away)? Both hypotheses are so unlikely that either would be automatically rejected were it not that that would mean automatically accepting the other!

Fortunately, we are not compelled, in these wide-view chapters where we rise above the problems of individual lifetimes, to take a stand on questions of this nature. This is not a history, nor even an attempt at a history, but rather an experiment to see to what degree it is possible to write a history, in the present state of knowledge, of the Second Millennium B.C. And we are not obliged to pretend that problems have been resolved which are still *sub judice*. In fact this problem is not even *sub judice;* it is at a stage where, to continue the metaphor, there is not sufficient evidence to bring the case to trial. But there will be, and some day soon a judgment will have to be given. And when that day comes two lines of evidence are likely to be of decisive importance.

One is the question of the working of copper and bronze in Middle America. The earliest use of copper in America has been pushed further and further back in time as archaeological research into the earliest civilizations of Mexico, Guatemala, and Nicaragua has extended in scope. If it should appear that the working of copper in fact commenced in the Second Millennium, the case for contact across the Atlantic at this period would be greatly strengthened.

The second line of evidence would involve search for connecting links along the route between the entrance to the Mediterranean and the Gulf of Mexico. There is a strong case for research along the northwest coast of Africa, in the Canaries (where Bronze-Age carvings have been found) and the Azores, in the West Indian islands, and on the coasts of Venezuela. In these areas even negative evidence would be of importance—until it can be said that these areas have been explored and *nothing* of Second Millennium date discovered, the question of contact between the old world and the new must remain open. Until then all that can be said is that, if there is one single theme which runs through this book, it is that during the Second Millennium people were traveling more widely than ever before, trade goods were traveling even farther than people, and ideas even farther than trade goods. And that if ever there was a period in the millennia before our own era when America might have been reached from Europe or Africa, that period was in the centuries between 1650 and 1300 B.C.

Anyway, in these centuries there *were* maize-growing communities living in Middle America. And they *may* have been visited, very infrequently, by long galleys out of the eastern sea. Certainly their legends thousands of years later say that they were.

In Europe we are on surer ground. Three hundred fifty years ago, when we last looked down upon the continent, we saw a mixture of peoples of widely different origins and modes of life in the process of adjusting to each other. Bronze traders and prospectors from Spain, cattle-herding charioteers from the south Russian steppes, coastwise congregations clustered round stone-built communal tombs which had their origin in the eastern Mediterranean, communities of corn-growing farmers who had been settled in the interior for two thousand years or more, and forest hunters who had been there almost forever—all were acting and reacting upon each other.

Now, three hundred fifty years later (a period, let us again remember, as long as from the Pilgrim Fathers to our own day), the reaction has stopped effervescing. An equilibrium has been established, though how stable the equilibrium is, only the future will show.

Europe consists now of a plethora of nations. The fifteen different groups with sufficiently distinctive fashions in artifacts to be designated as "cultures" by the archaeologists can be subdivided almost without limit. And there is little reason to believe that even such areas as are archaeologically homogeneous were necessarily united under a single rule. Yet there is an underlying similarity throughout. A similar way of life—even a similar standard of living—is found over the greater part of the continent.

Europe is in the hands of the beef barons. Aristocracies of cattle ranchers, by now very likely riding horses where their grandfathers drove chariots, rule the small nations, and are probably at daggers with each other. There is still some agriculture, mainly by now barley growing, along the river valleys, but it is in the hands of the lower classes, descendants of the original farmers. Any man with self-respect rides the range. But he is no longer armed with the stone tomahawk of his forefathers centuries ago, nor even with the flint or bronze dagger that he was wearing when we last saw him. Now every gentleman wears a sword, a long light cut-and-thrust weapon of bronze with inlaid hilt and oval chased pommel. He is clean-shaven, if the number of keen bronze razors to be found in the graves of the period are anything to go by. And we know how he dressed, for oak coffins in Denmark have, in favorable circumstances, preserved the complete finery. His woolen tunic reaches to his knees and is belted at the waist. Over it he wears a cloak, fastened at the shoulder with a bronze toggle pin. Around his neck is a bronze or gold necklet, and on his head a close-fitting pile cap. We can imagine his clothes patterned in the yellows, greens, and blues of vegetable dyes, possibly in tartan patterns.

His wife and daughters are no less striking, in a half-sleeved blouse and an openwork skirt reaching well above the knee, a knitted lace hair net, and a belt with a circular eight-inch plate of ornamental bronze at the front.

These are the inheritors of the new Europe, warlike and proud—too proud to speak the language of their subjects. For it must have been in these centuries that the language of the herdsmen from the east came to be the languages of Europe. Just as Anglo-Saxon and Norman French fought for dominance in England in the centuries after the Conquest, so the Indo-European language brought by the battle-ax invaders six hundred years ago had been fighting the original languages of Europe. But by now Indo-European was clearly winning out (every language in Europe is now Indo-European or else known to have been introduced later, save only Basque).

With its new language, new social stratification, new semi-nomadic economy, new tools and weapons of metal, Europe had suffered a revolution in the last third of a millennium. But a third of a millennium is a long time, eleven overlapping generations of birth, growing-up, marriage, and new births, and it is unlikely that the revolution was ever even as much as a consciousness of change to the people to whom it happened. Things they would notice, though, were the fluctuations of trade and the growth of manufacturing and marketing.

Traders and prospectors, of course, had been known for generations, as long as tradition went back, since long before the millennium opened. But never had trade been organized as it was now. Since the Achaeans of Greece had sacked great Knossos a hundred years ago—and Europe still reverberated to its fall—the lords of Mycenae and of the lesser Greek cities had taken over and expanded the organized supplying of primary products from the hinterland of Europe to the markets of the Near East. And with the ending of the long wars in the Levant and the recovery of Egypt, the eastern markets seemed insatiable.

Many luxury goods were shipped and portaged along the coasts and the great riverways of Europe, furs and amber and gold and silver and semiprecious stones. But trade ran largely on staples such as hides and salt and metal, copper and above all tin. The metal trade was now well organized at the source. Prospectors had hundreds of years ago located the ore-bearing regions and trained the local populace in their exploitation. Gold was panned on a commercial scale in Ireland and in Spain; on the northern slopes of the Alps in Austria and in southern England open-cast mining for copper and tin had long ago exhausted the surface outcroppings, and the lodes were being followed ever deeper. The metal was smelted at the source and traveled south in ingots or was fashioned into heavy necklets, convenient to carry and easily refashioned at the end of the route. The metal-producing peoples had grown wealthy on this export trade. And as a subsidiary which was rapidly outstripping in importance the primary production, they had gone into the manufacturing line, producing tools and ornaments and weapons of bronze which were bartered to the surrounding peoples in exchange for other wares. Even the ingots were not now all sent southwards. For the rich amber lands of the Baltic were great buyers of raw metal, and had their own schools of itinerant smiths producing distinctive wares of high quality, which in turn were bartered to the lands beyond.

Caravans of traders, families of wandering smiths and tinkers, coastwise trading vessels and river barges, and convoys of ships on the long hauls were moving in all directions over the lands and seas of Europe, supplied by the mining and smelting villages whose ever-smoking furnaces stained the sky.

But this incipient industrialism was still a fragile thing. The local European market was limited, for the bulk of the population, herding its cattle and reaping its barley, was too poor to purchase bronze, and there was a limit to the quantity of metal that the ruling classes could absorb. The metal industry depended still on the main market, the wealthy nations of the civilized Near East. And in central Europe the incoming wealth had already occasioned an increase in population that was beginning to press heavily on the available land.

But while Europe and the Near East, with much of Africa and of central Asia, were in these middle centuries of the Second Millennium knit together as never before into a commercial and manufacturing unity, farther east a "bronze curtain" had descended. The charioteers of the Russian steppes, whose western cousins had played and were still playing a dominant role from Europe to the valley of the Euphrates, had wiped out the civilization of Meluhha, with its cities of Mohenjo-daro and Harappa. Throughout the Indus valley and into the valley of the Ganges the Aryan invaders roamed with their cattle and horses, settling in temporary villages while the blackened ruins of the great brick cities stood deserted. In central India some semblance of the Meluhhan civilization survived precariously, but all connection with the west had ceased. Ships no longer sailed the Indian Ocean between Mesopotamia and the east, and the civilized world ended at the Straits of Hormuz.

Some 2,350 miles, the distance from San Francisco to Pittsburgh, separates Memphis on the lower Nile from Harappa on the upper Indus. Approximately the same distance, in the

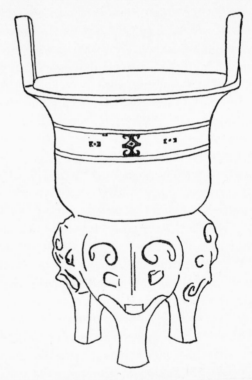

A BRONZE VESSEL OF THE SHANG DYNASTY, OF THE TYPE KNOWN AS "HSIEN." IT IS A DOUBLE VESSEL, A "STEAMER"; THE TRIPOD BASE, STANDING OVER THE FIRE, WOULD BE FILLED WITH WATER, AND THE STEAM, RISING THROUGH THE PERFORATED BOTTOM, WOULD COOK THE FOOD PLACED IN THE UPPER PORTION. SIMPLER VESSELS OF POTTERY OF THE SAME TYPE WERE MADE FOR HOUSEHOLD USE; THIS ELABORATE BRONZE VERSION WOULD BE USED TO PREPARE CEREMONIAL MEALS FOR ANCESTOR SPIRITS.

other direction, separates Harappa from the village of An-yang
on the Huan river, a tributary of the Yellow River in north China.
The distance is as the crow flies, and the unfortunate crow would
have to fly across the wildest part of the Tibetan plateau to reach
its destination.

In the year 1300 B.C. a city is rising at An-yang. The river
Huan, cutting deep into the loess soil, here makes a wide curve,
providing a natural moat around three sides of the chosen site.
On the fourth side, towards the south, the defenses are going
up, a broad wall of earth pounded to cement hardness within
the wooden shuttering, which is gradually raised as the wall rises.
Within the area cords mark out the streets, and along them plat-
forms, also of pounded earth, are being constructed, the floors
and foundations of houses, palaces, and temples.

The palace of the emperor and the temple to his ancestors
are almost completed. The rows of wooden pillars are erected,
and the crossbeams and ridge pole mortised into place. Now
while the roof is being thatched, the outer walls are rising to meet
it; they are built of the universal adobe, earth pounded to a hardness that rings under the mallets and then, when the shuttering
is removed, pared down to a glasslike smoothness.

The Emperor P'an Kêng, at whose orders the great city of
Shang is being built, visits the site but rarely. For days at a time
he is out with his army, on the hunts that provide the main royal
sport and at the same time the principal army training. In the
open woodland beyond the millet and rice fields to the east, on
the flood plain of the mighty Huang-ho to the south, or in the
wooded mountains three days' drive to the west, the foot soldiers
are deployed to envelop a large area, and to drive the game towards the waiting line of chariots, with the emperor in the
center. As the game begins to break cover, the two-horse teams
start forward, the drivers wheeling at the last moment to allow
the nobles to get in a flank shot with their sinew-backed bows, and
the spearman, crouched by the wheel, prepares to spring down
and finish a stricken beast. Excitement mounts as the animals
come in greater numbers and the chariots scatter in pursuit. The
game is mostly deer and hares, though boar—which it is generally agreed give better sport—are not uncommon, and oc-

casionally leopards or even a tiger will be flushed. Elephants are not unknown, but generally the chariot line divides to let them through when they are encountered. For elephants are scarce and valuable, potential additions to the army or the timberyards if they can be caught and tamed. But no other animals are protected. Bears and tapirs, even badgers and quail, go to swell the bag, which on a favorable day may well number over three hundred head. After the best of the bag has been set aside for offerings to the ancestral spirits and for the consumption of the court, the remainder goes to feed the army and the builders at work on the new city. Hunting is not only sport and military exercise; it is also a vital part of the system of supply, second only to the growing of cereals, and considerably more important than the herding of domestic animals.

The emperor also leads his army to war. The vassal kings on the frontier must occasionally be chastised, to teach them what vassalage means; and always there are incursions of nomads, the Ch'iang shepherds of the northwest, to be combatted. Punitive expeditions against Ch'iang encroachment are in fact hunts on a grander scale, and provide an even better bag: captives for enslavement and for sacrifice, and sheep for the commissariat. And the farmers in the frontier provinces are quick to send word when this human game is sighted.

P'an Kêng comes of a long line of emperors, and his empire is, at least in theory, large. He claims suzerainty over kings who rule in the deserts of Mongolia to the north and in the forests beyond the Yangtze-kiang to the south. His realm stretches to the sea in the east, and to the west an indefinite distance, into the lands of the nomad shepherds and of the barbarian charioteers of the Wei valley, beyond where the Yellow River turns northward. But the actual area that he personally rules is much smaller, from the Yellow River to the northern hills perhaps a hundred miles, and the same distance to east and west from his new capital.

His ancestors founded the Shang kingdom (some call it the dynasty of Yin) well over two hundred years ago, and in his new temple stand the tablets of nineteen former emperors of his line. At the time when Thothmes I of Egypt (of whom P'an Kêng has never heard) was campaigning north through Syria and erecting his boundary stone by the Euphrates, the first emperor of the Shang dynasty had led his troops into the valley of the Yellow River from their homelands in the south and east, and had overthrown the kings of the Hsia dynasty. But it was an uneasy kingdom into which the Shang emperors had come, constantly exposed to the marauding campaigns of the nomads to the north and west, and by no means always secure against the attacks of kinsfolk, and nominal vassals, in the east and south. The score of emperors in a score of decades was proof enough that kingship was a hazardous business; and five times the capital had been transferred to another town under the threat of invasion. Now there was to be an end to the movement of capitals. The Great City of Shang, with its wall and river moat, would be an impregnable bulwark against the western barbarians.

As the buildings of the city rise, the visits of the emperor and his court become more frequent. The ancestor tablets are now installed in the palace temple, and the ancestors must, of course, be consulted in all affairs of state. And the bronzeworkers, too, have set up their foundry in the city, and there are always sacrificial and ceremonial vessels to be commissioned from them.

Bronze is not a new thing in China. Though tradition says that the Hsia kings of the previous dynasty had no bronze, and though the coolies and peasants even today use stone tools and weapons, the knowledge of bronzeworking had reached the country in the early years of the present dynasty two centuries and more ago. And the native bronzesmiths, in addition to turning out weapons and ornaments for the nobles and their bodyguards, harness for their horses, and ornamental fitments for their chariots, are becoming adept at casting in bronze the complicated shapes of the ceremonial vessels, which, even within the memory of man, had previously been made of clay.

The bronze vessels are made for the ancestors, who demand and deserve the best of everything. In the family temples, of the imperial family as well as of the nobles, offerings of food and wine must regularly be made to each of the many ancestors, even when no especial favors are required. (When they *are*, the offerings will be supplemented by sacrifices of animals or of slaves.)

The presentation to one of the ancestors of a vessel for food or wine or water is a fitting way of commemorating any auspicious event, a successful hunt or battle, or a mark of imperial favor, a grant of land or of title. After all, the ancestors' influence determines the course of events for their descendants, and they deserve a reward for their efforts. The name of the ancestor thus honored will often be inscribed on the vessel in the pictographic script that, like bronze itself, has come into use during the reign of this enlightened dynasty. For many of the nobles can read; it is not an accomplishment confined to the oracle priests.

The priests are the interpreters between the dead and the living. Although they accompany the emperor on his travels in order to give him day-to-day advice from the ancestors, it is best to pose important questions within the ancestor temple in the city, where one is most likely to find the ancestors at home. Questions are submitted in writing, carved on shoulder blades of cattle or on tortoise shells, and the ancestors answer them, with a plain "Yes" or "No," by guiding the direction of the crack produced when the priest applies a red-hot bronze point to the back of the bone. It is a simple method, and the same bone or shell can be used over and over again. So the ancestors are asked about everything: tomorrow's weather and the best place to camp for the night, as well as the prospects for the harvest or the strategy to be adopted against an invading army. The answers are not infallible, for after all even ancestors are not all-powerful. But on the whole they know better than their living descendants, and sometimes the priest will triumphantly inscribe on the bone after the event the tally of the day's hunt or the laconic remark that "it really didn't rain."

It is these inscribed bones and tortoise shells and bronze vessels, together with the archaeological remains of the Great City of Shang at the site of An-yang, which have cast a flood of light over the civilization of north China in the latter half of the Second Millennium B.C. But the discoveries at An-yang pose as many questions as they solve, and one could wish that the ancestral spirits of the Emperor P'an Kêng were still disposed to give accurate answers to them.

The date of P'an Kêng and the building of Shang is disputed. The traditional date is 1395 B.C., or by another tradition 1324, but both traditions are of late origin. The evidence of eclipses recorded in the oracle bones appears to give support to various scraps of documents and later references which suggest that the date was actually the very year 1300 B.C.

The archaeological evidence for the origins of the Shang dynasty to the south and east of the Yellow River is slight and ambiguous, based mainly on the apparent introduction by this dynasty of the water buffalo and the tortoise to the north. But the big question which An-yang poses is that of the origin of Chinese bronzeworking and of the Chinese written language. Both are found at An-yang in a highly developed form, owing apparently nothing to influences from outside China. By what route the knowledge of bronzecasting and of writing reached China, if indeed both arts were not independently invented there, is still unknown. Certainly a considerable period of "native" experimenting with both media must have preceded the highly indigenous and formalized examples of both arts found at An-yang. Yet writing has been found at none of the many sites earlier than An-yang which have been investigated, and only one of these sites, the early Shang site of Chêng-chou, has produced bronzes earlier than those of An-yang.

The classical description of the finding and excavation of An-yang is given by H. G. Creel in The Birth of China. *The actual excavator, Li Chi, has given a more up-to-date interpretation in* The Beginnings of Chinese Civilization. *Much more than the development of Chinese art (a discussion of the problem of dating is included) is given in W. Willetts's* Chinese Art.

Book IV

Bronze and Iron

HORSEMEN WITH SPEAR AND SHIELD RIDE BENEATH THE SOLAR DISC
ON A SOUTH SWEDISH ROCK CARVING.

17

THE EXODUS

1300–1230 B.C.

A SCALON WAS a pleasant town to grow up in. It was not, of course, one of the larger cities of Canaan. Ugarit in the far north, in the Hittite-ruled lands, was much bigger, and Byblos, too, was larger. Even Gaza, ten miles farther south, was a busier city; and there must have been a score of towns along the Canaanite coast which counted themselves the equals or superiors of Ascalon.

But the burghers and their children regarded their town as second to none. Well situated, with ten or fifteen miles of fertile plain behind, before one reached the foothills of the mountains, and with the Mediterranean in front, it was far from being a backwater. The great coast road passed through the town, and along it moved in either direction the world and his wife. The children never tired of lying by the town gate, to the annoyance of the sentries, to watch the traffic, and they prided themselves on being able to identify the nationalities and religions of the passers-by at a glance.

The long-distance pack caravans were the most difficult, for among the drivers and merchants and passengers accompanying the long donkey trains were representatives of practically every nation of the world. Egyptians, of course, in their white linen kilts, and Hurrians in woolen tunics, were well known, for there were many Egyptians and Hurrians resident in the town, and most of the children could beg in Egyptian and Hurrian just as fluently as in their native Semitic. But it was not so easy to distinguish the Hittites from the upper-class Hurrians, who didn't speak Hurrian at all but a language closer to Hittite, while

Babylonians and Assyrians were almost indistinguishable, and you had to look at their loads to see whether they were carrying dates or wheat. Then there were all the peoples of the hinterland, coming in to trade with the caravans, Moabites and Midianites and Habiru and a score of others. But they were more local, and the children knew the slight differences of dialect or dress which marked them out. And sometimes there were convoys from deep in Arabia to the south, and it was always a red-letter day when *they* figured on the list. For they came with camels, huge ungainly beasts which the children's fathers said had only been hearsay when *they* were boys. Camels were said to be able to travel for days over waterless desert without needing food or drink. They had been tamed by the tribes of the deep southeast of Arabia and had only recently been introduced to the nearer Arabians.

Not all the travelers of the coast road were traders, though. Frequently—more and more frequently, it seemed—troops passed through, companies and battalions of Egyptian or Sudanese infantry, or squadrons of chariots, on their way to relieve the garrisons along the frontier by Byblos. And there were the couriers in their swift light chariots, and the upper civil servants traveling slowly and in comfort in palanquins, with creaking ox wagons carrying their household effects.

And then there were all the casuals, beggars of every nationality, strolling players and minstrels and acrobats, traveling bronzesmiths and jewelers and sealcutters, pilgrims and priests, doctors and painters and scribes.

Only one place could rival the town gate as a point of vantage for the children—and that was the harbor. Here, too, there was always something new to be seen. There was the fishing fleet, and the local vessels whose crews they knew. But there were also larger vessels from farther afield, galleys from Egypt and from the coast ports to the north, the big lateen-rigged merchantmen from Cyprus and Tarsus, from Crete and Greece, and even from farther away in the deeps of the Mediterranean. The children ran to secure the mooring ropes cast ashore, and then sat on the bollards along the quay, watching the booms swinging the cargo slings up from the holds and ashore. They interrupted the tally clerks with questions, as the cargo piled up on the quay, great jars of olive oil and wine, crates of the finer painted pottery of Greece, sacks of wheat and barley, balks of cedar and pine-wood, bales of hides and of woolen cloth, stacks of ingots of copper, and smaller consignments, carefully guarded, of tin or silver.

The narrow streets and multicolored bazaars of Ascalon were always full of strangers, and loud with the babble of a score of tongues. And they were alive with troops. The children used to cheer their own soldiers, the bodyguard of the prince. There were not many of them, as their functions were confined to sentry duty at the palace and customs patrol at the harbor. But they were all that was left of the proud regiments which had guarded the little city-state during its days of independence, before the Egyptians with their overwhelming strength had occupied the whole of south Canaan twenty years ago. With the troops of the occupying garrison the children waged a continuing feud, and the sentries and patrols, often tall thin black Dinkas from the Sudan with Egyptian officers and sergeants, were continually exasperated by the catcalling and mudslinging of the agile curly-headed boys. It was a large Egyptian garrison, not because Ascalon was important or difficult to hold, but because there was a large upland area to police. Patrols were continually being sent into the hills to keep order, and occasionally almost the whole garrison would be ordered out to deal with bandits in the mountains or the southern desert.

Before the boys who were born in 1300 B.C. were in their teens, the garrison was hurriedly called out one morning to help deal with trouble in the south. But only when they got back a week later, dusty and with a thirst that all the beer of the taverns could not quench, did the children, via the barmaids, hear the details.

The trouble had been in Egypt itself. Up on the edge of the delta, beyond the Bitter Lakes, were the grazing grounds of an Amorite tribe which had moved to Egypt many hundreds of years ago. They had already been in Egypt even before that glorious period of Canaanite history, the time when their princes, the Hyksos, had conquered and ruled all Egypt. They called

themselves the sons of Abraham, whom the Canaanites vaguely
knew as a mythical Amorite hero, or sometimes, to make it more
complicated, the children of Israel. At one time this tribe had
been wealthy, controlling much of the landward trade between
Egypt and Palestine, though they had never ceased to be sheep-
herders, nor had they mixed overmuch with the Egyptians.
But during the reprisals that followed the death of the infidel
king, Akhenaten, nearly seventy years ago, they had suffered
severely. For Akhenaten had forsworn his gods and proclaimed
that there was only one god. And apparently these sons of Israel
had the same unreasonable belief in a single god, and had been
tarred with Akhenaten's brush. Anyway, they had been heavily
fined and made subject to forced labor in the public works
projects, just as though they were ordinary bondsmen. And they
hadn't liked it.

The sergeants of the company that had stayed behind in
Ascalon, leaning over the tavern table as they listened to their
comrades who had been on the task force, signaled for more beer,
and the barmaids hung around to hear the rest of the story.

Well, the returned sergeants went on, there would probably
have been no trouble if it hadn't been for a firebrand with a
touch of religious mania, a young Egyptianized Israeli called
Moses. He had been well brought up; it was even said that he
had been adopted by one of King Seti's daughters, but he had
got into a scrape and had had to spend some years in exile among
the shepherd tribes of Sinai. And he had got the idea that the
sons of Israel would be better off a little farther away from Egyptian jurisdiction.

The authorities in Egypt had naturally refused permission
for the tribe to change its grazing grounds, but there had been
the usual red-tape tangle, with every official countermanding the
last. Then to cap it all, the peasants had got the idea that last
year's poor inundation, followed by the locust plague and widespread epidemics, was all the fault of Moses, who claimed to have
some sort of supernatural powers anyway. There had been a tense
situation, until suddenly the tribe had decamped without permission. And before breaking camp, they had raided the neighboring villages and carried off considerable booty.

King Rameses's viceroy in the delta had dispatched a regiment of chariots to round up the Israelis, and at the same time had sent word to the garrisons of Gaza and Ascalon to march south and head off the tribe. But young Moses apparently had an eye for country, for all his communing with spirits. He had shaken off his pursuers in the tidal flats around the head of the Gulf of Suez, where the chariots could not follow—many had been lost when the tide, coming in with deceptive swiftness, had turned the salt crust to quagmire. Then, instead of following the well-watered roads to the north, where he would have met the troops from Canaan, he had led his people into the mountainous desert of southern Sinai. And on the edge of the desert the troops had given up the pursuit and marched back into Canaan.

It was a routine incident, such a pursuit of a raiding tribe, made unusual by the fact that the tribe had so long been resident in Egypt. It only went to show, said one of the Egyptian sergeants, that you couldn't trust these Semites, however long they had been living in a civilized country. The barmaids sniffed and turned their backs demonstratively.

But the runaway tribe was soon forgotten by garrison and children alike. Traders and travelers from the south occasionally brought news of it, and it appeared that the Israelis had been accepted by the nomad shepherds of Sinai, with whom their leader, Moses, had established good relations during his earlier exile, and they seemed to be in process of assimilation. And that was that. There were other things to think about.

The most obtrusive of these was the coming war in the north. It was an open secret that Rameses II, the young pharaoh of Egypt, was preparing a large-scale campaign which was to break the Hittite grip on the rich lands of northern Syria and to re-establish the former frontier of Egypt on the Euphrates. During these years, while the class of 1300 B.C. was entering its teens, roads were being improved, stores collected at strategic points, garrisons increased and exercised, and troops recruited even from among the Canaanites. Many of the older brothers of the boys were attracted by the good terms of service and the prospect of plunder to join one or another of the mercenary companies that were being raised along the coast.

But business with the north went on as usual, and traders passing down the coast brought news of similar preparations being made in the part of the country held by the Hittites. There too Muwatallis, the Great King, was amassing troops, regular iron-sworded regiments of the Hittite army, squadrons of the heavy iron-tired chariots, and companies of mercenaries from all the peripheral states of Asia Minor. News of the coming trial of strength had spread abroad, and companies of freebooters were even arriving by their long ships from the more distant parts of Europe to take part, on one side or the other, in the struggle that would decide the supremacy in the eastern Mediterranean.

Some of the privateers came into Ascalon, and the boys of the town, who thought they knew all the peoples of the world, had new names and races to add to their list. Cretans and Achaeans they had met before, and occasional crews of Sicilians and Spaniards, and even, among these crews, a man or two of the flaxen-haired races who lived out on the shores of the north Atlantic. But these were none of them. They called themselves Shardanians and Dardanians and Philistines and Tekelians, and they were big, fair, brown-haired warriors with amber-mounted hilts to their long bronze swords. While the captains bargained for their sevices with the Egyptian district commander, the fighting men roamed the streets with predatory eyes on the goods of the bazaars and on the girls of the town.

It was the boys of the town, however, who attached themselves to the newcomers as guides, and made themselves approximately understood in the broken Achaean that both could speak after a fashion. They learned that these strangers were from inland Europe, from the headwaters of the great river called the Danube. That was the bronze-working region, and there was a large and growing population there, too large for the country to feed. Therefore, many of them had banded together and struck down the amber route to the Adriatic, and down the Danube to the Black Sea, and across the mountains to northern Greece and Albania. They had been fortune seekers when they left their homeland, and it looked now as though Canaan was a good place to make one's fortune. In the meantime they could draw a good ration of barley and fish and cheese as mercenaries to the king of Egypt, until such time as he should choose to use them.

Finally, in the spring of 1285, news indeed comes to Ascalon that pharaoh himself is on his way north. It is a brave sight, when the army of Egypt marches through Ascalon. It is not the whole of Egypt's might—the greater part of the army of upper Egypt has remained in the south, to guard the Sudan frontier. Only one regiment of six thousand men, the Pharaoh's Own regiment of Amon, comes with him from Thebes. But there are three regiments from lower Egypt, the regiments of Ra and Ptah and Sutek. In serried ranks they march along the great coast road, with standards borne aloft before them and with the squadrons of light two-man chariots in van and rear. And between the regiments come the free companies and the contingents drawn from the garrisons. The watchers by the road estimate the army at no less than thirty thousand men, surely the largest army ever to leave Egypt.

Rameses himself travels with the regiment of Amon, his four-horse chariot gay with waving plumes, and the chariots of his household troops driving two abreast before and behind. He stands straight and proud, with mace in hand, the double crown causing him to appear of more than mortal stature.

Behind the army come the long trains of pack asses and ox wagons bearing the supplies and tents, the bundles of arrows and spears, the fodder and the siege and bridging equipment. But this is only a small part of the supplies needed by the army. The greater part comes by sea; a large cargo fleet is on its way north, guarded by the lean galleys of the navy, to make junction with the army at the ports farther north, at Joppa and Tyre and Beirut, and to resupply the depots of arms and equipment which have long been assembled at the cities on the route.

The army passes on towards the north, and Ascalon seems empty when they have gone. For only a skeleton garrison remains, and the mercenaries and many of the young men of the town have gone with the army.

Now, whenever a ship or a party of travelers comes in from the north, they are eagerly questioned, and the news flies through the town. The reports at first are conflicting; it is said that some of the cities near the frontier, acting in concert with the Hittites, have closed their gates to the advancing army. But these stories are discounted, for surely no mere Canaanite princeling would dare to oppose the embattled might of the main army of Egypt. Then comes news that the Grand Army has passed the frontier and is advancing on the great city of Cadesh, on the Orontes. And then for two days there is no news.

But the next day a courier chariot, its occupants dusty and sweat-soaked, comes in along the highway, and while the horses are changed and the couriers snatch a hasty meal, they give the news from the north. A great battle has been fought, they say, by Cadesh, and the main army of the Hittites has been held and penned within the city. It was only by the grace of the gods and the personal courage of the pharaoh that the day did not end disastrously.

Captured Hittite scouts had reported that the Hittite army had withdrawn northward to Aleppo, and Rameses, leaving the Sutek regiment on the frontier, had pushed on with Amon and Ra, and with the Ptah regiment some miles to the rear. He had left Cadesh behind on his left and encamped for the night a little to the north by the river. But his information had been false. The whole Hittite army lay concealed on the blind side of Cadesh, and it now marched out and fell upon the rear of the regiment of Ra, which was approaching the camp. Ra, taken by surprise, had been routed, and the panic might well have spread to Amon, had not Rameses gathered his household troops and sallied out, rallying his demoralized soldiers as he went and breaking through the right wing of the Hittites.

Though he had had to abandon his camp, he succeeded thereby in making junction with his free companies of mercenaries who were following Ra, and, with his combined force, he turned and attacked the Hittites as they were plundering the camp.

Battle was now joined in earnest, and for some time waged indecisively. Then Muwatallis threw in his reserves, a thousand heavy three-man chariots. And the situation had been desperate. But Rameses had also a trump to play. At the first signs of the ambush he had sent a messenger back along the road to warn the regiment of Ptah coming up behind him. And now Ptah came, with its chariots flung forward in advance, and with the infantry coming on at the double behind. With trumpets braying, they threw themselves into the battle—and turned the day. As dusk fell, the Hittites broke off the engagement and retired within the walls of Cadesh.

The teen-agers of Ascalon cheered the couriers as they drove away, completely forgetful of their old enmity with the Egyptian garrison troops. Now they identified themselves with the gallant army that so lately had passed through the town, and rejoiced over the victory of its arms.

Their elders were more reserved. It sounded as though the "victory" had been by no means complete; Rameses had held the field, but his losses must have been immense. And the Hittites had clearly still an army in being, capable of taking the field again. Canaan could, of course, be indifferent to which of the two great powers won the war, but not to the worst that could happen— that the war should drag on indecisively, with armies marching and countermarching over the length of the country, pillaging and requisitioning, and at the same time strangling commerce. The elders of Ascalon, and no less those of the other market towns, desired neither to be protected nor to be liberated.

As further news came through, it was clear that there was to be no quick victory. Casualties coming down the line showed all too clearly that the losses in the battle had been severe. The two advance regiments had been practically destroyed, and the mercenaries and the third regiment, who had turned the tide of battle, had suffered heavily. There were many homes in mourning in Ascalon in those days. Neither power was now willing to risk its remaining reserves in another pitched battle, and the war developed into an affair of skirmishes and raids. With the onset of winter Rameses passed through again, this time on his way back to Egypt. And the crowds that lined the streets to watch him pass were silent.

The armies remained in Syria. The following spring rein-forcements went up the road to the front, and there was a summer offensive of a sort. Villages were sacked, prisoners taken, crops destroyed. But the main armies avoided battle.

In the following years the war in the north was an ever-present factor in the life of the coastal cities. It seemed likely to go on forever, with the armies based upon the fortified cities near the frontier, and the light chariotry and the mercenary companies probing the enemy line for weaknesses or withdrawals. The worst fears of the coast merchants were realized; trade along the land routes was practically at a standstill.

Not that there was any blockade, or prohibition of trade. The coastal shipping still carried goods between north and south. But armies in the field were notoriously uncommercial in their dealings with passing traders, and few caravans could be found to risk the passage through the lines, and still fewer merchants willing to pay the exorbitant freight charges they required for running that risk.

On the other hand, there were fortunes to be made in supplying the troops at the front. As the boys of Ascalon grew up and began to earn their livings, a very large proportion of them found their livelihood in connection with the long-drawn-out war. There were foundries and large-scale carpenters' workshops now in Ascalon, turning out equipment and munitions for the army, and there were continuous supply trains convoying goods to the depots behind the front. Jobs were available as storekeepers and cobblers and grooms and cooks. And always there were the ships plying up and down the coast, bringing equipment and reinforcements from Egypt to the northern ports.

Still the years went by, and the young men of Ascalon grew older and married and had young sons of their own. It became more and more clear that the Hittite-Egyptian war, most often cold but occasionally blazing up, was a useless drain on the resources of both sides. Rameses had long ago stopped coming north for the spring campaign, and was engaged in a grandiose program of buildings and public works in Egypt. He still held large forces at the Hittite frontier and along the coastal supply road. But he had withdrawn the Egyptian garrisons from the towns in the interior of Palestine, and relied for law and order there on the local militia of the tributary princes.

Travelers coming into Ascalon from the interior during these years brought constant tales of clashes between the forces of the princes and nomad tribes in the south. Apparently the chief troublemakers were the confederacy of nomads calling themselves the children of Israel, the people who a score of years back had left Egypt inches in advance of the chariots of pharaoh. Their leader, Moses, regarded himself as a man with a destiny, and even spoke of a god-given mission to carve out a country for his people in Palestine. He was apparently a general of some ability, and no mean organizer into the bargain. During the years since the escape from Egypt he had trained the men of his tribes in desert warfare, and had organized them in independent regiments after the model which he had learnt at the Egyptian court. In addition, he had imposed a strict code of laws on his confederacy, based, it would seem, on the law code formulated by Hammurabi of Babylon five hundred years ago, and had firmly established and codified the worship of the Israelis' unique single god. The portable temple to this god which they carried around was reported to be more magnificent than any of the shrines of any other nomad tribe.

During these years the Israelis had been moving from grazing ground to grazing ground in Sinai, and had frequently clashed with the settled peoples of south Palestine. The Amalekites in particular, southwest of the Dead Sea, had often had to repel raids in force from the nomads, and it was agreed that what was really required was a full-scale Egyptian punitive expedition.

But the Egyptians were tied up in the north, apparently forever. And they had other worries. The seafaring peoples who had enlisted in such numbers before Cadesh were becoming more and more troublesome. They still occasionally put in on the Palestine coast in their long ships, to do a little trading or to take temporary service with the Egyptians. But occasionally, too, they raided a coast village for supplies or plunder, making off before the nearest garrison woke up to the fact that they had been there. The ships that docked at Ascalon told that in the central Mediterranean these peoples from the wilds of Europe were becoming a menace. They were now sailing the seas in large fleets, putting out from their north-coast harbors with their families and household goods aboard, clearly intending not merely to raid but to settle. They had occupied a good portion of the coast of Libya and seemed bent on establishing a kingdom there on the western flank of Egypt.

When the men of Canaan whose lifetime we are following were about thirty, and the battle of Cadesh was an already dimming memory of their youth (as far behind them as the end of the Second World War is behind us), the situation drastically altered along the demarcation line where Canaan was divided into two states and the two world powers faced each other. Some six years ago the Great King Muwatallis had died, and behind the curtain of iron maintained by the iron-armed divisions of the Hittite army there had been a struggle for political power and the leadership of the empire. Since the Great King had withdrawn to his northern realm after Cadesh, the conduct of the Egyptian war had been in the hands of his brother Hattusilis, the viceroy of the eastern regions of the Hittite realm. And when Muwatallis's son Urhi-Teshub succeeded his father, Hattusilis tried first to use him as a puppet and then, finding the young king too independently minded, had deposed him and had himself assumed the throne.

Everyone expected that Hattusilis III would take the offensive against Egypt. The Kassite king of Babylon, Kadushman-Turgu, with his eye on the vigorous king of Assyria, Shalmaneser, even went so far as to offer his assistance against Egypt.

Thus it came as somewhat of a shock when the news spread in 1269 B.C. that the Egyptians and the Hittites were negotiating. Before the year was out, a peace settlement and a pact of mutual assistance had been engraved on silver between them. For in truth both Rameses and Hattusilis were tired of the costly and inconclusive division of the world into opposing spheres of interest. It was doing them no good, and was encouraging the rise of other potential enemies in their rear and on their flanks. Rameses was worried by the sea raiders in Libya, and even by the desert raiders in Sinai. And Hattusilis needed no reminder from Babylon to keep an eye on Shalmaneser of Assyria.

The men of Canaan were not informed of the terms of the treaty between the two monarchs, still less of the political factors behind it. But they were immediately affected by the reduction of military expenditure and the withdrawal of a large part of the Egyptian forces. And the great coast road began again to be crowded with merchants and tourists.

One result of the war effort of the Hittites had been an over-production of iron armaments, and now with the opening of the frontier this new metal was available for sale to the south. The princes of south Canaan hastened to equip their private armies with this new tactical weapon, and could soon look with pride on regiments bearing iron swords and chariot squadrons with iron-tired wheels.

The next year news came with the caravans from the north that Hattusilis had marched against Assyria, and had recon-quered the old territory of the Mitanni kingdom, re-establishing it as a buffer state between Assyria and the Hittite-colonized kingdoms of Carchemish and north Syria.

Peace was a novelty in Palestine. Not since their early teens had the now middle-aged men of Ascalon known a time when the roads and the seas were open in every direction. Now the world came to them, and they went out into the world. The Ca-naanite merchants and craftsmen traveled in these years the caravan routes of the Middle East ever more widely, seeking markets and raw materials.

More than one of them during the next fifteen years visited the camps of the Israelis in the Negeb, in south Palestine. These nomad shepherds were often on the move between their grazing grounds, but they were most frequently to be found in the neighborhood of Cadesh on the edge of the Sinai desert (not, of course, to be confused with the famous Cadesh of the battle), a region which they had long ago conquered from the Amalekites. Though they were received hospitably enough, and found a ready market for their manufactured goods in exchange for wool and mutton on the hoof, the Canaanite commercial travelers were disturbed by the Israelis. Here was clearly a nation or-ganized for war. They were divided into tribes, and each tribe encamped around its standard in military order like regiments around the headquarters camp where the tent temple was erected. Raiding and scouting parties were continually out on the flanks, under their two renowned generals, Joshua and Caleb.

And at the center, organizing everything, was the general staff, dominated by the powerful though elderly figure of Moses.

Moses, whom they found quite approachable, was pleasant and courteous enough in speech, but behind his words could always be sensed an inflexible purpose. Everything he said and did appeared to have one single aim, to persuade his fraternity of tribes of their own corporate identity, of their difference—as much in quality as in race—from all the peoples around, and of their destiny to carve out for themselves a kingdom in the agricultural lands to the north. The Canaanite visitors found this calm assumption that the Israelis were a master race, destined to rule over lesser peoples (among whom they were themselves included), an ominous sign. For there was no doubt that the children of Israel were a force to be reckoned with.

Still, the years passed without serious disturbances on the southern frontier. Not until the generation that we are following had passed the age of fifty, with grown sons who had taken over the more active side of the family firms, did the first signs come that the Israelis were on the move. The news arrived from the other side of Jordan, beyond the Amorites of the mountains and the easternmost Canaanites who possessed farmlands along the river.

Beyond the coastal plain inland from Ascalon rose the white limestone mountains of the hill country, green with olives and with vines. Scattered among these mountains were the small walled cities of the Amorite princes, each controlling and protecting its surrounding farmlands and villages. Farther to the east the land fell steeply below sea level, descending by precipitous gorges of brown sandstone to the sweltering plain of Jordan, with its well-watered gardens, and to the deep blue waters of the Dead Sea. The cities and villages lying on the edge of this escarpment, to the east of the venerable city of Jerusalem, saw, in the course of two or three weeks, column after column of black smoke rising on the other side of Jordan, the easily recognizable smoke of burning towns. And as the refugees began to come in, it became possible to piece together what had happened.

The Israelites had appeared in force from the southeast, in a full-scale migration, bringing with them their women and children, their flocks and herds, and their famous tent temple in which their god was said to dwell. By a daring march along the fringe of the desert to the east they had bypassed Edom and Moab, the powerful kingdoms south of the Dead Sea which so long had held the desert tribes in check. And they had come out of the desert into the Amorite kingdom of Jazer to the north of Moab. In a pitched battle they had defeated the king of Jazer and captured his capital, Heshbon, and a number of surrounding towns. Stopping only to plunder and burn the towns, they had passed on to the north, and at Edrei had met and defeated the king of Bashan, the land lying to the east of the Sea of Galilee. They now held all the land to the east of Jordan from the Sea of Galilee to the Dead Sea, and they had returned south, laden with plunder, to encamp just north of the Dead Sea, across the river from the great fortress city of Jericho. Their intention of crossing the river Jordan and invading the lands between the river and the sea was painfully obvious.

There was consternation in Ascalon and the other cities of the coast. Though Jericho was all of fifty miles away, there was no army in the hill country capable of checking the redoubtable Israelis if once they established a beachhead across the river. And while Egypt would undoubtedly see to it that the coast road remained in their hands, the Egyptian garrisons were far from strong enough to guarantee the safety of the ports, still less of the cities of the interior. It was poor consolation that the Egyptian army would certainly recover and revenge them.

In the hills the princes made feverish preparations for defense, and almost forgot their feuds with each other as they sought allies against the invader. In Jericho the fortifications were hastily strengthened, and the people of the surrounding farms made ready to retire into the city the moment there was any sign that the Israelis were about to cross the river.

Then suddenly a respite was granted. News came across the river (by way of Moabite noncombatants who were allowed to fraternize with the Israelis) that Moses, the aged but terrible leader of the Israeli confederacy, was dead. He it was who had founded the military strength of the sons of Israel and who had promulgated the laws, religious and secular, which had held

them together against the centrifugal forces that normally lead
nomad tribes, as they grow larger, to disintegrate and go each
fragment its own way. Time after time during Moses's leadership there had been crises and schisms, and it had taken all his
religious authority, court-learnt diplomacy, and cold-blooded
ruthlessness to hold the tribes together. Now the Amorites of the
hills and the Canaanites of the plains weighed the chances that
the confederacy would break up. Already three of the tribes
had settled down on the rich pasturelands of the newly conquered territory in Transjordan, and had openly lost interest in
invading Canaan proper.

For a while indeed it looked as though the immediate danger was past, and the established burghers of the cities of Canaan
had leisure to look at the world beyond their own doorstep. This
was admittedly little more encouraging. Their agents and branch
managers and business associates in the Hittite-colonized cities of
the Syrian and Lebanese coasts were pessimistic about the future. Assyria had been extending its domains to a threatening
degree, and was now a very present danger. It was twenty
years since the Hittites had made peace with Egypt and had
occupied Mitanni, hoping thereby to confine Assyria within its
frontiers on the upper Tigris. But Shalmaneser of Assyria had
succeeded only a few years later in recovering the lost
province. Shalmaneser had died ten years ago, but his son
Tukulti-Ninurta had proved himself a vigorous and competent
general. He had struck again and again in yearly campaigns
against the eastern provinces of the Hittite empire, and his
latest campaign had resulted in the capture of Carchemish, a
city which had been Hittite since the time of Suppiluliumas. He
was now within striking distance of Aleppo, and in addition controlled, and could tax or interrupt at will, the trade passing
along the great Euphrates route between the Mediterranean and
the Persian Gulf, between the far west and the far east. However, trade still moved, and the latest reports were that the
Kassite king of Babylon, Kastilias, was prepared to dispute
Assyrian interference with the route on which Babylon's livelihood depended. And Babylon was still strong enough to cause
an Assyrian king to think twice. Why the Hittites had not

reacted more vigorously to the Assyrian attack was less clear. The Great King never showed himself in the southeastern provinces, and it was said that he was fully occupied dealing with the raids of the Achaeans, who had been strongly reinforced by the European freebooters from farther north, upon his western provinces.

On the stage of world politics the new nomads beyond Jordan played but a minor role, and they had by now been quiescent for nearly two years.

Then one morning news reached the coast that the Israelis had crossed Jordan and were encamped outside Jericho. They were commanded by Joshua, their most renowned general, who had succeeded Moses. Joshua was one of the few who had been of military age when the Israelis left Egypt, and during the nomad period he had been a famous raiding chieftain. Now, in his sixties, he was still as active as ever. After a week's siege he led a direct assault on the walls of Jericho, and captured and burnt the town.

The news of the fall of Jericho threw the princes of the hill cities into a panic. Many met together to swear alliance against the invader down in the river valley below them. Surely a united front could hold the steep escarpment.

The following year, after the crops were in, Joshua struck up from the valley with a small probing force, was met outside one of the smaller cities, and forced back. But he returned with a larger force, captured the city, and made an example of it. Its prince was executed, its inhabitants killed and enslaved, and the town itself razed to the ground. This measure had its effect; the prince of one of the major cities, Gideon, lost his nerve, and sent overtures to the new power in the land, offering peace and alliance. It was the breach in the ranks which Joshua had been looking for. He accepted the alliance, and withdrew to his permanent camp in the Jordan valley outside Jericho to await events.

To the inhabitants even of the coastal cities it was now clear that the situation was critical. But the Egyptian military governor saw no reason to take action. This was after all an affair of minor tribal warfare between vassal princes. The Israelis in the valley and the Amorites in the hills were of the same stock and spoke almost identical dialects. And who ruled whom was immaterial. Admittedly the Israeli confederacy made up a stronger and more united entity than was customary among these quarrelsome minor princes, but they could never be a threat to Egypt. And the garrison troops were intended for guarding the coastal route and could not be dissipated in futile punitive expeditions against the desert tribes in the interior.

The Canaanites of the coast were heartened by the ordering of a state of readiness in the garrison troops and by the token arrival of a squadron of Egyptian warships. They watched the situation in the hills closely, and sold munitions to the princes while it was still possible.

It was an attack on Gideon that set the hills aflame. The ruler of Jerusalem, at the head of an alliance of five cities, determined to affirm the necessity of a united front against the invaders, and led the attack on the traitor city which had made an alliance with Joshua. But Joshua had been waiting for just this move. He entered the hills and engaged and defeated the allied army. Thereafter he did not leave the hills. One after the other in the course of the next two years, he invested and reduced the cities of the alliance. Only Jerusalem, with its sheer walls rising from the steep escarpment, held out against him.

Israeli troops now patrolled as far as the edge of the foothills overlooking the plains that belonged to Ascalon itself. But they made no attempt to provoke the Egyptian forces by entering the plains. Instead they consolidated their gains, expropriating and enslaving the conquered Amorites and distributing the captured lands, cattle, and booty among their own people. And Joshua made preparations to campaign northward.

His attack, when it came, was as brilliantly successful as his earlier raids. Pushing beyond the Sea of Galilee, he met and defeated the combined forces of the northern princes at Lake Merom.

During the three years that Joshua and the main Israeli army were absent in the north, the burghers of Ascalon breathed more easily. Admittedly news came down the road of the taking of one city after another, and of the occupation by the Israelis of an ever-widening area of the hill country as far as Mount

Hebron. But it seemed that the coastal plain was outside Joshua's plans. Even when he returned there was no war, though the peace between the plains and the hills was uneasy. Joshua had enough to do, holding and organizing his new dominion.

Once it became clear that the new state on either side of Jordan had no immediate designs on the Canaanite cities of the coast, normal intercourse was rapidly resumed. Canaanite merchants visited the markets of the upland cities, and young men of the hills came down to the ports to look for work and to savor the cosmopolitan atmosphere of the seaport towns.

The men born in 1300 B.C., when Rameses II had just come to the throne and the long-ago Hittite war was brewing, were now sixty years old and had retired from active work. But they kept a close eye on the businesses and shops and warehouses of their sons and grandsons, and on the course of events in the world outside. Egypt was wealthy and peaceful. Rameses II had been on the throne for sixty years and seemed a permanent institution. The revolutions of over a hundred years ago, which had brought his grandfather to the throne, were long forgotten. Returning travelers from Egypt told of the colossal temples which Rameses was building, and in particular of the rock-cut temple of Abu Simbel near the Sudanese frontier, hewn nearly two hundred feet into the living rock, with four seated statues of the pharaoh, each over sixty feet high, flanking the entrance, and with the walls within covered with reliefs of the events of pharaoh's life, including the battle of Cadesh.

Looking in the other direction, the old men of Ascalon saw trouble in the distance. Tukulti-Ninurta of Assyria clearly intended to build an empire. While still holding Carchemish and the old Mitanni country as buffer states against the Hittites, he had now turned south, and during these years news came that he had captured great Babylon itself and taken prisoner its Kassite king, Kastilias. Opinions were divided as to whether he could hold Babylonia, whose people were not accustomed to being any man's vassals. And ancient Elam, still farther to the south and east, had of late been growing once more in strength and might well dispute the rule of the land of the Twin Rivers.

The Hittites were unlikely to dispute Carchemish, though it

was one of their oldest possessions. In the northwest, in Asia Minor and in Greece and out in the Mediterranean generally, things were going from bad to worse. The mid-Europeans, who had first come down the amber route some fifty years ago and taken to the sea, were by now a menace not merely to shipping but to any land with a coastline. Apart from their settlements in Libya, they had imposed themselves in force on many of the coastal cities of Greece. They had even taken mighty Mycenae itself, and their new dynasty there was organizing a confederacy among both the old Greeks and the new settlers (who were closely related, anyway, both in tongue and in race). And the sea raiders had been stirring up trouble on the Aegean shores of Asia Minor, in the Hittite province of Arzawa. The new king of the Hittites, Tudhaliyas IV, who had succeeded his father Hattusilis, had been forced to lead his armies into the west to restore order, leaving for a while his main interest, the temple he was constructing outside Hattusas on the model of Rameses's new temple at Thebes.

The old freedom of the seas was a thing of the past, complained the old men. Rarely now did the long-distance deepwater craft come in from Greece and the Adriatic and the west, and even the fine pottery of Crete and Mycenae was seldom on the market and when it did come was correspondingly high in price. Things were not as they had been in the good old days, they said.

It seemed a sign that an era was ending when, in 1234 B.C., Rameses the Great died. And almost at the same time came the news that Joshua, the Israeli leader, was dead. Rameses, who had lived to be over ninety, was succeeded by his eldest surviving son—his thirteenth—Merenptah. But there was no designated successor to Joshua. The component tribes of the Israeli confederacy showed signs of splitting up, and their Amorite subjects took the opportunity to rise in revolt and to seize many of the cities which they had formerly owned. In this they were actively encouraged by the princes of the Canaan shore.

The Jebusites of Jerusalem, who for years had maintained their precarious independence within the Israeli-occupied area, in secret organized the revolt, and city after city succeeded in containing or destroying its Israeli garrison. To the princes and elders of the coastal cities it appeared that the rule of the invaders was tottering and, abandoning their policy of nonintervention in the affairs of the interior, they ordered out their chariotry and infantry to assist the liberation movement. Many of the sons and grandsons of the elders of Ascalon were among the troops who guided their iron-tired chariots through the city gates and, joining the regiments from Ashdod and Gaza, disappeared across the plain towards the foothills.

The old men turned anxious eyes towards the hills in the ensuing weeks. At first all went well, and news came back of further liberations. But it was known that the nearest Israeli tribal units, those of Judah and Simeon and Benjamin, were gathering their forces for a counterattack. And one day the first stragglers came back across the plain with news of the disaster at Bezek. There the Canaanites and their mountain allies had met the Israelis in open battle and had been defeated with heavy losses.

On the coast hasty defenses were organized and new levies recruited, as refugees came in from the hills from city after city reconquered by the tribal armies. Finally came the news that Jerusalem itself had fallen and that the Israelis were moving towards the coast.

When Ascalon heard that Lachish to the southeast and Ashdod to the north had fallen, the citizens knew that there was no hope any more, and the evacuation began. From the little harbor fishing vessels and coastal tramps and even the small pleasure craft sailed for the north, crowded with women and children and old men. Among them were such as still lived of the men who had been children at the beginning of the century, and they looked back with scarcely comprehending eyes at the stout walls running down to the shore bastions, still manned by their sons and grandsons. And inland they could see the pillars of smoke rising from burning villages, very close to the city.

It was a long pull up the coast, in the overburdened galleys, to Tyre or Sidon, Byblos or Beirut, where they could hope to be safe. And there, housed reluctantly in the homes of relatives or business associates, they received the expected but unbelievable news. The towns had been stormed, Ascalon and Gaza were taken by the enemy, the whole of south Canaan was in Israeli hands, the troops of Judah held all the coast from Joppa to the Egyptian frontier—and the Egyptians had recognized the new rulers. Though many of the troops had escaped in the naval vessels which had remained to take them off, and were full of plans to regain the lost cities, the old men shook their heads. They knew that this was the end. Israel was there to stay.

THIS SCENE, TAKEN FROM AN IVORY INLAY FOUND AT MEGIDDO IN NORTH PALESTINE, SHOWS PRISONERS OF WAR BEING ESCORTED BE-FORE A CANAANITE KING. IT IS DATED TO THE EARLY TWELFTH CEN-TURY, AND IS THUS CONTEMPORARY WITH THE WARS BETWEEN THE CANAANITES AND THE ISRAELITES FOR DOMINION OVER PALESTINE.

It has long been agreed that the Exodus is a historical fact. While the only written authority for it is the Old Testament (which was admittedly first written down some six hundred years later), the very detailed and circumstantial account given in the Pentateuch and in Joshua agrees so closely with the archaeological record that there seems to be little reason to doubt that the conquest of Palestine by the Israelites did in fact proceed as there described. The only major point at issue is the date. The evidence seems strongly in favor of Seti I being the pharaoh who knew not Joseph, and his son Rameses II the phar-aoh who let Moses's people go. (Earlier and later dates, which would make the two pharaohs either Akhenaten and Horemheb or Rameses II and Merenptah, run into difficulties of nonsynchronization with the archaeological evidence for the destruction of such towns as Jericho and Lachish.) Thus the main events of the Palestinian conquest can be dated with high probability within limits of perhaps thirty years. For the purpose of the story it has been necessary in this chapter to pinpoint the dates more closely than that, and it should be realized that such pinpointing is in advance of the evidence—in other words, guesswork.

18

THE SACK OF TROY

1230–1160 B.C.

T HE TWO BOYS had grown up together within the great rambling fortress of Mycenae. Agamemnon was the elder by a couple of years, and tended to be vaguely protective towards his fair-haired younger brother. Menelaus accepted this attitude, and cheerfully followed his brother's lead in games and weapon training, even though by the time he was ten he could outstrip Agamemnon in the races and throw his spear with greater accuracy though not so far as his sturdier brother.

They were left much to the care of the womenfolk and the older men, for of course their father Atreus was away from Greece most years with the long ships and the fighting men, raiding somewhere or other along the Mediterranean shores. In fact one of Menelaus's earliest recollections was of the return of his father at the beginning of the winter in which his fifth birthday fell. Menelaus had been picked up by a burly bearded giant whom he gradually came to realize was his father, and forced to sit on his knee while Agamemnon stood straight and serious beside his chair. And, only half understanding, he heard the story of the voyage from which his father had just returned. It had lasted all of three years, that voyage, for it was not one of the private plundering ventures. No, this had been a large-scale assault on the Egyptian seaboard, organized by their cousins, the kings of Libya. It was from Libya that the greatest number of fighting men had come, but when the news of the planned campaign got around, free companies had assembled from almost all the seafaring peoples of Europe and Asia Minor. In addition to Atreus and his Achaeans, there had been Etruscans and Philistines from Asia Minor, and Sikels and Sardinians from their new settlements in the west. It had been a great host that advanced, by sea and by land, against the Nile delta. And they had captured many towns and taken rich booty, before Merenptah, who was king in Egypt, could assemble an army to oppose them. It had doubtless been foolhardy to meet a professional army like that of Egypt in pitched battle, said Atreus, but the king of Libya had been overconfident and had paid the penalty. He had lost his army—and even his plumed helmet—and had had to flee with all speed back to his own kingdom. The freebooter companies, what was left of them, had escaped aboard their ships, to which their share of the booty had already been transferred, and had sailed off on an expedition of their own. Rumor had it that there might well be openings for mercenaries up on the Levant coast, as there so often had been before. A few years back a collection of desert tribes of the interior had come down from the hills and captured the coastal plain and the ports of southern Canaan, and the rulers of north Canaan and the refugees from the south were said to be raising a force to win back the lost provinces.

This had indeed proved to be the case, and there had been a number of brisk and satisfactory combined operations against the Israelite hillmen, who really had no idea how to defend a coastal town and who couldn't run a fighting galley to save their lives. So the Canaanites had got their coastland back again, with their ports of Ascalon and Gaza, though admittedly Merenptah of Egypt had taken advantage of the war to send an army up the coast to assert his overlordship over Israelite and Canaanite alike. But he had been satisfied with a nominal tribute and had withdrawn to Egypt.

At this point Atreus had drawn his share of pay and booty and sailed for home, together with the rest of the European freebooters. But the Philistines had stayed on in Canaan, ostensibly to garrison the newly rewon cities against a renewal of the war by the Israelites. "But," said Atreus with a chuckle, "it would really quite surprise me if the Canaanites ever again have very much say in the government of their country. For the Philistine

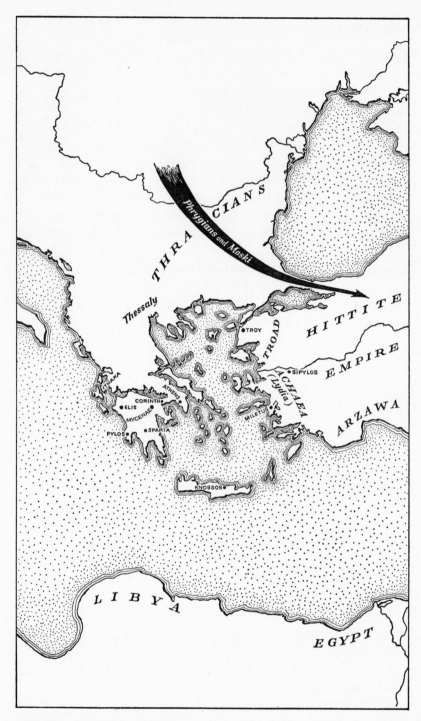

GREECE AND THE AEGEAN AT THE TIME OF THE TROJAN WAR.

captains were already apportioning themselves estates—and wives—when I left."

Menelaus had a lot of questions to ask his elder brother when they went to bed that night. How the kings of Libya, where the people were black, could be cousins of his fair-haired father, and who the Etruscans and Philistines were, and whether the Canaanites would now hire the Israelites to drive out the Philistines from their cities. And Agamemnon explained that the Libyans were no more black than they were, and that their rulers were people of their own race from the coasts of Europe who had settled there a hundred years or so ago. Certainly their kings were cousins of theirs. Mother was the great-granddaughter of Andromeda, who was daughter of Cepheus, king of Libya, and had been rescued from a dragon by their great-great-grandfather Perseus, way back in the days when the Achaeans had destroyed the might of the sea kings of Crete. Perseus had brought Andromeda back as his queen, and had been the first king of Mycenae in their own line. As for the Etruscans and the Philistines, they were cousins too, living on the coasts of Asia Minor just across the Aegean, not far from where Atreus's grandfather Tantalus had been king. But there had been famine in Asia Minor in the last year or two, and many people were emigrating to other parts of the Mediterranean. The Sikels and Sardinians were in process of establishing colonies on the islands south and west of Italy, and the Etruscans were said to have an eye on Italy itself. Whether the Philistines would be satisfied to stay in Canaan none could say; probably if they married Canaanite wives they would have to, he added with the matter-of-factness of the eight-year-old. Nor did Menelaus question this, for he already knew that men settled where their wives lived, just as his own father ruled Mycenae because he had married their mother, the daughter of the last king of Mycenae. "When I grow up," he said, "I'll marry a king's daughter and be a king myself; you can be king of Mycenae."

The days passed pleasantly enough for the two young princes, and built up with astonishing rapidity into years. In summer there was hunting and fowling and hawking, in winter the long evenings by the deal tables, where the returned freebooters would tell tales of raids and booty, storms and sea battles, and the old men would cap them with waves made larger and fights made fiercer by an extra generation of recounting. And the court minstrel, or one of his guild passing through on a visit, would silence them all by a lute-accompanied lay of the loves and battles of the gods and the deeds of the heroes of old, heroes even earlier than Perseus the dragon killer and Theseus the slayer of the Minotaur.

But winter and summer alike there was always weapon training for the boys. Under the harsh-tongued guidance of the drillmaster, they spent long hours casting at marks with the bronze-tipped throwing spears, shooting with the short sinew-backed bow, and fencing with man-sized swords and the light round shields. When they were ten years old they began on chariotry, and from then on had to use bow and javelin from the two-man cars, taking it in turns, the one to drive while the other shot. And two years later they graduated to ship fighting, driving in the early morning the nine miles of road from the castle to the harbor town and spending the day in ten-oared boats manned by the sons of the citadel troops, learning how to handle and maneuver the long galleys of the battle fleet. It was a long and well-organized training, interspersed—when the fleet was home—with specialist courses in siege warfare, deployment, bronze casting, and the equipment and provisioning of expeditionary commandos.

It was an exhaustive education, but the brothers knew that warfare was to be their life, as much as commerce and seafaring was the life of the people living in the harbor town, and farming the life of the men of the hamlets scattered through the valley. That town and those hamlets were theirs to defend, and beyond them was a whole rich world to plunder. And, more immediately, there was the prospect, in a very few years, of sailing out with their father on their own first expedition.

In the meantime, in their earliest teens, they took their chariots and an escort in the summers and went visiting over the hills to King Tyndareos in Sparta or the young King Nestor in Pylos on the east coast; and most often to their old grandfather, King Pelops of Elis just south of the Gulf of Corinth.

It was a great disappointment for Menelaus when Agamemnon, at sixteen, was given command of a ship and sailed with his
father, while Menelaus must wait the two years until he, too,
was old enough. And even more when Agamemnon returned with
the first of the autumn storms, bearing the beginnings of a
beard, and a notched sword, and tales of skirmishings with
the Arzawans and Hittites deep in Asia Minor behind Miletus.
Menelaus knew, of course, that their family held lands in Asia
Minor inherited from their great-grandfather Tantalus, who was
king in Lydia. They had recently been troubled by a Hittite freebooter, and Atreus had crossed the Aegean to assert his rights.
But it took more than one campaign to discourage what was
clearly a disguised Hittite attempt to win the Aegean coast of
their peninsula, and in the third year Menelaus, too, received
his command and sailed with the fleet. It was a heart-stirring
sight for the young prince, as the score or so of long beaked galleys sailed before the wind, with their crews resting at the oars,
over the incredibly blue summer sea. One by one the green and
white islands of the Cyclades passed astern, and after three
days the ships ran up the beach of the bustling town of Miletus.
As they passed through the streets to the palace where they were
to be lodged, Menelaus forgot his princely dignity and gaped
around, at the stone houses and temples, shops and warehouses.
He had expected Asia Minor to be barbarian and primitive, but
here was a city far surpassing the greatest towns of Greece,
Mycenae, or Sparta, or even Corinth. He caught himself won-
dering if it were not Greece that was primitive and barbarian.
And the journey into the interior, with the chariots clattering
over paved roads that wound up the hillsides past well-kept
vineyards, reinforced the impression of a tamed and civilized
countryside, contrasting with the crags and woods and goat-
pastures of inland Greece.

Menelaus saw his first fighting on that campaign. The
Hittite brigand, Maduwatas, who had invaded the Achaean possessions in Lydia and had been driven out by Atreus two years
before, was now commanding a border province as the official
Hittite governor, and still laid claim to Atreus's realm of Sipylos. This practically amounted to an official Hittite claim to the

Achaean lands and could not, of course, be tolerated. Atreus raised a force of a hundred chariots and nearly a thousand infantry and crossed the border into the Hittite empire, burning crops and cutting down vineyards as he went. As he had expected, this brought out Maduwatas with his Hittite garrison, and the two forces met in one of the narrow valleys.

Menelaus never forgot his first battle: the rush of the two-horsed chariot at the tensely waiting line, the shock of the encounter, and the sudden transformation of the orderly ranks into a melee where it was hard to distinguish friend from foe and where a throwing spear proved to be the ideal weapon for in-fighting. The confused stabbing and thrusting lasted only a couple of minutes (though it seemed longer), and then the charioteer had swung his horses and retired to re-form and charge again. In the middle of one of the re-forming maneuvers a squadron of the Hittite heavy chariots, massive four-horsed battle-wagons, had taken them in the flank, and Menelaus had a stand-up fight with a big black-bearded Hurrian with iron sword and figure-of-eight shield which was only interrupted when the wheel horse of the Hurrian received an arrow in the rump and bolted.

It had been a good fight, Agamemnon agreed that evening, as they lay rolled in their cloaks by the bivouac fire. Admittedly the Achaeans had had to retire when the Hittites brought up their heavy chariots, but they had done a great deal of damage and driven off much cattle during their raid, and Maduwatas would think twice about claiming a second time to be ruler of Achaean lands.

On the approach of winter Atreus and his sons sailed home by the northern route, by Troy and the Thracian coast. Menelaus was even more impressed by Troy than by Miletus. It was smaller, but it rose on a hillock high above the surrounding plain, and its sheer walls, newly built after the earthquake ten years ago, made the town look impregnable. They spent some days as the guests of King Priam and his many sons, who took the two princes to their hearts, trying strength and speed and skill with them in all forms of sport and weapon use, and capping their casually told tales of battles in Lydia with equally casual accounts of trading expeditions to the Caucasus and the Crimea and wars against the nomads of the great plains who sat their horses so one might think that they were half man and half horse.

The great castle of Mycenae seemed dark and damp and depressing when the expedition returned, and the winter tasks of tithe collecting and caulking of the ships and arranging for

REPRESENTATION OF ACHAEAN INFANTRY (SURELY A CARICATURE) FROM A VASE FOUND AT MYCENAE AND DATED TO APPROXIMATELY THE TRADITIONAL DATE OF THE TROJAN WAR.

renewals of weapons and rigging and supplies were boring in the extreme. Only the evening sessions in the great hall, where the bards sang of adventures long ago and far away, could bring back to a degree the fascination of the summer campaign.

Thereafter scarcely a summer passed without the young princes sailing forth, on diplomatic or warlike missions, or on undisguised plunder and slave raids. Most years they visited Asia

Minor, to collect the tribute from the viceroy of their Lydian kingdom and to show their standards on the border of the Hittite lands. And one splendid year Atreus left his two sons, with half his force of warriors from Greece, to spend the winter in Sipylos and to watch the frontiers of the Achaean lands. That summer reports had come that some of the nations of Thrace had crossed the Bosphorus in force with all their possessions, their horses and cattle and womenfolk. They were clearly prepared to fight for new areas to settle, and no one knew in which direction they would strike out. Nothing came of the danger, though. The new people, Moski they called themselves, settled down to the northeast, and apart from a few refugees the frontier remained quiet, quieter even than usual, for the Hittites moved their main garrisons farther north to cover the new threat.

Another year Menelaus was instructed to remain behind in Mycenae, much against his inclination. There were rumors that his exiled uncle Thyestes was raising a force in the north, preparing to try to recover his share of the Mycenaean kingdom from which he had been expelled by Atreus a score of years back. But that threat, too, came to nothing.

It was a standing disappointment to Menelaus that they never, in these years, ventured a raid against the greatest prize of them all, Egypt. When the news was brought by a Cypriote trading vessel that Seti II, King Merenptah's son, had been assassinated, and that southern Egypt had refused to recognize the usurper, Siptah, and had set up a rival pharaoh of their own in Thebes, called Amenmeses, Prince Menelaus had urged in council, with all the forthrightness of his twenty-one years, that they should take the opportunity of plunder while it was offered. And they even sailed south to Libya that year to confer with their royal cousins there. But the Libyan kings could still recall the disastrous campaign of fifteen years before, and were of the opinion that another raid in force now would unite Egypt against them. It was better to wait, they said, and let the Egyptians fight among themselves without outside interference. So Menelaus and his brother had to content themselves that year with a slave raid on a village in Sicily which hardly paid the expenses of their voyage, and a long stern chase after an unusually fast merchantman coming down from the Adriatic, which turned out, when they eventually close-hauled her, to have a free pass from Laertes of Ithaka. And Laertes was an ally who must not be antagonized, so they got nothing more out of that than an amber necklace each which the captain thought it wise to offer as insurance for the future.

They commented then on the increasing scarcity of prizes to be picked up at sea, and that fall they went to the trouble of discussing it with the merchant who was just about the biggest importer in Mycenae. He was quite outspoken about it. "You're ruining your own trade," he said, "—and mine. Of course, there've always been privateers on the trade routes, and even some of the traders haven't been averse to fighting for a cargo instead of paying for it. But now it's reached a pitch where it hardly pays to send a ship on a long trip at all. There's not an even chance of it getting back in safety, and even the bankers in Byblos won't touch marine insurance these days."

He poured out Egyptian wine for his princely customers, and went on. "When my great-great-grandfather founded the business after Knossos fell, things were different. The merchantmen had the legs—and the teeth—of most other craft, and anyway the Cretans had policed the seas from Trieste to the Nile. You could sail for years and never meet a pirate. It was in my father's time, with all the new people pushing down from the north, that the long ships began really large-scale raiding. And it's not merely the merchantmen that suffer. Any town near the sea is fair game, and a port is lucky if it doesn't get plundered and burnt at least once in a generation. Of course it keeps goods in circulation—I make a good thing out of selling your plunder for you—but it isn't the same thing as steady trade." He shook his head at them. "You're living on the accumulated fat of generations of steady trade," he said. "One of these days there's going to be no fat left." The two princes laughed. "It'll last our time out," said Agamemnon.

Only three years later, with less than a score of followers, many badly wounded, they sought refuge and sanctuary from Tyndareos, king of Sparta. Atreus, their father, had fallen in action, and Thyestes held Mycenae.

It had happened while they were away in Asia Minor. With a fleet of northerners Thyestes, the old pretender to the throne, had landed on the Peloponnese and, helped by a fifth column within the palace, had taken Mycenae. A courier had reached Atreus in Lydia and they had sailed straightway, landed, and marched on the castle. But Mycenae, which they had been to such pains to make impregnable, was not to be taken. Atreus and most of his force had fallen in the assault, and the young heirs, scarcely out of their teens, had been routed by a chariot assault from the sally port. They had scarcely escaped with their lives.

Dynastic struggles and palace revolutions were no unusual events among the kinglets of Greece, and the courts of the Achaeans were full of kings in exile. Still, this was a little different, for Mycenae was the richest town of the Peloponnese, and Atreus had been the head of the rather nebulous Peloponnesian confederacy. And Agamemnon and Menelaus were popular figures, already experienced leaders of troops. Tyndareos of Sparta willingly gave them shelter and full support in their plans for the recovery of their kingdom.

But an open attack on the fortress of Mycenae had been proved impractical. It took several years of undercover plotting before the only practical alternative, the assassination of King Thyestes, could be planned and successfully carried out. In the meantime the two princes, grown to full manhood, were figures of distinction at the Spartan court. And none was surprised that their return to their kingdom, supported by the whole army of the Spartan king, coincided with the announcement of their marriage to the two daughters of Tyndareos.

Helen of Sparta, Menelaus's new bride, was a raging beauty, and, as the elder daughter, conferred by age-old tradition the succession to the Spartan throne. It was considered right and proper, therefore, that Menelaus take up residence in Sparta, while Agamemnon, with his wife Clytemnestra, assumed the throne of his father at Mycenae. Even so, the two brothers worked closely together, re-establishing the Peloponnesian confederacy, making treaties of friendship with many of the princes north of the Gulf of Corinth, and sailing once more across the Aegean to

At Abu Simbel, three hundred miles along the Nile south of Thebes and close to the borders of Nubia, four colossal statues of Rameses II (1301–1235 B.C.), each sixty-seven feet high, flank the entrance to a temple cut in the living rock to a depth of over two hundred feet. The great pillared hall within is adorned with reliefs depicting the pharaoh's exploits, including his war against the Hittites and the inconclusive battle of Cadesh.

PLATE XXV

Among the reliefs on the walls of the temple of Rameses II at Abu Simbel (PLATE XXV) occurs this scene of the young pharaoh dispatching a Libyan warrior. The Libyans were at this time just beginning to be a serious threat to the Egyptians, a threat which was to culminate a century later in the attacks of the people of the sea.

PLATE XXVI

The burial bouquet, which had been placed close to the entrance of the antechamber to Tutankhamon's tomb.

Not far from Hattusas in Asia Minor lies the open-air temple of Yazilikaya, where the sheer walls of several interconnecting canyons are carved with representations of all the gods of the extensive Hittite pantheon. The temple was executed by order of the Hittite king Tudhaliyas IV, who lived at the time (thirteenth century B.C.) when Rameses II was also expressing his greatness and his piety by carving the living rock of Abu Simbel.

PLATE XXVII

The main entrance to the citadel of Mycenae, at the western end, passes through a gateway twice the height of a man, surmounted by a single capstone weighing twenty tons. Above the capstone stand the famous lions of Mycenae, cut in deep limestone relief.

PLATE XXVIII

The visitor to Mycenae, entering through the Lion Gate, sees on his right, as Agamemnon must daily have seen, the great circular enclosure which contains the shaft graves of the earlier kings. It must originally have stood outside the walls of the earlier citadel, for its graves date to about 1520 B.C., while the wall that now incorporates it was built, together with the Lion Gate, about 1400 B.C.

PLATE XXIX

This boundary stone from Babylonia bears a portrait of Marduk-nadin-ahhe, the successor to Nebuchadnezzar I of Babylon, and the king who was overthrown when Tiglathpileser I of Assyria conquered Babylonia in 1107 B.C.

This statuette is carved from amber, the whole figure being only ten inches high. It represents one of the kings of the beginning of the Assyrian empire, at the end of the Second or the beginning of the First Millennium. Just as plate III, top, is normally identified with Sargon and plate IX, top, with Hammurabi, this figure is generally considered to represent Assurnasirpal II (883 B.C.).

PLATE XXX

This rock, at Cemmo in the Camonica valley, is covered with rows of deer, horses, and daggers, all apparently sacred objects to the Second Millennium inhabitants of the Alps.

PLATE XXXI

At Naquane in the Camonica valley this rock face is covered with hundreds of carvings superimposed one upon another. Religious significance seems sometimes here to be subordinated to a plain love of the chase.

PLATE XXXII

their Lydian dependencies. The death of Tyndareos not many years later, and the accession of Menelaus to the throne of Sparta, only served to strengthen the Achaean alliance.

They had been married seven years—Agamemnon had three children growing up in his palace and Menelaus a single charming daughter—when news came to Menelaus, visiting in Mycenae, of the abduction of his wife. Half out of his mind, and unable to imagine how a slave raid could have penetrated so far inland as Sparta, Menelaus urged his horses over the sixty miles of rocky road separating Mycenae from Sparta. Beside him drove his brother.

The full story reduced them to speechless fury. It was no slave raid which had carried off Helen. She had been kidnapped (and, some whispered, not against her will) by a guest, visiting under the laws of hospitality, Prince Paris, the son of Priam of Troy.

Pursuit was scarcely practical. Paris had a two-day start, and in any case the guard commander had sent a squadron down the valley road as soon as the abduction was discovered. But, for what it was worth, the brothers drove on, with a change of horses, the twenty miles to the coast. And there confirmed that Paris had sailed two days before, for Crete and Asia Minor.

There, in the royal lodge by the harbor, the two kings sat down to discuss what their next step must be. The matter could not be ignored, and whether Helen had acquiesced was irrelevant. Not merely their honor but the sacred laws of hospitality, and therewith the gods themselves, had been mocked. And any guest who had ever enjoyed the hospitality of Sparta would be under an obligation to avenge the sacrilege. In any case, honor demanded that the Achaean kings avenge the insult to their family. But all this Paris must have known. And unless he was completely blinded by infatuation, there must be a deeper meaning behind the abduction.

The more Agamemnon speculated, the clearer it became that the action of the Trojan prince must be intended as a challenge. And the challenge could only be concerned with one thing—the Achaean provinces in Asia Minor.

Now everything began to fall into place. Asia Minor was in

the melting pot these days. The Moski, and the Phrygians who had followed them from Thrace, had of late been pushing deep into Hittite territory, and the Hittites had withdrawn their garrisons from the outer provinces to man a defensive line not far west of their capital, Hattusas itself. The princedoms of western Asia Minor, formerly tributary to Hattusas, had banded together for protection into a loose confederacy. Of this confederacy Troy, which had never been subject to the Hittites, was perhaps the most influential member.

But in the heart of this confederacy lay the Achaean realm of Lydia. In the coming war between the Peloponnesian and the Trojan confederacies, for which the gauntlet had here been thrown down, the prize was to be not only the queen of Sparta but also the Achaean kingdom in Asia Minor.

It was in the year 1193 B.C. that the confederate army embarked for Troy. Menelaus was thirty-seven years old, his brother a couple of years older, his wife ten years younger. It was the greatest army, and the greatest fleet, that had ever sailed from the Greek mainland. Not merely the men of the Peloponnese were there, but also allies from many of the other princedoms. The redoubtable Odysseus, son of Laertes of the Western Isles, had brought his warriors, and young Achilles, rather a mother's darling and an unknown quantity, led a contingent of north-country men whose fighting qualities no one doubted. The Achaean king of Crete had thrown in his lot with the mainlanders, as had many of the princes of the Aegean islands.

They sailed against Troy in 1193, and in 1183 they were still encamped about its walls. In the absence of trained siege engineers, the walls of Troy had proved as unscalable as they looked. Trained siege engineers could only be found in the armies of the Hittites and of Egypt, and both countries had other uses for their troops. In 1192, and in 1190 and again in 1186, the kings of Libya had organized the seafaring peoples of the Mediterranean in their long-awaited attacks upon Egypt. But for all that Egypt had been weakened by ten years of civil war, it had proved impossible to develop the raids into a bridgehead, still less an occupation. Setnakt, a resolute general of Tanis in the delta, had reunited the country by a defeat of the pretender from Thebes, and had founded a new dynasty, the twentieth by Egyptian reckoning. And now his son, another Rameses, was king, and still strong enough, it seemed, to hold off any invaders. Even the invasion of 1190, when the Libyans and their maritime allies had joined forces with their cousins, the Philis-

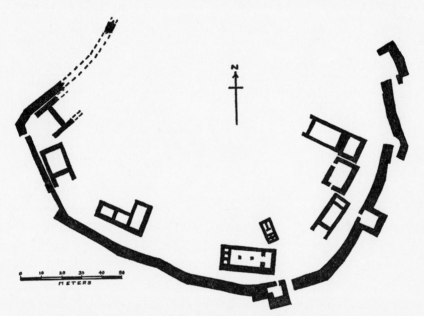

PLAN OF THE EXCAVATED PORTION OF TROY VI, THE CITY WALLS AND BUILDINGS OF WHICH STILL STOOD, CROWDED AROUND WITH REFUGEE SHACKS, AT THE TIME OF THE SIEGE OF TROY. NOTHING IS LEFT OF THE CENTRAL AREA, WHERE THE PALACE OF PRIAM MUST HAVE STOOD—IT WAS CLEARED AWAY WHEN A GREEK CITY WAS BUILT THERE ABOUT A THOUSAND YEARS LATER.

tines of the Canaan coast, and with those experienced desert fighters, the Israelis of the interior of Palestine, had been beaten back. They had attacked from Palestine in a combined land and sea operation across the Sinai desert and had reached the isthmus between the Gulf of Suez and the Mediterranean. But at Arvad near the eastern edge of the delta they had been decisively defeated by the army of Rameses III and had retreated in disorder.

In these attacks some of the allies of Agamemnon had taken

part. Though a containing force kept permanent watch around
the walls of Troy, the remainder of the fleet had sailed regularly
on other operations, striking at many points along the coasts
of Asia Minor and even farther afield. For it was clear that the
reduction of Troy was going to be a long-drawn-out affair. It
was not easy to starve the city out. Admittedly all the farmers for
miles around had sought refuge in the city (and spies told of the
hovels which now blocked the once-broad streets of the citadel),
but though the slaves and captives of the Achaeans now sowed
and reaped the fields for the sustenance of the attackers, food
still reached the defenders. With the prevailing northeast wind,
the Greek ships could not blockade the coast of the Dardanelles
to the north of the city, and small craft, hugging the coast, came
in regularly with supplies. And these supplies got into the city,
sometimes slipped in past the sentries at night, sometimes brought
in openly in the teeth of the besiegers by an organized sally.

It was during these sallies that the fiercest fighting took
place. Losses had been severe on both sides. Both Agamemnon
and Menelaus had been wounded, and Achilles, who had proved
himself one of the greatest of strategists and in-fighters, had been
killed. Among the Trojans Hector, the crown prince, had fallen,
and Paris himself had been killed only recently. But the fall of
the city seemed as far off as ever, and some of the allies, particularly the more loosely confederated northerners, were ad-
vocating breaking off the siege, now that honor had been satisfied
by the death of Paris. Matters had reached a stalemate, where
Troy could neither be taken by assault nor starved into surrender.

But now a side result of a greater war to the eastward showed
the way out. The Moski and the Phrygians, the two great tribes
from Europe which had crossed the Hellespont many years before
and carved out for themselves kingdoms in the western provinces
of the Hittite empire, had for years been fighting the Hittites
in one summer campaign after another. Now they had defeated
the main Hittite army in the field and had advanced on Hattusas
itself. And the news came that Hattusas had fallen and was
burnt. The Great King, a Suppiluliumas who had nothing but
his name in common with his almost legendary ancestor of nearly

two hundred years before, had died in the flames of his palace, and the Hittite empire was no more.

The greater part of the great Hittite army had succeeded in escaping to the southeast, to the surviving Hittite provinces around Aleppo. But even so Asia Minor was full of wandering soldiery, scattered remnants of the Hittite grand army. And among those who reached the Aegean coast were a number of officers and men of the Hittite corps of engineers.

It was Odysseus who suggested that these be recruited to build siege engines against the walls of Troy. And they were glad of employment within their trade. A mighty wooden engine was constructed under their supervision by the ships' carpenters of the Achaean fleet. Mounted upon wheels, it had a hide-covered roof to conceal and protect the attackers, and underneath swung an iron-shod ram. From a fanciful resemblance the Achaeans called it a wooden horse. . . .

Supported by archers to give covering fire, the wooden horse moved forward, and all day the thud of the ram against the stones of the wall could be heard throughout the city. Towards evening a section of the wall slowly crumbled and fell in a cloud of white stone dust. Agamemnon gave the signal for the assault. All night street fighting went on. Flames rose from sector after sector of the city, lighting up the desperate groups of defenders, the fleeing terrified women and children, and the ranks of the attackers, intoxicated with victory. Resistance gradually was broken and ceased, and the sack commenced.

Dawn rose over a city in flames, with bands of prisoners being herded out through every gate, laden with the treasures of one of the richest and oldest cities of the world. There were bowls and flagons innumerable of gold and silver, chests and furniture with inlay of ivory, bronze swords with hilts and scabbards inlaid with gold and amber, rich hangings of gold brocade and purple dyes. There were furs and fine clothing and jeweled ornaments. There was a whole armory of weapons, including nearly a hundred swords of iron. There were inlaid chariots, and such of the famous horses of Troy as had survived the siege and the sack. And there were prisoners beyond count, half-naked and seeking frantically from group to group to unite their scattered families. All was assembled outside the walls to await the great distribution, while working parties of the Achaeans unhinged the great gates and demolished the mighty walls.

And to Menelaus, as he stood gazing gloomily at the scene of his triumph, came a party of Ajax's Locrians, uncertain whether they were acting as an escort or a guard, bringing Helen to her husband. Menelaus was at a loss what to say. But Helen looked him straight in the face and said: "At last." And thereafter ten years of warfare and separation were never mentioned between them. Undoubtedly, thought Menelaus, it would save public embarrassment if it were officially assumed that Helen's abduction and sojourn in Troy had been against her will. But he had an uneasy feeling that for all future time his wife would be known, not as Helen of Sparta, but as Helen of Troy.

Nor did he feel that, after these years, he could face the mockery of a triumphal entry into Sparta with its errant queen. After the division of the spoils, he took his share and his wife on board and sailed south with his long ships for Crete and Egypt.

There was at this time an uneasy peace in the eastern Mediterranean. Although Egypt still claimed Palestine as within her sphere of influence, Rameses III had made no attempt to reimpose the garrisons in the coastal cities which had been expelled during the Philistine war seven years before. North of Palestine, the former Hittite provinces of the Lebanese coast had been left without a master when Hattusas was destroyed. They would just as lief, of course, be without a master. Huddled between the mountains of the Lebanon and the sea, they had always lived on sea trade and had been profoundly disinterested in who ruled the hinterland behind them, if only those rulers did not tax them too heavily and did not interfere with the free passage of goods by the Euphrates route from the Farther East.

Sea trade was still the preoccupation of the mixed peoples of these Lebanese cities (whom people were beginning to call Phoenicians), and of the mixed Philistine and Canaanite population of the Palestine coast towns—and indeed of the cities of the Nile delta. But the seas were dangerous as they had never been before. The freebooters of Libya and Cyprus and the

Aegean, whom the Egyptians so appropriately called the people of the sea, raided far and wide, and no merchantman dared any longer venture out of sight of land. To protect their merchant fleets, every city of the coast had by now established a navy, long heavy galleys with bronze-clad rams projecting below the prows which could hole and sink the swifter but more flimsy raiders. And they also turned the raiders against each other, by recruiting mercenary fleets from among the people of the sea.

It was in this honorable service that Menelaus spent the next seven years, with his squadron of ships chartered by the Egyptian navy and himself under contract as admiral. He had

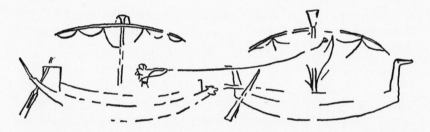

THE RELIEFS ON THE MEDINAT HABU TEMPLE OF RAMESES III GIVE, UNFORTUNATELY, VERY LITTLE IDEA OF THE APPEARANCE OF THE SHIPS OF THE PEOPLE OF THE SEA. SUCH REPRESENTATIONS AS THERE ARE SHOW THEM TO HAVE BEEN COMPLETELY DIFFERENT FROM EGYPTIAN VESSELS. THE RESEMBLANCE OF THE SHIP ON THE RIGHT TO THE SHIPS OF THE SWEDISH ROCK CARVINGS (PAGE 207) MAY NOT NECESSARILY BE ENTIRELY FORTUITOUS.

his shore base at Tanis, the greatest city of the delta, now called the city of Rameses since pharaoh had taken up residence there. And most of his service consisted of convoying merchant fleets up to Gaza and Ascalon, Tyre and Sidon, Byblos and Beirut and Ugarit. But on occasion he had the opportunity to take the river route, south to Memphis and even to Thebes, where Rameses still had a royal residence and where he was building his grave and mortuary temple in the traditional manner in the Valley of the Kings. And there, like any other tourists, he and Helen visited the great new temple at Medinat Habu, to see the carvings recording the victories of Rameses over the people of the sea.

Although it had been Menelaus's life ambition to visit Egypt, he had never intended to stay so long away from his own kingdom of Sparta. But within a year of his arrival in Egypt, he had received dispatches from home telling of his brother's death. While Agamemnon had been absent at Troy, a cousin of theirs, Aigisthos, son of the rebel king Thyestes, had established himself at Mycenae, with the aid of Agamemnon's wife, Clytemnestra. And Agamemnon had been struck down on his return and killed. With Aigisthos holding Mycenae and dominating the Peloponnese, Menelaus could not return to his kingdom without a greater fleet at his back than he was able to raise for a campaign which promised little in the way of booty. And all he could do was bide his time in Egypt, keeping in touch with the resistance movement in the Peloponnese, which was pinning its hopes to the exiled prince Orestes, the son of Agamemnon.

In 1178 B.C. Menelaus received word that the time was ripe. And he sent what ships he could spare north to Greece. The following year news of the successful revolution reached him at Tanis. Electra, Agamemnon's daughter, who had been held almost a prisoner at Mycenae, had raised a faction that had been joined by Orestes, landing secretly from the north. They had overpowered Aigisthos's guard and killed both Aigisthos and Clytemnestra. And Menelaus's fleet had been sufficient to overawe the allies of the usurper king and prevent any counterattack.

Next year Menelaus and Helen left Egypt and, laden with parting gifts from friends and officials in Egypt, returned to their kingdom of Sparta.

Menelaus was at this time fifty-four years old and felt that the time had come to leave adventuring to younger men. With the spoils of Troy and the considerable wealth that he had gained in Egyptian waters, the old palace at Sparta was remodeled and furnished in almost Egyptian splendor. In the great hall the twin thrones were of Egyptian manufacture, inlaid with ivory. On the high table the drinking cups and serving platters were of silver, and the walls were hung with priceless weapons, the gifts of many an eastern prince, swords and shields gleaming with silver and gold, onyx and amber. The private rooms which led off from the dais of the great hall were furnished more comfortably though scarcely less magnificently, with tapestry hangings and inlaid chairs and bedsteads, with fur rugs on the wooden floors, and with stores of fine linens in the painted Egyptian chests along the walls.

Every evening, when the large household gathered to dinner in the hall, and the maidservants moved along the tables with the platters of pork and mutton, and the cupbearers poured out the wine and beer, minstrels would sing to the tones of the harp of the deeds of the sons of Pelops and the great epic of Troy.

Menelaus had no sons (apart, of course, from his unofficial issue with slave girls and maidservants) and the throne of Sparta would pass, after his day, to his daughter's husband, just as he had received the kingdom with the hand of the former king's daughter. Years ago, while they were encamped outside Troy, he and Achilles had agreed to the betrothal of his daughter Hermione, then a child of seven, to Neoptolemos, the young son of Achilles. And now that Hermione was seventeen and a grown woman Neoptolemos sent an escort of his wild Thessalians to fetch his bride. And it was at the farewell feast before Hermione's departure that young Telemachos of Ithaka suddenly arrived, seeking news of his father Odysseus, who had set off for home from Troy and had not been heard of since.

Some two years later Odysseus himself came visiting. He had in the meantime returned home, and he had hair-raising stories to tell of ten years of incredible adventure in the Western Mediterranean. Menelaus was too polite to express his doubts at the time, but he had difficulty believing in the clashing rocks, and sirens and beautiful goddesses and one-eyed man-eating giants which Odysseus claimed to have met west of Sicily. For Menelaus had met Sicilians and Sardinians and even Spaniards at the courts of Libya and Egypt, and they appeared to be quite ordinary people who regularly sailed the whole length of the Mediterranean without meeting navigational hazards other than storms and sea rovers.

He was more disposed to believe the account given some years later by this nephew Orestes of a voyage which he had undertaken to Tauris in the Crimea, to fetch home his elder sister Iphigeneia, who had been sent to Tauris twenty years before as priestess of a shrine of Artemis at an Achaean trading colony there. Orestes had sailed past Troy, and could report that the site was deserted, except by shepherds who had made roughly habitable some of the burnt shells of buildings. Farther on, on the Black Sea coast of Thrace, he had met princes of half-nomadic nations who were planning to move southward with all their possessions, and to cross into Asia Minor like the Moski and the Phrygians before them who had overthrown the Hittite empire. From the mouth of the Danube Orestes had crossed direct to the Crimea, and there, in the little half-Achaean half-native trading colony, he had spent several months. He described the bands of farmers and herdsmen who would come into town, brightly clad in their best embroidered felts and homespuns, to barter their hides and wolfskins and sacks of grain for the wine and olive oil and bronze jewelry of Greece.

In truth, though Menelaus in his old age sat at home, there was no lack of visitors to tell him how it fared in the world outside. When he was sixty-five he heard from a Cypriote sea captain that his former employer, Rameses III of Egypt, was dead and that another Rameses had succeeded. But it all seemed far away and long ago. He was more interested when his son-in-law Neoptolemos visited him, and talked of his plans to move his Thessalians, or a large part of them, south to settle in the hill country of Sparta, which was still sparsely inhabited. For the people living north of Thessaly had been getting more and more restless under pressure from tribes expanding into and along the Danube valley; and it would be good policy to put the Gulf of Corinth between his people and possible invasion. Menelaus wondered what the original farmers of Sparta would say to the sudden arrival of several thousand wild Thessalians, but he was now an old and failing man, and Neoptolemos was his heir. It seemed as though the future presaged movements of whole peoples, instead of the swift raids of bands of young men which had been *his* way of fighting in his day.

As he sat by the hearth in the great hall of Sparta, his thoughts went back to the weapon training of his youth in Mycenae, to sparring bouts and chariot racing with his brother Agamemnon, now twenty years in his grave, and to the thousand ships assembled at Aulis waiting for a favorable wind to sail against Troy.

THE CRETAN TRADITION OF VASE PAINTING LIVES ON AMONG THE ACHAEANS, BUT THE FREEDOM OF EXPRESSION IS GONE. COMPARE WITH PAGE 238 THIS MYCENAEAN VASE FROM THE ISLAND OF RHODES.

This chapter is an attempt to make a coherent whole out of a series of dischoate events. A lot of very revolutionary occurrences take place during this lifetime: the Hittite empire is destroyed, and Hattusas, its capital, burnt, by persons unknown; the Philistines replace the Canaanites as the dominant power on the Palestinian coast; Egypt suffers its most serious invasions since the Hyksos, a series of inroads of wandering nations whom the pharaohs call the people of the sea. And of course there is the Trojan War, traditionally dated by the Greeks to 1193–83 B.C.—and archaeology agrees with them.

The people of the sea are a mystery. They are described in detail, named by name, and even illustrated, in the Egyptian records. While the list of peoples is not always the same for every invasion, it comprises nations called Teresh, Meshwesh, Shardana, Shekelesh, Akaiwash, Dainiuna, and Peleset. There is good reason to believe that these are the people later known to us as Etruscans, Maxyas, Sardinians, Sikels, Achaeans, Danaeans, and Philistines, settled in historical times respectively in Italy, Tunisia, Sardinia, Sicily, Greece, and Palestine. But it is unlikely that, at the time of their attacks on Egypt, all these peoples were already settled in the countries in which we later find them and to which they in many cases gave their names. This is at least true of the Philistines, who first occupy Palestine after they are driven out of Egypt, and is very likely in the case of the Etruscans, who are not clearly attested in Italy until about 750 B.C. The Egyptian records state that in some of their attacks they were accompanied by their families and possessions—in other words, that they were migrating. And it is probable that their attacks on Egypt are part of the migratory movement which eventually brought them to the lands where we later find them. (An analogy with the Vikings is very tempting.) But where did they come from? A certain amount of evidence points to western Asia Minor and to Greece, with the rider that they do not appear to have been long in these lands. (Apart from the doubtful case of the Achaeans, for example, none of them are mentioned in the Hittite records.) I have here assumed that the people of the sea are peoples of southwestern Europe, the Balkans and the Danube basin, who in the century or so before this chapter opens have pushed south to the Adriatic and Aegean coasts, and into Asia Minor, and who there have taken to a sort of Viking existence, combining farming with freebooting. And that during this chapter and in the following generations they are still spreading out, particularly towards the central Mediterranean, Libya, Tunisia, Italy, and the islands. And I have assumed that the invaders who destroyed the Hittite realm were part of the same movement; certainly when records again become available we find the Moski and the Phrygians occupying the territory of the

Hittites, and they are known to have come from southeast Europe.

The picture Homer gives us of the Achaeans is, in fact, of just such a collection of sea pirates, living on plunder, and with roots in the land that rarely go back more than two generations. The Trojan War does not appear to have been part of the irruption of European "Vikings" into Asia Minor, but rather it seems to have been an internal quarrel between two groups of these invaders; and we have no reason to doubt the story that Helen's abduction caused the trouble. On the other hand, the irruptions were going on at the time, and the Achaeans did take part. They are listed by Merenptah of Egypt among the peoples of the sea; the Hittites mention frequently the Ahhiyawa in western Asia Minor, and even name a certain Attarissiyas at this time, who is believed by some (but not by others) to be Atreus himself. Even Homer recounts that Menelaus spent seven years in Egypt and in Libyan waters before returning home after the fall of Troy, just at the period of the main onslaught of the peoples of the sea on Egypt.

Many ingenious attempts have been made to explain away the story of the wooden horse of Troy. It has never seemed a likely story as it stood; and yet it is at least as early as Homer. The theory here put forward is no more than a further addition to the list of rationalizations. It is no more likely than most others to be true.

One very considerable assumption has, of course, been made in this chapter, the assumption that the Homeric epics, the Iliad *and the* Odyssey, *are substantially true. This would perhaps appear to be a rash assumption, since they are works of poetry first put together in the form we know some time in the eighth century* B.C., *some four hundred years after the events they purport to describe. However, though the epics are works of poetry, they do not represent themselves as, nor were they ever believed to be, works of fiction. And though compiled long after the event, they bear many indications of being based upon, and to a great extent incorporating, a large body of earlier lays, some of which appear to go back almost, or exactly, to the time they deal with. Moreover, modern archaeological investigations at Troy, Mycenae, and Pylos have confirmed the central fact that Troy was taken by storm at a date which could well be the traditional one of 1183 B.C., and at the same time have disclosed parallels to many of the minutiae of the epics: vases and bowls and swords and shields and house types and burial customs corresponding exactly to those described by Homer. Finally, the decipherment of the Cretan Linear B script has enabled us to read many tablets found at Knossos, Mycenae, and in particular Pylos. These tablets, though largely inventories and storekeepers' records, tell of a political and social structure existing at the time of the Trojan War which corresponds very closely to that depicted by Homer, and tell of it moreover in turns of phrase so similar to those found in the epics that it has seriously been suggested that the bards of the Achaeans were also the court scribes and storekeepers.*

The whole question of the historicity of the Homeric poems, and particularly the Iliad, *is discussed in detail in D. L. Page's* History and the Homeric Iliad.

19

THE WOLF ON THE FOLD

1160–1090 B.C.

To the Assyrians living in their capital of Assur the sea was a distant fable. In fact the Achaeans used to say that, if you took an oar upon your shoulder and walked inland from Aleppo, by the time you reached the Assyrians they would be asking you why you were carrying a winnowing fan. That was a libel, of course, for the Assyrians were well acquainted with oars and paddles from the boats and rafts which carried men and merchandise along the broad waterway of the Tigris. But it was true that few Assyrians had ever seen the sea. Three hundred fifty miles away across the mountains to the northeast, they knew, lay the Caspian, and three hundred fifty miles away across the mountains to the northwest lay the Black Sea. Three hundred fifty miles away across the desert to the west lay the Mediterranean, and even farther to the southeast lay the Persian Gulf. Though farther away in distance, the Persian Gulf was in many ways closer to them than the other seas—for it was to that sea one came if one followed the great Tigris downstream, and it was from there that the barge loads of dates came up the river. But on the whole they were not interested in the sea; they preferred to graze their cattle and horses and to grow their wheat and barley on the broad plains at the foot of the mountains.

Not that they were provincial, of course. If fact, they would protest with some heat whenever Babylonians from the south (who, it was well known, thought Babylon the navel of the world) made the accusation. They reminded the visitors that, on the contrary, Assyria had kept the ancient culture of Mesopotamia intact for nearly three hundred years while Babylon lay supine beneath the foreign yoke of the Kassites. It was only five years since the Kassite kings had been driven from the throne of Hammurabi, and even that had not occurred through any action of the Babylonians themselves, but by the intervention of the king of Elam.

The Babylonians were not convinced. It rather amazed them to meet a people who still regarded the Kassites as foreign newcomers. They had been in Babylon for nearly five hundred years, and they were still there. Apart from the language, they could not be distinguished from "native" Babylonians, and most of them talked more Babylonian than Kassite anyway. Their gods and their dress and their customs were long ago absorbed into Babylon, and most Babylonians had a Kassite grandmother tucked away somewhere, and were by no means ashamed of it. As for Elam, admittedly they had called in Shutruk-Nahhunte of Elam to help them overthrow the Kassite kings (who *had* retained their language and family fairly unmixed), but the Elamite king had returned to his country four years ago, and the king in Babylon was as Semitic as even an Assyrian could wish. Why, even though he lived in Babylon he had begun to call his family the Second Dynasty of Isin, to recall the almost legendary kings of Isin who, in the days before the great Hammurabi, had fought the Elamite kings of Larsa, Warad-Sin and Rim-Sin.

Babylonians and Assyrians always quarreled, whenever they met. It was too easy for them. For they were two people divided by the same language. The small boys who were growing up in Nineveh and Assur between 1160 and 1150 B.C. would troop behind any Babylonian they saw in the streets, caricaturing as loudly as they dared the drawl and the soft consonants with which the southerners spoke their language. And the Babylonians winced at the harsh dialect and brash manners of the northerners, regretting the necessity of having to come upriver to trade their goods against the cattle and hides and wheat of Assyria, and looking forward to their return to the civilized life of their towns and date plantations.

They had not of course been entirely honest about Elam.

It was not really true that the Babylonians had called Shutruk-Nahhunte in. He had come unasked with a magnificently equipped army and had besieged Babylon for three years, in the meantime burning and plundering towns and villages throughout the land. And when Babylon fell, he had by no means contented himself with massacring the ruling house. Babylon had been plundered with a thoroughness that called to mind the great sack of olden days, the time four hundred thirty years ago when Mursilis the Hittite had taken the city. The Elamites had taken everything of value, gold and grain and slaves, ivory and wine and cattle, arms and horses and craftsmen. They had taken the great statue of Marduk, the guardian god of Babylon, and they had taken the black column on which Hammurabi had carved his laws six hundred years before.

Shutruk-Nahhunte had left his son with a garrison to rule in Babylon, but the following year the garrison was hurriedly recalled, and Kutur-Nahhunte, the viceroy, had thought it wise to return to Elam with the troops. It was one of those movements of the new peoples that had caused the Elamite to leave Babylon. One never really knew where one was these days, with wandering peoples moving down from the northwest and the northeast, upsetting all the established frontiers and established diplomacy and balances of power. It was forty years since Hattusas had fallen to these incoming tribes, but that Moski and Phrygians now ruled where once the Holy Hittite Empire had stretched was still something the older generation found difficult to assimilate. New peoples had occupied much of the coast of the Upper Sea, and many an old trading house in Lebanon and Canaan boasted new partners, sons-in-law with strange names and languages, who knew little about trade (though they were learning fast) but who knew how to sail and fight, as was more and more necessary for a trader in these troubled times. Then of course there were the Bedouin, who were really becoming a menace these days.

Anyway, the Elamites had left Babylon because of a sudden threat to their own northern and eastern frontiers. A whole confederation of new peoples had come down into the mountains that ringed Elam from up by the Caspian Sea. Persians, they called themselves, and Medes, and half a dozen other tribes besides. From Luristan, and from the borders of India, they were pushing south towards the Persian Gulf. But unlike their cousins in Asia Minor they were not, it seemed, anxious to try conclusions with the old empires, and they had bypassed the eastern frontiers of Elam. So one didn't really know whether the new king in Susa, Shilhak-Inshushinak, might not now try to regain Babylonia. Really it was madness, said the Babylonian traders to themselves, this mutual suspicion of Assyria and Babylonia. Only in alliance could they hope to survive in these dangerous times, and yet alliance seemed impossible, and would doubtless only come when one of the two countries had conquered the other.

The boys in Assur knew nothing of the anxious speculations of the Babylonian traders, and cared less. They didn't like Babylonians, and that was that.

The children of Assyria did not, like their elders, regard the times as dangerous. They had known nothing else in their short lives, and even the reminiscences of their fathers concerned little other than the struggles of rival kingdoms and the depredations of roving nations of mountaineers in the north and desert dwellers in the south. Since Tukulti-Ninurta, their great king, had conquered Babylon ninety years before and been murdered seven years later, there had been no peace; the old days of the great empires, when Hittite and Egyptian had held the Near East in balance, were nothing more than a fable to this new generation. War was the natural state; whichever country was the strongest campaigned almost yearly against its weaker neighbors, and the only important aim in life was to be the country that was strongest.

So there was no surprise in the minds of the ten-year-old boys when the news came that the king of Elam had crossed his western border with a large army and was burning crops and villages along the lower Tigris. The main attack, of course, was aimed towards Babylon, but the young men of Assyria were called to their regiments all the same, and marched south, with their bows on their backs, to strengthen the southern frontier.

They were needed. While one contingent of the Elamite

army crossed the Tigris and the land between the rivers and laid siege to Babylon, another force marched north along the Tigris. They pushed the raw Assyrian levies back from the border, breaking up their rallies with massed charges of heavy chariotry, and outflanking their lines with swift-moving auxiliaries who—surprisingly—*rode* upon their horses. Many of these auxiliaries were Persians, the new race from the north, and in the lands from which they came, it was said, the riding of horses was a commonplace, and people practically lived on horseback.

Back went the Assyrian forces, until for the first time in their lives the boys of Assur could see from the walls of their city, perched as it was on a spur of the hills, the army of an enemy encamped on the plain beneath.

There was confusion in the city as the nobles and the richer of the free families hurried to evacuate their children and wives and possessions to Nineveh, a good seventy-five miles farther north. Such wealth as could not be sent north disappeared underground, cached in all sorts of unlikely hiding places until the danger should pass. Amid the confusion detachments of troops were working to strengthen the fortifications, adding courses to the walls, building emplacements to cover the gates, and piling depots of arrows and slingshots at intervals along the parapets. The boys, organized to assist in fetching and carrying, had the time of their lives.

But the danger passed. Assur was too strong to be easily taken, and the Elamites dared not press on to the north and leave the city, intact and manned by the intact Assyrian army, across their rear. Symbolically they burnt the crops and cut down the fruit trees up to the very walls of the city, and then they retired. But they continued to hold the southern provinces, with strong garrisons within the cities they had captured. All the wide plain of the Tigris south of the hills was barred to the Assyrians. The river merchants, as always, found ways and means to pass their cargo rafts and boats through the occupied territories, but they had to pay heavily in bribes and taxes for the privilege, and freight and insurance charges went up to unheard-of heights.

It soon became known that the Tigris was in Elamite hands

all the way to the Persian Gulf. Though Babylon had withstood
the siege, the old cities of Ur and Eridu on the lower Euphrates
had fallen to Elam.

The boys of Assur grew to manhood with Elam an ever-
present—and often visible—threat to the southward. The lost
provinces were not to be forgotten, for many of their fathers had
owned farms in the river valley, and Assur itself was full of
refugees, reduced to menial occupations and even to debt slavery,
who once had been free landowners. And almost yearly the
Elamite occupation troops raided north, to reap crops which
they had not sown and to take slaves and cattle.

In their early teens the youths were conscripted to their
military service, learning to handle the bow and the slingshot
and the throwing spear, training in close-quarter fighting with
shield and sword and battle-ax. And the sons of the nobility
joined the chariotry, as was their privilege. Mostly their weapons
were still of bronze, but more and more iron was coming in by
devious means from the west. The great ironworks in Asia Minor
were now in the hands of the Moski and the Phrygians, but
the iron masters were still, of course, Hittites of the old stock,
who took a pride in circumventing the Phrygian embargo on
iron exports.

While some of the young Assyrians joined the regular army,
most served only during the campaigning months of summer,
between sowing and harvest. The rest of the year they plied
their trades, learning from their fathers and elder brothers the
occupation to which by family tradition they belonged. For nine
months of the year they were farmers or ferrymen, carpenters or
tanners, goldsmiths or merchants or millers, greengrocers or cobblers or bankers. But for three months they were all soldiers.
And these three months, of sweltering marches over the dusty
sun-parched foothills, of sharp skirmishes and sudden ambushes,
of the scared exhilaration of the massed battleline, and of the
cool nights by the bivouac fires, replete with millet cakes warm
from the embers, brought a sense of comradeship and purpose
unknown in the nine months of civil life. The young soldiers,
combing their incipient beards in the hope of inducing the
tight curls of the spade beards of the seasoned warriors, talked

with bloodthirsty inexperience of what they would do to the Elamite if they once got loose within the walls of Susa.

In 1140, when they were just out of their teens, they heard of a new king in Babylon, called Nebuchadnezzar, but the news made little impression. They had their own dynastic troubles at the time. The year before, the old king of Assyria, Assur-dan, had died, and the throne had been taken by a man whose legitimacy was far from straightforward, a certain Ninurta-tukulti-Assur. He had sufficient support within the royal family, the army, and the priests of Assur and Ishtar, to enforce his rule within the city; but outside, the legitimate successor, Mutakkil-Nusku, was gathering his forces. The people of Assyria were uncertain whom it was safest to support, and at the same time apprehensive that the Elamites would take the opportunity of a civil war to attack Assyria in force. It was therefore some relief to hear that the new king of Babylon had opened his reign with a campaign against the Elamite-occupied territories. The subsequent news that the campaign had been unsuccessful occasioned no surprise—everyone knew that the Babylonians were decadent—but at least the Elamites had been distracted in the crucial months that it had taken Muttakil-Nusku to overthrow the usurper.

But as the months passed it became clear that Nebuchadnezzar was showing unusual spirit for a Babylonian. His army, reorganized and strengthened, had definitely taken the initiative in the ten-year-old war with Elam. Undeterred by lack of decisive victory, he campaigned yearly against the Elamites occupying the lower Tigris valley, keeping them on the defensive, and gradually wearing down their strength.

For some years an unaccustomed peace descended on Assyria. Elam had no time to spare for campaigns in the north and, while many voices in the Assyrian army urged that now was the time to strike for the lost provinces, Mutakkil-Nusku preferred the comforts of his palace to the hardships and dangers of the field. The reservists were still called periodically for training or for frontier patrols, but no longer every year. The young men of this particular generation were by chance allowed to pass from youth to manhood undisturbed by the usual constant warfare.

Individually, of course, each of the young men born in Assur in 1160 B.C. experienced personal problems and adventures much more immediately exciting than the reports of Babylonian victories and defeats. They settled into their place in the life of the community, growing richer or poorer, becoming owners of slaves or traders in slaves or even, via debt and bankrupcy, slaves themselves (though there were not many slaves in Assur in these peaceful times, and those there were were mainly foreigners, Lullubi or Urartians raided or bought from the hill country to the east and north). In these years the young men lounged purposefully of an evening at the corners of the narrow city streets or at the open windows of the beerhouses, their eyes following the slim dark-eyed girls who passed along the streets bearing the water jars on their heads. And sooner or later, after considerable bargaining over the bride price between the fathers, a marriage would be solemnized before the priests of Assur, the city god, and another girl would join the ranks of the matrons, for the rest of her life going veiled along the streets.

Outside the city the small holdings of the free farmers and the estates of the nobles were once more flourishing, with the crops stretching green as far as the eye could see, and the new generation of fruit trees already bearing well. To the north, on the rolling hills, grazed the flocks of sheep and the herds of cattle and horses, watched by herdsmen armed with spear and bow against wolves and lions and raiding hillmen. Even trade began to pick up, and small well-guarded caravans of pack horses and oxcarts and ass trains followed once more the age-old route along the foot of the northern mountains towards Carchemish and the Mediterranean. This route was still comparatively safe, though no longer as it had been in the long-gone days when the empires of the Mitanni and the Hittites had maintained their garrisons along the road, taking their tolls from the merchants, true enough, but keeping the ways free from more rapacious brigands.

The southern route, from Babylon along the Euphrates to the Upper Sea, was, on the contrary, almost unusable these days. Within the last generation the desert raiders had increased in numbers and boldness beyond belief. They called themselves Aramaeans, and they came from the deserts of Arabia, bringing with them their new riding beast, the camel. The peculiarity about the camel was that it could go for days without water. Thus the Aramaeans had the freedom of the desert in a way that the Amorites, who had come the same way in the generations before Hammurabi, had never had. They could, and did, appear anywhere out of the waterless wastes, attack a caravan far from the nearest garrison, and disappear again with no possibility of pursuit. And now, secure in their increasing numbers, they were taking advantage of the preoccupation of Babylon and Assyria with Elam to settle down around the oases along and to the south of the Euphrates route. Flourishing Aramaean principalities were already springing up at Palmyra and Damascus, new towns which promised to dominate completely the southern trade route from sea to sea. And they were pushing into the old Mitanni lands north of the Euphrates, dangerously close to the northern trade route which was to the Assyrians the lifeline towards the west. For by this route came the silver on which their currency was based, and the iron which was becoming more and more important to their economy.

In this period of armed peace and armed commerce came the great news that Nebuchadnezzar of Babylon had the Elamites on the run. It was a blazing July, when even the uplands of Assyria lay parched and yellow beneath the sun, that Nebuchadnezzar took the field in the sweltering humidity of lower Mesopotamia. And this time the Elamites broke before his attack. The Babylonian envoys who brought the news to Assur read out in the market places Nebuchadnezzar's own graphic dispatch telling how the Babylonian army had pursued the enemy, "with the road like a furnace underfoot, and the blades of their weapons too hot to touch"; how they had smitten the rallying Elamites at the Karun river, well within enemy country; how Hulteludish, king of Elam, had been slain in flight; and how his capital, Susa, had been taken and sacked. And the statue of the god of Babylon, Marduk, which had been carried off in triumph to Susa by Shutruk-Nahhunte thirty years before, was in triumph borne back to its temple in Babylon.

The Assyrians were not as enthusiastic over the victory as they might have been. That their lost provinces should be liberated by the Babylonians was a blow to their pride, and it was not at all certain that a strong Babylon was to be preferred to a strong Elam on their southern frontier.

In the following years Nebuchadnezzar did nothing to relieve their suspicions. He campaigned northward from Elam into the hills on punitive expeditions against the hillman allies of the Elamites, the Lullubi. The Lullubi, in the mountains overlooking Assyria, were the private and special enemies of the Assyrians. It was almost an affront for any other nation to attack them, and this move of the Babylonians began to look very much like encirclement.

Worse was to follow when Nebuchadnezzar turned to the northwest, attacking the new Aramaean nations along the upper Euphrates, on the other flank of Assyria. As well as being another step in the encirclement of Assyria, the attack promised to reopen the Euphrates trade route, the direct road from the Persian Gulf to the Mediterranean. Assyria would thereby be bypassed, relegated to the position of provincial cul-de-sac, which the Babylonians had always claimed that it was.

The nobles of Assyria began to raise their voices. It was the general feeling in Assur that something would have to be done about the sluggard Mutakkil-Nusku—when he was suddenly considerate enough to die.

Assur-resh-ishi, who succeeded him, was a man of another stamp. He had no illusions about the aims of Nebuchadnezzar of Babylon, and he mobilized his army for general training. Once more the men of 1160 B.C. found themselves practicing with bow and sword and throwing spear, marching and countermarching and learning the intricate drill of the formed battleline. Now it was they who were the veterans. The year was 1127 and they were in their early thirties, their curled spade beards and their reminiscences of the Elamite wars the envy of the young recruits. By the bivouac fires they boasted of what they would do to Babylon, as they had boasted a dozen years before of what they would do to Elam.

They had their chance two seasons later when Nebuchadnezzar demanded recognition from the Assyrians of his overlordship of the whole of Mesopotamia. Assur-resh-ishi refused, and the Babylonian marched north and laid siege to the frontier fortress of Zanki. Assur-resh-ishi marched to meet him, and for the first time in fifty years or more Assyrian and Babylonian met in battle.

The Assyrian army found their opponents no soft-living southerners. Nebuchadnezzar's army was the army that had conquered Elam in the heat of summer, and the troops had since been hardened by seasons of desert and mountain warfare. It was ten years since the Assyrians had engaged in anything more than garrison duty and patrols against brigands. The battle went hard and indeed ended undecisively. But the weary Assyrians, counting their dead and binding their wounds after nightfall had ended the fight, could grimly agree that their king had done well to play a drawn game against an old campaigner like Nebuchadnezzar. And their good opinion of themselves and their commander was confirmed when the Babylonians raised the siege, burnt their siege train, and withdrew across the frontier. The Assyrians expected a respite until the next campaigning season.

But in a matter of weeks Nebuchadnezzar had gathered reinforcements and once more crossed the border, encamping in Assyrian territory. Assur-resh-ishi, though, now had the measure of the Babylonians. Their strength was in their mobility. It was this that had defeated the Elamite, and had enabled them to mount this second surprise campaign. But man for man the Assyrian was the better warrior. He led his troops in a direct attack on the Babylonian camp, knowing that within the ramparts the chariotry of the Babylonians would be useless. And the Babylonians broke and fled, abandoning their camp and forty chariots and even a captured general, in the hands of the Assyrians.

Assur-resh-ishi knew better than to try to follow up his success. Assyria needed an army of quite another caliber before it could seriously try conclusions with Babylonia. It must have both striking power and mobility. Above all, it must have chariots. And he set to work to create such an army.

Once again, as in the days when Elamite armies lay a day's march from Assur, the young men of Assyria spent every summer with the colors. At the same time, the number of regiments in the

standing army was greatly increased, and many of the thirty-
year-old veterans chose to take permanent service with the army,
seeing opportunity for promotion and plunder.

But the years went by, and while promotion came their way
plunder was but scanty. Assur-resh-ishi was a cautious man, and
was content to hold his southern frontier in strength, employing
his army actively only against the less well-organized countries to
west, north, and east, the Aramaeans and the Urartians and their
old enemies, the Lullubi. And from these less civilized nations
there was little to be gained in the way of plunder.

As the company and platoon commanders of the new army
reached and passed the age of forty, they began more and more
to pin their hopes to the young crown prince, Tiglathpileser, who
was being trained to generalship by his father and who was
known to have ambitions. They had hopes that he would lead
them south in 1117 B.C., when news came that Nebuchadnezzar of
Babylon was dead. But Assur-resh-ishi was also ailing at the time,
and it was wise of the prince to stay by his father's side—as was
proved the following year, when the Assyrian king died and
Tiglathpileser ascended the throne.

The next year the Assyrian army was unleashed.

The veteran company commanders, watching regiment after
regiment wheel away from the review ground outside the walls of
Assur, were convinced that this was the greatest army that had
ever taken the field. They had no means of knowing how large it
in fact was, but their estimates ranged from thirty to a hundred
thousand men. And while most of them, as always, were archers,
it looked as though at least one man in twenty was a charioteer.
Nothing, this time, could stand against the host of Assyria.

And nothing did. They marched north and west along the
Tigris, past Nineveh, and on towards the mountains. There they
swung onto the Great West Road, the road to the sea, with the
mountains on their right and the rolling plains stretching on their
left to the horizon, and beyond the horizon to the Euphrates.

The rumor soon spread that they were going to the old
Mitanni land, Hanigalbat, as they had always called it, to re-
establish the Assyrian frontier where it had stood in Tukulti-
Ninurta's day, at the city of Carchemish. That, they knew, would

not be achieved without fighting, but fighting was what they had trained for all their lives. And they inspected with extra thoroughness the arms and equipment of the men under their command. They would soon be needed.

Before they had been on the march three weeks, reports came back from the screen of chariots ahead of the main force that they were in contact with the enemy. And Intelligence, interrogating prisoners and digesting reports from its agents, gave news that a coalition of five kings of the mountain tribes had assembled an army to oppose their advance. They were outlying tribes of the Moski, who now ruled at Hattusas and claimed all former Hittite territory.

There was no attempt on either side to avoid battle. The mighty Assyrian army turned north into the rugged mountain country, formed line, and enveloped and overwhelmed the enemy. Clearly the Moski had no idea what they were up against. Tiglathpileser's official communiqué claimed the defeat of an army of twenty thousand men, and certainly the heaps of severed heads which the Assyrians piled on the battlefield as a trophy and a warning might well suggest that this number was not exaggerated. And the long lines of prisoners might well have numbered the six thousand that was claimed.

There was no need for further demonstration. The cities of the trade route, even great Carchemish itself, hurriedly sent envoys to express their appreciation of being liberated and to promise payment of whatever tribute their Assyrian overlord considered fitting. Tiglathpileser left adequate garrisons in the newly won territory and turned for home.

That winter the slave markets of Assyria were busy, as the returned troops disposed of their share of the prisoners to the farmers and manufacturers, who were already experiencing a shortage of manpower as a result of the almost universal conscription of men of fighting age. And the following spring the army again marched out.

They followed the same route, for the conquest of the previous year had proved by no means so decisive as it first appeared. The mountain cantons and the cities along the trade route had, it seemed, no intention of paying Assyrian tribute except in the presence of an Assyrian army. They had expelled their garrisons, and no tribute had been sent. But again they had underestimated the striking power of the new Assyrian army. This time Tiglath-pileser was going to teach them a lesson, and the soldiers, furious at having to conquer the same people twice, were not disposed to interpret his orders leniently. They carried fire and the sword along the length of the west road, and forayed up every valley of the steep brown hills to the north. Everything that could not be carried off was burnt, everyone who could not escape into the upper mountains was enslaved or slaughtered. This time there was to be no clemency.

But one lesson the rebels had learnt. Their army avoided a pitched battle and retreated into the hills, crossing the Tigris near its source and making an alliance with the Kurds, those dour warriors of the mountains who had never accepted Assyrian rule. And there, in a pass of the mountains, on territory which gave them every advantage, they did at last turn and fight.

It was a long and bloody battle, the infantry stubbornly advancing up the rocky slopes under continuous arrow fire, gaining a ridge only to meet new fire from the ridge above, and only the overwhelmingly superior numbers of the Assyrians won the day. But won it was, and the paramount chief of the Kurds was captured, with considerable booty. Again envoys came in from the city-states to the north and west, on the borders of Asia Minor, promising submission and friendship.

And again in the winter that followed, while the snow lay on the mountains that ringed Assyria, the unconquered countries took heart and repudiated their submission. Again the army took the road in the spring, to redo the work they had twice done. Again the week-long marches, again the sacking and burning of towns and villages, the indiscriminate slaughter of all who were not active enough to escape to the high hills. But this time there were no battles. The rebel armies kept their distance, and the countries beyond the ravaged lands were abject in their protestations of submission.

After another winter at home, and the spring sowing, Tiglathpileser led out his army once more, but this time to the east. It was necessary to show the independent mountaineers of

Luristan that he was not so occupied with the west that they could raid the lowlands with impunity. And deep into the hills his infantry and chariotry pushed up the stony tracks, the engineers in the van building bridges and clearing rockslides as they went. It was more a demonstration march than a war. The Lullubi and the tribes beyond, who were of the new Persian

SOLDIERS OF THE ARMY OF CARCHEMISH, PORTRAYED IN RELIEF ON A STONE SLAB.

stock, submitted without demur and were assessed for a tribute which everyone knew they had little intention of ever paying. But their teeth were drawn; most of the young men were forthwith pressed into service with the Assyrian army.

It had clearly been a mistake to give the west a year's respite. Carchemish and the countries beyond had always regarded Assyria as a very distant threat. An Assyrian army might, once or twice in a thousand years, adventure outside its allotted sphere, and such a catastrophe, like any other act of god, had to be endured while it happened and forgotten as soon as possible when it had passed by. Tiglathpileser had demonstrated his power, with unnecessary severity, they felt, and now he was demonstrating elsewhere. It could not be his intention to establish a permanent dominion over the countries at the western end of the routes from Mesopotamia, for by tradition these belonged to the Hittite, the Asia Minor sphere of influence. Hattusas, admittedly, had fallen a lifetime ago. But Carchemish and Aleppo and Hama and Ugarit were no less Hittite for that—in fact the fall of the old country had left them the heirs to the traditions and glory of Great Hatti. Hittites had never submitted to Assyrians, and they were not going to start now. Though they had lost the north to the Phrygians, the Hittites of the south would keep the standard of Suppiluliumas aloft.

Tiglathpileser took the Great West Road again.

His soldiers were now seasoned campaigners. They could cover twenty miles a day and still fortify a camp at the end of it, grumbling, of course, at the scouts who had picked a site where stones had to be carried two hundred yards and at the commissary that never got the provisions up until halfway through the night. They were adept at picking up a goat or two on the march, or knocking over hares and bustards and even an occasional gazelle with arrow or slingshot, to supplement the eternal buckwheat and dates. They could act as beaters when the king and his staff called a holiday to hunt lion in the desert, or wild oxen and even once elephant in the marshes of the Khabur, and they enjoyed the chase as much as the king did. And they were expert sackers of towns and villages, quick to size up the objects that could profitably be carried home and to destroy and burn the rest, to distinguish between the prisoners who were healthy and comely enough to make slaves and those who were only good for executing. They were good at massacre by now, competently setting up the sharpened stakes and impaling the captives cleanly and without fuss. Without pity or squeamishness, too, for the captives were rebels, who had brought their own fate upon themselves. They could have submitted and saved their lives. Not to do so was to play hazard with their lives, and they could not complain if they lost the game. Anyway, the Assyrian soldiers hazarded their lives, too, and *they* did not complain if they lost. Many of the soldiers who had stood in their time against Elamite and Babylonian had died in the western marches, and Assur and Nineveh were full of widows and orphans, eking out a miserable existence on the charity of the families of their dead husbands and fathers. And there were wounded and crippled comrades, too—not many, for a man wounded on campaign had little hope of reaching home. A gathering of halt and maimed and blind veterans was always waiting when the army returned, hoping that old comrades would spare them something of the booty which they brought back. And certainly these poor destitutes were more deserving of pity than the rebels awaiting a clean execution.

This time the army was as determined as their monarch to crush the west beyond all possibility of renewed revolt. This time they would go on until there were no unconquered territories beyond in which the seeds of rebellion could remain. While the main force marched solidly west along the well-trodden road, the chariotry, by now built up to be capable of operating independently, acted as a mobile striking force on the flanks. Pushing north, it scattered a confederation of twenty-three Kurdish chieftains in a single swift engagement, and still managed to rejoin the main force before Carchemish. This city was the richest on the whole road and one of the centers of the neo-Hittite movement. Time and again its king had submitted to Tiglathpileser and then annulled his submission. Its fortifications could still have withstood a long and costly siege, and once again the ruler used this bargaining counter to obtain terms. But this time, although the city escaped destruction, the king was deposed, an Assyrian governor and a large Assyrian garrison stationed in the citadel, and a punishing annual tribute of three tons of silver and a hundred twenty pounds of gold imposed.

From Carchemish the King's Road ran northwest towards Hattusas and the heart of Asia Minor. Along that road the Hittite armies had marched in days long past, to the conquest of Mitanni and nearly five hundred years before to the sacking of Babylon.

Now it echoed to the clash and rumble of an Assyrian army marching north.

The central lands of Great Hatti had long been in the hands of the Phrygians, and now the *coup de grâce* was to be given to the southern lands which still called themselves Hittite. Halfway to Hattusas, a hundred eighty miles along the Royal Road, lay Kanesh and Kumana, the last strongholds of the Hittites. And a week's march and a swift assault now placed them in the hands of the Assyrian king. There was an old tradition that Assyrians had once lived and traded at Kanesh, seven or eight hundred years ago, before ever the Hittite empire had existed. And here Tiglath-pileser laid, with some ceremony, the western boundary stone of his empire, on the very edge of Phrygian territory. And then he turned south, to Ugarit and the Mediterranean.

It was with awe that the Assyrian soldiers looked out over the limitless blue waters of the Upper Sea. They had been brought up on tales of the exploits of the legendary Samsi-Adad, who seven hundred years before (equivalent to the time of the Crusades for us) had led his Assyrians to the shores of the Upper Sea. Now, for the first time since those heroic days, an Assyrian army could again dip its standards in the Mediterranean. In triumph they marched south, to receive the submission of the cities of the formerly Hittite Levant.

The campaigning season was well advanced, and Tiglath-pileser returned home with his regiments of household guards. But for once the bulk of the army remained, to winter in the coastal cities. At Ugarit and Tyre and Arvad, at Byblos and Beirut and Sidon, the Assyrian officers quartered themselves on the richer merchants, keeping their companies handy in requisitioned barracks and warehouses. On the whole they were well received, for the coastal cities were accustomed to entertaining strangers and took a foreign occupation in their stride, providing it did not interfere with business. And the Assyrians had money in their pockets and soon learned to spend it.

The middle-aged Assyrian officers, seated at the tables of their hosts, or drinking resined wine in the harbor taverns, found themselves in a new world, their horizons broadening daily. They met new races, Egyptians and Greeks and Philistines, and heard of new lands and wars and politics that hitherto had been beyond their experience.

Egypt of course had never been beyond their experience. They had known of it all their lives, as the oldest and largest and richest kingdom in the world. In olden days it had been the most powerful, too, and it had more than once helped Assyria against her enemies—or the reverse. But now everyone knew that Egypt was the sick man of the East, finished as a great power, with no possessions or influence any longer beyond the Isthmus of Suez. It was a surprise to the Assyrians to find the Lebanese coast full of Egyptians all the same. There was a flourishing temple of Amon in Byblos, and Egyptian merchantmen were frequently to be seen in the harbors, though their officers had bitter tales to tell of brushes with Philistine pirates (calling themselves customs cutters) off the ports of the former Egyptian province of Canaan. The Assyrian officers tried to find out what they could of the political position in Egypt, but it was all very confused. There was a pharaoh in the delta, at Tanis, claiming to be the ruler of all Egypt; it was he who had recently sent a crocodile as a present to Tiglathpileser, "knowing how interested his majesty is in hunting and in exotic animals." But the Amon priests at Byblos denied that Nesubenebded, the usurper of Tanis, ruled more than the delta, and even that only at the pleasure of his Libyan mercenaries, descendants of sea rovers who had previously often attacked Egypt. These mercenaries now held in force the oases to the west of the delta, and could take power in the delta itself whenever they wished. It would be best, said the Amon priests, for Tiglathpileser, if he wished to enter into diplomatic relations with Egypt, to address himself to Hrihor, the high priest of Amon in Thebes, who spoke for Rameses. The pharaohs of Egypt—at least the upriver pharaohs—were always called Rameses, and the present one was the eleventh of the name. But the actual rule upriver was exercised by the high priest of Amon, whom the Byblos priests did not hesitate to name with full royal titles.

But whether Hrihor or Rameses or Nesubenebded or the Libyans were the rulers of Egypt, there was no doubt that they were powerless outside Egypt. Even just across their eastern frontier, in Palestine, the Philistines—distant cousins of the

Libyans, incidentally—were taxing and plundering Egyptian ships at the same time as they were fighting a war with a stubborn inland nation called Israel. They had just captured one of the Israeli champions, a man called Samson, and they told jubilantly how he had been blinded and was working as a slave in Gaza.

The Assyrians soon learned to recognize Egyptians and Philistines, and Aramaeans from the new kingdom of Damascus, when they saw them in the bazaars of Tyre or Beirut. But they never managed properly to distinguish between the various peoples from the far west, whose ships frequently called in at the ports. They were the people who brought the olive oil and resined wine that had occasionally in the past come along the trade routes to Assyria, together with exotic trade goods such as amber and sponges, and the Assyrians now learned that these people lived across the sea, on islands and peninsulas beyond Asia Minor. They spoke a completely unintelligible language—it was they who called the Hittites of the Lebanese coast Phoenicians, for example—and many of them were fair-haired, just like the new Persian tribes in the mountains to the east of Assyria. They were great drinkers and used, in their cups, to sing interminable songs which, the interpreters said, were about the sack of an Asian city called Troy about a hundred years ago. The Assyrians, great sackers of cities themselves, could not understand why such a fuss should be made of the fall of one city, but the interpreters suggested that it was because the sack of Troy was the last exploit of these Achaeans, as they called themselves, before they in their turn had been subjugated. For Achaea had recently been overrun by tribes from the north, called Dorians, who claimed a divine right to rule Achaea because they were descended from an old Achaean hero, Hercules. And the Achaean princes had been forced out of their country, and had settled in Cyprus and Asia Minor—not at Troy though, for another northern tribe had crossed into Asia Minor and occupied that site.

It was all very confusing, but without significance to a land power like Assyria. Obviously no king of this place called Greece would ever invade Asia or conquer Mesopotamia. The world could safely ignore Greece.

It was almost with regret that the Assyrian garrisons re-

ceived news that Tiglathpileser was on his way to join them
again. The fleshpots of the west had proved unexpectedly pleasant, and they had little desire to be relieved by the new troops. It
proved an arduous campaign, too, that year, for after Tiglathpileser had superintended the change-over of garrisons and made
a triumphal tour of the coast—including a porpoise hunt—he led

ONE OF THE EARLIEST REPRESENTATIONS OF A RIDING CAMEL, FROM
THE ARAMAEAN SETTLEMENT AT TELL HALAF IN NORTH IRAQ.

them into the desert behind the Anti-Lebanon, deep into the
territory of the Aramaeans, to the oasis of Palmyra far south of
the Euphrates.

Just why they should be tackling the Aramaeans they did not
at first understand. It could hardly be solely to acquire the camel
corps which the king recruited from his captives. But then the
rumor got around that the aim was to dominate the country on

both sides of the Euphrates trade route, the southern route which crossed the continent by way of Babylon. Then they understood. At last they were to try conclusions with Babylon. At last they were going to show the world who was master in Mesopotamia.

All the same, a year went in preparations after their return, in the fashioning of iron weapons and iron-tired chariots from the stocks of metal acquired in the western campaigns. And in the next year Tiglathpileser contented himself with establishing bases on the lower Zab in northern Babylonia, using as pretext a Babylonian border raid which had carried off some cattle and two temple statues. But in 1107 B.C. he marched southward in force.

He was met by the main Babylonian army at Marrili in upper Akkad, and the issue was never in doubt. The veteran Assyrian army, a hundred thousand strong, was the greatest fighting machine of the age. And the tough desert campaigners broke the Babylonian line in a single charge. The rest could be left to the engineers and the specialist storm troops. Dur-Kurigalzu, Opis, the two Sippars, and finally Babylon itself were taken by assault. The rest of the campaign was organized plundering—and the Assyrians reckoned themselves without equal as plunderers.

Never had Assur been so full of portable wealth as the following winter. Slaves were a glut on the market. Silver and gold flooded the imperial coffers and overflowed into the pockets of the troops. Cattle and sheep could almost be had for the asking. The wealth of the world streamed in on unending ass trains and convoys of laden barges. Tiglathpileser bestrode the world, and the following year, for the first time in ten years, there was no campaign.

At about this time the majority of the men born around 1160 B.C., the veteran backbone of the army, retired from active service. They were in their middle fifties, and their sons were already in the ranks. They could afford now to take the grants of land, at home or in the conquered territories, which were the payment for long service, and with the captured livestock, and the captured slaves to herd them, they could and did settle down to pass the rest of their days as gentlemen-farmers.

Tiglathpileser, too, had no more worlds to conquer. He had

surpassed his great predecessor, Samsi-Adad, and like the mythical Sargon of old he ruled from the Upper to the Lower Sea.
Occasional campaigns were still necessary, more police actions
than regular warfare, but now he could devote himself to the
pleasures of empire, to the magnificent lion and elephant hunts
which were seriously reducing the numbers of these beasts in the

HUNTING WAS THE PRINCIPAL RECREATION OF THE ASSYRIAN KINGS
AND NOBLES, AND THIS SCENE, FROM AN ASSYRIAN CYLINDER SEAL,
SHOWS A PLEASING INCIDENT FROM AN OSTRICH HUNT. THE OSTRICH,
LIKE THE LION AND THE ELEPHANT, WAS AT THIS TIME TO BE FOUND
IN THE SYRIAN DESERT.

river valleys, and to the building of temples and palaces. With
the wealth of his empire available, with the silver of the Taurus
and the cedars of Lebanon at his disposal, he rebuilt at Nineveh
and Assur the temples of Bel and Ishtar and Adad in magnificent
style, laying out parks with deer and ibex and foreign plants and
trees. On their infrequent visits to town, the aged veterans looked
with proprietorial pride at the national evidence of the success of
their arms.

But mainly they were content to live on their estates, or to visit the estates of their comrades in arms, reliving across the winecups the battles of their youth and middle age, the defensive wars against Elam and Babylon, the desert marches and the mountain assaults, the halcyon days on the Phoenician coast, and, always, the storming of Babylon, the crowning achievement of a life in arms.

In this chapter there is little or no fiction or guesswork. The Annals of Tiglathpileser give as detailed an account as one could wish of the later period, and Nebuchadnezzar of Babylon has also left his own account of the events of his reign. He is not, *be it said, the well-known Biblical Nebuchadnezzar (II), who ruled in Babylon some five hundred years later (604–562 B.C.).*

20

THE CELTIC DAWN

1090–1020 B.C.

To THE SOUTH marched the mountains of the Caucasus. From sea to sea they marched, from the Black Sea to the Caspian. Their peaks reached up grey against the blue of the sky, and they were crowned with eternal snow, as eternal as the mountains themselves, as the great rolling plains, as the people of the plains.

The people had always lived on the plains. Their farmlands stretched along the valleys of the great sluggish rivers, and up the streams into the foothills. Between the rivers were the grasslands, where the herdsmen wandered with their immense herds of cattle and horses. But herdsmen and farmers were one people, had been one people since time began, and the barrows that lay thick over the plains covered the bones of their common ancestors.

As befitted an ancient people, they had long traditions. In the morning of their race, sang the bards, they had sent out their sons to the north and the south, the east and the west. To the ends of the earth they had gone, and where they came they had ruled. There was a time when a young man of their people could travel from the Yanisei to the Rhine, from the Indus to the Baltic, from the Mediterranean to the White Sea, and travel among kinsfolk all the way.

But those days were gone. Their kin had married among their subjects, had forgotten their common language, had quarreled among themselves and lost their coherence, lost even the memory that their ancestors were of the steppes. Foreign nations now bordered their grazing grounds.

The borders were uneasy. The kings and councils of nobles

met constantly to make plans to cope with the unrest in the south and east. But it was more and more difficult to hold the troubles in check.

The southlands, across the mountains, had always been the lands of opportunity. There lay the wealthy kingdoms of the city dwellers and thence came the merchants, bringing weapons and ornaments of iron and bronze, bronze caldrons and ivory-inlaid furniture, wine and dates and fine cloths, incense and spices and jewelry. The merchants came every year to the great horse fairs, held on the open plain by Maikop, and they bought horses by the hundred, loading them with bales of felt and furs and hides for the journey south. And many of the young men of the people went south with the horses, as they had done from time immemorial, to serve a term as drivers and horse trainers and mounted archers in the armies of the southern lands.

During the last thirty or forty years the recruiting and remount officers from the south had been particularly active. For there had been war across the mountains. The new kingdom of Urartu north of Lake Van had been fighting for its life against the Assyrians in the northern plains of Mesopotamia. Tiglathpileser, the great king of Assyria who had recently died, had campaigned deep into the mountains, inflicting defeat after defeat on the Urartians, whom they called the Na'iru. There had been attractive opportunities for mercenary service during those years, and the people had gone south in large numbers. They had served, of course, on both sides, for they had no interest in either part and went wherever the pay or the prospect of booty was greatest.

In the course of the wars hundreds of refugees had fled across the mountains to the country of the plains, and now that Tiglathpileser was dead many of the young men of their own people, now no longer so young, were returning, bringing with them their wealth and their outlandish acquired customs and their foreign wives. The country, in fact, was getting dangerously overcrowded—particularly as a result of the loss of the eastern grazing grounds.

They had known the nations to the eastward for generations. These nations had always been there, and always been uncomfortable neighbors. They had long claimed rights to grazing grounds which traditionally were not theirs. There had been clashes of mounted archers, cattle-raiding—in both directions— and horse-thieving and woman-snatching. Occasionally a wagon camp was burnt and its inhabitants massacred and scalped. And in the midst of it all there had been parleys and trading, cere- monial visits of chieftains accompanied by impressive presents and protestations of good will, exchanges of captives and sur- render of political refugees. All the usual bickering and chaffering of a border between two loose confederacies.

They were even willing to count the eastern tribal confed- eracy as their distant cousins. The eastern tribes were descend- ants of the clans that at the time of the great expansion, perhaps a thousand years ago, had ranged east and north, to the Urals and beyond, and they still retained the fair skin and intelligible speech of their ancestors, though up on the Yanisei they had ac- quired a foreign strain, which showed itself in lank black hair and yellow skin and high cheekbones.

The tribes of the eastern confederacy had many names, and the confederacy was generally known by the name of whatever tribe was paramount for the time being. But now, after the Per- sians and the Medes and the other southern nations had hived off a couple of generations or so ago and migrated south into the Iranian plateau, the remainder of the confederacy had gradually adopted the generic title of Scythians, in much the same way as the people north of the Caucasus would call themselves Cim- merians.

The Scythians were being troublesome. The adoption of a common name was only one symptom of a greater coherence and unity of purpose, and their paramount king was not merely re- newing the traditional claims of his people; he was enforcing them. He claimed, it was true, that he was being pushed by his own eastern neighbors, a Sarmatian confederacy related to the yellow men of Siberia, but whatever the pretext, he had occupied the disputed grazing lands in force and could not be dislodged.

The council of the Cimmerian chiefs met on the Maikop plain, at the time of the great horse fair. Among the corrals and booths and wagon camps their great curved tents of embroidered felt rose like the grave mounds of their ancestors hard by. Where their standards rose at the place of assembly they could be found deliberating, seated upon their saddle blankets and surrounded by a vocal throng. Every free man could listen to the deliberations of the chiefs, and speak if he could attain a hearing.

In these years there were many and serious complaints. The eastern natives of the confederacy, who had lost their pastures, had been encroaching on their western neighbors. Ranges were being overgrazed twice in one year, and the grass was failing. The hungry herds had broken into the plowlands of the farmers and eaten the young grain, and it had come to blows between settlers and herdsmen. The returning mercenaries were claiming family grazing rights that had been reapportioned in their years of absence. Too many people, too many flocks and herds were competing for too little land.

The traditional solution to such a situation (which after all was known to have recurred every few generations) was to seek more land. And no time was wasted in deliberating that point. Even the question of direction involved little discussion. For the south was blocked by the armies of Assyria and the not inconsiderable might of Urartu. And the Scythians in the east had already shown themselves too strong to be pushed back. To the north the grazing became progressively worse until the swamps and forests began, a country only suitable for hunting and marginal farming.

But the west was, as it had always been, a land with possibilities. And the debate turned to ways and means of exploiting its promise.

The west was in a turmoil unparalleled in the memory of man. Ever since the central Europeans had established their own bronze foundries and armament industry three hundred years or more ago they had been pushing out to the Mediterranean coast, to raid the rich shipping and richer cities of the mercantile empires there. But since, just a hundred years ago, the Achaeans of Greece had sacked Troy, the guardian of the gateway leading from Europe to Asia, and incidentally weakened their own power in the process, the nations of Europe had been moving south in organized bodies to loot and occupy the exposed lands.

The main work was already done. The Phrygians and the

Moski had crossed into Asia Minor and broken the Hittite empire. And to their west the Dorians had pushed south into Greece, and had captured the key fortress of Mycenae less than twenty years before. Since then all the peoples south of the Danube had been emigrating unchecked into Greece and Asia Minor, eager to seize what plunder remained and to stake out a claim in the rich and fertile valleys of the fabulous Mediterranean coast. And behind them the Thracians had been able to spread from their home-lands north of the Black Sea into the almost deserted plain of the lower Danube.

And the Thracians were the immediate neighbors of the Cimmerians to the west.

They had not, of course, completely deserted their home pasturelands. But many families, and even chieftains with their whole peoples, had trekked southwest. Land was available, then, in the Thracian territories, at the price of acknowledging the suzerainty of a Thracian king, or—if the situation warranted it —defying his authority. The assembly broke up after a formal decision that, although war with their old friends, the Thracians, was not to be contemplated, the western border was henceforth to be regarded as open territory. Any of the peoples who wished might move across it and make what arrangement they could with its inhabitants. And if they were opposed with force, the king and his chieftains in council would decide in what way support might be given.

In the following years a considerable portion of the Cim-merian nations crossed the open frontier. It was no organized movement. When a territory was heard to be vacant or sparsely held, a subtribe or a group of families would strike through the intervening lands and occupy it. Sometimes there would be skirmishes with other aspirants; sometimes the matter could be settled by the payment of a few score head of cattle or by the promise of an annual tithe. Sometimes the new settlers were thrown out, and returned or went elsewhere; sometimes they were defeated and enslaved. But on the whole the movement was constant and successful.

Always in the van were to be found the veteran mercenaries from the Assyrian campaigns. They were hard-riding, hard-fighting, hard-living warriors, accustomed to living off the country and not too particular about loyalties, except to each other. Although they were now accompanied by their families and possessions, they tended to form free-lance squadrons in the old manner, collecting under the banner of an experienced and popular officer and moving wherever war or rumor of war offered a chance for a profitable period of service.

A whole new generation of soldiers of fortune grew up in the mercenary camps of eastern Europe in the middle years of the last century of the Second Millennium.

The horsemen picked their way along the stony pack-horse trail by the clear blue waters of the glacier stream. Ahead of them the mining village was out of sight around a pine-clad spur, but its presence was marked by the pall of smoke, a thousand feet or more higher up the mountain, which veiled the icy peaks of the Salzkammergut and marked the site of the actual mines and foundries of Hallstatt. There was always smoke in the evenings at the copper mines, said the mule drivers, who had been there before. In the evening the smelting pits were raked out, and new fires were banked at the lode faces of the galleries anywhere up to a hundred yards into the mountains, to split by their heat the ore that was to be mined the following day. The captain of the escort nodded thoughtfully, and stored the information away, together with the other details he had gleaned on the way.

His accoutrements were unusually rich for a commander of a mounted escort. Beneath his embossed leather saddle, a saddle-cloth of appliquéd feltwork almost swept the ground with its woolen tassels. Silver buckles and the silver-inlaid bit set off the intricate pattern of the leather bridle and breastband. The rider's cloak was tossed back to reveal the bronze scales of his body armor and the gold-plated scabbard of his long sword. And he bore a helmet of bronze plates mounted on red felt and supporting a plume of ermine.

He was indeed more than an escort captain. At the court of the king by the Danube he held the office of Master of the Horse, and for all that he was a foreigner he ranked with princes of the blood. But he had learnt as a young man in the army of Tiglath-

pileser the importance of seeing things for himself, and when the
king determined to send a pack train south to the mountains to
bring bronze, he had taken the opportunity to see with his own
eyes the source of the metal. Bronze was essential to the equipment and armament of his troops, and he needed to know whence
it came, how much could be produced, and how vulnerable was
the route along which it came. All the same, he was dissatisfied
with bronze, as anyone must be who had once been accustomed
to the bite of iron weapons. Bronze was at most a second best, and
no commander likes to equip his troops with second-best materials. That was another matter that he could discuss with the
foundry masters on the morrow.

But the subject came up that evening, at dinner at the high
table in the house of the royal superintendent of mines. It was the
son of the Master of the Horse, provoked by a chance reference
from his father to his service with the Assyrians—irritatingly
frequent, those chance references were—who ventured to protest. Tiglathpileser had been dead these thirty years, he said, and
half Europe and half Asia lay between Assur and the Salzgebirge.
What did the Tigris have anyway, or come to that the Nile, which
the Danube did not have?

He was a very young man, scarcely out of his teens, and very
sure of himself. He was of a new generation, brought up in the
cavalry camps of central Europe, and, like all his generation,
completely divorced from his tribal origins on the steppes. He
affected to despise everything Cimmerian; having been born in
Nyrax in the territory of the Danubian king, he preferred to
consider himself by birth a Celt. Like the native Celts he cultivated a flowing mustache and swept his fair hair back in a carefully pomaded mane. Though as a concession to utility he went
so far as to wear the trousers of the steppe people rather than the
European tunic, he professed to regard felt armor and horse
cloths as positively Scythian, and himself affected the local
woolen homespuns. The massive gold torque around his neck and
the horned bronze helmet hanging from its peg on the wall behind him both proclaimed his assumption of the fashions of the
Celtic court.

But for all his youthful extremism, he was known to his

father as a brave warrior, a brilliant horseman, and a skilled patrol commander, and his outburst was treated as worthy of serious reply. The valleys of the Tigris and the Nile, his father said soberly, were political unities in a way that the Danube was not—yet. Admittedly Mesopotamia had split up again, after the death of his old commander Tiglathpileser (his son shuddered at the name), into the age-old rivalry between Assyria and Babylon; and admittedly since the death of the last Rameses Egypt too had been divided into north and south, with apparently unending civil war between rival pharaohs. But any king who was also a competent general could unite each of the valleys, because there was a historical background for unity. On the Danube that historical background was still for the future to create. The king ruled the upper reaches of the Danube and the Drave, and his sovereignty extended loosely into Thracian country, the great plain of the middle river. But that was all.

Then, too, the Nile valley and Mesopotamia were densely populated, with rich cities, whereas the deserts surrounding them were only sparsely inhabited, however warlike the inhabitants might be. The farmers of Europe had never developed anything larger than wooden market towns like Nyrax along their rivers, and their upland was comparatively thickly populated by half-settled herdsmen, who could be neither ignored nor easily incorporated in an empire. It could be done perhaps, but if his son contemplated a Celtic Empire—and he smiled slightly—he would do well to try to win the herdsmen of the Alpine foothills to the idea first.

The Nile and the Tigris, anyway, had something else which the Danube had not. They had iron. In fact, everyone in the east had iron by now. Even insignificant nations like the Philistines and the Israelites in Palestine fought their unending wars with iron swords. And the Danube valley could never hope to compete as a power among powers by pitting bronze weapons against weapons of iron. They could not even hope to prevail against smaller and nearer nations who possessed iron, the Dorians of Greece, for example, or the new Etruscan colonies in Italy. What were the possibilities, the Master of the Horse asked, turning to the superintendent on his left, of converting the smelting pits here in Hallstatt to the production of iron?

The technical discussion that followed was continued the following day, in consultation with the leading mining engineers and the smelting masters of the guild. They were disposed to dismiss the whole idea as impractical. Admittedly, there was iron ore in quantity. It had been located in outcrops years ago by prospectors from Asia Minor who were looking for silver and tin. But the process of smelting was completely different from that of copper. Iron would not melt even at the highest temperatures that could be produced in the open bronze-smelting pits. Only a sort of malleable slag could be achieved, and this, even if it were beaten into crude shape, produced an edge much softer than bronze. The smiths simply did not know how "hard" iron was produced, but they suspected that some other constituent was introduced, just as tin was mixed with copper to produce bronze. They demonstrated in the following days what could be done, puddling a cartload of iron ore in one of the bronze-melting pits beside the stream near the mines. There was no doubt that the results were unusable, coarse-grained coagulated lumps, resembling stone rather than metal, which flew to pieces when hammered cold. They even managed, by building a turf roof over the pit and stoking feverishly, to raise the temperature to a point where they could run off a little molten iron into a mold. The experimental cast iron shattered as soon as they tried to give it an edge. Yet clearly iron could be worked. The general could recall the blacksmiths of Assyria pounding red-hot iron bars to produce swords and knives, and chariot tires that could be bent into a complete circle without snapping. A manufacturing secret was involved, and somewhere it could be acquired.

Hallstatt had at this time not been long under the protection of the Celtic king. And its dour miners and foundry hands were not displeased at being able to show the easterners that some, at least, of their newfangled ideas were impracticable. These dirt farmers of the middle Danube plain had not been interested enough to bring their orders for bronze to the Alps before, so long as they had had the Carpathian mines at their beck and call. But

now that the Thracians and the other nations from Russia had occupied the Transylvanian mining districts, the Danubians were
glad enough to come to Hallstatt. And they expected the Hallstatt foundries, if you please, to produce Hungarian specialities
for them, broadswords instead of rapiers, and caldrons, and
jingle-jangle ornaments. It was just like them now to send this
foreign trooper from the Caucasus, expecting Hallstatt to stand in
for the ironworks of Asia Minor as well, and to produce Assyrian-
type weapons of iron for his armies.

Though the Celts were newcomers to the mountain uplands,
and the name they gave themselves was new, they were not
strangers. For centuries their ancestors had been farming the rich
cornlands of the Hungarian plain, growing most of the barley
without which the cattle and sheep ranchers of the uplands would
have had neither cakes nor ale. For this reason, and also for a
certain grim courage in defending themselves and their homesteads, and for their broad-bladed swords, which—though they
were not horsemen—they could wield so devastatingly against
mounted men, they had been tolerated in spite of their odd
customs. And their customs were very odd indeed. They did not
bury their dead under a mound, as other Europeans had done for
a thousand years, but burned them and put their bones in a pot,
and the pot they placed in a simple hole in the ground. And their
gods were not the gods of the open spaces and the open heavens,
the sun-god and the wind-gods and the god of thunder; they were
not even, as one might have expected, farmer deities, corn spirits
and fertility goddesses. No, these Celts worshipped older gods
(somehow, one knew that they were older), gods of the forest
and the hunt, gods with deer antlers or with three faces, gods who
lived in oak trees and in the mistletoe, gods that were worshipped
by moonlight.

For over a hundred years now nation after nation of the
steppe people had been pressing in from the east, and the farmers
of the plains of the middle Danube had stood full athwart their
path. They had had much use for their broadswords, and for
their courage, in that hundred years, and many a horde from the
east had turned away to seek easier lands to the south. Three
generations had stood to arms, while Phrygians and Moschians,

Ionians and Dorians and Thessalians had tried their mettle, and then turned south to Greece and Asia Minor. And still new nations appeared out of the east.

Before the Thracians, at last, the farmers had broken. Scarcely a generation ago their eastern defenses along the Transylvanian mountains had been overrun, and the Thracian horsemen had poured through the Iron Gates into the plain beyond. And the farmers, withdrawing northwestward before them along the narrowing valley of the Danube, had joined the number of the nations seeking a new home. They were still a force to be reckoned with, stalwart land-hungry men, well armed with Transylvanian bronze and well trained in its use. They had established themselves in the plain of Vienna and the Carinthian hills, more united and more dangerous now that they had lost their roots. And they were still pushing westward, reinforced by these mounted mercenaries recruited from the peoples of the steppes. They were now a united nation and, though composed of many tribes, had a single ruler and more and more freely used the common name of Celts.

There was a trade route that crossed the Alps, following the course of the river Inn through the Tyrol and climbing to the Brenner pass. South of the pass it divided, to follow the Alpine valleys southward to the swamps and forests of the Po, and thence to the Adriatic. It was a well-worn route, still with paved or brushwood causeways crossing the marshy patches and with the trees cut back where it passed through the forests. Now the brushwood and brambles were thick where the road had been, leaving only a narrow trail still trodden clear. Many of the hospices along the way were gone—heaps of tumbled stones or charred mossgrown logs, where invaders had passed by and paid for their lodging with the sword.

It had been a busy road in its day, the old men said. They called it the Amber Road, for along it had come the sea gold of the far Baltic as well as the copper ingots and the tin from nearer home, and furs and hides and slaves and cattle, bales of wool and casks of honey and sacks of salt. And the other way, from the south, had come the fine wares of the east, ornaments of gold and

bronze, jewelry of faïence and topaz and ivory, fine weapons and
fine tools, woven linen and damask, skins of wine and of olive oil,
drugs and dyes and incense. And with the traders had traveled all
manner of men, smiths and tinkers, acrobats and priests, wheel-
wrights and prospectors and physicians. There had always been
life on the road in the old days.

Now few used the Amber Road. Since the Dorians had taken
Greece, no ships came up the Adriatic from Mycenae and Crete
and Pylos. Only an occasional coastal vessel brought to the mouth
of the Po a scanty cargo, bought on speculation from the Phoenician ships that called in farther south. And the merchants of the
estuary towns put aside their plowshares and organized a hasty
and expensively escorted pack train to defy the brigands of the
Alpine passes and bring the goods through to the Danube markets, where they were sold at exorbitant prices.

The Master of the Horse was interested in the Amber Road.
It ran only some eighty miles west of Hallstatt, and in the ten
years since his abortive attempt to process iron at the bronze
foundries there, the Celtic dominions had been extending westward along the northern foothills of the Alps almost as far as the
valley of the Inn.

They had been ten years of almost ceaseless fighting. As he
had forecast long ago, any attempt to form a strong kingdom
along the upper valley of the Danube depended upon the support
or subjection of the Alpine hillmen who dominated the valley,
and the hillmen had resisted subjection stubbornly. Their villages, stockaded or when possible built on a wooden platform
supported by piles in the marshes of the shores of lakes, were
difficult to attack. And when they were eventually taken and
burnt, the inhabitants preferred to move rather than submit. The
western expansion of the Celts seemed, in fact, merely part of an
unending chain reaction, uprooting the peoples they met, who in
turn wandered westward to uproot others. Report had it that as
far as the Rhine valley and the plains of France people were
pressing on people just as in the youth of the Master of the Horse
the Scythians had pressed on the Cimmerians on the far-off Russian steppes.

It was a pity that the Alpine peoples should migrate. They

were good material. And the Master of the Horse suspected that they must have come, generations ago, from his native steppes. For, like his ancestors, they built barrows for their dead, and their language had many words recognizably the same as his own. At the court of the king, now established near Vienna, he was a staunch advocate of a policy of conciliation and alliance

ROCK CARVING OF A MOUNTED WARRIOR FROM VAL CAMONICA IN THE ITALIAN ALPS.

that would incorporate the Alpine herdsmen peaceably into the Celtic confederacy.

One of his chief arguments was the importance of the old Amber Road. It was along this route that a few iron objects, knives and bracelets and axes and an occasional sword, reached the Celtic regions from the south. They did not come by the sea route but directly up the Italian peninsula, across the Apennines, from the country of the Etruscans in central Italy. It would be

important to gain control of this route and establish a more
regular trade with the Etruscans.

His arguments had carried weight, and now he was once
again riding into new territory, this time as an ambassador, with
an escort and a herald carrying a white-painted staff, on his way
to confer with the chiefs of the Alpine cantons at their religious
center in the southern Alps.

They had crossed the Brenner pass yesterday, and now they
had turned off the Amber Road, crossing an even higher pass into
the vale of Camonica, which ran down, a hundred miles it was
said, to the Po. The path by which they rode, following their
guide on his shaggy pony, was little more than a sheep track,
winding down and down into the narrow bare valley between
snow-clad peaks. But gradually, as they dropped, the air grew
warmer and the valley widened and straightened. They passed
summer pastures with grazing cattle and then, as the trees began,
patches of fenced plowland and an occasional timber house with
reed-thatched barns. Farther down, the cultivated land was wide
in extent, covering the whole valley floor, and on the southward-
facing slopes were terraced vineyards. It was here that they came
to the first of the painted rocks. Their guide reined up where the
path bent around a sloping rock face, and pulled off his close-
fitting cap. And as they followed his glance, they saw that the
rock was covered with pictures, carvings incised in the rock and
painted in vivid reds and yellows.

At first sight it was difficult to make head or tail of the pictures on the rock; they were a jumbled mass of figures, some
freshly painted, others scarcely distinguishable. But gradually
details could be made out: figures of dancing men, of men
brandishing axes, of daggers, of oxen, and of horses. At many
points could be seen the rayed disc or the four-spoked wheel
which even the Danubians knew represented the sun. Slowly the
Master of the Horse realized that these were holy pictures, and
he pulled off his own ermine plumed helmet, remembering the
sun-worship of his own people.

As they rode on, past more and more of the carved rocks, he
questioned the guide about the pictures.

This was a holy valley, the guide explained, for the Thun-

derer—he touched the dagger at his belt—dwelt often upon the
jagged peak of Mount Concarena, which frowned down upon
the valley. Here, beneath the abode of the gods, the dwellers in
the valley had from time immemorial carved the symbols of the
gods upon the rocks, and figures of men worshipping the gods,
and of sacrificial animals, and other such things as it would de-
light the gods to see.

SOLAR DISC, AX, AND DAGGER; RELIGIOUS SYMBOLS CARVED ON THE
ROCKS OF VAL CAMONICA.

The valley had thereby become even more holy. And here,
therefore, the free people of the Alps—he laid a little emphasis on
the word "free"—assembled every four years, for games and
religious festivals and discussions of matters of common interest.
And it was there, though this was not a year for the games, that
the chiefs of the cantons had now assembled, to confer with the
envoy of the Celtic king and hear his proposals.

It was not long thereafter before they came in sight of their
goal, a widening of the valley, where other roads came in from

east and west and where there was a sizable town. On the slopes above the town the guide pointed out the small timber temples, each belonging, he said, to one of the cantons, and, down by the river, the shingled roof of the imposing hall of assembly. There, on the following day, after they had eaten and slept, they met the chieftains of the Alpine confederacy. They were noncommittal men, in homespun cloaks and tunics, and deeply suspicious of the motives of the Celtic king. They even seemed disturbed by the fact that his envoys wore trousers, a sign that the Celts had forsaken European ways and in spirit allied themselves with the hordes from the Russian steppes.

But the Master of the Horse turned the point against them. One could move with history, he said, or one could stand fast with tradition. The future lay with the trousers, which were designed for horse riding, just as the future lay with the riders of horses rather than the drivers of chariots. The Alpine cantons could remain a tunic-wearing backwater if they chose. But the future lay here in the central mountains of Europe, where the road from east to west crossed the road from north to south. If all the peoples of the Alps stood together, they could dominate Europe.

Three days later he took, as he had expected, a noncommittal answer back to the capital. But among the concessions granted to the Celtic nation was freedom of passage along the Amber Road.

In the course of the next ten years, the younger generation throughout the Alpine cantons did in fact adopt trousers. And contingents of the Alpine peoples served with the Celts in the campaigns that in those years were waged against the inhabitants of the upper Rhine valley and the Bavarian forests. The Amber Road was opened for trade once more, and blond-mustached Celtic tradesmen chaffered with Phoenician ship captains and Etruscan importers in the half-Asiatic markets of Tarquinii in Etruria, or even as far as the new Phoenician colonies in Sicily. In these years the Celts took part in the Val Camonica games, and themselves added carvings of their warriors and their gladiators to the picture book of the rocks.

Before the Master of the Horse died, he finally saw the two peoples merged into a Celtic confederacy, and saw Celtic customs adopted in ever-increasing measure by the inhabitants of the lakeside villages. But though he had been one of the prime movers in the union of the two peoples, it pained him somewhat to see the Alpine people abandon the custom of barrow burial and begin, like the farmers, to burn their dead and bury them in cemeteries of urns. He left strict instructions to his sons that he, at least, was to be buried in the manner of his native land beneath a barrow, with his horse and his weapons by his side.

FOUR-WHEELED OXCART FROM THE VAL CAMONICA ROCK CARVINGS.

This chapter, if not pure myth, is at best extrapolation. The peoples mentioned in it, Celts and Cimmerians, Scythians and Sarmatians, Thracians and Dorians and Etruscans, are historical facts. But they are first named in history some hundreds of years later, when histories of these areas first came to be written. For the majority of them this means the writings of Herodotus, about 450 B.C. But these nations of early Europe did not appear out of a vacuum in 450 B.C. According to their own recorded traditions, they had been around for hundreds of years by then. The Scythians claimed to be the oldest race in the world; the Dorian invasion of Greece occurred by tradition two generations after the Trojan war; the Etruscans had a calendar going back to 935 B.C., and Vergil's story of the coming of Aeneas to Italy after the sack of Troy is a reflection of an old Etruscan legend. It has been one of the favorite pursuits of archaeologists to seek to identify the recorded peoples of Europe with particular "cultural complexes," types of artifacts, layouts of settlements, methods of burial and of ornament, and then to trace these cultural complexes back in time, justifiably assuming that the name associated with the complex in the historical period would be the name of the people as far back as the complex remains basically unchanged.

This chapter is fiction based on these archaeological facts. The later so widespread culture called Keltoi by the Greeks and Galli by the Romans does appear in fact to have originated among the farmers of the upper Danube at just about this period, and there is direct evidence that one of the factors in the rise of the Celts was an influx of a very small number of horsemen from the south Russian steppes. Since the Scythians are recorded as having, not much later, driven the Cimmerians from this area, it is reasonable to believe that these horsemen were Cimmerians. Certainly at this time cremation burial, long practiced among the farmers of the Danube valley, spreads to the herdsmen of the lands north of the Alps, and later, in the form of huge urn-fields, to much of central Europe. And this urnfield culture is believed to be the stuff out of which the Celtic empire of First Millennium Europe arose. For an elaboration of this argument, one should go to T. G. E. Powell's The Celts.

The origin of the Etruscans is much discussed. But they said themselves that they came from Asia Minor, and their civilization shows sufficient traces of Near Eastern traits to make this claim likely. It would appear from the archaeological record that they were already in Italy by 1000 B.C., and it is not unlikely that the appearance of the Teresh among the People of the Sea who attacked Egypt in the twelfth century B.C. marks their first settlement in Italy. This, however, may have followed later.

Iron was in fact first worked on a large scale in the Hallstatt area about 700 B.C., but copper and bronze had been worked there in quantity for centuries before that. And since some iron was imported in the years before 1000 B.C., it is very unlikely that the metalworkers of this region had not tried to manufacture this new and superior metal, though clearly with only limited success. Certainly Europe was highly interested in iron at this time.

The rock carvings of Val Camonica exist to this day, and are well described by Emmanuel Anati in Camonica Valley. The fact that they are only found in this one valley (and in the Monte Bego area three hundred miles to the west) strongly suggests that Val Camonica was a religious center for the peoples of the Alps throughout this millennium. The precise form that this centralized worship would take is unknown, but it seems reasonable to imagine it not very different from the centralized worship instituted not much later by the Greeks beneath Mount Olympus, where the Olympian gods looked down upon a periodic festival comprising a political congress, religious ceremonies, and the Olympic games.

21

THE END OF AN ERA

1020–1000 B.C.

THE WARRIOR KING WU was dead, and it seemed as though all his conquests, and all the planning of his father before him, were to go for nothing. The dynasty of Chou appeared to be ending before it was begun, and the next few months might well see a Shang emperor again seated firmly on the dragon throne of China.

The new king of the realms of Chou, King Ch'êng, was only a child, but his empire, now falling to pieces, was not even as old as he. It was a bare seven years since his father had led the chariots of Chou and her allies eastward down the river and captured the Great City of Shang—though the conquest had been planned long before, as even the simplest Chou farmer knew.

It was King Wên the Wise, father of King Wu, who had conceived the plan, a quarter of a century ago, when he had succeeded to the throne of Chou. Chou was then an inconsiderable kingdom, and from its capital at Fêng the king ruled only the farming villages of the Wei valley, from the foothills of the western mountains to the junction of the Wei with the Yellow River a hundred miles east of the capital. The Chou kingdom was not rich, for though in a good year the valley could give fair crops, the rainfall was erratic and famine an ever-present fear. But the people were hardy, and had learnt through long experience with border skirmishes to use with effect the heavy four-horse chariots that they had acquired from the nomads of the steppes and deserts to their west.

But Chou, though poor, was independent, or liked to think

itself so. Admittely, its eastern border marched with the Shang empire, and the Shang kings had claimed a general suzerainty over the land, but the Shang dominion was not enforced and was hotly denied by the court at Fêng.

King Wên's mother had been a Shang princess, and it was said that she had never reconciled herself to living among what she considered to be western barbarians, and filled her son with tales of the splendors of Shang and the glories of its empire. Certainly the prince grew up with a determination to show that Chou was superior to Shang in every way. And indeed all Chou knew that the kings and nobles of Shang lived a life of decadent luxury, and that their own hardy and frugal farmers were, man to man, worth two of the soft winebibbers of the lower river.

When the prince ascended the throne in 1045 B.C., he made no secret of his ambitious plans to conquer Shang and extend his rule as far as the mouth of the Yellow River, the eastern sea, and the sunrise. And to that end he set to work to train and equip a large army, and at the same time instituted a rule of austerity, forbidding the use of wine except for sacrifices and at certain festivals. But King Wên's reign had been short, only seven years, and in that time he was unable to complete his preparations, though he campaigned against the nomad chariot-eers to the west, exercising his army, capturing the horses that his heavy chariots would need, and at the same time securing this frontier in his rear.

When his son, King Wu, had succeeded just eighteen years ago, he naturally prepared, as a good son should, to carry out the wishes of his father. Even so, nine years had passed before he felt that he was strong enough to venture against the mightiest empire in the known world. And then it was only a probe, a swift thrust across the Yellow River which formed the boundary between the kingdoms.

Two years later, in 1027 B.C., his father's spirit finally informed him by means of the oracle bones that the time for attack had come. He had gathered his chariots and those of his allies and struck home. It was nearly four hundred miles from Fêng to the great city of Shang, and over half this distance was through enemy territory. But the army of Chou was irresistible, and the millet and rice fields of the Yellow River valley provided ample provision for men and horses. Near the city the invading army had been met by the vastly greater army of Shang, but the superior training of the men of Chou and their heavier chariots (for Chou used four horses to a chariot, whereas Shang generally had but two) had won the day. And the sybaritic emperor of Shang, Chou-hsin, had committed suicide with refined courage, retiring to a summer palace, arraying himself in his finest robes and jewels, and setting fire to the palace. He had perished in the flames, and his two favorite concubines had hanged themselves.

Since then, for the last seven years, King Wu of Chou had ruled the lands of the Yellow River, in truth as far as the eastern sea. He had rewarded his generals and his allies with grants of estates and with dukedoms throughout the conquered lands, enjoining that for their fiefs they should supply contingents for his army. What to do with the actual district of Shang had been somewhat of a problem. The enmity of spirits as powerful as those of the deceased Shang emperors could not be risked, and their malevolence towards the new rulers would be certain unless the supply of sacrifices to them was continued. And it could, of course, only be continued by one of their own line. Fortunately the son of the last Shang emperor was willing to co-operate. He had been left as vassal king in the city of Shang, with the task of continuing the offerings to his ancestors, and with two brothers of King Wu, the dukes Kuan and Ts'ai, to take the actual burden of ruling off his shoulders. A younger brother of King Wu was at the same time created Duke of Chou itself.

For seven years thereafter there had been peace in Chou, though the earls and dukes of the border marches were kept busy repelling raids or extending their domains, and incidentally those of the Chou empire, ever farther to north and south.

But now King Wu was dead and his son was only a boy. And the great dukes, with their personally loyal armies, needed a warrior king to keep them in order. News soon reached the capital at Fêng that Duke Kuan and Duke Ts'ai of Shang had refused to acknowledge the young king, and were claiming the throne for the king of Shang, their protégé.

It was in this crisis, in this very year 1020 B.C., that the Duke of Chou took the scene. He had not previously been noted for any ambitions for power or military glory. On the contrary, he was a philosopher of note, a man of powerful intellect and integrity. And—though many doubted it in the first years—he was completely loyal to his nephew, the young king. He assumed the regency in the original state of Chou, quelling by sheer force of personality the spirit of defeatism that the presence once more of an emperor in Shang had engendered. And assembling his barons and their retainers and their chariots, he took the road against Shang.

This time it was no lightning campaign. His brothers, the two rebel dukes, had gained the adherence of many of the nearer nobles, particularly former dependants of the Shang emperors, who by speedy submission to Wu had been confirmed in their fiefs. But others of the dukes and barons were wavering and could be won to one side or the other by diplomacy, threats, or blandishments. In this Machiavellian game of winning adherents, the Duke of Chou soon showed himself to be a natural master, and gradually the Dukes of Shang found themselves isolated and surrounded by hostile nobles.

After three years they were defeated in the field, and the Duke of Chou entered the city of Shang in triumph. Duke Ts'ai escaped beyond the borders of the Chou realm, but Duke Kuan and the Shang king were captured and put to death.

The danger was past, and the dynasty of Chou again secure upon the throne. But the duke was determined to prevent a recurrence of the trouble. It was necessary to prevent Shang from ever again becoming a focal point of rebellion. The mighty city that the Emperor P'an Kêng had built just three hundred years before was evacuated of all its inhabitants and destroyed, its great pisé wall leveled to the ground. Its inhabitants were settled at a new, unfortified town at Ch'ao Kê some thirty miles to the south. Ch'ao Kê became the new capital of a new state, called Wei, which comprised but a portion of the former state of Shang, and another brother of the duke, K'ang, was given the new state in fief. Both the city and the state of Shang ceased to exist.

But the spirits of the former Shang emperors could not be so easily disposed of. Some member of the Shang dynasty had to be given the means and rank necessary to permit the offerings to these dangerous spirits to continue. Finally the duke decided to recall from exile Chi Tzǔ, a half-brother of the last Shang emperor, who had quarreled with his brother years ago and fled beyond the borders. He agreed to take over the ancestral sacrifices, and was appointed Duke of Sung, a tiny principality south of the Yellow River and a safe hundred and fifty miles away from Shang.

FIGURE OF A DRAGON FROM A RITUAL WINE VESSEL OF BRONZE, OF THE SHANG OR EARLY CHOU DYNASTY OF NORTH CHINA.

It had taken seven years to restore and consolidate the empire of Chou. And in 1013 B.C. the duke could feel that his work was done. King Ch'êng was now a grown man, and—somewhat to the surprise of more ambitious nobles—the duke now handed over to him the reins of government, giving, however, one piece of final advice. King Wu, he said, had been strongly of the opinion that the realm of north China could not be ruled from a capital so far to the west as Fêng, and the events that followed his death had proved him right. It was always well to follow the wishes of one's parents, and the king would do well to consider building a new capital farther to the east.

King Ch'êng agreed, and a site was chosen on the Yellow River some hundred and fifty miles southwest of the millet fields that now covered the ruins of Shang. In the peaceful years that followed, the duke spent much of his time superintending the building of this new city of Lo-yang and the raising of the massive wall of beaten earth around it. But most of his time he spent on his estates south of the river Wei, hunting and working on his philosophy of Right Conduct. From there, looking across the valley to the plateau beyond, he could see the great mounds that covered the graves of his father King Wên and his brother King Wu. There, when the time came, his own tumulus would rise.

In these years the Duke of Chou is laying the foundation of a realm which already stretches to the sea and which, with the favor of the spirits of his ancestors, may well one day extend from the South China Sea to the steppelands of Asia and the Roof of the World; and in barbarian Europe the warriors of the Celtic confederacy are dreaming of an empire covering the valleys of the Rhine and the Danube, and who knows how far beyond. But in the lands between, where once the great empires had stretched, chaos is come again, small kings fight for small stakes, and the farmers plow with sword at belt and one eye on the nearest horizon.

In Egypt the last Rameses, the eleventh of the name, had died sixty-five years ago, and at his death the high priest of Amon in Thebes, who for so long had held the real power in the south, had officially assumed the title of pharaoh. But at Tanis in the delta a rival line of pharaohs continued. War between the two centers of power had been avoided, largely because neither could trust his mercenary armies, and it almost seemed at times as though there was a tacit agreement that the title of King of the Two Lands should be held alternately in the south and in the north. Now, in 1020 B.C., Menkheperre ruled in Thebes as high priest with royal powers, but recognized the title of pharaoh assumed by Amenemopet of Tanis. The people of Egypt were well content that weak and rival pharaohs should court their support, while the lands beyond their frontier breathed easily, knowing that neither of the rivals dare embark on foreign ventures that would give the other a chance to seize the whole country.

In Assyria there have been five kings in the fifty-eight years since the great Tiglathpileser died. Now his great-grandson, another Shalmaneser, had succeeded to the throne, but to a vastly depleted heritage. For in the past lifetime the Aramaeans of the desert had won all the empire of the great conqueror, and even carved out kingdoms for themselves from the land of Assyria itself. It had gone even worse with Babylonia, where an Aramaean chieftain, Adad-apal-iddina, had captured Babylon itself and assumed the throne. And now the Aramaeans of Babylon and their cousins the Chaldeans of the southern cities were themselves being assailed by the Sutu, another desert tribe.

The situation in Palestine is typical of the whole of the Middle East. The peaceful days when Palestine was a colony of Egypt are more than two hundred and fifty years in the past (as long ago as the reign of William and Mary). And there is a tradition that, all of seven hundred years ago (the time of the Crusades, to us), a people from Palestine had even conquered and ruled Egypt. But the people who now live here feel no tie of blood with the Hyksos (though strong ties there must in fact be). Palestine is divided. The hill country of the interior, and the deep plain of Jordan, are held by tribes of the children of Israel, shepherd farmers whose forefathers, they say, entered the country eight generations ago, after a long period as desert nomads and an even longer period settled in the Egyptian delta. The coastal lands and the plain as far as the foothills belong to the Philistines, who know that their great-great-great-grandfathers, some hundred and fifty years back, came in by sea from Asia Minor in the course of the great migrations. They have inherited from their Canaanite predecessors (whose language they speak and whose blood runs strong in theirs) a tradition of war with the Israeli hillmen, and as far back as man's memory goes there has never been more than a year or so without a punitive expedition into the hills or a plundering raid into the plains. Yet both sides fight with one hand only. To the Philistines the hillmen are unruly brigands who prevent honest seamen from devoting their full attention to building up the overseas trade, which is now beginning to show signs of picking up again. And the Israelis must forever keep a watchful eye on the desert to the east and south, where the raiding Bedouin, on their swift camels, are always ready to take advantage of an army engaged elsewhere.

At the moment Israel is split into factions, while the Five Towns of Philistia are in close alliance. Some thirty years earlier the hillmen had been decisively defeated, after a battle at Ebenezer, where their rallying point, a sort of portable shrine called the Ark of the Covenant, had been captured. The Ark had later been restored, as a gesture of good will, but this may well have been a mistake, for the good will had not been reciprocated.

Priests had always been powerful among the Israelis, ever since the days of Moses, their almost legendary priest-king. And now the archbishop in charge of the Ark, an old man called Samuel, has long been preaching rebellion against the Philistine dominion, which is anyway hardly more than nominal. But at the same time a guerrilla leader called Saul has arisen, and a struggle for power is going on between the priests and the guerrillas. Saul had made his reputation recently by a brilliant march to relieve the city of Jabesh, east of Jordan, which had been attacked by Bedouin, and he had been anointed king by the archbishop himself. A secular leader is something new for the children of Israel, and the priests do not appear adequately to have considered the implications of their appointment. For almost immediately Saul begins to act with complete disregard for the wishes of the priests. From his camp in the Jordan valley, not far from Jericho, he sends an army into the hills under his son Jonathan, and the army attacks and cuts to pieces the Philistine garrison in the town of Geba. The Philistines, of course, dispatch a punitive expedition into the hills, which burns several villages in reprisal. But Saul avoids battle and retires southward, to attack and defeat the Amalekites in the northeast of the Sinai peninsula.

Local warfare of this sort was, of course, endemic in these years all along the border between the desert and the farming country, and the Philistine kings were not unduly troubled by

Saul's successes and his assumption of royal titles. And they certainly paid little attention to a clash between another of their expeditions and the army of Saul, in which the only encounter of note was a single combat between a tall swordsman of Gath called Goliath and the armor-bearer of Saul, a young warrior called David. Admittedly they suffered a trifling loss of prestige when their champion fell, but they were confident that in the long run their superior weapons, swords and spears of iron and iron-tired chariots, would prevail against the old-fashioned bronze weapons of the Israelites. It seemed, in fact, as though Goliath's death had resulted in an unexpected advantage to the Philistines. For David became at a stroke a popular hero among the Israelis, and the priests began to build him up as a rival to King Saul. The internal dissension that so often before had prevented the hillmen from combining against the coastal cities appeared to be breaking out again.

And indeed during the following years much of the energy of the turbulent hillmen was dissipated in internal strife between the two parties. The Philistines, in the cities of the coast, digesting the reports of their agents in the hills, could never really make out whether David was in active rebellion against Saul. His friendship with Saul's son Jonathan was proverbial, and several times Jonathan succeeded in reconciling the two leaders. But though Samuel by now was dead, the open support given by the priests to David time and again provoked quarrels between the king and the popular guerrilla captain, and David was again forced to withdraw with his companions from the court and go into hiding in the hills.

Then one day (it was in the final year of the millennium) David appeared with six hundred followers at the gates of the Philistine outpost city of Gath and requested sanctuary. King Achish of Gath gave him permission to settle in the town of Ziklag close by, and sent word to the kings of the Five Cities that the Israelites were now seriously at odds with each other and that the time had come to crush them once and for all.

The winter passed in preparation, for not merely the Five Cities of the Philistine League but all the towns of the coast as far as the lands of Phoenicia were to combine to provide an overwhelming expeditionary force. And the following spring the Philistine army—horse, foot, and chariots—moved inland from the coast south of Mount Carmel. Not far from the ruins of the ancient city of Megiddo they met the army of Saul and routed it utterly. And Saul and three of his sons, including Jonathan, died in the battle.

As the new millennium opened, David went up from Gath to contest the kingship of the defeated people of Israel.

The dating of the accession of Saul at 1020 B.C. and that of David at 1000 B.C. is only an approximation, but a close approximation. And the Bible account of the wars of the Philistines and the Israelites is closely borne out by the testimony of archaeology, as is clearly set out in W. F. Albright's The Archaeology of Palestine.

The dating of the fall of Shang and the establishment of the Chou dynasty in China is disputed, and the dates adopted here are based on the arguments already set out in the discussion following Chapter 16, where further suggested readings on the subject are listed.

22

THE BEGINNING OF AN ERA

Over all the world many individuals of many nations glance briefly at the sunset of an ordinary day, and do not know that by our reckoning the sun that day is setting upon a millennium. It is an ordinary day in an ordinary year, and the sun will rise again tomorrow. And life will go on.

A thousand years have passed since we watched the sunrise of another ordinary day, and now the sun sets on a very different world. Thirty generations lie between the people upon whom the sun of the Second Millennium B.C. rose and those upon whom it sets. And the people have changed. Over much of the world the language and the physical type, the dress and the equipment have changed completely. Especially the equipment. Whereas the knives and nails and hammers and saws that we use today are recognizably the same as were used in King Alfred's day a thousand years ago, the people of Europe in 1000 B.C. use swords of bronze where a thousand years before their ancestors used flint spearheads, and in the Near East the farmers use sickles of iron where their forefathers used bronze. Our own millennium of progress has seen not a single new domestic animal, but the horse and the camel—and perhaps the llama—have come with the Second Millennium B.C. And it may be that the Sword is as great an innovation as the Bomb.

Looking back on thirty generations (as no one alive in 1000 B.C. could have done) we can trace trends and movements, and perhaps even causes and effects, whereas in the preceding chapters we have only recorded events.

At the opening of the millennium there exist in the Middle East civilized cities and peoples, with an economy based on bronze and a tendency to coalesce into three or four larger units, one on the Nile, one on the lower Euphrates and Tigris, one on the upper Tigris, and one on the Indus.

In Europe there are farming communities, reasonably self-sufficient, with flint implements and too small an agricultural surplus to support large armies and all the apparatus of conquest and empire.

Between these two, the primary producers and the "industrialized" civilizations, trade tends to grow up, vastly encouraged by the advantages of bronze over stone and the geographical accidents of the location of copper and tin lodes.

This is a picture of a fairly stable, progressive, expanding economy.

But upon it is superimposed the pressure of nomad pastoralists, Indo-European-speaking in eastern Europe and south Russia, Semitic-speaking in the Syrian desert and the Arabian peninsula. These are forced outward from their homelands by population—and perhaps climatic—pressure, attracted towards the farmlands and the civilized regions by the lure of a higher standard of living, and given the means to expand by the domestication first of the horse and later of the camel.

Both the civilized communities of the Middle East and the farming communities of Europe have a stable and resilient culture that can absorb and assimilate quite a considerable influx. Nomads invading the farmlands automatically become farmers, nomads invading the civilizations automatically become civilized—providing the pressure is not too great.

We see it happening in this millennium. The Semitic speakers push into the civilized regions of Mesopotamia and then of Egypt and, after no more than a slight pause for absorption, actually stimulate Mesopotamia and Egypt to a higher degree of cultural integration. The Indo-European speakers press into farming Europe from the east and into the civilized east from the north.

In Europe they are first absorbed without difficulty, though their cattle-herding mode of life remains overprinted upon the agriculture that preceded it. In the Middle East they assimilate civilization, mix with (and often rule) existing peoples, or else form their own states on the pattern of the civilized nations. Only in the isolated Indus valley do they destroy a civilization without themselves being infected by its virus. There they retain their herding life, nomadic or settled in villages until, at the end of the millennium, the cult of city life is again introduced from the west.

The invasion of Indo-European speakers into Europe and Hither Asia does not even disrupt the steady growth of trade. On the contrary, they provide a new market, and their nomad traditions, like those of the Semitic speakers earlier, encourage the free movement of goods. Where they meet the sea and seafaring peoples, they take to the sea themselves, and seafaring and sea-trade flourish as never before (oddly enough, especially in the areas where *both* Semitic-speaking *and* Indo-European-speaking strains have mingled with the original inhabitants).

But the Indo-European speakers and the Semitic speakers keep on coming, not in a continuous stream but in waves. And there is a limit to the amount of armed incursion that a settled culture, "industrial" or farming, can take without breaking.

This limit is reached about 1200 B.C. The edges of the civilized area crumble, with the fall of Troy and Mycenae and the Hittite homelands. The shock waves reach even to Egypt and to England. Trade is interrupted, retrenchment and local self-sufficiency are perforce introduced. Local warfare becomes endemic, and nations war for survival and supremacy rather than for wealth. The spread of the knowledge of ironworking helps, though it does not cause, all these processes.

It was to happen again at the collapse of the Roman Empire, and then, as now, it was followed by a Dark Age, though then, as now, seeds of the renaissance began to sprout even in the midst of the collapse.

That is the story of the millennium in terms of trends and movements. But we should not forget that the story is in fact not one of trends. It is a story of people, of lifetimes, of births and deaths and sorrows and happinesses. The trends are merely superimposed upon these, and no one alive in this thousand years, lacking the knowledge of his own past and his own future which we now have, could have recognized the trends while they were operating.

The millennium ends with the sound of nations warring in the night, with a Dark Age following upon the enlightened imperial brilliance of the Bronze Age. There is little to suggest that in less than five hundred years a Persian Empire will stretch from the Dardanelles and the borders of Libya as far as India; and in Greece sculpture and rhetoric, philosophy and architecture and lyric poetry and dramatic art will be approaching heights that have still not been surpassed; and in Palestine and India and China three of the great living religions of the world will already be flourishing. There is little to suggest it—but there is something.

In China, for example, the Duke of Chou is, even as the millennium ends, formulating a philosophy which Confucius himself regarded as the foundation of his system of ethics, a philosophy which for the first time suggests that man must look in his own heart to know what he should do.

In India the Aryan invaders have by now settled down into the clusters of warring principalities such as are portrayed in the *Mahābhārata*. It is not apparently a society conducive to philosophical meditation. But already it is clear that the extrospective religion of the steppes, with its anthropomorphic gods, is giving way to another religion with other gods, which can hardly have come from any source other than the overwhelmed Indus valley civilization. And this religion contains the idea of the cycle of lives and a soul striving through many existences towards an ill-defined perfection. It is a religion fraught with possibilities for the future.

The Israelites have long been monotheists. They were in Egypt in Akhenaten's time, and his doomed experiment may after all have influenced the future. The idea of a single, invisible, and universal God is a new factor of quite incalculable potency.

North of Israel, at the end of the millennium the Phoenicians on the Lebanese coast are beginning to reopen the seaways to trade. Their ships are venturing out towards the western Mediterranean and the almost mythical Straits of Gibraltar, which are the gateway to the outer world. And they are thinking seriously of founding a colony at a place they will call Carthage, on the coast of Tunisia. And they have invented that insignificant device, the alphabet. It is quite a useful little gadget, its chief advantage being that it allows any reasonably bright person to learn to read and write, whereas hitherto the scribe has been a specialist with a lifetime's professional training. And it is, incidentally, the key to democracy, and philosophy, and history, and half the arts.

INDEX

(PAGE REFERENCES IN *italics* ARE TO ILLUSTRATIONS)

A NOTE ABOUT THE AUTHOR

THOMAS GEOFFREY BIBBY has in recent years been one of the leaders of a series of expeditions to the lands bordering the Persian Gulf, investigating prehistoric settlements which he discovered shortly after the Second World War, when he was stationed in Bahrain Island. These expeditions have revealed two entirely new civilizations of the Second and Third Millennia B.C. and cast new light on the commercial connections between the Sumerians of Mesopotamia and the cities of the Indus Valley and on the whole problem of the spread of civilization eastward from its Mesopotamian cradle.

Mr. Bibby was born in 1917 in Heversham, Westmorland, and educated at Cambridge University. During World War II he served in the Intelligence Corps of the British Army, and was awarded King Christian X's Liberation Medal for his work with the Danish underground movement. From 1947 to 1950 he was Executive Officer of the Iraq Petroleum Company, stationed on Bahrain Island. He later made his home in Denmark and is now Director of Oriental Antiquities at the Prehistoric Museum of Aarhus, Denmark. He has traveled widely in Europe and the Middle East and has taken part in many archaeological excavations in Scandinavia, Great Britain, and the Middle East. His book *The Testimony of the Spade* (1956), about life in northern Europe from 15,000 B.C. to the time of the Vikings, was a pioneer work in turning prehistory in the heartland of Europe into history.

September 1961

A NOTE ON THE TYPE

THE TEXT of this book is set in CALEDONIA, a Linotype
face designed by the late W. A. Dwiggins (1880–1956),
the man responsible for so much that is good in contemporary book design and typography. Caledonia belongs to
the family of printing types called "modern face" by
printers—a term used to mark the change in style of type-
letters that occurred about 1800. Caledonia borders on the
general design of Scotch Modern but is more freely drawn
than that letter.

*Printed and bound in the United States of America
by The Haddon Craftsmen, Inc., Scranton, Pa.
Typography and binding based on designs by*
W. A. DWIGGINS